Need and GREED

Stewart L. Weisman

Need and GREED

The Story of the Largest Ponzi
Scheme in American History

Syracuse University Press

All figures and tables courtesy of the author unless otherwise noted.

The paper used in this publication meets the minimum requirements of American National Standard for Information Sciences—Permanence of Paper for Printed Library Materials, ANSI Z39.48-1984.∞™

Library of Congress Cataloging-in-Publication Data
Weisman, Stewart L.

   Need and greed : the story of the largest Ponzi scheme in American history / Stewart L. Weisman.—1st ed.

     p.   cm.

   Includes bibliographical references and index.

   ISBN 0-8156-0610-9 (cloth : alk. paper)

   1. Bennett, Patrick. 2. Bennett, Michael A. 3. Bennett Companies. 4. Commercial crimes—United States—Case studies. 5. Commercial crimes—New York (State)—Syracuse —Case studies. 6. Securities fraud—United States—Case studies. 7. Securities fraud—New York (State)—Syracuse— Case studies. I. Title.

HV6769.W45   1999

364.16'8—dc21

                                     99-049298

Manufactured in the United States of America

For my beloved daughter Ange, may her soul
be bound up with the Eternal.

Stewart L. Weisman has been practicing law for more than seventeen years. A graduate of Syracuse University Law School and Brooklyn College, he specializes in corporate investigations, bankruptcy, and employment discrimination litigation. He lives with his wife, son, and four dogs in Manlius, New York.

Contents

WHY?

THE ANSWER?

APPENDIXES

Illustrations

Figures

Tables

Acknowledgments

Unlike our criminal justice system, which theorizes it is better to let ten guilty persons go free than to send one innocent person to jail, at the expense of forgetting someone who should have been mentioned, it is better to thank than not to thank.

With that in mind, I thank Professor of Law Christian Day for critiquing the manuscript. Many of his broad suggestions were incorporated.

I thank Syracuse University Press as a whole, and in particular, Director Robert Mandel, for believing in the project. Tom Seller did an excellent job editing the entire work.

The Lugbara people of Africa do not have a word for "friend" because one is a friend by virtue of deeds not description. I am, however, privileged to know two of the best people on this planet, Deborah and Timothy Rodrigo, and thank them for friendship, support, and reviewing drafts of the manuscript.

Most of all, I thank Sara, my wife, for helping me keep going and for her contributions, such as the subtitle. My son Samuel, the copy master, deserves thanks, as do my parents for teaching right from wrong.

Lastly, I thank U2 and Mozart for audio support.

WHO?

He that is greedy of gain troubleth
his own house. . . .

   —Proverbs 15:27

A Grimm Tale

GEORGE GRIMM was a financial consultant from New City, an afflu-ent community just north of the Big Apple.[1] Although George had been edgy for the first two weeks of April 1996 because large investments soured, neither his wife nor children could tell it ate away at him like un-treated cancer.

As accounts of the losses began to be publicized,[2] ratcheting exposure a thousandfold, George contemplated suicide. Like George Bailey in *It's a Wonderful Life*, he simply couldn't tell clients their money was gone.

On April 16 George emerged from his office at midmorning and told his secretary he was going to an appointment. He drove his gold BMW to Harriman State Park, about ten miles away.

Although spring had arrived, few people visited Harriman that Tues-day. George, 44, drove aimlessly throughout the park oblivious to new leaves on trees, evergreen boughs, and blooming buds rising out of the strips of grass that grew alongside the winding roadway.

As the sun began to set, George parked the "beamer" near Lake Skan-natati and watched its breeze-stirred ripples diffuse into the shore. He squinted as the rays of the dying sun glinted off the water.

George sat in the car for several more hours amid the stirrings of noc-turnal woodland animals, hatchlings, and the white noise of insects as the first stars became visible.

He gulped down a handful of sleeping pills and waited till they worked into his bloodstream. George got out and walked across the beach, stopping at a point that separated the dry sand from the wet. He looked in all directions to ensure privacy. His eyes fixed on the BMW with a contemptuous glare as if he blamed it, or more properly, what it represented, as the reason for being at Lake Skannatati in the middle of the night.

Ignoring despondency and the cold sting of the lake water, George waded in. He walked until natural buoyancy compelled him to start swimming. With every stroke the interaction of the coldness and the chemicals began to numb his limbs. About twenty yards out paralysis set in.

George's systems began to shut down one by one as he slid under the surface of the starlit lake. The 220 pounds on his six-foot frame felt like a million tons. Water filled his lungs squeezing out the last breath of life. As the final exhale of air bubbles floated toward the surface, his thoughts turned to the upcoming appointment with God. Would he go to Heaven or be found sinful and sent to Hell?

At last, with no angel to save him, George could ponder no more. The spark of life left his body and joined the great procession of souls.

A missing persons report was filed by his wife on April 17 with the Town of Clarkstown Police Department.[3] After receiving a copy of the report over the wire, park police at Harriman remembered seeing a BMW parked at Lake Skannatati the previous day.

Dispatching a patrol cruiser, police found the unlocked car. A one-page note on the front seat read, "I'm sorry." The note also had private instructions to the family.

Tracing an imaginary path into the lake from footprints in the sand, police divers swept the bottom and recovered his body wrapped in a business suit shroud.[4]

George made the ultimate atonement for advising clients—friends, neighbors, and religious institutions—to invest some $5 million into an obscure family-owned company in Syracuse, New York, The Bennett Funding Group, Inc. George himself pumped in more than $10,000. He had earned $182,000 in commissions.[5]

Not long after the last investment dollar was paid to purchase tax-free municipal leases, federal regulators shut down Bennett Funding and several affiliates for perpetrating "the largest Ponzi Scheme in American history."[6] Most of the $5 million was forfeited.

George Grimm was but one victim of what Justice Department officials deemed "a massive, carefully executed investment fraud,"[7] which fleeced more than 12,000 individual investors, 10,000 trade creditors, and 245 banks and financial institutions nationwide of more than $1 billion.[8]

Until the clampdown, Bennett Funding was owned and controlled by Bud, Kathleen, Patrick, and Michael—the Bennetts. The family members also held controlling or substantial interests in more than seventy other corporations, partnerships, proprietorships, and their subsidiaries, affiliates, successors, and assigns. Just about all of these "Bennett companies" have been implicated in the investment fraud as well.

In the halcyon days, the Bennetts, through their corporate counterparts, owned assets in almost every state, including hotels, office buildings, a racetrack, floating casinos, the stream of payment from 100,000 or more equipment leases and 25,000 or more consumer installment notes, a Nevada casino and related gaming property, a shopping mall, fifteen time-share and membership resorts, hundreds of thousands of copy machines, fax machines, computers, pieces of office furniture, scores of large-ticket commercial mortgages, stocks and options in publicly traded corporations, artworks, antiques, luxury cars, houses, and boats.[9]

During their reign, the Bennetts hobnobbed with and financed politicians, including New York governor George Pataki, and celebrities, such as Debbie Reynolds. They employed Big Five accounting firms Price Waterhouse and Arthur Andersen to produce audited financial statements. They struck deals with international financial giants, such as ING Bank from Holland and Assicurazioni Generali, S.P.A., an Italian insurance company. Yet, despite their lofty appearances and impressive connections, the Bennetts looted and depleted their employees' retirement plans.

The Bennetts' world came to a screeching halt on March 28, 1996, when the Securities and Exchange Commission, the SEC, sued Bennett Funding, three affiliates, and their chief financial officer, Patrick Bennett, for securities fraud and related offenses.[10]

In a vain attempt at self-preservation, Bennett Funding and the three affiliates filed chapter 11 the very next day,[11] one of the largest bankruptcies in New York State history outside New York City.[12] The pervasiveness of the fraud and its cover-up necessitated the appointment of the former chairman of the SEC as the bankruptcy trustee.[13] Over time, the family has been forced to disgorge its booty.

Within a year, nine federal indictments were issued.[14] Eight of those indicted pleaded guilty. The last, Patrick Bennett, rolled the dice and was convicted by a federal jury.

After six years of government investigations, civil lawsuits, and criminal proceedings, the hunger to know what really happened at Bennett Funding gnaws at the bellies of the thousands of victims and their families. The collective conscience screams out for knowledge to prevent such things from happening again. There comes a time, therefore, when the pangs must be satiated and the story told as the last stone is set upon the pillar of justice.

For twelve years, from the beginning of Bennett Funding's expansion in 1984 to its demise in 1996, I was general counsel to the Bennetts' conglomerate of corporations.

From commencing lawsuits because of bad credit decisions, to buying and selling nonperforming commercial realty, to handling employee problems engendered by poor management, to correcting misfilings, to forming useless corporations, and to giving unheeded advice, all of the Bennetts' problems seemed to end up on my desk.

Since the bankruptcy filings in March 1996, I have worked with the powers that be to investigate the fraud, assist in the preparation of bankruptcy-related documents, and collect assets for the benefit of creditors and investors.

In the performance of these duties, I have interviewed witnesses, reviewed documents, prepared analyses and reports, taken the witness stand, suffered through depositions, and drafted and filed affidavits.

Although secure in my belief in ultimate dispensation through the slow but steady march of legal practice and procedure, with a tale of so many victims I oftentimes wonder whether one should simply adopt reincarnation as a theory of justice.

Reincarnation is a simple belief people can grasp as they struggle to cope with the bad things visited upon them: raging disparities, broken promises, waste, shattered faith, unrequited love, premature death, economic ruination and loss. It is a system in which things done in one lifetime will be accounted for in the next—karma.[15]

It seems my karma to clean up after the Bennetts, who broke the hearts of so many souls. My incarnation as a corporate attorney must have been the payoff of a huge cosmic debt my past lives owed to a whole family, a fate inexorably intertwined with the Bennetts' rise and fall from power and grace.[16]

Beginnings: My Path to Bennett

AFTER GRADUATION from Syracuse Law School in 1980, I secured a position with a general practice firm in Queens, New York.[1] The firm's offices commanded a view of Queens Boulevard—a never-ending flow of cars, buses, taxis, pedestrians, and their commingled honks, screams, screeches, and exhausts.

The firm mostly represented established commercial entities and landlords, that is, paying clients. The office suite was decorated with obligatory famous legal-scene prints and functional furniture.

Consigned to litigation, I spent most of my time preparing for and appearing at motions, hearings, depositions, pretrial conferences, settlement meetings, calendar calls, and even a bench trial or two—those tried by a judge without a jury—throughout the five boroughs of New York, Long Island, and Westchester.

In New York, unlike most states, the Supreme Court is the court of general jurisdiction. It hears all types of cases, including breach of contract, negligence, and divorce. Losers in the Supreme Court could appeal the adverse decision to the Appellate Division. Losers there could appeal to the Court of Appeals, New York's court of last resort.

Many of the buildings that house the supreme courts were built early in this century in the neoclassical tradition, when blocks of stone and thick columns were all the rage. Although their facades have darkened and discolored through years of caustic city air, the courthouses' innards witnessed extensive renovations in the 1930s under President Roosevelt's work projects.

Comprised of materials that would be prohibitively costly today, the interiors are spacious with cathedral ceilings and decorated ornately with large-scale murals, ceiling relief, wooden judge's benches and scrollwork bars, wainscoting, inlays, large wooden counsel tables and chairs, marbled stairs with brass banisters, and tiered and fluted bulbed candelabra.

Called the "zoo" by the local bar in the early 1980s when I practiced there, the Brooklyn Housing Part, a specialty court, provided a forum for the resolution of housing complaints and landlord/tenant disputes.

At the time, Brooklyn's population approached 3 million people. As most rented apartments, or so it seemed, the zoo was continually in session. If nothing else in common, people from all walks of life had housing complaints.

The place was alive with languages: Puerto Ricans spoke Spanish; Haitians, a French patois; Hasidim whispered in Yiddish; and Chinese argued in Mandarin or Cantonese or other dialects. The lawyers and the judges spoke legalese. Unidentifiable languages wafted in the air.

The zoo lay in *toto caelo* from the Sistine Chapel–like supreme courts. Its once powder blue walls were city-blue peeling—a mixture of dirt, snot, fumes, shoe scuff marks, newsprint, water leak residue, and the trapped, unanswered complaints and curses of the aggrieved. Its low flat ceiling contained rows of recessed sputtering fluorescent lights protected by plastic shields. City-gray linoleum covered the floor.

In the summer, the air circulated by the occasional working fans was oppressive. A few people even collapsed from the heat, the pressure of the burgeoning crowd of litigants, and the overpowering smells from unwashed bodies, booze and beer, perfume, cologne, scented deodorant, and moist polyester.

The landlords and tenants along with their lawyers sat in institutional interlocking plastic and metal chairs. Some chairs were cracked or had pieces missing making them sharp and dangerous. I snagged a suit once. The overflow lined up against the walls and alongside the opened windows. People even sat on the sills. The zoo was rife with patent housing code violations, the same code it was ironically bound to enforce.

As a rule, the housing judges brooked no bullshit from the litigants or their lawyers. During one marathon session, a lawyer, on behalf of a single landlord client, succeeded in evicting six tenants, extracted full payment from two others then and there, had one shaky case adjourned, and received partial payment from the last two with emotional promises in Spanish to pay the balance within seventy-two hours, that is, before the city marshall would throw them, their families, and their possessions out unto the street. Although his partners ought to have been very happy, his bar mitzvah teacher would have died from shame.

As much of my time was spent scurrying from courthouse to courthouse within the firm's sphere of influence, I learned the routes of the various subways. It was always a delight walking down long flights of stairs to the platform like descending through the nine levels of Dante's Hell.

One had to navigate around other passengers, musicians, token takers, panhandlers, small-shop owners, and patrolling transit police because, after all, people did not act so differently below the surface.

With their rumbling, screeching of metal feet, and dripping fluids, the trains were like great prehistoric carnivores, which continually stopped, started, slowed, and sped as they searched for prey.

Car travel was not much better as rush hour and crosstown traffic were choking. As I spent upward of three to four hours on some days in trains or cars, traveling began to weigh heavily on body and soul. My paycheck reflected not so much compensation for services rendered but for incremental bodily destruction. Maybe that is the nature of wages, as people are so rarely paid for the true value of their labors. I became rapidly disenchanted with this unexpected part of the practice of law. Travel 101 was not a required subject at law school.

The relationship with the Queens firm lasted a year. New York's subways, gut-jarring potholes, pollution, dilapidated courtrooms, crowds, violence, high rents, racism, and inordinate waiting scored another victim.

Hearkening to an inner voice, I recalled my days at Syracuse University.[2] Contrary to the heroic images portrayed in Grisham novels, as most law students, I led a cloistered existence: attending classes, studying, going to the library, studying, shopping for food, studying, doing the laundry, and studying.

Yet, the little I did get around, Syracuse offered enough to sustain me on both professional and personal bases, and it was far enough from New York City's ways and means. I moved to Syracuse in 1982 without first securing a position. I guess I had had enough.

Within two weeks I landed an associate counsel position with a five-lawyer firm and was assigned to consumer bankruptcies.[3] The firm was one of the first in the country to employ advertising techniques and went as far as soliciting accident victims by offering them "free" advice as to their rights with "no strings attached." After acclimating to the firm's culture, I found I did not like the overriding entrepreneurial spirit of the senior partner.

He treated the firm as a business almost to the exclusion of everything else. All firm decisions were first run through the sieve of profitability. Billings were the alpha and omega of existence.[4] The pressure to maximize bore down like being submerged five hundred fathoms deep.

Many years later, the senior partner ran into a few difficulties himself, including the demolition of his house for violating zoning restrictions, a criminal conviction for theft of services, and disbarment. Karma must have been on overdrive in his case.[5]

From a legal perspective, consumer bankruptcy work is routine. The forms are the forms. The fee is the fee. The discharge of debt is the discharge of debt. The monotony drones like a merciless metronome. *Tick form tock form tick form . . .*[6] But even this innocuous, vapid work had moments of sublime clarity into the human condition—the stories of degradation of so many average people caught in the throes of destitution.

I began to dread the frightened and desperate looks in the clients' eyes and the sad heaviness in their voices as they told their stories of financial ruination while shifting uneasily in chairs across my desk.

Their sounds of despair and resignation resonated in the audible exhales between pursed and defeated lips. *Sssssssss.* The dread of the publication of their names in the local newspapers under the bankruptcy section. *Shame. Shame. Shame.* The moral wrestling that no doubt preoccupied their spirits because of the unwelcome welching on legitimate debt. Such was the world of bankruptcy. You pay your fee and you discharge your debt. Perhaps this was one of the lessons my soul needed to learn, for them.

The right to file bankruptcy is found in Article 1, section 8, of the United States Constitution.[7] For the record, most people do not file bankruptcy because they want to cheat creditors or to live well beyond their means—or on fantasy island. They file because crushing uninsured medical bills, loss of a job, divorce, death of the breadwinner, or other catastrophic event forces their hand.

People do what they have to do to stop the collectors, the hounders, the lawsuits, the garnishments, the foreclosures, the replevins, the bickering at home caused by economic impotence, the unbearable debt, the accruing interest, the threats, the demand letters, the repo men, the hang up calls in the middle of the day and night, the lack of stability, the fear of the future, the cursing of the past, the blame, and the guilt.

"O God, help me through this," the young wife sobs, sitting at the kitchen table amid piles of unpaid bills.

When I was four, my younger brother, Andrew, of blessed memory, died from Tay-Sachs disease. Tay-Sachs is a particularly horrible infantile disease that destroys the nervous system and leads to death. For some reason it is virulent among Ashkenazi Jews, those of eastern European origin.[8]

The medical bills crushed my parents. The debt collectors were savages. At the time, the Fair Debt Collection Practices Act,[9] which prohibits and punishes unethical collection techniques, was not yet in existence. Had it been enacted earlier, the relentless hounding my parents took, particularly my mother, would have been eliminated. The process drove them into bankruptcy.

After a year of bankruptcy work, I left the firm and became a sole practitioner. At this time I met and fell in love with Sara, who became my wife. We started life's journey together without any money. Clients were developed through word of mouth, through friends and referrals. I accepted contract work from other lawyers. I did the night court thing. I chugged along.

Although it is good to be one's own boss, I lost the protection of the weekly paycheck, what one colleague terms the "W2 syndrome." I did not have enough money for any type of insurance, health, life, or malpractice. Life was lived on the edge. Times were tough. I lost weight. "Lean," they say. But love sustained us then as it does now.

One day in June 1984, while defrosting the refrigerator by chipping away at ice with a screwdriver, I punctured the sidewall effectively killing it. We purchased a new refrigerator, which depleted our meager savings. It was time to find suitable employment. Once more I entered the fray.

That very Sunday, I read with interest an advertisement in the local paper: "Corporation looking for attorney with 2–3 years experience for collections."

A résumé was cobbled and forwarded. An offer of employment was made and accepted after the second interview. I had never worked for a corporation before and knew not what to expect. I was twenty-eight.

Bennett Land

IN THE SUMMER of 1984, The Bennett Funding Group, Inc. ("Bennett Funding" or the "Company") employed twenty people in a cramped suite of offices on the outskirts of Syracuse. The place was literally filled beyond capacity, supersaturated. The hiring of one more employee would have precipitated a fallout from solution.

Until we all moved to larger and nicer accommodations in the Hotel Syracuse four months later, I did not have an office. I used the desks of employees who were absent or on vacation. A day here, a week there. I felt as though I were transported back to the subway stations in New York commuting from court to court to court.

Bennett Funding was owned and run by the Bennetts: Edmund T. "Bud," the patriarch, chairman of the board and chief executive officer; his wife, Kathleen, board member and president; and their sons Patrick, the chief financial officer, and Michael, the deputy chief executive officer. Both were on the board as well. Years later, as Bud eased back, Michael became known as "deputy dog."

The Bennetts. *Left to right:* Bud, Kathleen, Patrick, and Michael inspect renovations to the Atrium. Photo by Carl Single. Copyright © The Syracuse Newspapers.

At that time, Bennett Funding's business was strictly small-ticket office equipment leasing. I was hired to supervise the collection of delinquent lease accounts, including the commencement of legal action to enforce rights under the lease agreements.

I remember being handed a box of leases and told to go after the lessees for payment. No other guidance was given. I went to work chasing deadbeats. I was the collection department, the hammer, the enforcer. This was important work. Ensuring the continuity of payments is critical to every business. It is the ichor by which all employees live ultimately.

As their leasing business grew in the late 1980s, the Bennetts parlayed the revenue and expanded operations. At first, the Company made forays into real estate development, recreational campground financing, and hotel ownership. As those interests stabilized, the Bennetts enlarged their

Table 1. The Bennett Companies that initially filed bankruptcy petitions

Bennett Company	*Filing Date*	*Docket No.*
Aloha Capital Corporation	April 25, 1996	96-61934
American Marine International, Ltd.	April 19, 1996	96-61829
Bennett Management & Development Corp.	March 29, 1996	96-61379
Bennett Receivables Corporation	March 29, 1996	96-61377
Bennett Receivables Corporation–II	March 29, 1996	96-61378
Cordoba Corporation	May 15, 1996	96-62330
Resort Service Company, Inc.	April 19, 1996	96-61830
The Bennett Funding Group, Inc.	March 29, 1996	96-61376
The Processing Center, Inc.	April 26, 1996	96-61977

investors to purchase post–World War I European currency coupons at face value for dollars. Because of the runaway inflation befalling many European countries, Ponzi preached that the investors could make a killing when the coupons matured.

To prime the scam pump, Ponzi had the initial investors tell others they received returns in excess of 50 percent within a two-month period. Soon, almost forty thousand suckers purchased the coupons. Eventually, investigators were able to prove Ponzi did not make the claimed profits from the redemption of the coupons, and the actual investment income would be insufficient to pay all the investors.

Ponzi was arrested, jailed, released, rearrested, released again, and deported. He died in 1949. Ironically, the name of his company was the Securities Exchange Company, the "SEC."

According to language in an opinion by the U.S. Second Circuit Court of Appeals in 1995,[4]

A Ponzi scheme is a scheme whereby a corporation operates and continues to operate at a loss. The corporation gives the appearance of being profitable by obtaining new investors and using those investments to pay for the high premiums promised to earlier investors. The effect of such a scheme is to put the corporation farther and farther into debt by incurring more and more liabilities and to give the corporation the false appearance of profitability in order to obtain new investors.

In other words, as in Charles Ponzi's, a pyramid scheme involves cash from new investors, who are promised a return greater than others. The money is used to pay and keep happy earlier investors,

fiefdom to include time-share financing, turnkey construction loans, and even software development.

The last growth spurt in the nineties came in gambling, euphemistically known as "gaming," with purchases of a racetrack, floating and fixed casinos, and gaming equipment leasing. Ultimately, the Bennetts' empire extended to virtually every state of the Union, Canada, the Caribbean, and Ireland.[1]

Necessarily, the scope of my duties expanded to keep up with the scores of new ventures and to maintain a handle on existing ones. Although for the first several years Bennett Funding's Legal Department comprised myself and a secretary, it eventually grew to fifteen people, including attorneys, paralegals, law student interns, secretaries, and administrative support staff.[2]

Before it went belly-up in March 1996, twelve years after I began chasing commercial lessees, Bennett Funding and its more than seventy related entities grew to about one thousand employees. The mainstay businesses of equipment leasing and time-share financing employed at their zenith about 275 people at the downtown Syracuse headquarters.

Because equipment leasing is such an important part of Bennett Funding and integral to this story, its mechanics need mentioning.[3] To preserve scarce resources, take advantage of favorable accounting treatment, and avoid equipment obsolescence, many businesses and governmental entities lease equipment rather than purchase it outright. Airplanes, copy machines, computers, rolling stock, automobiles, and fax machines are commonly leased.[4]

In essence, leasing allows the lessee to have the full use of needed equipment for relatively little money down. In 1998, revenues in the equipment leasing industry exceeded $183 billion.[5]

The process commences with a lessee's selection of office equipment from a dealer. The terms and conditions of their arrangement are incorporated into a lease agreement. The equipment is then delivered to the lessee triggering monthly payments. To pay the manufacturer of the equipment, and to get a lump sum of cash, the dealer may sell the lease agreement to a third-party leasing company, such as Bennett Funding.

Bennett Funding paid the dealer the highest list price for the equipment, because the cost was hidden and passed through in the monthly payment from the lessee. In leasing circles, as long as the amount of the monthly payment is low enough, the purchase price of the leased equipment seems unimportant to the lessee.

Fig. 1. Bennett Funding and the Aloha Capital equipment leasing business

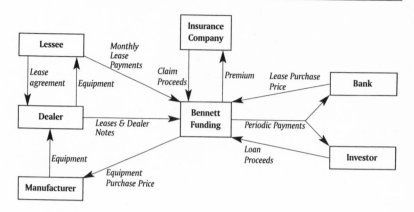

After payment of the purchase price to the dealer, Bennett Funding would take title to the equipment and service the account. To raise capital for the purchase of the lease agreement from the dealer, Bennett Funding offered lease-backed financial products, directly or through broker/dealers, to investors who received a return, in theory, commensurate with prevailing rates.

In many cases, the lease payments were insured against default in payment by a third-party insurance company, thus, as the literature boasted, guaranteeing the payments from the lessee. The insurance was to be assigned to the investor who purchased the lease-backed security.

Bennett Funding's profit was in the spread, the difference between the interest rate inherent in the lease agreement and the interest rate it paid to the investors. Bennett Funding also made money by billing miscellaneous charges, such as risk fees, document fees, and late fees, all blended into the monthly lease payment. These charges were retained by the Company.

If one makes prudent credit decisions, keeps tight reins on the performance of the portfolio, gets the cheapest sources of funds, a leasing business can be profitable. According to records reviewed by the forensic accountants Coopers & Lybrand, who were hired by the bankruptcy trustee, the Bennetts' leasing business was at best only marginally profitable.[6]

The Bennetts compounded their ineptitude by expanding into so many areas without the requisite economic foundation nor, as it turns

out, moral underpinning. The Bennetts were Midas in reverse; whatever they touched turned to lead.

To illustrate, in 1995, deputy dog Michael Bennett, the younger son, spent about $500,000 to rent a hospitality tent at the 1995 Ryder Cup Golf Competition hosted in the nearby city of Rochester, New York.[7]

Michael anticipated that other, and much larger companies that did business with Bennett Funding, such as Konica, Savin, and Monroe, would help defer the rental cost by purchasing the complimentary tickets issued to tent renters. This would be accomplished through Michael's ability to schmooze with his counterparts at those companies.

Two things stopped him. First, we advised him such activity may be considered ticket scalping, an illegal activity in New York at the time.[8] Second, and perhaps more important, not one of the other companies purchased a ticket. To fill the tent and avoid embarrassment, Michael wound up giving away the tickets to any interested employee.

Similar planning went into the Company's purchase and refurbishing of the Hotel Syracuse for $20 million in 1993 and, in 1994, the loan of $3⁵ million for the construction and development of a mall in Aroostoʳ County, Maine.[9] Both projects will net less than half of the mⁱ invested.

The Incident

ON MARCH 28, 1996, the economic equivalent to bombing exploded in Syracuse when the S Bennett Funding, three affiliate corporations, anⁱ curities fraud.[1] Aftershocks were felt the next dⁱ and the three affiliates filed for "protection fⁱ ter 11 of the Bankruptcy Code.[2] As it turⁿ protection from the Bennetts. Within tⁱ companies filed petitions as well.

So ended the reign of the Benⁿ cronies, orchestrated what Justiceⁱ deemed a Ponzi scheme of epic pⁱ

The infamous Charles Ponzⁱ active in the 1920s in the Bostⁱ

who were made similar promises. In reality, no product or actual investment exists. The scheme organizers siphon the largess like leeches.[5]

All goes well until new money stops coming in—that is, until the investor pool is sucked dry. In some cases the size of the number of older investors or base of the pyramid becomes so large that all of the money that there ever was or ever will be is insufficient to fuel the monster. It collapses into itself like a black hole.

Ponzi schemes usually do not last long. Someone talks, investors become skittish, the initial payouts are too large relative to new money, the perpetrators become too greedy and tap the cash at inappropriate times and in inappropriate quantities like so much maple syrup.

Defying statistics, the Bennetts survived nineteen years because they intertwined the traditional Ponzi scheme with legitimate businesses.[6] The Bennetts boasted a good-looking facility in a modern office building in the heart of downtown, a large workforce, state-of-the-art equipment, and a dog and pony show that should have been on Broadway.[7]

Brokers, bankers, investors, insurance companies, rating agencies, accounting firms, and law firms toured the headquarters, met employees, and performed audits. Nothing. No crack in the armor. Although the Bennetts were naked, everyone saw them clothed. It seems people see what they want to see, especially when money dangles before their eyes.

The combination of the tangible testaments to wealth and success and the psychology of greed coupled with the charm of the Bennetts enabled the scheme to live long and prosper, way beyond the short-term nature of such structures.

It is not known whether the Bennetts started out with larcenous intent. It is not known whether the Ponzi was triggered by need and fueled by greed or both. In what lifetime the Bennetts' souls became corrupted is known only to the Great Conscience that rules us all. What is known is that a great mass of people was victimized.

From the decision of one of the leading cases on the subject: "A Ponzi scheme cannot work forever. The investor pool is a limited resource and will eventually run dry. The perpetrator must know that the scheme will eventually collapse as a result of the inability to attract new investors. The perpetrator nevertheless makes payments to present investors, which, by definition, are meant to attract new investors. He must know all along, from the very nature of his activities, that investors at the end of the line will lose their money. Knowledge to a substantial certainty constitutes intent in the eyes of the law . . . and a debtor's knowledge that

Table 2. The network of Bennett brokers

Broker	Code	Broker	Code
Bob Bryant	**100**	Dean Pelton	512
Mid-State Advisors	101	Joel Yohay	513
Professional Money Management	102	Ron Levin	514
Jameson Dewitt & Assoc.	103	Robert Perry	515
Karpus Investment Mgmt.	104	George Gomez	516
First Interregional Equity	105	American Business Systems	517
The Investment Center	106	Burton Sivin	518
Joseph Jackler	107	Ray Krieger	519
Underhill Financial Advisors Inc.	108	Elizabeth A. Diamond	520
Jay Jackler	109	Mark Kuttler	521
American Eagle Financial Services	110, 118	Bruce Brigandi	522
Walnut Street Securities	111	Alfred Tucker	523
Wolff Investment Agency	112	Syracuse Partners	524
Reich & Company, Inc.	113	Americorp Securities Inc.	525
Financial Synergy	114	Randy M. Kornfeld PC	526
Jules E. Levine, Esq.	115	Bennett Financial Services	527
Chirchill Securities	116	E. Russell Ives, Jr.	528
First Montauk Securities Corp.	117	Ira Rothman	529
Princeton Financial	**200**	Michael Foti	530
Allan Eyre	201	William Vezo	531
D,G,H,N,P, & S	**300**	Thomas Murray	532
David Elias	301	Investor Associates	533
Gilbert Dorfman	302	Paul Shein	534
Nevoso & Pivirotto	303	Jaron Equities	535
Anthony DelSpina	**400**	Winward Partners, Ltd.	536
Genovese & Company	**500**	Seth Wager	537
Dennis Mair	501	**Kurt Rosenberg**	**700**
Neil Wager	502	**Kenneth Kasarjian**	**800**
Peter Rosenbaum	503	Sima Insurance Company	801
Alvin Rapp	504	Horizon Securities, Inc.	802
Jerold D. Cohn	505	Halpert & Company	803
Arlene Resnick	506	Brede Investment Mgmt.	804
George Grimm	507	Monarch Financial Corp.	805
Barry Berg	508	Richard Howe	806
Diane Steele	509	First Miami Securities	807
Richard Lewis	510	Stoever Glass & Company	808
Professional Group Mktg.	511	FAIC Securities Inc.	809

The boldface entries indicate chief reporting broker for that particular numbered grouping. For example, Genovese & Company, Code 500, is the reporting broker for brokers numbered 501–537.

Table 2 *(continued)*

Broker	Code	Broker	Code
Emanuel & Company	810	Equity Services Corp.	903
Herbert Gerstein CPA	811	Townsley & Associates	904
Martin Kaiden Company	812	Sage-Rutty & Company	905
Kurz-Liewbow & Co., Inc.	813	Bankers Financial Corp.	906
Aegis Capital Corporation	814	Summit Financial Securities	907
Corporate Securities Group	815	Hefren, Tillotson Inc.	908
Solomon Associates, Ltd.	816	S. C. Parker & Company	909
J. B. Hanauer & Co.	817	McGinn Smith & Company	910
Lew Leiberbaum & Co., Inc.	818	R. Seelaus & Company	911
Weiner Abrams & Co., Inc.	819	Cheevers Hand & Angeline	912
Ferris Baker Watts	820	Allen & Company	913
American Eagle Investments	821	**Richard Kelley**	**1000**
David W. Jenks	**900**	**Crawford & Associates**	**90**
Genna Brown	901	**House (Employees)**	**80**
Brighton Securities	902		

future investors will not be paid is sufficient to establish his actual intent to defraud them."[8]

In an ideal world, investors make investment decisions based on informed choice, free from fraud, overreaching, duress, and mistake. In this best of possible worlds, however, issuers and their agents do not always make full disclosure, financial statements are often wrong or misleading, projections are frequently pipe dreams, and fraud and mistake are all too common.

The one-two punch of the commencement of the SEC suit and the bankruptcy filings hit square in the face more than 12,000 individual investors,[9] 10,000 trade creditors, and 245 banks and financial institutions along with their employees and shareholders nationwide.

The banks and financial institutions immediately hired large law firms to protect their pecuniary interests. Most cut deals with the bankruptcy trustee. The remainder joined battle in Bankruptcy Court. In any event, they certainly appeared able to sustain the losses and fend for themselves.

The investors, however, like punch-drunk boxers meandering about

Table 3. State-by-State Listing of Aggregate Investor Liabilities

State	Investment	State	Investment
Alabama	658,000	Montana	0.00
Alaska	0.00	Nebraska	3,000
Arizona	5,352,000	Nevada	539,000
Arkansas	602,000	New Hampshire	858,000
California	14,059,000	New Jersey	211,846,000
Colorado	2,551,000	New Mexico	146,000
Connecticut	10,797,000	New York	195,002,000
Delaware	4,125,000	North Carolina	5,927,000
Florida	87,711,000	North Dakota	687,000
Georgia	1,072,000	Ohio	4,873,000
Hawaii	80,000	Oklahoma	970,000
Idaho	0.00	Oregon	42,500
Illinois	4,752,000	Pennsylvania	56,123,000
Indiana	1,980,000	Rhode Island	581,000
Iowa	0.00	South Carolina	393,000
Kansas	1,543,000	South Dakota	103,000
Kentucky	144,000	Tennessee	1,238,000
Louisiana	2,042,000	Texas	25,348,000
Maine	134,000	Utah	47,000
Maryland	8,802,000	Vermont	550,000
Massachusetts	5,820,000	Virginia	4,284,000
Michigan	10,970,000	Washington	805,000
Minnesota	1,309,000	West Virginia	321,000
Mississippi	533,000	Wisconsin	157,000
Missouri	3,816,000	Wyoming	973,000
Total			$680,668,500

the ring, were lost, cast adrift, and caught in the swirling tide of misfortune.

The devastation ravaged people from Florida to Maine and from Massachusetts to California. Like the Mongol hordes encircling their enemy, nothing caught inside the circle survived. The losses of life savings, retirement money, huge chunks of income, trust endowments, and death benefit proceeds were all too common. The effect upon the aged, the young, the widowed, the divorced, the rich, the poor, the college student, the worker, and people from all of God's creation gushed forth like a real-life Miss Lonely Hearts.

Just after the bankruptcy was filed and announced publicly, my office phone rang constantly.[10]

One investor related the following: "When my husband died in 1994, my broker convinced me I should place all of the life insurance proceeds into leases at Bennett Funding. He said the leases were insured. 'Guaranteed,' he said. So I did. The payments came like clockwork. Then, all of a sudden in January 1996, one of the checks bounced. I called and they told me not to worry, just a printing error. But then I got a letter. It said that for the next two months the Company was exercising an option just to pay interest, no principal. I don't remember any option like that. I didn't like it but it seemed that there was nothing I could do. Then the March payment didn't come. I got nervous. Then I heard about the SEC and the bankruptcy and lawsuits, and . . . [crying]. I was living off of the monthly payment. I don't have any other money. I don't work. I'm too old to start over. My husband took care of everything. What am I going to do [crying]?"

Another shouted: "I lost everything in that fucking company. My God, everything."

An elderly woman: "I lost my family in Europe. You know, the Holocaust. I came to America and lived with some cousins. I worked and saved. I put all of the savings into Bennett. My advisor was such a nice young man. I retired and lived off the Bennett investments. The monthly payments pay my rent and my food. I'm not a healthy woman you know. I can't walk so easy. The landlord needs his money. Hey, mister, when can I get my money?"

A young college student: "My parents set up a trust account for me. The money was placed into leases and the income was used to pay tuition and the rest for very basic living expense. Jesus, I lived like Spartacus. Now I can't pay tuition. Thanks a lot, assholes."

Many businesses invested their pension funds in Bennett. What liabilities will the owners have? Were the investments safe and prudent? And, especially, what of their employees who salted away years of retirement money that was invested into Bennett?

One imperative we followed in the aftermath of the bankruptcy filing was to speak with investors, to calm them, reassure them, hear their worries and fears, let them vent rage and frustration, let them cry on our shoulders electronically, give them news and hope, particularly hope. Hope is so very important in our existences. Sometimes, it is all we have.

In his classic book *Man's Search for Meaning*,[11] Viktor Frankl describes his survival at Auschwitz and the origin of his theory of psychoanalysis called logotherapy: the product of Frankl's attempts to deter fellow inmates from committing suicide. A recurring theme throughout Frankl's writings is hope. A "helpless victim of a hopeless situation, facing a fate he cannot change, may rise above himself, may grow beyond himself, and by so doing change himself. He may turn a personal tragedy into a triumph."[12] I can only hope that those who have fallen victim triumph as well.

The losses, though, were not limited to outside investors. Legitimate brokers, advisers, and similar businesses went bankrupt or out of business, taking, in their wake, the dreams, aspirations, and livelihoods of all of their employees.

Several equipment lease vendors who relied upon leased equipment maintenance, service, and supply money billed and collected by Bennett Funding folded through lack of cash flow.[13]

Many of the employees of Bennett Funding were also burned badly. More than half of the employees lost their jobs in the wake of cessation of business. Virtually all of their $2.5 million of pension money was "loaned" to outside associates of the Bennetts or improperly invested in products of dubious quality. Mandatory employer contributions to the 401(k) plan were not made for years. Patrick even sold double-pledged and fake leases to employees who invested with the Company.

One Bennett Funding employee, who worked in the finance department and handled cash-outs, invested all of her savings in leases. She also had her immediate family place all of their savings into the Company as well. All was lost. She related a story that a corporate director and officer liquidated all of her investments just before the Company tanked. When she asked the director why the money was being cashed out, she was advised the director's family was starting a business and needed all the cash that could be mustered. Mother guppy eating her hatchlings.

Daze of Reckoning

M Y FAMILY and I live in Manlius, a town about twelve miles east of Syracuse. Just up the road is a dairy farm, a Christmas tree farm, and a horse-boarding ranch. The property taxes are high, primarily to support the local schools. Both of my children are graduates of the local high school. The school is a powerhouse in lacrosse. For those unfamiliar, lacrosse is a game invented by Native Americans. The word derives from the French for *stick,* which is used by the players to shoot a ball into a goal in hockey fashion. It is fast moving with moments of great athleticism.

The small cul-de-sac in which our house sits has good neighbors and no fences. Raccoons, deer, groundhogs, weasels, chipmunks, squirrels, rabbits, blue jays, cardinals, robins, and even a red fox have walked over, nested in, burrowed in, and run on the property.

Human beings begin to stir from 7:00 to 7:30 A.M. as children go off to school and spouses to work. Until then, the silence envelops the households like Saran wrap.

On March 28, 1996, the phone rang about 5:30 in the morning. The sharpness of the ring pierced the protective quietude. It busted me out of sleep.

Who the hell is that? I wondered as calls at strange hours tend to be harbingers of bad news.

"Hello," I answered, the sleepiness still evident in my voice.

"What do you think?" was the reply.

"Michael, is that you?"

"Yeah, what do you think?"

"What do I think about what? What are you talking about," I asked Michael Bennett, the younger son of Bud and Kathleen. Indeed, he rarely if ever called me at home and certainly not at that hour.

"I guess you didn't hear," he said.

"Hear what?" I demanded. My voice began to show exasperation at this game of twenty questions so early in the morning.

"The SEC is filing suit today and the Justice Department is filing criminal charges against Patrick," (the older son) Michael finally blurted out.

"Holy shit. What happened?" I asked.

"The SEC sent a copy of the proposed suit to our counsel last night and said that they were filing it today. Patrick has to drive down to New York City and turn himself in."

My mind was spinning. Bennett Funding was under inquiry by the SEC about two years, and investigation one year. We were all assured by management of the routine nature of it. Lawsuits and criminal prosecutions were never mentioned. What could have triggered this god-awful thing? I thought. *Lord, save us from the fury of the Norse.*

"I'll be right in," I said to Michael. I got dressed and drove to work.

The SEC is a watchdog agency of the federal government.[1] Its mission is to protect the investing public from fraud and manipulation in the highly regulated world of securities. It is charged with investigating and, if warranted, taking enforcement action against issuers and dealers who violate the securities laws. True, the purchase of securities is not risk free, but it should not be a crapshoot either.

The SEC has several layers of enforcement proceedings against individuals and entities suspected of securities violations. The first level is the informal inquiry. At this stage, the SEC will notify the suspect, or target, that it is making inquiry into practices that may run afoul of the securities laws. The inquiry asks for voluntary cooperation.

If the inquiry shows promise, a formal investigation is instituted in which the full police powers of the SEC can come into play, including the issuance of subpoenas for documents and the taking of depositions of witnesses, that is, testimony under oath.

If the investigation turns up dirt or is met by stonewalling by the target, the SEC can commence a civil action. The civil action is often accompanied with a demand for the appointment of a receiver to take control of the wayward business.

The SEC's enforcement powers are strictly civil in nature. It does not have jurisdiction in criminal matters. That privilege is reserved for the Justice Department.[2]

At this level, the U.S. Attorney's Office and the FBI, both under the auspices of the Justice Department, may also commence companion criminal proceedings and lay siege to the targeted entity.

In the Bennett matter, the "Order Directing Private Investigation and Designating Officers to Take Testimony" was signed by Jonathan Katz, secretary to the SEC, on October 11, 1994.

Michael met me at the office. He stands five feet, nine inches. His complexion is fair. His nickname is "Opie." I suspect he might have had freckles as a kid.

Michael's parents were at home. They have not returned to the office since that day. Patrick was en route to New York to "check in" at the intake facility. We called Edmund T. "Bud" Bennett, the patriarch, on a speaker phone.

"Hello," Bud said.

"Dad, it's me and Stu," Michael responded.

"Listen, Stu. Rick Marshall struck some kinda deal with the SEC. We gotta file bankruptcy immediately. It is the only way to keep the Company from receivership and liquidation," Bud declared.

Rick Marshall[3] was the former senior associate regional administrator in the New York office of the SEC. After leaving the SEC, he became a highly priced securities lawyer at Kirkpatrick & Lockhart,[4] recommended by those in the know.

Rick had been representing Bennett Funding for the past year of the SEC investigation. His firm co-counseled with Robinson, St. John & Wayne of New Jersey. Several prominent members of that firm had been representing the Company in securities matters since the mid-eighties.

Allegedly, the brusque style of the Robinson, St. John & Wayne[5] securities litigation attorney assigned to the matter rubbed the SEC the wrong way. In response, the SEC turned up the heat. Therefore, new counsel was needed, or so the story goes. More likely, the probe was coming dangerously close to home. Scapegoats were needed.

"Mr. B. [as Bud was known]," I said, "filing a chapter 11 petition is a big deal; we should get real good bankruptcy counsel to help us."

"Maybe Gordon from Shaw Licitra,"[6] Michael added.

"Shaw Licitra?" Bud questioned. "Is that those assholes who worked for the other side when we bought the Hotel Syracuse?"

Several years before, Michael had purchased the stock of the company that owned the Hotel Syracuse. The hotel is the largest in the area and a downtown landmark. The holding company was in chapter 11 bankruptcy.[7] Shaw Licitra represented the seller. They did an outstanding job in representing their client and, in the process, earned the court approved $1 million fee—a fee, as it turns out, paid indirectly by the investors through the Ponzi scheme.

Bud hated Shaw Licitra. He blamed the firm, the former owners, and all connected with the transaction for the financial loser the Hotel Syracuse purchase turned out to be. His hatred was groundless. If he felt the deal was bad at first, he should not have permitted it to proceed. Michael, though, had to have the Hotel Syracuse, and like Lola, whatever Michael wanted, Michael got.

At the closing of the Hotel Syracuse in 1993, Michael had agreed to place about $250,000 into escrow with Shaw Licitra. The money was to pay certain creditors once their debt was reconciled by our accountants. Bud did not like the seller, and through illogical extension did not "trust" the firm. He reneged on the placement of the money with Shaw Licitra as escrow agent.

Taking umbrage at the slight, namesake partner Stanley Shaw commenced a suit against the Company. Under the circumstances, Shaw had no recourse but to sue; after all, his firm's reputation was called into question. Fortunately, the matter was settled, but Bud, usually the successful bully, was beaten down and bore a grudge.

"Yes, Gordon represented the seller," I answered.

"I don't like them, but I will leave that to you two. The bottom line is that we have to file the petition immediately," Bud said, his voice becoming increasingly louder and colder. Bud, like many CEOs, was a "bottom line" kind of guy.

"Okay, but let me speak to Rick Marshall first and coordinate things," I responded.

"Listen, goddamn it. You don't have to talk to him, just file the fuckin' petition," Bud thundered in reply.

"Dad, calm down, we'll do it," Michael interjected.

"Michael, don't give me any crap," Bud said, and slammed down the phone. Michael looked at me woefully. Wallowing in self-pity engendered by his father's ruthless public display of lack of confidence in him, Michael acquiesced to my taking charge. I felt sympathetic to Michael's plight.

Although Patrick was the accused criminal at the time, Bud and Kathleen still did not have faith in Michael's ability to carry on the business even though his advice concerning the retention of expert bankruptcy counsel was correct.

"Mike, I'm calling up Marshall to see what's going on," I said.

"Okay," Michael agreed robotically.

I touched the keys. The electronic tones sang melodically.

"Kirkpatrick & Lockhart, may I help you?" the receptionist asked.

"Rick Marshall, please." Rick's secretary picked up after two rings.

"Mr. Marshall's office," she said.

"Hi, this is Stu Weisman, may I speak with Rick, please."

"One moment, please." Ten seconds later Rick Marshall got on the phone.

"Rick Marshall here."

"Hi Rick, Stu Weisman."

"Hi Stu. I guess you know what's going on."

I related the morning's conversations with Michael and Mr. B.

"Okay," Rick said. "Well, the SEC is moving to appoint a receiver, Richard Breeden, the former chairman of the SEC [ironically, Rick's former boss]. We can't let that happen. It would just devastate the business."

Devastate the business? Did Rick think the lawsuit would look good on the financial statement? I thought, my mind still trying to come to grips with the suit and the criminal charges.

"Stu," Rick continued, "the deal is that the SEC will back off if Bennett Funding files chapter 11. We've got to do that immediately. It's the only way to save things. Can you handle that?"

"Save the business," I almost blurted out in a spasm of bemused incredulity. Rick did not know Patrick Bennett lied to him concerning the financial condition of Bennett Funding and the status of a hundred thousand equipment leases. Rick, in the course of representation of the Company, related the erroneous information to the SEC.

"Yes, I can file the petition," I said, "but I think we need to have some expert advice. Michael and I were thinking of Shaw Licitra. They represented the Hotel Syracuse when we purchased it. They really know bankruptcy law, Rick."

"Sure," Rick said. "But the filing must be done quickly. Anything else?"

"Yeah," I responded. "What caused the suit?"

"The SEC found out about the bogus New York City Transit Authority Leases and decided to close Bennett Funding down."[8]

"What bogus leases?"

"I'll fax you a copy of the suit and you can read it yourself."

"Fine," I said, and hung up the phone. I looked at Michael. He looked forlorn. "Don't worry, Mike, we'll get through this," I said reassuringly.

"I know, I know," he said, tears welling.

"Okay Mike, let's call Gordon." I pushed the buttons. The tones sounded a different melody. "One day I should explore phonetone music," I thought. Funny how with the world going to shit, the mind can think of such things.

"Mr. Gordon's office," the receptionist answered with a slight Queens accent, transporting me momentarily to my first job on Queens Boulevard. I guess you can never leave home.

"Hi, this is Stu Weisman and Michael Bennett and it's real important that we speak to Mr. Gordon."

"Hold on, please." she said. About forty seconds later Gordon answered the phone.

"Hello, Gordon," I said.

"Hi," Michael echoed.

"Hey, guys, how are you?"

"Good, good. Listen Gordon, we got a real situation here. The SEC sued Bennett Funding for securities fraud, and criminal charges have been filed against Patrick," I rattled off. I knew I was going to be repeating that sentence many more times during the next few days.

"My God," he responded simply.

"Our outside counsel cut a deal with the SEC," I continued. "If we file chapter 11 they will not move for receivership. We want you to handle the case for us."

"Wow. This is unbelievable. Michael?"

"Yeah."

"Michael, does your family agree with retaining our firm?" Gordon asked.

"Yes," Michael responded sheepishly.

"Okay. How much time do we have?" Gordon asked.

"We have been ordered to file now, today," I responded.

"That's impossible. What do you mean ordered? Who ordered you?" Gordon asked.

"Bud and his outside securities counsel," I answered.

"Well, there's a whole bunch of planning that needs to go into these filings. First-day orders, creditor lists, asset schedules," he said in bullet-like fashion. "Today's Thursday," he continued, "at least you need to give me through the weekend," Gordon implored.

"The best I can do is to try to talk to Mr. B," I offered.

"Okay, I'll wait to hear from you then," Gordon said hanging up the phone.

I looked Michael in the eye. "Let's call your father."

"I don't know. Rick Marshall said it was important to file today."

"I know, but Gordon's the expert. Marshall doesn't know shit about bankruptcy, he's a securities lawyer."

"Well, you call my father then," Michael said and left the room. "Damn it, he crumbled," I thought. Michael, as usual, was afraid to confront his father. I didn't blame him. Mr. B. yelled like a sand tortoise in rut. Every corpuscle of his six-foot, one-inch frame blasted his message like a drill sergeant to boots. One could imagine Bud's arm tattoo rippling in anger. Like Ronald Reagan, Bud showed barely any gray on his head of dark hair.

Before Bud's quadruple bypass, Michael and he had bloodcurdling blowouts right in the office. Generally, the fights would start with Bud ordering Michael to "get in here" (his office). Michael would obey like an automaton. Just as Michael crossed the threshold, Bud would slam the door rattling all wall hangings. Then the screaming would start in earnest—deep, dark and loud, spewing hatred like a volcano spitting flames and lava and ash and toxic fumes.

The fights were ostensibly about the right way to conduct business, but really the fighting was over money. Money. Money. Money. Money seemed to be their only true link and excuse for communication. Yet, it was hard to believe these two men, father and son, would engage in mortal combat over money. Maybe their souls needed to learn there was more to life than the acquisition of money and power and things.

The fights sometimes grew so loud that the secretaries would vacate the area. Eventually, Kathleen Bennett, the "peacemaker," would enter the room and try to calm everyone down. Sometimes she was even successful. I dreaded the call.

"Mr. B?" I queried innocently.

"Yeah, Stu," he answered seeming somewhat distantly.

"I spoke with Gordon. He suggested we put the filing off for a few days so that he can prepare better."

"Goddamn it. I don't care what he said. I want that petition filed now."

"I think it's better we wait," I challenged. Even Hans Solo evading Darth Vadar's fighters paused to calculate the coordinates before jumping into hyperspace so he didn't materialize inside of a planet.

"No, goddamn it, file now." I pictured him kicking a door and pounding his fist onto the tabletop like Kruschev pounding his shoe at the UN.

"Okay." I backed down. After all, it was his company, he was the boss and the client. I also figured he was nervous about the allegations against Bennett Funding and the criminal charges facing his son. I learned later he broke down when he heard the news of the double whammy.

I completed four bare-bones petitions and had them filed the next day in the U.S. Bankruptcy Court for the Northern District of New York in Utica.[9] It was March 29, 1996, my mother's birthday.

The Bennett bankruptcy is the largest bankruptcy ever filed in the northern district,[10] the largest federal district in New York. It extends from Albany westward to just before Rochester, and from just above Westchester northward all the way to the Canadian border. The bankruptcy seat is in Utica.

The Bennett bankruptcy has generated so much litigation that it has its own motion day. So many people made inquiries concerning the status of the proceeding and the filing of proof of claims that the Bankruptcy Court Clerk's Office set up a special Bennett hotline. So did the Justice Department.

The Bankruptcy Court is in an old combined federal building and post office in Utica. The courtroom is accommodating but not large, designed in the minimalist tradition of basic geometric forms with few frills.

Under normal circumstances, a debtor, one who files a bankruptcy petition in a chapter 11 proceeding, acts as its own trustee and is known as a debtor-in-possession, a DIP.[11]

In those cases in which the debtor cannot run the business or in which fraud, mismanagement, or the like are suspected, any party in interest may petition the Bankruptcy Court for the appointment of a trustee to run the business and the affairs of the debtor.[12]

Alternatively, there is precedent in bankruptcy law that permits a debtor to appoint a responsible person in lieu of a trustee. A responsible person runs the company like a trustee but is friendlier to the existing owners and management. In those cases in which the debtor's activities need to be further investigated because of suspected criminal activities, the court can also appoint an independent examiner,[13] who works in tandem with the responsible person.

Soon after the petitions were filed, Gordon and Al Marder from Shaw Licitra encamped at Bennett Funding's headquarters in Syracuse. Matthew Harrison[14] joined them later to act as the responsible party. Harrison was well versed in the business of running a distressed company suffering from the throes of corruption. He had been involved in cleaning up WedTech, the scandal that brought down a thriving, but crooked, government contractor and a prominent congressman.

Harrison is a West Pointer, a recipient of a Silver Star, five Bronze Stars, and two Purple Hearts for heroism in Vietnam. He also authored *Feeding Frenzy: The Inside Story of WedTech*.[15]

Before accepting the position, Harrison needed approval from the owners of the Company, Bud and Kathleen. In essence, the Bennetts needed to place the voting rights of their shares of the Company into an irrevocable voting trust proxy and execute the relevant enabling instruments. Harrison would serve as trustee of the voting trust, that is, vote the Bennetts' shares of Bennett Funding as he deemed fit and proper.

With these in hand, Harrison, in running the Company, could act as required with authority and impunity and without concern that Bud and Kathleen would trump his judgment by threatening to revoke or actually revoking his authority.

By this time, Bud hired a new set of lawyers from a local firm, Scolaro Shulman,[16] to represent him and Kathleen in this mess. I recall attempting to negotiate with the new counsel to convince them of persuading the Bennetts to put their shares into the trust proxy and make some other concessions to make the plan feasible. Bud refused to do as suggested. He refused to execute an irrevocable trust.

Instead, he and his counsel came up with some tortured revocable trust proxy document, which, by its very terms, provided a "back door" provision to allow Bud and Kathleen to oust Harrison and reassume shareholder control—a legal shedding of crocodile tears.

As no further compromise could be reached, Bud and Kathleen signed a revocable trust proxy. Harrison then assumed his position as responsible person in early April 1996, subject to ultimate Bankruptcy Court approval. In all of this, Harrison never met the Bennetts.

During his roughly ten days on the job, Harrison was in early and put in iron days. Trying to be as helpful as possible, I paralleled Harrison's hours. I practically lived at the office. The press was merciless. Daily accounts of various aspects of the Bennett scandal were plastered on page one. The story was run on television in a seemingly endless loop of videotape. On the way into work, sound bites from the radio filled the air. I dared not venture out of the office for fear of someone yelling, "There goes one of them."

Harrison and Shaw Licitra performed admirably dealing with the press, enraged investors, bank counsel, the Bankruptcy Court, the omnipresent eye of public scrutiny, and others who laid siege to the Company's assets like ocean fowl and sand crabs ripping the living and dying flesh off a beached whale.

Even with Harrison on the scene, confusion ran rampant. Justice Department attorneys and FBI agents dropped in unannounced and had "chats" with us. We handed them documents and reports that, in theory, helped the continuing federal investigations and, ultimately, the prosecutions of truly responsible persons.

We met with SEC attorneys, particularly Barry Rashkover. Rashkover, along with Alistaire Bambach, senior accountant Herbert Cohen, and the rest of the posse,[17] had stopped Bennett Funding in its tracks from fleecing any more investors by the imposition of the SEC lawsuit that triggered the bankruptcy filing and the flight of the Bennetts. Like baby shampoo, no more tears or victims.

The SEC did not like the concept of a responsible party to run the Company. As was its statutory right[18] and duty, the SEC filed a motion to appoint a trustee.[19]

On that motion day in April 1996, the courtroom was packed with lawyers, bankers, investors, and the press. Before hearing the SEC's motion, the chief U.S. bankruptcy judge, Stephen D. Gerling, allowed various parties in interest to make short statements concerning the proceeding.

Among those who spoke was Bud's lawyer from the Scolaro office. He spoke passionately about Bud's and Kathleen's innocence and their contribution to the community. His words fell on deaf ears. The assemblage was in a hanging mood and did not take kindly to the rhetoric of strangers.

Toward the end of his soliloquy, the lawyer said that once matters were settled and everyone was paid off, Bud was willing to allow the investors to share in the future profits of the Company. That woke people up. They buzzed like angry hornets forcing Judge Gerling to demand, "Silence!"

The scene was reminiscent of Shakespeare's Antony addressing the *hoi polloi* at the reading of Caesar's will, "Friends, investors, fellow capitalists . . . not only will you get all of your money back but you will still make a handsome return."

These things did not, will not, and cannot come to pass. Alchemy notwithstanding, it is simply impossible to convert the known and recovered assets to cover the anticipated $1 billion or more shortfall.

Just before severing ties, Scolaro Shulman filed a lien against Bud's and Kathleen's Syracuse home for fees, which exceeded, reportedly, $150,000.[20] The house sold eventually for $109,000.

Shaw Licitra fought valiantly to oppose the SEC's motion for the appointment of a trustee. If successful, the firm would be in line to receive millions in attorneys' fees from a grateful Harrison, who would earn a similar amount.

Gordon argued a responsible person could run the Company and an independent examiner appointed to investigate the alleged wrongdoing. "A trustee," Gordon said, "is not necessary."

"Nonsense," SEC attorney Alistaire Bambach argued. Surely, this largest of all Ponzi schemes cried out for a trustee. A responsible person and an independent examiner are simply insufficient in a case of this magnitude. Moreover, inasmuch as Harrison was "picked" by the Bennetts, the SEC argued, he was, practically speaking, unfit and not eligible for the position, with all due respect.

Harrison, Gordon, and I sat at the debtor's counsel table during the motion. Because battles are not static, a good general knows when to scrap the plan and "ride to the sound of the guns." Motions can be similar experiences. After years of practice, one develops a battlefield sense, knowing when to change tactics, feeling when the judge has heard enough. Toward the end of oral argument, I passed a note to Harrison: "We're outta here."

Predictably, the SEC prevailed. Judge Gerling agreed with the SEC's position and held that a trustee was required under the circumstances. Harrison was ordered to immediately wind down his appearance at Bennett Funding, then was summarily booted. My sympathy toward Harrison's loss of employment was short-lived, however. On the way back to the office he received a call on his cellular phone, which turned out to be an offer to run another distressed company.

Before he left Bennett Funding, Harrison gave me some advice like Washington's Farewell Address: "Make yourself as useful as possible."

After Harrison's departure, confusion again reigned supreme for the next several days. Prematurely, the local U.S. Trustee's Office, a division of the Justice Department, announced that James Hassett had been selected as chapter 11 trustee for the Bennett bankruptcy.[21]

Hassett was an excellent choice. He had experience as bankruptcy trustee with several large leasing companies who were chapter 11 debtors, including CIS,[22] a local leasing company, and the infamous OPM Leasing, which is cited as precedent in many bankruptcy and nonbankruptcy leasing cases.

Hassett arrived the next day and toured the facility. I thought, Here we go again. More ungodly hours. More "making myself useful." Something, however, went wrong. The SEC lobbied against Hassett, opting for Richard C. Breeden, their former commander in chief to be the trustee—ironically, the same man the Bennetts feared would have been appointed receiver had they not filed bankruptcy.

Several days later, on April 17, 1996, it was announced Breeden was appointed officially as trustee and Hassett was out.[23] The assistant U.S. trustee who made the erroneous announcement was transferred. I called Rick Marshall and advised him of the turn of events.

"That's not good," he said.

"Why? What's going to happen?" I asked.

"He's going to lock the place down, fire everyone, then prosecute them," he said ominously. As Marshall worked for Breeden, I assumed he knew whereof he spoke. I dreaded the occasion and the even more "making myself useful."

On April 18, 1996, most everyone at work was lolling about, unsure of the future, not knowing what to do, wondering whether they would continue to draw a paycheck, and asking who's in charge.[24] Harrison had already left the scene. By five o'clock, everyone but Gordon, Marder,[25] and I had left, awaiting the inevitable.

Breeden and his team of lawyers from Simpson Thacher & Bartlett, a Manhattan-based megafirm,[26] and a team of forensic accountants from Coopers & Lybrand[27] swarmed in like Vikings who sailed from fjords to raid coastal towns. Breeden also brought a squad of Pinkerton guards.[28] The Pinks, as they are called, went to work immediately to secure the perimeter and the mainframe computer, and to change all of the locks. The Pinks were armed. They were polite but exuded the feeling that if you screwed around they'd shoot you.

While the Pinks were doing their thing, the rest of us went to the boardroom and sat around the twenty-foot long and eight-foot wide table. Breeden's entourage fired questions at me, sometimes all at once. At one point, Breeden made the time-out sign with his hands and took over the questioning until about ten o'clock that night. Although it was a grueling meeting, I got the sense that Rick Marshall was wrong; Breeden had no intention of mass firings or prosecutions. I went home to steal some dreamless sleep.

Kathleen McCarthy and Edmund T. "Bud" Bennett

FOUR PLAQUES signed by the pope, the governor of New York, the Onondaga County executive, and the mayor of Syracuse, proclaiming the Bennetts as "Family of the Year" hung prominently in the main reception area in the Bennetts' office building, the Atrium.

Adjacent to the plaques in a small alcove were various civic awards, *Inc.* magazine's prestigious three-time recognition of Bennett Funding as one of the "Top 500 Privately Held Companies in the US,"[1] and assorted pictures of the Bennetts hobnobbing with the rich and famous during the glory years.

In remembering the minichapel dedicated to the worship of the Bennetts, Lincoln's admonition comes to mind that "you can fool some of the people all of the time and all of the people some of the time, but not all of the people all of the time."[2]

The Atrium is a three-story class "A" office building dripping with marble and brass.[3] Each suite of offices has windows that face into the interior atrium, which is illuminated by large skylights. Every square inch of the perimeter of the open area is covered with lush, well-groomed vegetation.

As part of a $4.3 million like-kind real estate exchange,[4] the Atrium was purchased from an affiliate of the cash-strapped Olympia and York in 1994. The Bennett companies occupied portions of each of the Atrium's four floors. Other tenants occupied the balance. The third floor contained the companies' main reception area, the executive area, the boardroom, the finance department, and, in separate areas, lease sales and credit.[5]

Except for the sales area, the third floor was filled with paintings, antique furniture, vases, and other artwork repossessed from a lessee from Texas who defaulted on various big-ticket leases to the Company. All of the leases were insured against default.

Bennett Funding filed claims with the insurer, CIGNA, on the "Texas leases" and received the proceeds. CIGNA alleged the Company never tendered the value of the repossessed furniture and artwork until a suit and countersuit were filed years later.[6] More on this later.

Edmund T. "Bud" Bennett, age 67 on the petition filing date, is a self-made man.[7] A product of foster homes, Bud joined the marines early and was stationed in the Pacific at the end of World War II. After the war, he obtained a "business degree" from DeVry Institute in Chicago and went back to Syracuse. He married Kathleen McCarthy. The couple has two sons, Patrick and Michael.

Bud started out as an electronics technician and opened his own sales and repair store. His prosperity ran with the burgeoning technology. He even made an unsuccessful bid for public office.

In the mid-1970s, Bud had an inspiration: microwave technology was the way of the future in the transportation industry. He founded a small company specializing in his vision. Eventually, it grew and attracted Venrock Investors, a Rockefeller-backed group. Venrock made a large capital contribution to the venture.

Although the story isn't clear, somehow suits and countersuits among and between Bud, Venrock, and the other shareholders were instituted. Bud and his group were accused by Venrock of stock fraud and financial statement manipulation, a harbinger of the very accusations that have been leveled against his company some twenty years later.

The suit lasted years. Venrock eventually settled, deciding to simply pay Bud off and discontinue mounting legal costs. One of the lawyers[8] who put Bud through hell in the Venrock litigation in the 1970s became Bud and Kathleen's attorney in the bankruptcy and was present at the meeting concerning the attempt to get Bud's signature on the irrevocable trust proxy to Harrison.

As the story goes, through the Venrock settlement proceeds, Bud started Aloha Communications Systems, Inc., in 1977.[9] The name was changed to The Bennett Funding Group, Inc., in 1984, before my employment as corporate counsel.

To help in my efforts to get money from delinquent lessees, Bud was fond of reciting the following paradigm of collection philosophy: "I remember my first boss. If someone owed him money on a TV, he would go to their house, repossess the TV, and then smash it right in front of them."

In November 1995, when the Bennetts' mighty world began to break down, a rash of actual and threatened resignations from non-Bennett family officers started and continued until the filing of the petition in March 1996. The rank and file was losing morale and becoming nervous because so many key people were leaving. I heard a pool was started to name the next resignee.

In January 1996, when I was bitten by the resignation bug, Bud and Kathleen, desperate to stem the tide of resignations, asked me to visit them at home on the north side of Syracuse. We had a real heart-to-heart. We met for more than three hours. To sum up, I was told how I was "like a piece of furniture, always there, dependable."

I was a table. An armoire. After granting me certain assurances and securing my continued employment, Bud took the liberty of telling me his worldview of business: "a Jewish lawyer from New York, an Irish salesman."

I was typecast. How naïve I had been for all those years. In me, Bud thought he had another foreclosure specialist from Queens. I was not hired because of the content of my character, my youthful energy and aggressiveness, several years of litigation experience, and general good looks. I was hired because of my religion. Let me tell you affirmative action does no wonder for the hired person's self-esteem. Really big debt service.

Bud was a "show" marine. He loved being with and in the company of other marines. He loved the trappings. When angry or trying to prove a point, he threatened to "talk like a marine." He would marine-schmooze with other famous marine personages, such as F. Lee Bailey.[10]

Bud had met F. Lee while their yachts were docked alongside at the Bahamas. F. Lee was representing a time-share developer from the Bahamas who was looking for capital. As Resort Funding, a Bennett Funding subsidiary, was in the time-share finance business, the two had much to talk about.

Shortly after the meeting, F. Lee flew to Syracuse to negotiate a deal and review documents. I met him for breakfast before getting down to business. With the Sam Sheppard and O. J. Simpson cases to his credit, F. Lee is one of the most famous American lawyers. Who hasn't asked an inquisitorial person, "Who are you—F. Lee Bailey?"

F. Lee lived up to my expectations. He was animated, charming, and told interesting stories. We finished breakfast and went back to the Atrium to deal. Although the parties did not have a meeting of the minds, F. Lee spent several hours making a pitch.

Bud had a host of marine paraphernalia in his office, including small statues, a diorama, flags, and books. He even flew a marine flag on a huge staff just outside the Atrium. He was *semper fie.*

But when Bennett Funding filed the petition, and his son faced criminal prosecution, Bud was nowhere to be found. He and Kathleen fled to Florida to live in a double-wide trailer Kathleen had inherited. This was even before Bud himself was sued by the trustee and the investors for $1.8 billion.[11]

During the infant stages of the bankruptcy, I heard Bud exclaim that he "wished he was younger to fight back tooth and nail." But whom did he wish to fight? The investors who were fleeced? The employees who were robbed of their future? The banks that were swindled?

Surely, with such statements Bud was sensing realities that did not exist and wishing to act upon them. He was seeing the world as he wanted it to be rather than how it really was. The poetic Muses will not grant his request for rejuvenation, to hold him harmless, and dub him a victim under the circumstances he, mostly, engendered.

Bud Bennett left the employees to fend for ourselves. He deserted us. He left us to face the onslaught of reporters, disgruntled investors, class action attorneys, and the uncertainty of the future. He left us with underfunded and depleted pension plans. He left us all to face a world we did not create. Investors who know somebody say that Bud calls a mean line dance in the trailer community.

But what great doctrine, revolutionary idea, or liberating philosophy underscored Bud and Kathleen's flight to Florida like stealth bombers gone astray? Their flight supported no deontological principle. Despite the bad press and pressure from all sides, their very family name was at stake. They should have stayed and helped sort out the mess, and maybe in so doing, redeem themselves amid their community and peers who had supported them throughout the years.

If only Bud had taken an interest in his son's nefarious doings. If he had spent only a nanosecond on the status of the pension plans. If only he had been a real marine, that rare breed willing to make the ultimate sacrifice in defense of their country and comrades. If he had acted, so many things would be different now.

Two years after their flight to Florida, Bud and Kathleen had their big chance to set the record straight at their court-ordered depositions in Syracuse. Their counsel continually maintained they were too ill to travel and appear. Granted, Bud did have heart surgery years before and Kathleen had her stroke.

But who would be healthy when faced with public disgrace, the fear of imprisonment for their sons, economic ruination, and the overnight fall from grace and a weekly paycheck, which is the fate they so unmercifully employed against the workers—the constant fear of loss of job?

The sideshow of the elder Bennetts' health slipped in and out of focus until the local paper reported the couple drove to a Florida airport then flew to Syracuse on at least two occasions within one year after the filing of the bankruptcy.

Judge Gerling finally ordered Bud and Kathleen to appear at depositions by the end of March 1998 under the penalty of contempt, which
can lead to fine or imprisonment or both. They pleaded the Fifth
Amendment right against self-incrimination and refused to answer any
of the trustee's counsel's questions about what happened at the Company.[12] Like Pharaoh before them, the Bennetts' hearts were hardened and
their lips were sealed.

Bud used to say there are two ways a business can make money: increase sales and decrease costs. As part of the implementation of that
philosophy, in 1991, Bennett Funding did away with bonuses, curtailed
the rate of annual raises, and switched from employer-paid health insurance and pension plan to employee-contributed ones.

In that same year, Bud and Kathleen purchased a yacht, later named
the *Lady Kathleen*. Owing to a glut in the market for such luxury items,
the purchase price was only about $630,000.

The *Lady Kathleen,* as described in the brochure, was sixty-nine feet
of luxury, with stateroom appointments usually associated with those
depicted on "Lifestyles of the Rich and Famous." Not happy with the size
of the *Lady Kathleen,* Bud had an eight-foot extension added to the forward section. The dingy was named *Lil Bud.*

The yacht had its own captain and small crew. Although Captain Don
had some other chores, such as supervising the construction of a 236'
gaming boat in Florida, his first and foremost duty was to the *Lady Kathleen.* Bennett Funding paid the captain's and crews salaries and expenses,
such as food, travel, and land-based lodging.

About one year before the bankruptcy, Bud told me the captain was
abusing his privileges by entertaining women on board without permission. When Kathleen finally had enough with Captain Don's seafaring
man's way of life, she had Bud fire him summarily by throwing him out
of his office like so much jetsam despite years of dedicated service. The
captain filed suit for breach of contract. I offered to settle for one year's
salary and medical benefits. The offer was rejected. The suit consequently, like so many others, became entangled in the net of the bankruptcy
and is of little value.[13]

As far as can be traced, virtually all proceeds used to purchase, refur-
bish, finance, and maintain the yacht came from one Bennett company
or another.[14] Despite the financial ownership, title to the *Lady Kathleen*
was vested in the names of Bud and Kathleen.

Capitalizing on being record owners, Bud and Kathleen's postpetition plan was to sell the *Lady Kathleen,* some local real property and personal assets, and flip the proceeds into a new house or some other "safe" and untouchable asset in Florida of comparable value. Thereafter, as the money and other assets were converted and residency requirements fulfilled, the couple would declare bankruptcy.

Florida allows people to shelter some of their "reported" booty by acquiring exempt houses.[15] As Florida has among the most liberal homestead exemptions in the nation, the Bennetts would have been able to keep their new home. We have all seen the news reports of palatial homes and sprawling landscapes, right in front of the noses of the local seniors who were ripped off: "I live on social security and some retirement money. I had investments. Investments that guy stole. Now look how he lives. Like a king. Justice is a sometime thing."

There is nothing wrong intrinsically with allowing an exemption for a person's house, if the house is truly a person's home and not some vulgar monstrosity acquired within six months of the filing of a bankruptcy petition. Although its law does provide a mechanism to set aside fraudulent asset conversion, for the most part, Florida seems to subscribe to the doctrine that a man's home is his castle.

Soon after the petitions were filed, Bud and Kathleen put their plan into action and sold the *Lady Kathleen.*[16] Although the net proceeds after paying the outstanding ship's mortgage and broker's fees were less than $80,000, the trustee got wind of the deal and sued immediately. Bankruptcy Judge Gerling ordered the money escrowed until a final determination was reached temporarily foiling Bud's plan to purchase a new residence.

During the hearing on the disposition of the proceeds, I was subpoenaed to testify by Bud's counsel. Treated as a hostile witness, I was accused of being a liar, a breacher of fiduciary duty, and every other contemptible thing one can think of while on the stand in open court. Bud even submitted an affidavit to discredit me as if I hatched the plot to rescue the proceeds.

The affidavit stated: "Stewart Weisman was personally responsible for the maintenance of the yacht."[17] Besides the fact Bud never invited me on the boat, I have never seen the boat, and I get seasick—how ludicrous to suggest I maintained the boat. Did I sneak out of my office from Syracuse and repair the engines in Florida? I'm good with a hammer, but I don't know my ass from my elbow about boats. As the adage goes, "Des-

The *Lady Kathleen* with the 8' dinghy *Lil Bud* suspended above the stern. Courtesy of "Captain" Don Carroll.

perate people will take desperate measures," no matter the desperation was bred in evil and brought about by corrupt behavior.

Finally, on August 3, 1998, Judge Gerling awarded the trustee $456,500 against Bud and Kathleen for reimbursement of expenses paid by the Bennett companies toward the yacht.[18] Bud and Kathleen have not yet filed bankruptcy.

After Bud purchased the *Lady Kathleen* in 1991, all he could do was talk about the yacht. His braggadocio came partly at the expense of employee bonuses that had been given every year at Christmas since the Company's inception. The cut came without warning a day or two before the holiday just as in Chevy Chase's movie *National Lampoon's Christmas Vacation*.

To assuage her conscience, Kathleen even convinced herself that the employees who complained their meager bonuses would be missed were to be dealt with.

"How dare they expect bonuses!" she yelled to a group of stunned managers at a meeting.

"They should be lucky they have jobs," Bud added as he poured over plans for extending the forward section of the yacht. All managers were expected to tow the line and trickle down the grinch philosophy to their staffs.

Lord knows what prehistoric sensitivity training or management school they attended, but the Bennetts even held up a newspaper story that AT&T was to lay off six thousand workers to invoke foxhole mentality relief from their own workforce.

"Thank God I have a job!"

Some cost cuts were necessary, such as reducing travel allowances and restructuring reimbursement guidelines for car and mileage allowances. But most of the cuts impacted directly on payroll and the employees' perks. Such cuts should not have been borne on the backs of the workers.

While Bud and Kathleen were busy counting pennies saved, Patrick was diverting tens of millions from widows and the employee pension fund. While Bud and Kathleen cut back raises, Michael was spending $20 million for the Hotel Syracuse. While the family lounged aboard the *Lady Kathleen,* brokers were selling fake leases to senior citizens.

Year after year, during the first weeks of December, the Bennetts' Christmas party topped the Company's agenda. Although the Bennetts' hotels, Vernon Downs, and other affiliates had their own parties, the main party was held for Company employees, their spouses, and the Bennetts' inner circle, about five hundred people.

The Bennett Funding Christmas parties were fun because one was among coworkers. No airs were needed. One simply ate, had drinks, did a little dancing, told or listened to stories, and went home.

Several weeks before the party, the employees chipped in to buy a gift for Bud and Kathleen. The presentation occurred midparty. Generally, the employee who championed the gift took the mike, made a brief acknowledgment, and invited the Bennetts to the podium to receive their gift.

The Bennetts were genuinely touched; after all, how many chief executives received gifts from the entire workforce? How many shareholders were as beloved as Bud and Kathleen? The gift giving went on year after year with the value of the gift increasing apace with the cost of luxury living.

One year it was a weekend trip to New York City to see a Broadway play. The trip included airfare, limousine service, food, swank hotel accommodations, and the tickets. Another year an artist was commissioned to paint their portraits.

Yet, into this Eden, a serpent did slither. Somehow, attendance at the parties was taken. One did not dare miss the Christmas party for fear of winding up on Mrs. B.'s shit list of undesirables. Even the absence of spouses was duly noted. Unbelievably, the gift giving went on despite the elimination of bonuses and the de-perking of the employees' benefits.

I recall an incident involving former associate general counsel Thomas Kingsley, Bud, and a turkey. Tom worked for the Bennetts from 1989 to 1994. His primary responsibility was enforcing the terms and conditions of the leases against wayward lessees. Tom was the former law librarian at Syracuse University Law School, holds a master's degree in library science, a B.A. in Spenserian English, and is one of the few men I know who looks good in a bow tie. In the sterile Bennett world of business, we talked about art and literature. We were a good team.

There came a time when Tom was trying to settle a rather large litigation. Seizing upon a window of opportunity, Tom was able to hammer out the terms of a settlement. Instead of saying nice job in collecting, say, 75 percent of the debt, Bud Bennett, who disdained settlement because he could not walk away the clear victor, had asked Tom whose side he was on. He said that to his litigation counsel who had brought in millions of dollars in collected funds, and had nothing but the best interests of the Company at heart. On another occasion, Tom had won another action for a substantial sum of money. When told of the victory, all Bud could ask was, "Where's the check?"

In the business of lease litigation, it is always preferable to settle, get your money, get out, and move on. This is not to say we accepted low amounts in full satisfaction of claims, or that we did not pursue remedies to the fullest extent under the law. Indeed, we aggressively pursued all who owed us money, but we applied cost/benefit analyses to do so.

The philosophy of settlement recognizes the economic realities inherent in the operation. Inasmuch as the spread in the leasing business at the Company was small, every day that passed without income generated by lease payments had a negative multiplier effect upon the financial health of the Company. Bills had to be paid in timely fashion regardless of cash flow.

We were under tremendous pressure to sue, to win, and to collect. As any litigation lawyer can tell you, winning can be at times easy, but collecting can be another story. We lived in a dichotomy: management demanded results but chastised us for spending too much in outside legal fees or settling accounts for too little.

In 1991, just as they announced bonuses were no longer to be paid because of unanticipated costs associated with operations, the Bennetts started an annual tradition of handing out Thanksgiving turkeys to the employees.

As Thanksgiving 1993 approached, Bud became increasingly anxious because the turkey-in-lieu-of-raise was at hand. The ritual involved a truck stuffed with turkeys waiting at the loading dock. The employees would line up and be handed their twenty-pound birds. Their names would be checked on the master list.

As a protest against the metamorphosis of our bonuses into a feathered thing, Tom and I refused to accept our turkeys. Not wanting to let food go to waste, however, we decided to donate our birds to a food bank. Tom offered to fetch the birds from the loading dock. Dutifully, his name was checked as having received two turkeys.

That same afternoon, Bud called Tom into his office and basted him for taking two turkeys. Bud said Tom had ruined the joy he felt during the giveaway. Tom's days were numbered. I guess Tom had some debt service as well. He resigned not long thereafter and opened his own, now successful, practice.

By the way, our two turkeys were donated to the Rescue Mission. Two years later, the Rescue Mission itself fell victim to investor fraud perpetrated by John Bennett, no relation, the founder and former president of the Foundation for New Era Philanthropy.[19] New Era specialized in swindling money from charities. Although much of the money was ultimately recovered, the Mission still lost a bundle and incalculable public faith in its operations.

The Bennetts, selected officers, and favored employees who worked at the Atrium parked in the adjacent Company-owned lot. Other Atrium tenants were allocated the remaining spaces. A swipe card was needed to access the gated lot, except on the weekends. All other employees parked about two blocks away in a Bennett-owned garage.

The garage was poorly designed and in a general state of ill repair. Cars were routinely damaged by concrete pieces falling from the roof. Even the staircase had rusted metal shards hanging like malevolent stalactites. Especially in the winter, it took an inordinate amount of time to exit.

Because parking assignments were doled out by the Bennetts, the lot became a source of petty jealously and bitterness among the employees, as there seemed to be no logical reason why certain people were given lot spots and some consigned to the garage.

One early October, a major tenant moved out leaving about fifteen spaces open in the lot. A few days later, an early snowstorm dumped about a foot of snow in the area. Although Syracuse gets hellish winters, this early season storm was unexpected and pernicious.

A longtime employee who had recently been promoted to vice president assumed he was in line to receive a lot assignment. Obtaining an extra swipe card, he gained entry and parked his car in one of the spots left open by the former tenant. After he entered the Atrium from the lot, the employee was told that Fred, the building engineer (superintendent) wanted to see him. Fred stood about 5'11", thin to the extreme and bespectacled. Fred always wore jeans and a short-sleeve shirt with breast pocket and numerous pens.

In front of three outside contractors, Fred told the employee to move the car. The employee asked for a break because of the snowstorm. "Besides, there are plenty of open spaces," he pleaded.

"No way," Fred said. "You better move the car." His tone was menacing. The three contractors looked at one another in embarrassment and began to back away, like the Magi in reverse, sensing the impending clash.

"But, Fred, be reasonable," he pleaded, repeating the litany of open spaces and storm.

"Just move the car," he responded.

"C'mon, Fred, give me a break. You know I'm a new officer of the company," he said hoping to appeal to Fred's sense of propriety.

Fred, sitting behind his desk with hands folded behind his head and elbows jutting in front like a ram said, "I don't care who you are. You better move that damn car."

"Listen, I'm not moving the car," the employee shot back.

"Yeah, I'll have it towed."

"Don't touch that car if you know what's good for you," he finished and stormed out, blood coursing hotly. He went to his office and cooled down. A bit later, he told me the story and asked me to intercede on his behalf with Fred. I did and the matter was thought to be concluded.

Bud and Kathleen came into work later that morning. As Bud walked into his office, which at the time was diagonally across from mine, Bud yelled to his secretary to get the employee up to his office. The secretary made the call, and after a minute or two, the employee went into Bud's office.

"Who the fuck do you think you are?" Bud screamed as he slammed the door.

The employee went into shock. He didn't know what Bud was talking about.

"Fred said you walked into his office and said you were an officer and could park anywhere you want," Bud roared.

"I . . . I didn't say that. That's not what happened," the employee stammered.

"You move that fucking car now or I'll have it towed myself," he screamed.

The employee walked out of Bud's office quickly with head hung down and all hope of posture gone. Apparently, Fred reneged on our agreement and got to Bud first. It seemed the Bennetts believed whomever told the story first. FLIB, first lie is believed.

I called the employee in his office and asked if he was okay. We agreed to meet later for lunch. He relayed Bud's treatment.

"I felt naked and humiliated. There was no spot in the universe in which I could seek shelter. There was no comfort zone," he told me.

"I want to storm into Bud's office and tell him he can't talk to me like that," the employee fantasized. He even thought Bud would apologize and he could return to work with a sense of euphoria that must have been felt by Neil Armstrong on the moon and Sir Edmund Hillary on the summit of Mt. Everest.

Bud, the classic bully, was playing tough. He was demonstrating that he was in charge, that he signed the paycheck. From the episode, my innate understanding that strength of character is not derived through money and its corrupting power was reinforced. Bud's personality was his problem, his karma. Belittling others forces a repeat through the next lifetime.

I gave the employee some advice. "Any real confrontation with Bud will not be a fair fight considering the impact of immediate job termination upon your wife, the kids, the payment of bills, the job market, the mortgage." I told him that "sometimes as an employee you have to eat shit, mounds of shit."

Despite the appreciation of the inner reality, I told the employee that as he was still employed at Bennett Funding, he needed to clear the air. I advised him to speak with Kathleen, knowing she would understand his feelings in this matter.

I could not have been more wrong. Although she agreed, in principle, Bud was perhaps a little rough, she supported wholeheartedly the point he was trying to accomplish. What point? The pursuit of absolute power over people? Instant humiliation? A fair and evenhanded policy toward automobile parking?

The employee never regained favor in the Bennetts' eyes and eventually left the Company.

Kathleen McCarthy Bennett, age sixty-three on the petition date, is of Irish-German stock.[20] Her mother was part of the Kuhl (cool) clan of Syracuse, a prominent local family. With nondescript hair color that seemed to change hues from week to week, Kathleen stands barely five feet tall in sharp contrast to Bud's six-foot frame. Through a stroke suffered a few years before the bankruptcy, Kathleen lost the functioning of an eye and ear.

Kathleen seemed incapable and unwilling to forget or forgive a slight, be it real or imagined. One treaded lightly about Kathleen with the knowledge that many a career lay in shambles because of her whims. Once fallen from grace for whatever trivial offense, it took years, if at all, to regain favor.

As a young wife, Kathleen suffered unfortunately a couple of miscarriages. Instead of showing mercy, compassion, and understanding, her form of feminism tended to be very tough on women who needed extra time off because of a new birth or miscarriage.

Kathleen expressed the view that women in the workplace should be strong and not have special considerations because of maternal needs. In this fashion, the logic went, women will be treated as equals, although the women involved were basically nine-to-fivers who were not interested in a career, just putting food on the table.

Kathleen was a shareholder, director, president and manager of personnel of Bennett Funding. She took her roles seriously: special shopping days at Bonwit Teller, midday beauty salon visits, charity balls, boating aboard her namesake yacht, and attendance at lavish parties.

Kathleen was one of the women invited to attend a special luncheon with Hillary Rodham Clinton when she visited Syracuse in the mid-nineties, prior to Hillary's senatorial bid.

"Mrs. B.," as she was known by the employees, was confident in her ability to assess people, to delve into their hearts, and to get to the essence of their beings. Despite her Kreskin-like talent, it has been said many of Bud's decisions, particularly those affecting personnel, were as a result of Kathleen's all-night-long nagging.

Although Kathleen publicly denounced those who spread scuttlebutt, rumor, innuendo, and the other horsemen, she employed spies throughout the Company. The toadies reported to her every infraction, every bit of gossip and dirt the interaction of 275 people at the home office could muster. She was addicted to the stuff. It seems true one hates in others what one does wrongly himself or herself.

Kathleen's habit included reading the insurance claim forms of her employees thereby learning all of the medical and psychological problems of her workforce.

As one reflects upon Bud's and Kathleen's boorish behavior as typified in the handling of the car incident, in the final analysis, under any circumstance, one should not and cannot allow another to define one's worth or value as a human being.

I am reminded of the poignant passage in *Night* by Nobel Prize winner Elie Wiesel. Wiesel's father, who ultimately died in a concentration camp, told young Elie that wearing the dehumanizing and demeaning yellow Magen David, the Star of David, would not kill him. Elie reflected, "Of what then did you die, father?"[21]

In a strange manifestation of karma, about one year later, the officer who was savaged by Bud drew the duty to fire Fred, the building engineer, for, among other things, keeping the "good luck" change dropped into the Atrium's fountain.

From Bennett Funding's incorporation in November 1977, all 31 of its issued and outstanding common shares were owned by Kathleen. Then, in January 1994, Bennett Funding increased the amount of authorized shares from 200 to 10 million.[22] The corporation accepted Kathleen's offer to purchase such additional shares. In turn, Kathleen transferred half of the newly acquired shares to Bud—5 million shares of common stock each.

Later, in December 1995, as the heat intensified and to show the SEC they "meant business" and were "serious in their efforts to rout problems," and maybe to insulate their assets, Bud and Kathleen placed their 10 million shares of Bennett Funding into a revocable trust. Unlike an irrevocable trust, the Bennetts' trust could be discontinued at will and the shares returned, no questions asked.

David Barrett, a well-known and well-connected Washington, D.C., lawyer served as trustee.[23] He also represented Bud and Kathleen as part of the coterie of counsel before the SEC. He resigned three months later on March 28, 1996, as a result of the allegations against Bennett Funding and Patrick Bennett by the SEC.

In his resignation letter Barrett stated: "When I agreed to be Trustee of the Trust which was established December 28, 1995, it was our under-standing that it was for estate purposes for your children and grandchil-dren. Now, it appears that there are potential considerations far beyond those of mere estate planning. . . ."

On first blush, it appeared Barrett deserted his clients at the time they needed him most. Upon closer inspection, however, he did the right thing. Bud and Patrick lied to him as they did to the SEC, their outside counsel, their auditors, the employees, me, and to themselves about vir-tually everything concerning the Company's assets and liabilities. In the end, it proved unwise to have lied to the very people defending them.

Alms to the Poor

TRADITION HOLDS that there are eight levels of charity:

• to give grudgingly, reluctantly, or with regret;
• to give less than one should, but with grace,
• to give what one should, but only after being asked;
• to give before one is asked;
• to give without knowing who will receive it, although the recipient knows the identity of the giver;
• to give without making known one's identity;
• to give so that neither giver nor receiver knows the identity of the other;
• to help another to become self-supporting, by means of a gift, a loan, or by finding employment for the one in need.[1]

When I asked a rabbi[2] about the levels of giving, he said simply, "Any giving is better than not giving."

By all accounts, the Bennetts were a charitable family. They donated money, conducted and attended fund-raisers, and were involved with sponsoring children from Belfast for the summer. Bud even hit us up to buy rather expensive raffle tickets on behalf of his favorite church.

Just as almost every personal asset of the Bennetts was bought by the Company through siphoned funds, just as their whole way of life was leveraged, so too was their charitable giving. Simply, large-scale giving is easy using other people's money.

Their charity had a face. Strings were attached—no anonymous giving. Every charitable act was orchestrated—publicity, splash, accolade, praise, worship. These were the essence of Bennett-giving, the handmaidens of demagogues.

The Bennetts did not seem to grasp the concept that true charity was faceless, that it is its own reward, that it is divinely inspired. Nor did they give of themselves physically by rolling up their sleeves and pitching in.

One time during a meeting of the board of the local chapter of the Make-a-Wish Foundation, Mrs. Bennett bumped into associate counsel Tom Kingsley.[3]

"Why are you here?" she asked Tom.

"I'm on the board," he responded.

"Oh, really," Kathleen said snidely, and walked away as if only her family could do good works.[4]

The Bennetts preferred to donate money in the context of an affair, a dinner, an event requiring one to wear black tie or gown. To look handsome and pretty. To mingle with others similarly situated. To clink glasses. To recite toasts. To bask in the light of the privileged. To indulge in the mysticism of seating arrangements. To shop for clothing. This was charity for the Bennetts. And tax deductible too.

Years later, based on the premise that contributed funds were derived from the Ponzi scheme, trustee Breeden was compelled to sue all charities that received corporate donations from the Bennetts. Breeden did not go after the charities that received donations from the Bennetts personally, as the connections were tenuous.

He stated, "[W]hen a whole bunch of people are cheated in a bankruptcy situation, particularly a fraudulent situation, the law requires you to go after everybody, get back all the money you can."

Included in the actions against charities were those seeking "$5,950 from the Upstate New Chapter of the Multiple Sclerosis Society, $4,550 from the Crouse Hospital Foundation, $2,000 . . . [from] the Interreligious Council . . . and $7,500 from the Hiawatha Council of the Boy Scouts of America."[5]

Although such lawsuits seem to go against the grain, these cases posed no great ethical dilemma. The charities learned that the Bennett donations derived from a criminal enterprise that stole money from widows, orphans, and the elderly. The donations were not authorized by the

Ponzi victims. They could not even claim the deductions. The charities did nothing to earn the funds. They did not offer to pay them back. Breeden had no recourse but lawsuit.

The Evil Empire

PRESENTED BELOW is the lineup of the known corporations, partnerships, proprietorships, and their subsidiaries, affiliates, successors, and assigns[1] in which the Bennetts, individually or in combination, held controlling, substantial, or insider[2] interests at one time or another.

The businesses were incorporated in or organized under the laws of Alabama, Arkansas, the Bahamas, Bermuda, Delaware, Florida, Georgia, Iowa, Kentucky, Missouri, Nevada, New York, Ohio, Tennessee, Texas, Toronto (Ont.), Vancouver (B.C.), or from parts unknown.

Many were incorporated by the Bennetts or were the targets of takeover and acquisition like an amoeba engulfing its food.

Aegis Consumer Funding Group, Inc.
Aloha Capital Corporation
Aloha Leasing Canada, Inc.
Aloha Leasing, Inc.
Aloha Telecommunications, Inc.
American Gaming & Entertainment, Ltd.
American Marine International, Ltd.
Beaver Valley Resort, Inc.
Bennett Acquisitions Corporation
Bennett Atrium, Ltd.
Bennett Centralized Purchasing Corp.
Bennett Companies, Inc.,
Bennett Employee Benefits, Ltd.
Bennett Finance Incorporated
Bennett Finance I-V
Bennett Funding Corporation
Bennett Funding Group, Inc., The
Bennett Funding Limited
Bennett Funding of New York Corp.

Bennett Insurance Company, Ltd.
Bennett International Credit Corporation
Bennett Management & Development Corp.
Bennett Receivables Corporation
Bennett Receivables Corporation–II
Bennett Telecom Funding Corporation
Bennett Travel Management Group, Inc.
Bennetts' Northway Inn, Inc.
BFGSP
BFICP
Castle Office Systems, Inc.
Comfort Associates, Inc.
Comfort Financial Associates
Continental Recreation—Hidden Cove, Inc.
Continental Recreation—Lazy Creek, Inc.
Continental Recreation—Serendipity, Inc.
Continental Recreation—Tama, Inc.
Continental Recreation—U.S.A., Inc.
Continental Recreation Corp.
Cordoba Corporation
Crusa Shore-to-Shore, Inc.
Dollar Capital Corporation
Eagles Ridge, Inc.
Empire State Management & Development Corp.
Endless Trails Resorts, Inc.
Equity Guarantee Corp.
Equivest Finance, Inc.
Equivest International, Inc.
Exponential Business Development
Ferris Industries, Inc.
G.E.M. Financial Corp.
Hotel Syracuse, Inc.
Jameson-Dewitt & Associates, Inc.
Kenton Portfolio, Inc.
Lazy Creek Resort, Inc.
Liberty Helicopter
Liberty Helicopter Tours, Inc.
M. A. Bennett Associates, Ltd.
Mammoth Caverns Resorts, Inc.

Meridian Helicopter, Inc.
Mid-State Raceway, Inc.
Mutual Investors Funding Corporation
Okatoma River Resort, Inc.
Olympus Property Management Corp.
Pegasus Entertainment & Funding Corp.
Processing Center, Inc.
Resort Funding, Inc.
Resort Management & Development Corp.
Resort Service Company, Inc.
Scriptex Acquisition Corporation
Scriptex Enterprises, Ltd.
Shamrock Holdings Group, Inc.
Southern Leisure, Inc.
Standardbred Enterprises, Ltd.
TargetVision, Inc.
The Big South Fork
Troiano-Scerbo Productions, Inc.
Trapper John, Inc.
V.I.P. World Resort

Another Boat

DURING THE course of the bankruptcy trustee's suit against Bud and Kathleen for, among other things, breach of fiduciary duty in allowing their son Patrick to engage in a $1 billion Ponzi scheme, there came a time the Carver boat scandal surfaced. This matter perhaps more than any other epitomizes the corruption, backdating, document re-creation, stealing, and misuse of corporate privilege that ran rampant among the Bennetts. The facts are as follows.

In 1985, Resort Funding, Inc., nka (now known as) Resort Service Company, Inc., a subsidiary of Bennett Funding, purchased a 36´ Carver boat and motor for $105,000. Shortly thereafter, Bud had me draft a bill of sale from Resort Funding to himself. The title documents were prepared in his name and filed with the state. Postpetition investigation reveals Bud avoided paying the purchase price to Resort Funding.

Not long after the title transfer, the boat was leased to Bud by Aloha Leasing, the leasing division of Bennett Funding. It is a mystery how Aloha got ownership and title to the boat as the certificate of title remained with Bud and was not transferred to Aloha or any other Bennett company for that matter. How can a company lease something it neither owns nor has an interest in?

In any event, the lease was assigned a number and recorded in the Company's computer system. The record is not clear if Bud made any lease payments to the Company. Even if he did, the genesis of the cash used for such payments can be rightfully questioned given the track record of the *Lady Kathleen.*

About eight months later, Bud was cruising on a lake in New York. The boat was boarded by the maritime division of the Sheriff's Department. The deputies were performing routine title searches to ensure that the boaters had paid the appropriate sales tax to the state at the time of purchase. A computer inquiry revealed no sales tax was paid to New York during any link in the purchase or subsequent lease of the Carver boat.

Bud was given a citation and ordered to pay $9,000 for sales tax. Bud raided the corporate kitty to pay the fee. He made sure that the lessor, Aloha, paid the $9,000 sales tax. And he took an additional $45,000 in cash and had the lease payments increased accordingly. Imagine asking your Jeep leasing company to give you $10,000 in cash and write it into the monthly lease payment.

Bud had a new Aloha lease written to reflect the modifications, which was then backdated to the date of the original Aloha lease eight months earlier. He ordered the accounting records to be changed as well. All of his commands were followed.

After Bud bought the *Lady Kathleen* he gave the Carver boat to Michael. Michael wrote yet another lease with Aloha as lessor. The certificate of title, however, was still in Bud's name. During this time, as money was flying every which way but loose, Bud never divested title to the boat. Michael paid right up until March 1996.

During the bankruptcy, we learned the Carver boat was for sale. Through a court order, the proceeds of about $60,000 were placed into escrow. Bud and the trustee fought for the money, the trustee on principle and Bud for the money. Remember, the Carver boat was leased by Aloha to Michael, yet Bud claimed the proceeds. There was no legal basis for Bud's claim.

During the Carver litigation, a deposition of a former operations officer of Bennett Funding was conducted. She advised, under oath, on March 27, 1996, Bud was trying frantically to liberate funds from his Prime Conversion Account, the PCA.

The PCA was a particularly pernicious creation. People purchased leases from Bennett Funding as investments. In theory, no lease product no investment. But investors wanted leases in the worst way, and Patrick could not resist the lure of easy cash.

Investors turned over money to Patrick while awaiting application to leases or other products. Patrick placed the money into the PCA. Until the funds could be used to purchase a lease or other financial product, interest was to accrue, akin to a money-market account.

But to the chagrin of all who fell prey, the PCA existed as an accounting entry only—no bank or corporate account existed in reality. It was a virtual account existing in cyberspace. No interest was paid by any third party. The PCA was used to grease the Ponzi. The money was sucked into the giant cash vacuum cleaner known as the "honeypot," and was was used to buy toys for the Bennetts, such as stocks, a racetrack, floating casinos, and hotels.

Please note that on March 27, the SEC faxed a courtesy copy of its complaint to Rick Marshall, Bud's counsel, with a side comment that it was to be filed the next day, March 28.

So Bud knew on March 27 that the SEC was to sue on March 28. He was scrambling for his money from the PCA, as reported by the operations officer. While an explosion was about to occur equal to that which destroyed the island of Krakatoa, Bud was worried about his money. While investors and employees were about to have their lives ripped asunder, he schemed for his ill-gotten gain. While worlds were going to collide, he plotted.

The great and brilliant philosopher Immanuel Kant believed people should be treated as ends unto themselves and not as means.[1] The bus driver is not a means to get you somewhere. She is an ends, a person, a human being. The Bennetts did not learn this true and valuable lesson. They opted for the Machiavellian[2] side of life treating all as pawns in their never-ending grab for money.

Bud still maintains he paid the buyout for the Carver boat on March 28 with funds from the PCA, and consequently the boat and the proceeds are his. Fortunately, because of the pandemonium that broke out on March 28, the PCA funds were never transferred on the Company's books and records. Whatever money Bud gave to his son Patrick (to be deposited into the PCA) was looted. According to their counsel, Bud and Kathleen feel cheated because they believe the boat and the proceeds from its sale belong to them.

The Mastermind, Patrick R. Bennett

PATRICK BENNETT, the cherubic eldest son of Bud and Kathleen, was chief financial officer of Bennett Funding. He stands about 5′9″, portly with thinning gray/brown hair. Patrick has that pale and transparent skin of a man who sallies forth at night. Color-blind like his father, he needs other people to pick out suit-and-tie combinations.

At Bennett Funding, Patrick was the lord and master of cash in and cash out. He owned the Finance Department ("Finance") and was responsible for funding all of the Company's operations and cash dealings. All. Finance was Patrick's fiefdom. His manor. Its color scheme was green for money.

Finance was on the third floor, just off the main entranceway. It was separated physically from the rest of the Company by partitions and corridors, thick walls and doors. People could and did visit Finance and you'd never know they were in the building.

Ostensibly, Finance had a standard hierarchical structure complete with a manager and assistant managers. In reality, Patrick ruled with an iron fist. He controlled every decision made by the members of the department. When he wanted something accomplished his way, no feedback, no cross talk, no way but his was permitted.

Money ran Bennett Funding and Patrick controlled the money. If ever the expression "purse strings" had meaning, surely it was here. Patrick pulled those strings, made them sing like a harp. Patrick was given dominion and control over Finance like Adam over the beasts of the field.

"Patrick's the best financial officer in the country," Bud was fond of boasting at public gatherings such as Christmas parties and grand openings. He said it like he meant it. Bud was right. After all, Patrick ran the largest Ponzi scheme in American history—quod erat demonstrandum.

Despite the integration of the computer system Companywide, and what seemed like daily visits from bankers, brokers, investors, auditors, lawyers, CPAs, businesspeople and their associates, Finance, through

Patrick Bennett at the federal courthouse in Manhattan. Photo by John Berry. Copyright ©
The Syracuse Newspapers.

Patrick's manipulations, was allowed by the other Bennetts to operate
with billing, cash receipts, and cash disbursement systems independent
of those used by other departments and operations. This was propelled
indirectly by Patrick's brother Michael.

When I was hired in 1984, the Company also hired a computer programmer. Just as the Legal Department grew through the years, so too
did the computer department, Management Information Systems
(MIS). Programmers were busy all day writing software to support vari-

ous operations and administrative tasks. Soon, program requests over-whelmed MIS. Michael stepped in and took control. He triaged the pro-gramming requests, reserving approval and veto power unto himself.

Eventually, Michael split up MIS, sending the programmers to the various departments, like the Mongol seed offerings to the four winds. Thus, Finance got its own programmer. He wrote Finance-specific pro-grams or coordinated and troubleshot third-party proprietary programs that were newly installed. These programs were not accessible by anyone but Patrick and those Finance employees on a need to perform basis.

The trustee's complaint against the Bennetts and their allies stated that Finance, under Patrick, "ran free from any meaningful supervision or oversight by any other person from within the organization, including the other Bennetts."[1]

In other words, Patrick ran the whole show. Even during the end days when the monthly nut to crack was $15 million in and $30 million out, even when the feds were closing in, even when investor checks bounced in January 1996, Patrick was still in charge of the money.[2]

In a memorandum to investors in January 1996, Patrick advised the Company "would not make the principal and interest payments due to investors on either January 30 of February 15, but instead would make an additional monthly payment at the end of each Lease Assignment's term."[3] In some cases, the termini of assignments were five years down the road.

Patrick stated the Company needed to make this "adjustment" be-cause end users were not paying their leases on time to Bennett Funding. Patrick told investors they would be compensated for the "postponed payment by receiving a taxable payment equal to .75% of the investor's principal balance."[4]

By doing this, Patrick was able to substantially reduce payments the Company made to investors on January 30 and February 15, 1996. The other Bennetts permitted it.

Before the imposition of its complaint in March 1996, the enforce-ment staff of the SEC revealed it had concerns the Company "might not have sufficient cash flow to meet its obligations to investors."[5] According-ly, the SEC asked the Company to "quantify . . . outstanding obligations, and identify the source of funds that [Bennett Funding] would use to meet those obligations."[6]

Several weeks later, Patrick's counsel advised the staff it "had current outstanding obligations of approximately $438 million."[7] A computer printout was produced showing receivables of $273 million, a shortfall of some $165 million.

To mask the obvious chasm of unrequited debt, Company counsel told the staff "additional receivables were not reflected on the documents,"[8] which would cover the shortfall. Although given ample opportunity, the Company never supplied any evidence of the additional receivables.

Instead, in November 1995, counsel told the SEC Bennett "planned to retain an accounting firm, Richard Eisner & Co., to conduct a cash flow analysis"[9] and show sufficient cash flow.

Like so many things promised, the Eisner report was not produced to the SEC because Eisner and Co. was not permitted to conduct the audit. Patrick could ill afford an independent report that would verify the SEC's concerns.

As the pressure mounted, Patrick threatened to separate Finance from the rest of the Company. He told the other Bennetts, "I'll just pull the money out of here and go on my own. If Bennett Funding needs money it'll have to borrow it from me."

Bud knuckled under. He was scared of Patrick. He knew his son had the power of the purse. That fear, coupled with Celtic pride and stubbornness, and a healthy dose of greed, allowed him to turn blind eyes and to accept the bullshit Patrick fed him about why things were the way things were at Bennett Funding.

Just as other departments within the Company and other departments in all corporations, Finance relied upon several computer programs and applications and their corresponding databases in administering its business activities. Among the programs and applications used by Finance were the Finance system (FIN) and the Inventory system (INV). FIN was designed to track leases that were pledged as collateral to the 245 banks that made loans to the Company. INV tracked leases that were sold and assigned to the twelve thousand individual investors.

To help perpetuate his crimes, Patrick ensured those essential lease-allocating systems, INV and FIN—yin and yang—operated independently of each other. The information regarding bank loans and investor transactions did not intermesh in the systems or anywhere else for that matter. Cloisters within cloisters. The deliberate separation of the systems not only permitted double-pledging of leases without suspicion but also fostered the corporate culture of secrecy and compartmentalization so necessary to perpetrate the fraud upon an unsuspecting public.

In essence, because of the separateness of INV and FIN, one system could not detect whether the same lease was listed as assigned to an investor or pledged as collateral to a bank in the other system. As it turns it, FIN and INV, Tweedledum and Tweedledee, were electronic aiders and abettors in this most sophisticated part of the Ponzi.

In Patrick's methodology, the deliberate lack of integration of the FIN and INV systems carried over to the Finance employees who used them. Aping the INV and FIN systems on the computer, Finance had two subsections, the commercial and municipal, which in turn had their own employees.

Essentially, equipment leases are of two varieties, commercial and municipal. Commercial leases have lessees that are corporations, partnerships, sole proprietorships—commercial business enterprises. The Bennett Funding commercial leases were generally pledged to banks as collateral although many such leases were sold to investors as well. Because of the inherent risk involved in dealing with businesses, such as bankruptcy and slow pay, and the full taxation of the payments, the rate of return on these leases was relatively greater.

Municipal leases deal with political subdivisions of a state, school districts, and agencies, that is, governmental organizations. Although municipal lessees could cancel their leases if the budget ax chopped off appropriations for the next fiscal year, generally, municipal lessees were less credit risky than their commercial counterparts.

Moreover, municipal leases enjoy certain tax-exempt benefits, that is, the interest component on the monthly stream of payments is tax exempt.[10] Accordingly, the rates of return were lower than the commercial leases. These leases were generally assigned to investors by Bennett Funding, although, as it turns out, most were also pledged to banks as collateral.

Basically, the commercial subsection dealt with commercial leases, the banks that received them as collateral for loans, and used the FIN system in carrying forth its duties. The municipal subsection dealt with the municipal leases, with the investors who purchased them, and relied upon the INV system.

Finance employees performed tasks relative to the needs of their respective subsections. Like the FIN and INV systems on the computer, Finance employee chores simply did not overlap. That was Patrick's way; the left hand should not and could not know what the right hand was doing.

Fig. 2. The FIN and INV systems in theory

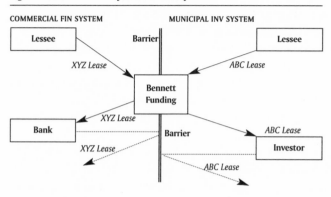

Fig. 3. The FIN and INV systems in practice

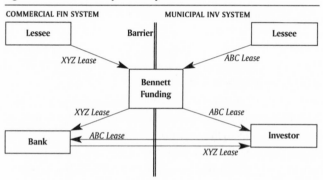

After leases were sold to investors or pledged to banks, the leases should have been removed from the daily inventory register of available leases. Somehow the fail-safe mechanism that would have prevented the reuse of the same lease was not programmed into the system.

Accordingly, leases were sold but did not come off the available lease register. Consequently, they were available to be sold and were sold again. In other words, municipal and commercial leases easily migrated through the blood-brain barrier of the computer system.[11]

Patrick himself doled out like Halloween candy the various leases to collateralize and support bank loans and investor sales. He sat there behind his large dark wooden desk defrauding people year after year after year. No emotion, no twinge of conscience. *What failed lesson, I wonder, did his soul need to learn?*

Individuals from MIS revealed to investigative counsel that in October 1994 "several major changes were made to Bennett's computer system, including changes affecting various functions of the finance department . . . to automate functions [previously done] manually."[12]

"During this time period, meetings were held to discuss the way the new system should and would work. Employees were asked to make suggestions to those in charge of developing the system. Several [people either] suggested or . . . heard others suggest adding a feature to the new system whereby 'sold' assets would be locked out of use for any other purpose."[13]

"This suggestion was prompted not [so much] by . . . concern with double-pledging, but . . . by a desire to automate certain bookkeeping tasks." The suggestion was ignored because Patrick indicated "such a device would slow down the implementation of the new system."[14]

At Patrick's trial in December 1998, Debra Brazier, the manager of MIS, testified Patrick Bennett directed that no such change was to occur to the system at that point in time.

Even before her testimony, we received a call from Brazier's predecessor, John Sullivan.[15] He said that in 1994 he specifically advised Bud and Kathleen the computer had the potential of, and was, allowing the same equipment leases to be pledged to both individual investors and banks.

Bennett Funding therefore was pulling in investment money at least twice on the same lease. This cash generator, this cyberfraud, went on for years. At the time, not one Bennett mentioned this little glitch to the bankers, brokers, investors, auditors, outside lawyers, CPAs, businesspeople, or any in-house counsel.

When Ma and Pa Bennett finally queried Patrick as to this seemingly major problem, he said, no doubt with bemused incredulity, that he would "look into it."[16] Patrick did as promised. He looked into it all right. His initial findings were that the "girls" in Finance were simply making mistakes.

Imagine, if you will, the misassignment of millions of dollars of equipment leases blamed on simple clerical error by the "girls of Finance." And the excuse was accepted! Swallowed hook, line, and sinker like some bloated porgy; incorporated into the very being of Bennett Funding. So much for Kathleen's feminism.

It has been said that, demographically speaking, Patrick surrounded himself with young entry-level female subordinates because they lacked the sophistication to question some of the bizarre requests from their boss. Was Patrick that good? That evilly brilliant?

When some of these women were hired, Patrick was in his late twenties. He attended some college classes but had no formal business education. He has a self-professed fear of flying and does not travel much. The Company was young and locally grown, so we had young workers from the available talent pool.

When the hard evidence materialized that double-pledging had occurred beyond simple mistakes, somehow Patrick convinced his parents that the problem should be fixed in stages. Stage I centered in blocking the commercial leases so that the FIN system would not allow pledged commercial leases to pass through to the investors on the INV system. Stage II was to fix the municipal lease migration from INV to FIN.

The Bennetts got around to implementing stage I so that only commercial leases were blocked or prevented from becoming available for resale on the system. Stage II never happened and was not allowed to happen. Consequently, the municipal leases were ignored allowing Patrick to go hog-wild.

Bennett Funding was also involved in financing time-share projects and resorts throughout the country, the Caribbean, and Ireland. So, to keep symmetry with the improper pledging of equipment leases, Patrick double-pledged the time-share consumer contracts to the banks and investors that Bennett Funding or a subsidiary or affiliate had purchased from developers. Bud and Kathleen also learned of this companion scheme in late 1994.

Under proper circumstances, in 1994, Bud and Kathleen should have removed Patrick, conducted an audit of all of the leases, conducted an independent investigation as to the facts and circumstances surrounding the double-pledging of commercial leases, and, based thereon, taken appropriate action. They did not.

During a meeting with the SEC in which issues relating to mistakes made in the assignment of leases arose, Kathleen stated the Bennetts would "totally audit the [Finance Department] . . . [t]otally, totally."[17] Except for placing the blocker into the commercial lease-allocation system, Kathleen's promise was forgotten, as in an amnesia victim not remembering that she once loved her husband.

After all, "at no time did any investor miss a payment," as Bud said ad nauseam. But in all of his denials, Bud never stopped to wonder where the money would come from to pay two or more banks and investors from the same monthly lease payment, especially after all excess cash was used to purchase large nonlease assets, such as hotels, boats, and a mall.

Although Bennett Funding did have investor offerings and other revenue sources that were not collateralized by leases,[18] did he think the Company was that prosperous?

The bury-the-head-in-the-sand attitude did them no good. The conversation with Sullivan concerning Bud and Kathleen's knowledge of the double-pledging was relayed to Simpson Thacher, the trustee's counsel. Based on this and other developments, the trustee amended his complaint in September 1996 and went after Bud and Kathleen in earnest.

At this juncture, one may rightfully ask how the accountants could certify that Bennett Funding's books were balanced as so many leases were double-pledged. In other words, when a lease was sold to more than one investor, the Company's books should not have been able to account for multiple sales of the same lease without detection.

Under basic accounting theory, the first sale of a lease to an investor increased the cash account and decreased the corresponding lease-receivable account, which recorded the amount owed by the lessee to the Company. These required entries could not be recorded if that same lease was sold or pledged again, because there was no lease-receivables account on the system to decrease, because it was expunged on the first sale to the investor.

Patrick relied on Bennett Management, an affiliate corporation, to hide the multiple sales. He treated the second and third sales of Bennett Funding leases to investors as though they originated with Bennett Management. Through this mechanism, Patrick was able to have Bennett Funding treat the cash it received as a debt owed to Bennett Management on its books, thereby eluding detection of the multiple sales of the same leases.

As Bennett Management's books were not audited, the accounting problems engendered by this sham went unnoticed. But, many believe that the accountants should have taken notice of this intercompany account structure and demanded an audit of Bennett Management, years before the bankruptcy.

The Mechanics of Lease Fraud

D URING THE course of its investigation, in the spring of 1995, the SEC and Patrick hammered out an agreement whereby the Company would immediately cease and desist from raising capital from investors through the use of private placement memoranda (PPM).[1] Before the agreement, the Company raised more than $200 million from investors for Bennett securities offered through PPMs. In form, a PPM is roughly equivalent to a stock offering prospectus.

The PPMs were issued pursuant to the *safe harbor* provisions contained in Rule 506 of Regulation D ("Reg. D") of the Securities Act of 1933.[2] This federal act along with the Securities Exchange Act of 1934 generally regulate the interstate selling of securities.

"Reg. D" allows private offering of securities to accredited individual investors to be free from registration normally associated with public offerings.[3]

"Accredited," as defined under Rule 501(a) of Regulation D, means, in part,

> any natural person who had individual income in excess of $200,000 in each of the two most recent years or joint income with that person's spouse in excess of $300,000 in each of those years and has a reasonable expectation of reaching the same income level in the current year ... any natural person whose individual net worth, or joint net worth with that person's spouse, at the time of his purchase exceeds $1,000,000.

In other words, someone with the financial wherewithal and savvy to afford and appreciate the nature and risk of the investment.

The SEC advised Patrick it was concerned with and was further investigating the financial information contained in the Bennett PPMs. The SEC maintained that erroneous financial information contained in the PPMs may taint the respective offering and, under the theory of integration, most of the other Bennett Funding offerings as well. Rather than risk immediate injunctive relief, Patrick acquiesced and stopped offering private placement memoranda.

Patrick, however, was not prevented from directly selling municipal leases to investors, as such issuances are also exempt from registration under another provision applicable to municipal securities.

To that end, Patrick obtained opinions from large and well-respected firms stating the sale of such municipal leases was within well-established exemptions from registration under the securities laws. The firms opined such sales were exempt under section 3(a)(2) under the 1933 act and did not have to be registered under section 5 of the 1933 act.[4]

Armed with the opinions and the knowledge that no fire wall was in place within the municipal-lease allocation system (only in the commercial system), Patrick could and did double-sell municipal leases to the investors and to the banks. This was most definitely not within well-established exemptions under the securities or any other laws. This was fraud most foul. He did this with the full knowledge he was under careful scrutiny by the SEC.

Through forensic accounting and legal investigation performed by Coopers & Lybrand, Simpson Thacher & Bartlett, the SEC, and in-house personnel, in June 1996, the trustee was able to file a massive civil action against the individual Bennetts and their accomplices.

The complaint was amended in September 1996 to include additional counts and parties, such as obtained from my conversation with the former MIS manager, John Sullivan. The complaint, a masterpiece of draftsmanship, sets forth exact descriptions of what can be termed the mechanics of lease fraud perpetrated by Patrick.

For example, as the trustee's complaint shows, in April 1995, Bennett Funding entered into a municipal lease for a copy machine with the U.S. Department of Agriculture as lessee. The lease was assigned number 95-04-1610, in which 95 is the year 1995, 04 is the month April, and 1610 is the sequential number of the lease.

The lease was registered in the INV system on the Company's computer, the municipal-allocation system used to track leases assigned to individual investors.

After the lease was inputted in the INV system, Patrick had a Company employee make a copy of lease 95-04-1610. The copy of the lease was then delivered to another Finance Department employee, who, under Patrick's watchful eye, was responsible for creating inventory lists of leases available for assignment to individual investors. The Finance Department employee would set forth identifying information for lease 95-04-1610 and for other leases as well on an inventory sheet.

The completed inventory sheet would be handed to Patrick, who, in turn, faxed the sheet to a broker for assignment to individual investors.

On August 24, 1995, a broker assigned the U.S. Department of Agriculture lease 95-04-1610 to an investor, Karl Ackerman of Roslyn, New York. Mr. Ackerman paid $6,587.16 to Bennett Funding for the lease.

After the U.S. Department of Agriculture lease was placed into the INV system for ultimate sale to an investor, Patrick gave the original lease to a different Finance Department employee. This employee, again under Patrick's direct supervision, was responsible for distributing leases to be pledged as collateral for bank loans.

Using the FIN system, the program used to record and maintain information for leases collateralizing loans from banks, the lease was grouped with a number of other leases procured under the same process. At no point did the INV system or the employees involved with servicing investor accounts interface with the FIN system or the employees involved with servicing bank loans.

On August 31, 1995, all leases under the grouping, including lease 95-04-1610, were pledged as collateral to obtain a loan from Wilber National Bank of Oneonta, New York. The loan was given Bennett Funding loan number 950832. The original leases associated with the loan were delivered to Wilber Bank along with enough documentation to choke a horse.

"Thus," as the complaint noted, "U.S. Department of Agriculture lease number 95-04-1610 was . . . assigned to Mr. Ackerman and pledged to Wilber National Bank."[5] In this fashion, through double-pledging of municipal leases, Patrick raised at least $95 million from December 1990 to the close of business on March 29, 1996. This averaged $1,484,375 per month for more than five years from this method of fraud alone. Actual income from the lessees under those leases was only $50 million.

Patrick was also daring. Because the scheme worked so well between the INV and FIN systems, why not try to double-pledge within the INV or FIN systems themselves? He choose the INV system.

The INV system could not prevent double-pledging between investors and banks because it did not interface with the FIN system. But the INV system was programmed to prevent multiple assignments to investors of the same lease within the system itself through a fire wall installed in 1994.

Under the Company's standard operating procedure, every municipal lease was to be entered into the INV system and assigned an eight-digit control number as described—year/month/sequential number. Once a lease was assigned to an investor, the INV system was "programmed not to allow the input of any further assignments to investors of the eight digit code representing that lease." As with the Highlander, *there can be only one.*

Patrick was able to circumvent the INV system fire wall by sending a list of available municipal-lease inventory to federal indictee and admitted coconspirator Kenneth Kasarjian in New Jersey.

Kasarjian, the dashing and well-dressed senior vice president of Bennett Funding from about 1990 through May 1995, was also a licensed broker headquartered in Mahwah, New Jersey.

After Kasarjian obtained the list and corresponding identifying information from Patrick, he would assign his own control numbers to the leases. The Kasarjian control numbers were radically different from the Bennett sequential numbers. This prevented the INV system and Finance Department personnel from detecting "the assignment of the very same leases," simply because the Kasarjian leases were not in the Bennett Funding system.

Kasarjian then sold the leases with his control numbers to investors through a network of brokers under his control.

Now for a triple whammy. In the normal course of its business, Bennett Funding entered into a municipal lease in March 1995 with Leon County Schools. The Leon County Schools lease was assigned number 95-03-0461 in the INV system.

After the lease was inputted in the INV system, Patrick sent a listing of available leases, including lease 95-03-0461, to Kasarjian. Kasarjian gave the Leon County Schools lease a new number, 921019-659M, on an independent system he maintained.

The Kasarjian/Leon County Schools lease 921019-659M was wholly independent from the Bennett Funding Leon County Schools lease 95-03-0461. Who says the same particle of matter cannot exist at more than one location at the same time?

A lease-inventory sheet containing Kasarjian product codes was sent to Halpert and Company, a New Jersey brokerage house. On May 10, 1995, Halpert sold Kasarjian Leon County Schools lease 921019-659M to the Edwin Golden Living Trust, Coconut Creek, Florida, for $31,361.23. In the wake of the lawsuits that followed the collapse of Bennett Funding, Halpert and Company filed bankruptcy as well.

As the Leon County Schools lease was breaking the laws of physics, Patrick had the original lease delivered to a Finance Department employee who worked with the banks in the FIN system. On June 5, 1995, the lease was batched with other municipal leases then pledged as collateral to secure a loan from Citizens Bank of Princeton, Missouri.

Eminently aware of the lack of fail-safe between the INV and FIN systems, on October 20, 1995, Patrick gave a copy of the Leon County Schools lease to another Finance Department employee involved with the INV system and assignment of leases to investors.

The employee placed the identifying information for the lease on an inventory sheet. The completed inventory sheet was given back to Patrick, who faxed it to Midstate Securities Corporation, another New Jersey brokerage firm.

Midstate, in turn, assigned the Leon County Schools lease number 95-03-0461 to Robert and Frances Cavalero of Mendham, New Jersey, for $31,361.23, the same way lease number 95-04-1610 was sold to investor Ackerman and then pledged to Wilber Bank.

In sum, the Leon County Schools lease was sold to the Edwin Trust, pledged to Citizens Bank, and assigned to the Cavaleros. The single lease generated double investment income of $62,722.46, and was also used as collateral to support a bank loan.

Patrick was pushing the envelope by engaging in this gerrymandering of leases just as he promised the SEC that he would "knock it off."

By the way, the record for a lease that was sold to investors then pledged to banks is seven. One investor even had the same lease sold to him twice under Bennett Funding and Kasarjian's different code numbers.[6] If only the masterminds harnessed their talents for the good of mankind instead of serving the god of greed.

During the chaos in the early postpetition days, Patrick and some of his friends loaded up boxes into vehicles parked in the lot adjacent to the Atrium and drove off.

Fortunately, one box, the Red Box, did not fit and was left at the lot, presumably to be picked up later along with other incriminating evidence. A Bennett Funding employee went outside, saw the Red Box, and brought it in. She advised me of the situation, and I took custody of the box and placed it under lock and key.

The Red Box was a standard ten-ream copy-paper box, measuring about 18″ × 12″. It was filled to capacity with substrates of municipal leases, copies of which, we learned later, were given to Kasarjian. With the connivance of Patrick, he sold them over and over again to investors loosening evil, like Pandora's box, upon an unsuspecting world.

The NYC Transit Authority
Needs Copiers

LIKE TREK BOERS, the Bennetts circled the wagons whenever things got tough. The employees, in retrospect, seemed like oxen with heads slightly bobbing as their bodies strained pulling those heavy wagons driven by their trekmasters, the Bennetts. The philosophy of the *laarger* became part of the corporate culture. It was us against them, no matter who the "them" were.

After I drafted the four bankruptcy petitions in March 1996, secured legal representation for the Company, and put out 1,001 brushfires that popped up like mechanical chipmunks at the midway at the state fair, the shroud of shock-ice that entombed me began to thaw. I could then read the SEC complaint for securities fraud, which triggered the cataclysm.[1] I was dumbstruck.

"Not my company," I bellowed as one of the oxen.

One of the counts of the SEC complaint dealt with the selling of bogus New York City Transit Authority (NYCTA) leases to investors.

"What the hell are the NYCTA leases?" I wondered. As the SEC complaint did not set forth enough information to answer my question, I also read the supporting affidavit of the NYCTA assistant chief facilities officer Martello.

Martello averred that in 1991 the NYCTA entered into a purchase order with Scriptex Enterprises, Ltd., a copy dealer with extremely close ties to the Bennetts, for scores of copy machines.

The purchase order called for the long-term financing of the equipment. The purchase price was about $2 million plus interest. Scriptex sold and assigned all of its right, title, and interest in and to the NYCTA purchase order to Bennett Funding.

Shortly thereafter, it was deemed to be in the NYCTA's economic best interest to buy the machines immediately rather than finance them over the long term. Accordingly, the NYCTA tendered the purchase price to Scriptex shortly after installation of the machines. Scriptex should have tendered the money to Bennett Funding and canceled the purchase order. That should have been the end of the transaction.

Through admissions by Kasarjian, the transaction was not concluded under commercially reasonable standards. Far from it. Patrick, with the

The SEC investigative team. *Front row:* Alistaire Bambach, Barry Rashkover, Barbara Bailin, Herbert Cohen. *Back row:* Ira Spindler, William Johnson, Andrew Geist, Al Troncoso, Eric Schmidt. Not pictured are Deputy Regional Director Edwin Nordlinger and Peter Goldstein. Photo by Dick Blume. Copyright © The Syracuse Newspapers.

help of Kasarjian, photocopied the NYCTA purchase order and repeatedly sold it and the stream of payments thereunder to investors through the Kenton Group, Inc., a brokerage firm owned, in part, by Kasarjian, through in-house brokers at Bennett Funding, and through outside brokers selected by Patrick and Kasarjian.

Bearing in mind the cloistered nature of the Finance Department, the brokers may not have known that competing brokers had the same purchase order to sell, which in the aggregate far exceeded the value of the purchase order in the first instance.

The affidavit of the NYCTA official went on to say no leases were entered into with Scriptex, Aloha, or Bennett Funding, and that in any event, the purchase order was paid as described above.

It should be noted municipalities transact all business with vendors through the purchase order system. Terms and conditions tantamount to a lease are referenced on purchase orders. In some transactions, a related lease agreement is executed as well. So when the SEC spoke of bogus leases with the NYCTA they missed the mark but only terminologically speaking.

The NYCTA entered into one or two more such purchase order transactions with Scriptex over the next two years. The purchase orders were assigned to Bennett Funding. The NYCTA paid each one quickly just as the first. The payoff was not forwarded to Bennett Funding. Instead, the purchase orders, worth $5–6 million in the aggregate, were photocopied and proportionate interests sold to investors, raising about $55 million.

I couldn't believe what I was reading. "How could this happen?" I dashed down to the microfiche room to research the NYCTA leases and other documents in connection therewith.[2] I felt like the character played by Charlie Sheen in *Wall Street* when he learned Gecko was selling out his father's airline company.

All of the documents and relevant entries were indeed microfiched. The purchase orders were there, equipment inventory sheets for the copiers were there, as was the approval of the assignment and purchase of the purchase orders from Scriptex by Bennett Funding. The approval was executed by Bud, Patrick, and Michael.

If Bennett Funding had legally entered into lease transactions in the numbers suggested by the sold purchase orders, then every motorman, every bus driver, every transit cop, every janitor, every worker in the New York City Transit Authority would have his or her own copier.

In reality, investors who were assigned NYCTA leases did not acquire obligations of a governmental entity paying tax-exempt interest and secured by office equipment as they were told. No, sir. The investors bought a pig in a poke. They simply acquired unsecured, taxable general obligations of Bennett Funding. As the investors exempted the interest component of the monthly payments from their returns, Lord knows what tax reporting ramifications this may engender.[3]

Other than Patrick and Kasarjian, no other Bennett Funding employee was involved in the shady NYCTA lease operation. This is credible because the bogus purchase orders were mass produced and sold off-site; funds for the purchase of the equipment were transferred between the

NYCTA and Scriptex; and investor payments flowed into Bennett Funding in the normal course.

Incredibly, Patrick and Kasarjian went on selling the municipal hotcakes right until the day before the SEC complaint was filed. A week or two later, I asked another lawyer who worked with Bennett Funding's securities lawyer, Rick Marshall, when did the SEC advise his firm and, consequently, the Bennetts of the NYCTA scam. He told me the scam was known ten days to two weeks before the SEC brought suit.

The Bennetts knew a considerable time before the shit hit the fan and did not tell anyone else. They let us continue in the day-to-day affairs without so much as an inkling as to what was going on, like oxen fit for slaughter.

What was the motivation for the nondisclosure? Embarrassment? Pride? Arrogance? Immature wish—if they didn't talk about it maybe the problem would go away? Or was the motivation pure greed? Let the oxen plug away while we secret our assets and get ready to move. Bud, the eternal optimist, maybe even thought he could win—beat the SEC and their phalanx of lawyers, investigators, and accountants.

The investigators also found other examples of selling outright fake Scriptex leases to investors.[4] These are summarized as follows:

Lessee	No. of Leases	Values
New York State–I	7	17,800,337
NYC Board of Education	1	3,504,922
State of New Jersey	12	32,358,963
State of New York–II	10	31,139,208
Total	30	$84,803,430

As it turns out, Scriptex, owned and operated by Kasarjian and coindictee and admitted perjurer Anthony Pavoni, was a front for Bennett Funding. Scriptex started off as a small-time copier dealer in New Jersey. Between 1985 and 1996, Scriptex managed to borrow, in the form of leases, cash payments, and inventory financing, approximately $80 million from Bennett Funding. Little, if any, of the money was paid back.

During most of the meteoric rise of Scriptex, its outside auditor was a firm controlled by fellow federal indictee and admitted felon, Charles Genovese.[5]

Genovese, a longtime friend and business associate of the Bennetts, was a trumpet-playing accountant cum "broker" also from New Jersey.

He raised tens of millions for the Company. Genovese's accounting firm "audited" Scriptex's books and produced financial statements that did not accurately describe, in either actual financial or legal terms, the relationship between Scriptex and Bennett Funding.

About the time of the 1992 presidential election, Kasarjian left Scriptex to become a broker. He passed the necessary tests and opened the Kenton Group, a New Jersey corporation. Kenton was owned jointly by Kasarjian and Tony Pavoni from 1990 through 1992, and wholly owned by Kasarjian since January 1993.

Kenton Group is the corporate entity through which Kasarjian managed sales of Bennett Funding financial products to investors. Tony Pavoni stayed with Scriptex and remained in charge. During this period, Kasarjian also became a vice president of Bennett Funding.

On April 10, 1997, the SEC filed a separate and independent complaint in Federal Court in Manhattan charging Kasarjian, then 52, and the Kenton Group with fraudulently offering and selling Bennett Funding securities through a network of broker-dealers.

According to the complaint, Kasarjian and Kenton participated in sham transactions that were used to materially overstate income on Bennett Funding's audited financial statements. Those financial statements were included in the PPMs used to offer and sell promissory notes to investors through Bennett Receivables and Bennett Receivables–II, Bennett Funding wholly owned subsidiaries. The financial statements were also relied upon by the lending institutions and investors who purchased leases directly.

Kasarjian and Kenton were also charged with fraudulently offering and selling, during 1995 and 1996, approximately $27 million in membership interests to investors in certain limited liability companies.[6]

The limited liability companies—Beckett Reserve Fund, Stafford

Fig. 4. The relationship among Bennett Funding, Scriptex, and Genovese

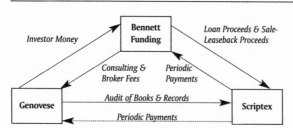

Fig. 5. The relationship among Bennett Funding, Kasarjian's LLCs, and the investors

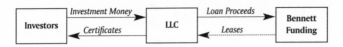

Fund, Parker Devon Fund, and Sterling Reserve Fund—were designed to make loans to Bennett Funding collateralized by equipment leases and other receivables.

According to the indictment, as of the date of the filing of the bankruptcy petition, Kasarjian had advanced more than $27 million from the limited liability companies to Patrick. However, Patrick had not provided any of the promised collateral to those companies. Accordingly, the companies became general unsecured creditors of Bennett Funding.

In other words, Kasarjian fraudulently advanced the proceeds of the membership interest offerings in the various limited liability companies to Bennett Funding and its affiliates without acquiring any such leases or debt instruments in return.

The hapless investors received a membership certificate, if that, in a noncapitalized, no-asset creature of fiction. Many of these investors have filed claims in the Bennett bankruptcy as well.

To give the appearance that the limited liability companies had a secured and priority status over the unsecured investors, Kasarjian and Patrick created, postpetition, bogus assignments of collateral.

As a reward for services rendered, Patrick established a $5 million line of credit for Kasarjian. Kasarjian accessed the line and built a multimillion-dollar house in New Jersey complete with riding stable.[7] The house was featured in *Architectural Digest*. Kasarjian and his wife executed a mortgage and a note back to the Company.

In an attempt to conceal the mortgage in the bankruptcy proceeding, Patrick returned the original mortgage and note to Kasarjian without receiving any payment in return. Kasarjian destroyed the documents.

Kasarjian no longer owns the house; the net sale proceeds, $1,329,642, were tendered to the authorities.

Watch What You Wish For . . .

O VER THE years the clamor for leases, particularly municipal leases because of their tax-exempt status, grew intense. Take the strange case of Investor-X.

Investor-X was told by an outside lease broker that there were no municipal leases to invest in at the present time. Instead, Investor-X could place funds in the Prime Conversion Account, the PCA, and earn interest until product became available.

Investor-X had pumped hundreds of thousands of dollars into Bennett Funding. He did not like what he was hearing from the broker. He did not want to tie his money up in the PCA.

He called the Company. Because of his economic clout he managed to get through to Patrick directly. Investor-X complained to Patrick that his broker was treating him unfairly and he wanted municipal leases now. Patrick gave in and allowed him to buy several municipal leases Bennett Funding had just gotten from the New York City Transit Authority.

Investor-X called the broker the next day, March 1, 1996, to gloat. Bennett Funding tanked twenty-eight days later.

What Did You Do in the War, Daddy?

C ORPORATIONS ARE artificial entities created by a grant of authority by a governmental agency.[1] Under the law, corporations are recognized as persons.

Corporations are entitled to some basic constitutional protections as are natural citizens. For example, a corporation has the right to exercise free speech and is protected against deprivation of property without due process of law. Although, for the present, corporations cannot vote, they make sizeable hard and soft money contributions.[2]

In New York, as in most states, corporations can sue and be sued, purchase and sell real and personal property, mortgage or pledge property, own bonds and securities, make contracts, incur liabilities, lend money, invest, make charitable donations, and pay pensions.[3]

Generally categorized by the manner of raising capital and the number and type of shareholders, corporations can be public or private. Although in the heart of every family-owned business beats a public corporation, there is a vast difference between the two.

Public corporations are those whose shares are traded by the general public through capital markets, exchanges, or over the counter. Public corporations are subject to strict reporting and disclosure requirements under the Securities Act of 1933 and the Securities and Exchange Act of 1934 as well as securities laws of the several states, known as "blue sky" laws.[4]

Reporting public corporations must file quarterly and annual reports with the Securities and Exchange Commission.[5] Their initial public offerings, IPOs, and subsequent securities issuances must be separately registered and well documented.[6] Material changes in positions of major shareholders must be disclosed. Proxy statements that contain information required by the Securities Act must be approved by the SEC as a prerequisite to solicitation for proxies. Proxies are instruments that authorize agents to vote on behalf of submitting shareholders.

The reasons for going public are legion. Chief among them is the ability to raise significant amounts of capital through the issuance of shares to the public. Public corporations can also allow stock to be used in lieu of cash for acquisitions and other business transactions, such as takeovers and mergers, be they hostile or courted.

"Going public" increases visibility and enhances credibility among existing and potential investors, customers, and business sources.

Another motivating factor is enrichment for certain key principals of public corporations through the selling of stock pursuant to recognized exemptions.

Going public, however, can be an expensive and time-consuming process. Public offerings, particularly initial public offerings, have underwriting fees, financial adviser fees, blue sky registration fees in the various targeted states, and legal and accounting fees keyed with the size of the offering.

The IPO process bears mentioning.[7] After working intensively with securities counsel, accountants, and financial advisers, the issuer files a registration statement with the SEC triggering the commencement of the public-offering process. After reviewing the statement, the SEC provides suggestions and required changes to the statement. Once the SEC's comments are received, the entire group meets again and produces an amended registration statement, which is refiled with the SEC.

During the filing of the amended statement, the issuer prints preliminary prospectuses and then distributes them to targeted institutional investors to gauge their interest. While the SEC is mulling over the amended statement, the issuer's financial adviser will commence "road show presentations" to the investors who may have expressed interest in the shares after reviewing the prospectuses. Such investors tend to be price setters and will advise the amount they are willing to pay for the shares.

From the information obtained during the road shows, the financial adviser recommends a price to the issuer. In an underwritten offering, the underwriter agrees to purchase the shares at the suggested public price minus a discount. The spread pays for the risk the underwriter takes in purchasing the shares to sell on the market.

As soon as practical after the underwriting agreement is signed, the underwriter commences the public offering.

Throughout the public-offering process, counsel to the issuer, financial adviser, and underwriter draft and redraft the required documentation to ensure compliance with the onerous requirements of federal and state securities laws to avoid civil liability and criminal prosecution for violations of those laws.

Privately or closely held corporations are vastly different from public corporations in almost all major aspects. Foremost is that the shares of private corporations are not traded publicly. They are typically held by a few individuals who are usually active in the management of the business.

With limited exceptions, private corporations are not regulated under the federal or state securities laws. They need not file quarterly or annual reports nor disclose issuances of stock to insiders with the Securities and Exchange Commission as do their public counterparts.

Private corporations do not have legions of lawyers, accountants, financial advisers, and underwriters reviewing records to ensure compliance with securities laws and regulations. Proxy statements are rarely required and are not solicited nor reviewed by the SEC.

Other than tax and labor matters, the government's policy toward private corporations is strictly laissez-faire. Indeed, the government encourages such entrepreneurial enterprises.

Bennett Funding is a private, nonregulated, nonreporting company. All of its shares are owned by Bud and Kathleen Bennett. Those shares have never traded on any market. The Company raised most of its capital through asset-based financing with lending institutions and by the sale of exempt securities to individual investors.

Hence, the Company did not need to have the elaborate internal controls traditionally mandated by counsel that would be installed in public corporations to ensure compliance with the myriad of federal and state securities laws.

As Bennett Funding was primarily a leasing company, most of the Legal Department's activities centered on the various elements that make up the legal aspects of such businesses on both transactional and litigation bases. One such important function was to create the commercial and municipal lease forms.

The process started with Legal researching applicable laws to insure compliance with statutes pertaining to leases[8] and to keep abreast of proposed legislation that could impact the industry. Legal also reviewed lease agreements from dozens of other leasing companies to keep up with the competition.

After drafting the initial form, Legal circulated it to other departments for comment and feedback. After the appropriate sign-offs by department heads, which usually took a couple of months, the lease forms would be sent to the printers, then distributed en masse to thousands of office equipment dealers to be used in almost a hundred thousand separate lease transactions nationwide throughout the years.

The terms of the leases and description of the leased equipment would be completed on site at the dealers. The executed lease agreements would then be submitted to Bennett Funding for credit approval and entry into the system.

Paralegals were called upon if the lessee sought routine changes to the lease agreement. Lawyers were consulted for material changes to the terms and conditions of the leases. Otherwise, there was no further involvement by Legal in the lease-application process.

Another important function centered on municipal leasing. When municipalities desire to acquire new equipment but do not want to encumber their coffers to any large extent, they may choose to lease the equipment. As with most things governmental, layers of bureaucracy and local ordinances control municipal leasing beyond the terms of the lease agreements.

For example, most state and municipal laws disallow the leasing of equipment above a certain value unless the matter is put to bid publicly.[9] The rationale is to prevent collusion, to encourage competition, and to obtain the best prices.

To facilitate the process, municipalities submit lease-bid proposals to various manufacturers and dealers. The proposals contain boilerplate information and set forth specifications, such as the number of copiers needed and the amount of copies per minute the machines must produce.

The manufacturers and dealers typically forward the proposals to leasing companies with which they do business, shopping for the best rate. As Bennett Funding, through its Aloha division, had built a reputation in the municipal lease niche, the Company was deluged with such bid proposals.

Bennett Funding's municipal-lease processing department reviewed the proposals. If a proposal contained specific legal requirements or unfavorable conditions, Legal would examine and make comment upon the bid.

To illustrate, municipalities can opt annually to cancel a lease if payments are not allocated in the budget for the next fiscal year. This is a known and accepted risk in the leasing industry.

Many municipalities, however, try to put one past the leasing company by including language that allows it to cancel the lease for convenience—at any time and for any reason.[10] Although this is an accepted practice in federal government leases, it is not generally permitted in the municipal sector unless the dealer is willing to take the transaction on recourse; that is, in the event the municipality cancels for convenience, the dealer will buy out the lease.[11] After Legal's review, it was a business decision as to the acceptance of the bid.

Legal also drafted or reviewed proposed agreements between Bennett Funding and the equipment manufacturers relating to programs with them or through their network of dealers. In this fashion, Bennett Funding did business with Konica, Toshiba, Panasonic, Canon, RISO, Monroe, Savin, A. B. Dick, Royal/Adler, and scores of others.

Interestingly, the agreements with the Japanese manufacturers such as Toshiba were in short form rarely longer than a few pages. Agreements with North American companies such as Monroe, however, were lengthy and unduly complicated. In the end, size did not matter because the bankruptcy superseded heretofore agreed-upon terms.

It is a fact of leasing life that many large and successful office equipment dealers require their lease financiers to accept subprime credit lessees as a condition to get "good business."

Although Bennett Funding accepted such subprime, or "B," leases, the flow of good quality paper did not necessarily follow from the dealers. It seemed the dealers knew whom they were dealing with.

Because of the disproportionately large amount of subprime leases in Bennett Funding's portfolio, thousands of leases were rendered in default because of nonpayment or other major breach.

Resultantly, much of Legal's efforts was geared toward the enforcement of the terms and conditions of the defaulted leases in federal, state, and bankruptcy courts across the country.

In lease litigation, Legal drafted summonses, complaints, answers, and replies in cases in which lessees filed counterclaims, responded to and drafted discovery demands, appeared at trials, motions, and hearings, and engaged in postjudgment collection efforts aimed at locating and liquidating lessee assets.

The in-house staff filed bankruptcy proof-of-claim forms and recovered equipment in lessee bankruptcies. Sometimes, the Company was compelled to retain local counsel to protect its interests with the Legal Department acting as liaison. Tom Kingsley and I even squeaked in pro bono representation of local indigents sponsored through the County Bar Association.

To forestall the crush of litigation, the Company used an army of in-house collectors who relied upon computer-driven collection technology as well as third-party collection agencies. Legal drafted the appropriate agreements with those agencies and advised in-house collectors of the do's and don't's of debt collection.

Over the years, the Company engaged in nonleasing businesses and amassed a portfolio of real estate and other noncore assets. Legal drafted and reviewed documentation, and attended closings of asset acquisitions and loans, at least the ones we knew about and were asked to participate in.

In time-share transactions for instance, we pulled together financial information, lien and judgment searches, and relevant documentation and disseminated them to other departments for review and analysis. This included the services of a local firm owned by the former regional director of the FBI to do background investigations of time-share project principals.[12]

Not until all of these documents, searches, and reports were compiled, disseminated, reviewed, and approved were the transactional documents prepared by and the closings attended by Legal.

In my role as general counsel, although I allocated most of the staff to the collection of defaulted leases, to avoid a rigidity that only paralyzes and compartmentalizes the workplace, I mandated overlapping of duties and instituted cross-training procedures.

From a management perspective, I found it favorable to advise staffers of the full scope of a project, subject to confidentiality guidelines, rather than so much as needed to perform the task. This allows individuals to feel part of the team and fosters a climate in which suggestions that may benefit the project as a whole are welcomed and encouraged.

To that end, we conducted department-wide meetings, meetings for just attorneys, and issue-specific meetings for those primarily involved with collections or a major transaction.

As a proponent of continuing legal education long before it became required in New York, I insisted the Company pay for department members to attend seminars and training workshops. Department members were also required to join bar associations and related organizations.

Believing that sexual harassment, all forms of harassment for that matter, at the workplace is not only wrong but can be economically devastating to a company, as early as 1993, I convened seminars on sexual harassment, instituted a policy on its prevention, established a mechanism for adjudicating complaints, and ensured that the Company's employee handbook contained such appropriate information.

Although the Company was not public, nevertheless, it was still obligated to comply with record-retention requirements under both state and federal laws as well as to maintain the privacy, integrity, and safekeeping of records in the normal course.

Based upon the maxim "when in doubt don't throw it out," Legal drafted the Company's Records Retention Plan and disseminated it to all department heads.[13] Although the plan urged employees "to contact the Office of General Counsel for guidance as to whether a particular document should be retained," we had few such requests.

Recognizing that because of the uncertainties of life, disasters are bound to happen from time to time, Legal drafted the "Business Interruption Preparedness & Continuation Plan of Bennett Funding."[14]

As the preamble to the disaster plan noted, "[e]ven as we move towards the 21st Century, disasters abound worldwide; the bombings in

Oklahoma in 1995, New York's World Trade Center in 1993, and London's financial district in 1992. But it is also a disaster when the air-conditioner on the floor above a company's MIS department leaks over a weekend and floods the mainframe computer." The plan, however, did not offer any guidance in the event the SEC, FBI, and Justice Department "come-a-callin'." Patrick Bennett had his own plan.

As general counsel, I ran the department from its nascency in 1984 until 1992. From 1992 through June 1994, the department was split into lease litigation and general corporate/transactions sections. I headed the general corporate section and another attorney litigation.[15]

When the litigation attorney was summarily booted in 1994, I regained control of the entire department. At that time the department was at its height, employing lawyers, interns, paralegals, legal secretaries, and support staff, some fifteen people.

Less than six months later, out of the blue, Bud distributed a companywide memorandum noting another restructuring of the Legal Department.

This time, the restructuring established a separate Office of General Counsel staffed by me, an intern, a paralegal, and a secretary. The rest of the department was split again into litigation and corporate divisions. Each division was headed by an attorney who was a former subordinate hired only the previous year.[16]

Bud advised the restructuring would free me from time-consuming management duties, such as reviewing bills from outside counsel retained by Legal, setting budgets, reviewing employee performance, monitoring attendance, and a host of related administrative chores.

Although Bud's explanation was perhaps sincere, at the core, the sudden stripping of management duties typically associated with general counsel functions without prior consultation must have been due to Bud and Kathleen exacting retribution for real or imagined peccadilloes by me—from their methodology, perhaps deserved.

The new restructuring lasted until fall 1995. At that time, the entire Company was split up, the two attorneys becoming general counsels in their own right.

Every upwardly mobile private company eventually needs to decide to "go public." If delayed too long, the dream of large dollars can evaporate and the company can become tapped out of resources in investors and lenders. It needs to expand to maintain viability.

Although the Bennetts took the art of raising capital by a private company to new limits—commercial bank loans, asset-based loans and direct sales with small savings and loans and regional banks, private placements, and securitizations—they decided to stay the course and not venture into the highly regulated public arena.

From the mid-1980s until the Company's demise in 1996, the Bennetts retained the services of outside counsel to render opinions concerning, and steer the course through, the securities aspects of its financial products.[17] Bennett received opinions from half a dozen firms regarding issues such as whether municipal leases were securities and whether the sale of campground membership agreements constituted the sale of securities.

Large securities firms drafted private placement memoranda, the PPMs, and researched the requirements of offering the PPMs in different states. Over time, the Company was able to use the PPM format created by the securities lawyers as models to draft its own.

The Legal Department reviewed some but did not draft these piggybacked PPMs. We filed the Form D exemptions relative to those PPMs with the SEC. All of the financial information concerning the offerings that needed to be contained in the Form D's was provided by Patrick. The Company used blue sky software, which facilitated registrations in those states in which the PPM offerings qualified.

We also fielded questions from brokers or the Finance Department as to whether a potential investor qualified as an accredited investor to take advantage of the Reg. D exemption. Sometimes we approved the individual and sometimes we did not.

Legal drafted some of the simple-form assignments of leases to investors, the terms of which were filled in by Finance and closed through brokers.

Other than that, we had no contact with investors. We never sent them opinions of counsel, although Patrick had an internal opinion copied and sent to investors on the "warehouse investment" without my knowledge or permission just as he and Kasarjian did with the off-site phony leases. When I heard a rumor this was occurring I stopped furnishing the opinions altogether.

The warehouse transactions continued right up until the bankruptcy. Those who continued to buy such investments without the heretofore illegally copied opinion would be hard-pressed to claim reliance.

Furthermore, Legal did not audit, was not in a position to audit, nor should have been expected to audit the financial and accounting books and records of the Company. The Company had in-house accountants and outside auditors do that.

We did not compile, review, or assign the lease or membership agreements as collateral; did not pick investors; did not attend individual investor closings (they were closed through the brokers like normal trades); did not pick brokers; did not pick lessees; did not pick manufacturers; did not pick lenders; did not become involved in the preparation of the annual financial statement; did not prepare tax statements or returns; did not participate in credit decisions; did not participate in executive committee meetings; and did not engage in nor aid and abet in wrongdoing.

If you rent an apartment, do lawyers attend the closing? If you lease a car, do lawyers show up at the dealer's? If the corner drugstore leases a copy machine, do lawyers negotiate the terms and conduct the closing? If you make a trade, do lawyers handle the transaction? Of course not.

In New York, as in all states, a lawyer's conduct is controlled, in part, by the Code of Professional Responsibility.[18] Lawyers-to-be must even take a separate test as part of the bar examination concerning their mastery of the code.

"The Code is designed to be both an inspirational guide to the members of the profession and a basis for disciplinary action when the conduct of a lawyer falls below the required minimum standards stated in the Disciplinary Rules."

The Code of Professional Responsibility consists of the Canons, Ethical Considerations, and Disciplinary Rules.

The Canons are the general concepts "expressing . . . the standards of professional conduct expected of lawyers in their relationships with the public, with the legal system, and with the legal profession."

"The Ethical Considerations are aspirational in character and represent the objectives toward which every member of the profession should strive." Lawyers are encouraged to rely on the Ethical Considerations for guidance.

The Disciplinary Rules are mandatory in character. They ascribe "the minimum level of conduct below which no lawyer can fall without being subject to disciplinary action."

A basic tenet of the code is loyalty to one's client to the extent "a lawyer should represent a client zealously within the bounds of the law."[19]

Professional considerations aside, my personality compels me to loyalty, but how can one be loyal to a corporation, a machine? To an ideal, perhaps, but not to a fiction, an amorphous creature created by statute. Loyalty to my client, Bennett Funding, was too abstract a notion. I needed flesh and blood. For ultimately, corporations are naught but the people who own them and run them.

As an attorney within the Bennett Funding context, I reported technically to the board of directors: Bud, Kathleen, Patrick, Michael, William Crowley, Kevin Kuppel, Joanne Corasiniti, and Richard MacPherson ("Coach Mac"). In practical terms, I reported to Bud then, much later to Michael.

Although I did go to formal dinners and luncheons with the Bennetts and other employees, I did not socialize with any of the Bennetts, and did not attend their private parties. Simply, I was not in the "inner circle." My workday path generally did not cross with those areas of the Company in which the fraud was perpetrated, that is, Finance and Accounting.

During the representation of my client, Bennett Funding, I made mistakes. But I endeavored to be loyal to the Bennetts and gave them the benefit of any doubt following the mandates inherent in the Code. That was my job and my duty practiced under the "highest possible degree of ethical conduct."

Since March 29, 1996, all of my files accumulated over the previous twelve years relating to the Company have been open to lawyers from Simpson Thacher, class action attorneys, forensic accountants from Coopers & Lybrand, the SEC, the Justice Department, and the FBI. The files are looked at without my presence required. I have not worried about this and can sleep at night. How many lawyers could say the same thing?

As stated under oath at the Bennett bankruptcy first meeting of creditors in May 1996, I did not know, could not have known, nor was in a position to know of the improprieties at the Company.[20] I did not, as some have suggested, fall asleep on my watch.

It's in the Air

S HORTLY AFTER the Bennett scandal broke in 1996, the SEC announced it was investigating a report of financial wrongdoing by the City of Syracuse itself. According to the comptroller of Syracuse, the city had issued prospectuses containing inaccurate financial information to investors to induce them to purchase city bonds. The report indicated the city's financial statement understated liabilities and overstated assets. Was there something in the air?

We figured as long as the SEC was in the neighborhood investigating Bennett, they might as well have at the city as well. After completing its investigation, the SEC found evidence of improprieties in the city's bond offering. But as strict enforcement proceedings may impact unfairly upon the citizenry, the SEC declined to take serious action.[1]

Despite the story in the local paper, the administration was swept back into office. This is the same administration that allowed former mayor Lee Alexander's body to lie in state in City Hall—the same Alexander who was prosecuted and convicted of an extortion and kickback scheme while in office. He served eight years.

Pennies from Heaven

I T WAS REPORTED Bud and Kathleen skimmed quarters from coin-operated copy machines the Company had leased in the field. A witness stated that bags of coins collected from the machines were routinely placed on Mrs. Bennett's desk. This allegation was denied by her counsel, who stated Mrs. Bennett "shall rest on her own credibility."[1]

One Thousand Cranes

CERTAIN ASIAN countries have evolved a custom of sending a thousand paper cranes to a patient to speed recovery. About five years ago, Bud was diagnosed with severe clogged arteries to the heart. The solution was a quadruple bypass operation to be performed at the heart factory known as the Cleveland Clinic.

Bud talked openly of the upcoming operation as if it was the new "rich man's disease" much the same way gout was once viewed.

Several weeks before Bud's operation, my wife, Sara, commenced making a thousand cranes. The method, commonly known as origami, involves the folding of paper into the shape of a crane about one inch in length. Small-scale objects are not easy to fold.

After Sara created a thousand red, green, gold, blue, and silver cranes from foil gift wrap, she mounted them on a structure resembling the shape of a lamp. The work was given to Bud with a couple of days to spare.

Bud pulled through the surgery. He said he felt stronger and younger from the procedure. Back at work, his screaming subsided, at least for a time. Bud was back on top of the world. He never thanked Sara for her contribution to his healthy and speedy recovery.

Oral Contracts Aren't Worth the Paper They're Printed On

BUD WAS fond of saying that "what you don't put in writing you don't have to defend." This bit of jurisprudence was cultivated during Bud's lawsuit with Venrock over the ownership to the predecessor corporation to Bennett Funding.

The trustee's attorneys came across a legal pad that included a statement in Bud's own hand: "What you don't put in writing you don't have to defend."

The Businesses of the Debtors

During its heyday, Bennett Funding was divided into four major operations groups each containing various departments.[1] The first group, "back-of-the-house," processed lease- and dealer-inventory financing applications, consumer campground/time-share applications, performed credit review of these same applications, entered data concerning payments from lessees under their leases, dealers pursuant to their inventory finance notes, and consumers under their vacation contracts, and engaged in collections of delinquent accounts.

The second group, "sales," was responsible for obtaining new manufacturers and dealers for the various equipment-leasing and inventory-financing programs and, under Resort Funding, new campground developers for the resort business.

The third group, "finance," was responsible for raising capital to make the equipment and resort receivable purchases as well as funds needed for operations.

The fourth group, "support," was responsible for providing logistics to the other groups, such as production of marketing brochures, reception, and mail services.

For the mainstay equipment-leasing business, the Bennetts used the trade name Aloha Leasing. Its logo, a stylized *AL,* was copyrighted and used on every form, lease, brochure, marketing propaganda, letterhead, and other written communication dealing with equipment leases and related business.

But was the choice of the name Aloha Leasing sensible in that the company was headquartered in the frigid climes of central New York?[2] The origin of the name is fairly easy to trace. While having a second honeymoon with Kathleen in Hawaii, Bud fell in love with the word *aloha,* the traditional Polynesian greeting. Armed with settlement money from the suit with Venrock over control of Bud's previous company, he started Aloha Communication Systems, Inc., a New York corporation, in November 1977.

In April 1984, several months before I joined the Company, the corporate name was changed to its present form, the Bennett Funding Group, Inc. Bennett Funding adopted the trade name Aloha to continue the goodwill it had built up under its former corporate name. Bud and Kathleen owned and still own all of the issued and outstanding shares.

The Aloha trade name was not used on the investor side, however. Patrick banked on the Bennett family name to draw the booty from the investing public. He separated the corporate/finance name of The Bennett Funding Group, Inc., from the trade name/leasing name of Aloha Leasing.

Since its inception in 1977, Aloha engaged in the business of small-ticket leasing of office equipment. As time passed, Aloha became a player in the niche market of municipal office-equipment leasing.

Aloha also assisted equipment dealers in the purchase of equipment inventory directly from manufacturers and distributors by providing interim financing to such dealers pursuant to short-term promissory notes.

In late 1994, Aloha Capital Corporation, formerly known as Bennett Leasing Corporation, was established to take over and continue the leasing and inventory finance business of Bennett Funding.

As Bennett Funding's lease portfolio dwindled, the valuation of the business would decrease proportionately. Thus, when the shares of Bennett Funding passed onto Bud and Kathleen's heirs, Patrick and Michael, the tax burden would be minimized.

At first a wholly owned subsidiary of Bennett Funding, Aloha Capital's shares were transferred to Michael in 1995, then transferred again to Breeden, postpetition, in May 1996.

Intrigued with the burgeoning consumer market for vacation hideaways, Bud incorporated Resort Funding, Inc., in Delaware in December 1984, seven years after Aloha was created. At first, Resort Funding provided equipment-leasing services to campground developments throughout the United States, akin to those provided by Aloha Leasing.

As the program matured, Resort Funding purchased membership agreements between campground developers and consumers. In consideration of the purchase price of the membership agreements, Resort Funding retained the revenue generated from the monthly payments made by the consumers much in the same fashion as Aloha purchased equipment from dealers and retained the revenue from the lessees. In some cases, the effective yield on the membership agreements exceeded 25 percent.

From the incorporation of Resort in 1984 until November 1987, Bennett Funding owned all of its issued and outstanding common stock. In

November 1987, Resort Funding issued a private placement memorandum. The Resort PPM offered both common shares and bonds to investors. Approximately 4.5 percent of the issued and outstanding common stock of Resort was purchased by the investors pursuant to the PPM. Bennett Funding retained ownership of the remaining 95.5 percent.

Thereafter, in or about 1993, records in the possession of the trustee indicate Bennett Management and Development, a Bennett Funding affiliate, repurchased all of the 4.5 percent issued shares from the investors.

Unfortunately, very few of the campground developments that did business with Resort Funding survived. Many were plagued by internal corruption and crooked and greedy owners—birds of a feather. Some of these campgrounds folded resulting in the cessation of payments from the consumers under their breached membership agreements. Other campgrounds were teetering with imminent foreclosure by other lenders and lawsuits by the various states attorneys general for fraud and breach of promise.

Rather than write off millions in receivables on Resort's books and risk continuing exposure to lawsuit, the Bennetts, without experience in the area, decided to take over the distressed campgrounds and enter into the campground business themselves. Sometimes the takeovers were peaceful and smooth. Sometimes the takeovers were hostile, resulting in litigation.

Through the acquisition campaign, the Bennetts wrested control of fourteen campgrounds in Missouri, Kentucky, Tennessee, Ohio, Alabama, Arkansas, Texas, and several other states.

It is theorized the massive collapse of the campground finance business, which cost the Bennetts more than $40 million, spawned the need that gave rise to the illegalities at the Company. Desperate corporations, like desperate people, can and do resort to crime to survive.

After several years of trying to be successful and compete in the slimy business, the Bennetts sold all of the campgrounds, receiving far less than their aggregate acquisition price.

As the campground business faded, Bud decided to take a step up to the time-share business. He reasoned a better class of developers would not lead to the same bad result as with the campground developers. Accordingly, Resort changed its name to its present name, Resort Service Company, Inc., and completed the wind-down of the campground business. The "discarded" name of Resort Funding was assumed by the time-share corporation, itself a Bennett Funding subsidiary.

With all of the names available in the universe, Bud's decision to use "Resort Funding" in the time-share business has been ridiculed by those now running that company. Analogous to Aloha Leasing in the equipment-leasing industry, Resort Funding had a reputation in the recreation and vacation industry. Bud adopted it for the time-share company to continue the goodwill Resort had in the campground segment. Not every decision the Bennetts reached was wrong, stupid, or downright criminal, just most of them.

In February 1996, just before the filing of the Bennett bankruptcy petitions, the Bennetts, through Bennett Funding, effectuated a modified reverse merger.[3] A reverse merger is an effective alternative to going public.

Basically, a privately held operating company, such as Resort, that seeks to become a public company is merged into a public shell, a corporation with little or no active operations. After the transaction the public shell is the legally surviving entity. The business of the operating company, however, continues unaffected.

Simultaneously, the owners of the operating company become the controlling owners of the public corporation. Thus, the private company in effect becomes the public company.

Such transactions have markedly reduced attorneys' fees and accounting costs, although an expensive fairness opinion from a bona fide investment bank is required to ensure that the resultant transaction is not a sham to existing shareholders.

In the reverse merger process the shares of the new Resort Funding, which were held by Bennett Funding, were swapped for shares in Equivest Finance, Inc., an insurance public corporation shell in Florida. After the reverse merger, Bennett Funding and Bennett Management became the majority shareholders of Equivest. Equivest became the sole shareholder of Resort Funding, its principal asset.

As a result of the stock swap, Equivest became controlled by Bennett Funding, or, more properly, the Bennetts. Early on, Kasarjian was appointed to the board of directors.

One month after the deal was consummated, the bankruptcy petitions were filed. In postpetition terms this means the trustee controls Equivest, because Bennett Funding and Bennett Management are its majority shareholders. Under that mandate, Breeden appointed a new board and slate of officers to run its affairs.

Indeed, the trustee is pinning his hopes of bankruptcy reorganization upon the success of the time-share company.[4] To that end, he flushed previous management except for several honest competent souls and has replaced them with talented high-caliber workaholics. The trustee has enticed several prominent businessmen to join the board. With such giants as Marriott, Disney, Ford Credit, and Finova (formerly Greyhound) leading the way with cheap cost of funds, competition is tough, very tough.

In articulating his position regarding the importance of Equivest, Breeden noted, "Since early in my tenure as Trustee . . . I have considered the . . . Estate's majority common stock ownership of Equivest and its wholly-owned subsidiary, Resort Funding, Inc. as a source of potentially significant value for the creditors of Equivest, even though the common stock was essentially worthless in the months immediately following the Debtors' bankruptcy filings in 1996."[5]

Because ING Bank, Resort's principal lender, was threatening to terminate its $50 million line of credit, Breeden maintained "a new lender . . . was absolutely essential to protect the debt owed to the Consolidated Estate, as well as to create further value in the common stock of Equivest."[6]

Responding to a request for proposals, six lenders expressed interest and submitted proposals for financing. After thorough review by Breeden and Resort management, Credit Suisse First Boston's proposal to lend $105 million was accepted, because it "had the best mix of low interest cost, most attractive cash advance rate on pledged loans, points and equity participation."[7]

Because the Bennett debtors owned about 86 percent of the common stock and ten thousand shares of Series 2 Preferred Stock of Equivest, Bankruptcy Court approval for the loan deal was required.[8] After the motion was granted to "restructure . . . Equivest's financial position," Breeden then needed to retire a couple of unsecured promissory notes from Resort Funding to Bennett Funding with an aggregate balance of approximately $25 million.

Accordingly, the next part of the master plan was to convert the promissory note debt of $25 million to common stock of Equivest. After meeting some opposition, the debt-equity swap was approved by the Court, partly because of the shares' rapidly rising value.

Consequently, Bennett Funding's and Bennett Management's ownership of Equivest climbed another three points to more than 89 percent in exchange for the cancellation of its direct monetary obligations.

In the next phase of the plan, Equivest acquired Eastern Resorts, a Rhode Island corporation.[9] As suggested by the announcement, Eastern Resorts is New England's largest time-share development and management company. Because of Eastern Resorts' experienced management, exposure in the industry, and time-share assets, it was envisioned that its acquisition would increase the real value of Bennett Funding's and Bennett Management's shareholder interests in Equivest.

The acquisition price of Eastern Resorts was 3,250,000 shares of newly issued Equivest common stock and $15 million in cash. As Equivest did not readily have $15 million in cash, that portion of the consideration was to be borrowed from Credit Suisse as well.

The Eastern Resorts acquisition loan was secured by pledging Resort Funding's interest in and to certain time-share receivables and mortgages, a cash sweep of all available cash, and cross-collateralization with other existing Credit Suisse facilities, including the master loan of $105 million. Additionally, Credit Suisse would receive a *structuring advisory fee* comprised of 180,000 warrants to purchase Equivest common stock at $8.00 per share for five years. Sound familiar?

With the $105 million loan from Credit Suisse in place and the acquisition of Eastern Resorts, the final phase of the plan was ready to be initiated: the sale of the Bennett companies' common stock interest in Equivest in a registered public offering.

After deducting the costs of the public sale and attorneys' fees, the proceeds will be placed in Breeden's trustee account at Chemical Bank for the benefit of the creditors.

One provision of the plan allowed Credit Suisse and the other underwriters involved in the public sale to purchase the offered shares of common stock at a discount of 6.5–7.0 percent off the price to the public.

To make the last phases of the plan fly, the trustee had to clear an earlier mistake in which about $27 million of mortgages and time-share receivables on Resort Funding's books were still held in the names of Resort Service Company and Bennett Management.[10]

Unless the titles to the assets were transferred to Resort Funding, Breeden's plan was doomed, because the financial information given to Credit Suisse would be inaccurate and Resort Funding would not be able to pledge certain of the time-share properties to support the $15 million Eastern Resorts acquisition loan.

Early in the time-share business as the campground interests waned, Bennett Management and Resort Service Company executed development loan and receivable financing transaction documents with various time-share developers with which they did business. Company in-house attorneys drafted the transactional documents, including the loan agreements, the loan promissory notes, the mortgages, and the receivables purchase agreements.

The time-share business as well as the concomitant development-loan promissory notes and receivables were subsequently assigned to Resort Funding, the subsidiary of Equivest.

Until those notes and receivables were sold or pledged as collateral by Resort Funding to third parties, however, the staff did not necessarily document the assignments internally, because Bennett Management and Resort Service Company were viewed simply as Bennett Group nominees. As no one envisioned a bankruptcy filing at the time, we did not view the use of nominees within the Bennett Group as a troublesome practice.[11]

For example, in 1995, ING Bank, the primary lender, was insistent the time-share assets be formally transferred to Resort Funding incident to any financing to that company.

Based on the de facto assignments and the fact that Resort Funding's records conclusively showed it had paid for and serviced the assigned assets, the Bankruptcy Court, over stiff opposition,[12] allowed the transfer of the $27 million worth of assets from Bennett Management and Resort Service Company to Resort Funding. And the rain fell.

During the middle of Patrick's criminal trial, two Equivest-related matters surfaced. First, in January 1999, Patrick turned over 1.2 million shares of Equivest to Justice Department attorneys. His lawyer claimed Patrick found them while rummaging through boxes. Justice turned them over to Breeden, who incorporated them into the Equivest offering.

Second, in February 1999, Equivest executed an agreement to buy six additional time-share resorts from the Kosmas Group International, Inc.[13] The resorts are in the U.S. Virgin Islands, New Orleans, Washington, D.C., and Ocean City, Maryland.

Unlike the Bennetts, who purchased fourteen campgrounds out of desperation, presumably the Equivest purchases were part of a coordinated business plan to increase market share and nip at the heels of the big boys in the industry.

With seven time-share resorts under its belt in record time, it seems Equivest's hunger for acquisition may not be satisfied. With ownership, though, comes the increased risk of liability from disgruntled consumers, lenders, various states attorneys general, the former owners, employees, and industry regulators.

Also, the blurring of Equivest's lending business and ownership of resorts may lead to allegations by developers and competitors of lender liability and unfair business practices.

"You know when my time-share development was a bit delinquent in paying Equivest, they made me an offer to purchase my resort. Maybe, you know, that was their plan all along." This was an allegation leveled against the Bennetts when they took over the campgrounds from owners who defaulted on their obligations to the Company.

And, if these things come to pass, whither the Equivest shareholders sue too?

Among the nine companies that filed bankruptcy are Bennett Receivables Corporation (BRC) and Bennett Receivables Corporation–II (BRC-II). These corporations were incorporated as wholly owned special-purpose subsidiaries of Bennett Funding.

Their "special purpose" was making loans to Bennett Funding that were to be collateralized by an assignment of a security interest in certain income-producing receivables—leases and inventory-finance promissory notes—generated by Bennett Funding.

Bennett Funding, in turn, would, hypothetically, use the loan proceeds to make purchases of new income-producing receivables. These corporations served as the models for Kasarjian's limited liability companies, Beckett and Parker Devon, for example.

BRC and BRC-II raised capital to make the loans to Bennett Funding by offering their promissory notes to individual investors through PPMs before the SEC prohibited such transactions.

According to the terms of the PPMs, the promissory notes were guaranteed by Bennett Funding. These companies had no other businesses. As Kasarjian after him, it appears Patrick forgot to collateralize the loans with the leases and inventory-finance notes. Accordingly, the investors purchased unsecured general obligations of companies with no assets guaranteed by a bankrupt corporation hopelessly insolvent.

American Marine International, Inc., (AMI) was established to own maritime assets of Bennett Funding. In particular, it was the assignee of Bennett Funding's rights in and to a 1994 shipbuilding contract for a gambling vessel known as the *Speculator* at Freeport, Florida. The construction costs have been about $14 million. The estate and the builder continue to duke it out in Bankruptcy Court over charges and counter-charges of incomplete payments and padded bills.[14]

When Judge Gerling granted the trustee permission to move the ship to another port, someone miscalculated its height, so it could not fit under a bridge. Like letting air out of tires, the *Speculator* had to be partly submerged to squeeze under the limbo bar.

AMI was also the assignee of Bennett Funding's rights in another gambling vessel and barge known as the *Sioux City Sue* in Omaha, Nebraska. That package deal cost $8.5 million.

The *Sioux City Sue* was destroyed by foul weather. The interior of the boat itself was vandalized. The estate sold the barge for $50,000 and was hoping to receive at least some of the $2 million in insurance proceeds.[15] The insurance company disclaimed liability and filed a declaratory action in federal court seeking a judgment that it had no duty to provide coverage for the vandalism.[16]

In June 1998, the court ruled the estate had no insurable interest in the *Sioux City Sue* and dismissed the claim.

The estate filed an appeal and is hoping to latch on to the proceeds through an assignment of American Gaming's rights to an insurable interest in the vessel. AMI engaged in no other business.

The sole purpose of debtor Cordoba Corporation was to take title to the *Lady Kathleen*. Sometime before the bankruptcy, Bud and Kathleen wanted to trade the seventy-foot *Lady Kathleen* for a new and larger yacht, the ninety-eight-foot *Spirit of Ecstasy*.[17] The *Spirit's* owner wanted to downsize to a smaller yacht, less costly to maintain and operate. Oh, the problems of the rich.

Their plan was to have Cordoba take title to the *Lady Kathleen*, then swap the stock of Cordoba with the stock of Jaru, Inc., the corporation that was to take title to the *Spirit of Ecstasy*. The plan was never consummated. Cordoba had no other business.

The Processing Center, Inc., (TPC) was incorporated to perform all "back-of-the-house" functions, such as billing and collecting, on behalf of Bennett Funding, Aloha Capital, and Resort Funding. Service agreements were executed by officers of the respective companies, who at one time were themselves officers of Bennett Funding.

Despite its incorporation in January 1995, TPC's employees were not in place until October 1995. Consequently, the company was not operational until the fourth quarter of 1995. In the bankruptcy, it continues to bill and collect on the leases from the lessees. The trustee was hoping to expand its operations by servicing accounts from third parties. After two years of wooing, the effort was abandoned.

In June 1998, about two years after the other nine Bennett companies filed petitions, Breeden threw Shamrock Holdings Group, Inc., into chapter 11 as well. Breeden had previously acquired the shares to Shamrock from Michael Bennett, the sole shareholder, who was in one of his cooperative moods.

Shamrock's major holdings are 87 percent of the stock of American Gaming and Entertainment, Ltd., a New Jersey company that served as Bennett Funding's gaming conduit, and the Harold's Club, a defunct casino in Reno, Nevada.[18]

The Bennetts acquired the seven-story pile of rocks formerly owned by Howard Hughes for about $7.75 million. Except for one tenant that operated a restaurant, Harold's Club has been vacant for years. To accommodate a serious buyer who wanted Harold's Club free and clear of all liens, Breeden added Shamrock to the ranks of the other debtors.[19]

With Apologies to Melville

I N THE brilliant winter rays of a cloudless blue midday sky, snow piled high and thick on hills and mountains and fields glints, glimmers, and glistens. Its whiteness is mesmerizing, compelling one to meld molecules with the great snow mass, to sublimate crystally.[1]

On a ski run down a slope, blowing snow and ice suspended in the air cleanse your face like organic sand blasters. The cold washes over you. It leaves you breathless. The metal edges of skis rip the slope as they grip, fighting for traction. The crunch of fresh corduroy. The squeak of gliding skis. The squealing of the lift machinery in gear. The smell of evergreens. Spines of smoke streaming from ski lodge chimneys.

On certain runs, one can achieve instant karma or so it seems.

My prejudice against downhill skiing started in college.[2] I was captain of the fencing team. Maestro Michel Sebastiani, the coach, warned of all things athletic skiing was perhaps the most dangerous.

The maestro was a specimen above mere mortal man. Six feet tall with deep Corsican accent, Michel could speak and write in French, English, and Arabic. It was said he was the youngest French officer in the

Algerian Civil War. He did not talk about it much save the time he re-called coming upon slain soldiers who had their genitals stuffed into their own mouths. The maestro was the soldier whom Bud pretended to be.

Michel could run a marathon, do a one-armed hand-stand, and per-form advanced gymnastics. Michel was a pentathlete, who excelled in running, swimming, horseback riding, pistol shooting, and one-touch épée fencing. The épée is a long, inflexible, four-sided strip of metal. It was said he knew a thousand single attacks on the épée alone.

Well, Michel said he broke his ankle skiing. That was enough for me. Anyway, there weren't many slopes in Brooklyn where I went to college. Skiing was also an expensive luxury back then. Truth is, I was scared shit-less to ski.

Despite this, I learned to downhill ski rather late in life. As true with all things learned in adulthood, lifelong accumulated baggage came up the slope with me. I needed to conquer the inborn fear of the synergy of heights and hurtling downhill on technoplanks. With the help and en-couragement of fellow Bennettite, Joe MacVittie, I succeeded. I now look forward to the winter, and winters in Syracuse are long, snowy, and bone-jarring cold. Skiing seems to help the beast pass quickly and enjoy-ably.

In early March 1996, Joe, I, and our two sons went on a weekend skifest in Vermont. At one mountain, Bromley, the sky was so darkly blue that it frightened me primordially. We all had so much fun—fathers and sons. A few weeks later Bennett tanked. That was the last good time I have had since.

The Quiet Company That "Made" Hundreds of Millions

ARCHITECT David Chase, a longtime associate of the Bennetts, de-signed the interiors of some of their properties and offices. His com-pany, Chase Architectural Associates, Inc., was also an equipment lessee of Bennett Funding and a recipient of loans. As with many a lessee, Chase could not make timely lease and loan payments.

But instead of lawsuit, and in partial consideration for the cancellation of debt, the Bennetts invited Chase to transfer undeveloped parcels, hotels, and commercial office buildings he had title to into a jointly owned start-up corporation, and ally forces with his former creditors.[1]

Thus, Chase Management & Development Corporation was born in April 1985. Bennett Funding owned 51 percent of its issued and outstanding common stock and David Chase the remaining 49 percent. Chase, along with the Bennetts, served on the board and was the company's first president.

Within a month after the incorporation, we received a call from the trademark counsel for Chase Bank. The Chase Bank lawyers threatened immediate and irrevocable action unless the name was changed to distance it with any possible connection to their client. With their approval, the corporate name was changed to Bennett-Chase Management & Development Corporation.

In July 1986, Bennett Funding had transferred its shares of Bennett-Chase Management & Development to Bennett Funding of New York Corp., another affiliate exclusively owned by the four Bennetts equally.

After a dispute evolved between the Bennetts and Chase in May 1987, Chase was forced to transfer all of his shares of Bennett-Chase Management & Development to the four Bennetts outright in equal amounts. As a result, the four Bennetts owned directly and indirectly through Bennett Funding of New York Corp., all of the issued and outstanding shares of Bennett Management.

During a meeting among Bud, Patrick, Chase, and me concerning the divestiture, Chase made certain representations that were not supported by the available facts. In the first display of temper I had ever witnessed from Patrick, he cursed Chase and left the meeting. Bud and I convinced Chase that it would be in his best interest to execute the appropriate documents, resign all positions with the company, and walk away.

With Chase gone from the scene, the name was changed again to its present style, Bennett Management & Development Corp. In March 1994, Bennett Funding of New York Corp. and Bud and Kathleen Bennett transferred all of their shares of Bennett Management to Patrick and Michael, such that the two sons each owned half of all of the shares.

Sometime during 1995, Michael transferred his shares to Patrick.[2] The consideration for the transfer was never disclosed. At the time of the filing of the bankruptcy petition, March 29, 1996, Patrick was the sole shareholder of Bennett Management.

Except for Chase and the Resort investors, who owned a meager 4.5 percent that was ultimately repurchased, at no time since the incorporation of any of the Bennett companies in 1977 did any person or entity other than members of the Bennett family or entities owned by members of the Bennett family have any ownership or voting rights in any of the companies.

Over time, in addition to the assets transferred from David Chase, Bennett Management acquired a plethora of nonlease holdings stretching far and wide. At the time of the bankruptcy, it was known generally these included a mall in Maine, large-ticket construction loan promissory note receivables, a loan receivable from a racetrack in West Virginia, and two gambling boats.

As the forensic accountants and investigative attorneys have discovered, however, Bennett Management had expanded its empire to include loans to and from cronies of Patrick, stock in public and private corporations, diversion of money to Patrick, as well as Patrick's house at Oneida Lake just north of Syracuse.

Patrick's house, known as Toad Harbor, was a former sixteen-acre inn on the lake. It contains numerous rooms, a full basketball court, swimming pool, and boat dockage. One summer, our family hosted a couple of French students. During a company clambake at Toad Harbor, I asked one of the students what he thought of the place. He remarked what a wonderful park it was. "*Mon dieu,* it belongs to one person?"

Several years later Patrick built an eight-thousand-square-foot country Victorian home and ninety-seven-acre horse farm near Vernon Downs, the racetrack he owned, so he could cut down on commuting time to be with his wife, Gwen, and their two young sons. An additional twelve-acre vacant lot lying across the road was also purchased.

According to Bankruptcy Court documents, Patrick gave Gwen $165,000 in 1992 to buy the land and another $600,000 to build the house in 1994. It is believed Patrick "borrowed" the money from Bennett Management for lot purchase and house construction. He made an accounting entry as if he sold Toad Harbor to Bennett Management to defray the loan for the new house. No appraisal nor paper work was associated with the ersatz payback of the loan, only a book entry in the amount of $1 million.[3]

Patrick was formally charged in 1996 with federal crimes. As part of his surrender terms to the Justice Department, Gwen allowed the government to file a $500,000 lien on the horse farm to secure his appearance at trial. As it turns out, Patrick never held title to the house but had it placed into Gwen's name from inception. Early on, it seems Patrick had good advice concerning preservation of assets.

With its known assets and hidden treasures, Bennett Management evolved into a gigantic slush puppy with icy goo oozing from its paper-cone wrapper. The Bennetts, particularly Patrick, clustered about the cone waiting to suck the drippings like wolf cubs at their mother's teats.

For most of its business life, Bennett Management had very little, if any, direct contact with the investing public or with banks that, as one attorney put it, "involuntarily invested with it."

Indeed, Bennett Management was a company that transacted in hundreds of millions of dollars of business no one knew anything about. Bennett Management was never audited, did not file tax returns, and had no financial statements. If no one knows of your existence you do not need to have audits or financial statements. Except, later on, something did care, even before the SEC became interested.

In the mid-1990s, West Virginia passed a law that allowed video lottery terminals (VLTs) to be installed at Mountaineer Racetrack.[4] In theory, the VLTs would boost track revenue, save jobs, increase the tax base, and so on—the usual bullshit that accompanies government expansion of gaming.

Learning of the Bennetts through American Gaming, the Bennetts' gaming alter ego, Mountaineer applied for and was granted a loan of more than $10 million. The loan documentation, including the mortgage, the promissory note and related instruments, were in the name of Bennett Management as lender.

West Virginia, as does every other state that sponsors gambling, requires lenders to meet certain suitability qualifications. The fear and dread of tainted money, drug money, Mafia money supporting such projects is distasteful and politically explosive. The fear of foreclosure by gangsters is unacceptable. If they only knew.

Bennett Management needed to present basic financial information and documentation to the West Virginia Gaming Commission to support its claim of lender suitability. You could just imagine the looks of incredulity on the faces of the commissioners when they were advised of the lack of even rudimentary financial documentation.

From that point on, the commissioners wanted Bennett Management to divest itself and get the hell out of the state. We took umbrage. Our credentials were okay to pump in $10 million but not good enough to

Patrick and Gwen Bennett's house and horse farm. Photo by Dick Blume. Copyright © The Syracuse Newspapers.

stay. We needed time either to divest or to present the financial documentation. It then became the old stall game. The stall carried right into the bankruptcy.

Eventually, partly because of the strength of the documents that were prepared and reviewed internally, the acumen of the trustee's counsel, and the integrity of the borrower, Mountaineer paid back $11,191,105 to the bankruptcy estate.

Patrick also purchased the controlling interest of Ferris Industries, Inc., a lawn mower manufacturer headquartered in the nearby town of Vernon.

Sometime in fall 1994, Patrick buzzed me.

"Stu, can you come to my office? I need you to look at something."

"Sure, I'll be right there," I said. A few minutes later, I was sitting across from Patrick at a round table in his office.

"Stu, I'm going to Rochester in a couple of days to close on a deal to buy shares of stock in Ferris Industries. I want you to review the closing documents and come with me. Okay?"

"In a couple of days?" I asked.

"Yeah, sorry for the short notice, but that's when we close."

"What about due diligence on the company?" I asked.

"All done. I just need you make sure the documents are all right at closing." Patrick handed me the proposed documents and I left.

Ferris Industries was founded in 1909 by the grandfather of its current president, David Ferris. In early 1994, the company had its lending sources dry up and needed working capital. Ferris, a neighbor, approached Patrick and discussed basic terms.

Patrick was intrigued. He thought a synergy could develop between the lawn mower manufacturer and Aloha Leasing in leasing. He also was interested in new golf course care technology developed by SubAir, Inc., a wholly owned subsidiary of Ferris that was supposed to do wonders keeping greens dry and verdant through a patented aeration process.

A few days later we drove to Rochester and Patrick came back to Syracuse with about 75 percent of Ferris stock in his pocket. The owner received $2,522,556.26 for the shares. The company received a capital injection of $2,525,000.00. Records indicate all $5,047,556.26 came from Bennett Management.

When the Bennett companies tanked in 1996, Ferris found itself bound up with the chapter 11 proceedings. About one year later, Dave Ferris bought back 65 percent of the shares for about $1.3 million. In October 1998, Judge Gerling approved the sale of the remaining 35 percent to a group of local investors for $1.4 million. Since 1996, the bankruptcy estate has received $2,944,622.00 on the resale of the stock, interest, and other consideration, a loss of $2,102,934.26.[5]

Substantive Consolidation and the Honeypot

B EFORE IT merged with Price Waterhouse in 1998, Coopers & Lybrand provided accounting and consulting services worldwide.

Table 4. Summary of Coopers & Lybrand's fees, 1996–1998

Total Fee Applications	Fee Adjustments	1996 Payments	1997 Payments	1998 Payments	Total Payments
9,410,673	1,463,650	1,295,000	4,708,271	1,941,326	7,944,598*

*Adjusted amount

Drawn from a pool of domestic and international talent, the forensic practice group of Coopers, led by Manny Alas, descended upon Bennett Funding on April 18, 1996.

Although Coopers' services to the estate have been minimized because of Breeden's resignation as a partner and the need to reduce administrative costs, for the first year of the bankruptcy Coopers' staff worked around the clock.

As a result of the Coopers' forensic team's work, the involvement of attorneys from Simpson Thacher & Bartlett led by James Cotter (Corporate), M. O. Sigal Jr. (Bankruptcy), and George Newcombe (Litigation), and the tireless and underpaid efforts of Bennett Funding employees and in-house staff,[1] a clear picture of the Bennetts holistic approach to corporate existence has emerged.

Saddled with dichotomous psyches, the Bennetts, on one hand, commingled corporate ownership, governance, operations, assets, liabilities, and cash to blur their existences and make tracking difficult, if not impossible.

Coopers noted that as a direct result of the commingling of all phases of the Bennett companies operations, and the "frequent failure to adhere to any degree of formality when transferring assets ... the books, records and business affairs ... are so entangled and intertwined that it is virtually impossible to delineate accurately the assets and liabilities of the individual debtors."[2]

On the other hand, their egos compelled them to seek publicity and bask in accolades. For example, the upper northeast facade of the Atrium had large brass letters spelling THE BENNETT COMPANIES. Perhaps fearing reprisals from investors, Michael Bennett ordered the letters removed immediately after the bankruptcy petition. Unfortunately, the Atrium is directly across from the Syracuse Newspapers' headquarters. The local media caught the removal in the act and splashed it over the news.

The only hope for investors to receive a decent dividend in the Bennett bankruptcy engendered by such pervasive fraud was for the trustee to substantively consolidate all of the Bennett debtors' assets and liabilities.

Substantive consolidation is a principle of bankruptcy law that enables a bankruptcy judge sitting in equity to consolidate the estates of two or more debtors that have filed petitions.

The bases for consolidation are to promote administrative ease, relieve judicial burden, promote fairness among creditors, and save scant resources by dispensing with costly forensic hairsplitting of where this dollar comes from and where that dollar went.

In the Bennett bankruptcy, without the equitable remedy of substantive consolidation, the trustee would be required to perform a painstaking analysis of available documentation in connection with each investment and loan to determine which Bennett company is obligated to each of the investors and banks.

This analysis would encompass a comprehensive review of all payments made to each of the twelve thousand investors and 245 banks since 1990 to determine "if the payments were recorded by the appropriate debtor and accounted for accurately."

According to Coopers, the trustee would also need to perform a similar analysis of all assets of the Bennett companies to determine legal ownership as well as the existence of mortgages, liens, security interests, and other encumbrances and clouds on the titles to those assets.

Additionally, the trustee would need to perform a reconciliation of "all inter-company balances," an "investigation [of] . . . inter-company cash" disbursements, and a review of "asset transfers for voidable transactions."

"Even if it were possible to untangle the affairs of the debtors," as suggested by Coopers, "the cost of any attempt to do so, and the resulting litigation, would be prohibitive."

To substantively consolidate the Bennett companies and avoid the mountain of work and incalculable expense as described, the trustee must establish the intertwining of the debtors' corporate ownership, governance, and operations, and the debtors use of the same well of money to fund their operations.

On paper, the seventy-plus Bennett companies served as special-purpose, asset-specific, or stock-holding companies. In practice, they had little or no indicia of separate existence.

All of the Bennett companies were ultimately owned and controlled

Fig. 6. Organizational structure of the major Bennett companies

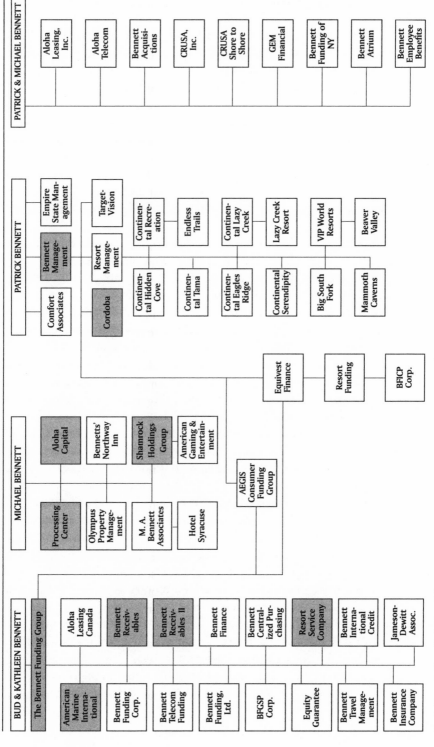

Shaded areas indicate bankruptcy debtor.

by members of the Bennett family.[3] Not only is the ownership documented in one form or another, but just ask any current or former employee "who ran the show."

Indeed, every material decision was made or approved by the Bennetts acting in concert or alone. Those decisions were made without regard to whether Bud, Kathleen, Patrick, or Michael was acting as an officer, director, or shareholder of any company. The Bennetts held all positions of power plain and simple.

To illustrate, the Bennett companies had common directors or interlocking directorates. Bud was a director of Bennett Funding, Bennett Receivables, Bennett Receivables–II, American Marine, Cordoba, and Resort Funding.

Patrick was a director of Bennett Funding, Bennett Receivables, Bennett Receivables–II, Cordoba, Resort, and Bennett Management. Michael was a director of Bennett Funding, Bennett Receivables, Bennett Receivables–II, Cordoba, Resort Funding, Bennett Management, the Processing Center, and Aloha Capital.

Likewise, the executive-level officers of Bennett Funding also served as executive-level officers of the other companies. Bud was the chief executive officer of Bennett Funding and of Resort, BRC, BRC-II, AMI, and Cordoba. Patrick was chief financial officer of Bennett Funding and of Bennett Management, Resort, BRC, BRC-II, and Cordoba. He was also chief executive officer of Bennett Management. Michael was deputy chief executive officer of Bennett Funding and of Bennett Management, Resort, BRC, BRC-II, and Cordoba; he was also president of TPC and of ACC. In other words, they held more positions than a Russian general has medals.

Other than in formal meetings of Bennett Funding and Aloha Capital, the requirements of shareholder and board meetings, and appointments and elections of directors and officers were generally ignored and, when done, were on intermittent bases.

From 1993, Bennett Funding's board comprised eight directors, the four Bennetts, and four executive-level officers. Bennett Funding conducted regular and annual board meetings, which I attended as corporate secretary and not as a board member. As corporate secretary, I was responsible to advise the board members of the meetings and keep custody of and prepare the corporate minutes book.

Serving on the board, however, was ceremonial and perfunctory. The meetings were pro forma and of extremely short duration, lasting as little as fifteen minutes. The record for the shortest meeting is seven minutes.

All proposed resolutions, including the installation of officers, were circulated ahead of time to the various members, who were free to comment to me or Bud concerning changes. Rarely, if ever, did I receive any such requests for changes.

At the meetings, although members were free to vote for or against resolutions and to discuss matters on the agenda, the board members generally read transcripts I had prepared ahead of time in consultation with Bud or Patrick as deputy chairman.

Bud told me the "real work" of corporate management on behalf of the Bennett companies transpired at the meetings of the Bennett Funding Executive Committee. This is supported by a promotional piece prepared by the Company in 1993 entitled *The Bennett Companies.*

The promo featured a picture of the Executive Committee with the subcaption "[o]perational issues at the Bennett Companies are dealt with in the monthly meetings of the Executive Committee."

The committee comprised members of the Bennett Funding board and, later on, the executive officers of Aloha Capital and the Processing Center, about ten people.

The attendees at the meeting were responsible for reports on sales, accounting, investors relations, tax, and financial matters. In preparation for the meetings, Bud required me to furnish him with status reports on major transactions I was aware of, and litigation affecting the Bennett companies.

Before 1995, the committee met monthly. Thereafter, its meetings coincided with Bennett Funding's board meetings that were conducted about five times a year. At the conclusion of the board meetings, Bud or Kathleen would give me the eye, a signal to get out of the room with all deliberate speed. Save for one meeting, the Bennetts did not want attorneys in the room while the Executive Committee met.

While tramping though the pampas grass of Company files, Coopers found "significant transfers of assets among the debtors . . . with little or no supporting documentation."[4]

After an exhaustive review of the Bennett companies' accounting books and records, Coopers stated such records often "lacked the formalities found in traditional companies." The books were not regularly maintained or updated, and intercompany accounts were not reconciled.

Indeed, certain Bennett corporations did not even maintain separate books and records.

Several notable examples of intercompany transfers are as follows:

Bennett Funding made more than 325 separate cash transfers to Bennett Management from December 1, 1993, through December 31, 1995. At the rate of approximately $19 million per month, the transfers totaled about $485 million. During the same period, Bennett Management reciprocated by making more than sixty-five cash transfers to Bennett Funding, totaling $104 million.

At Patrick's criminal trial Herb Cohen, a senior accountant with the SEC, testified that between 1990 and 1996, $1.2 billion was ultimately transferred from Bennett Funding to Bennett Management.

During 1993, Bennett Management along with other investors purchased about $11 million worth of 12b-1 trust certificates. The designation 12b-1 refers to the rule that regulates mutual fund fees.

Under the program, the mutual fund assigned to the 12b-1 trust all of the fund's right to receive marketing expense fees from its members in the future for immediate cash payment. The program was dependent upon the mutual fund making good on its promise to pay the fees to the trust.

In 1994, Bennett Management transferred the 12b-1 certificates to Bennett Funding "for no consideration other than simply recording an inter-company accounting entry on the books." Through the years, payments trickled in but not near enough to pay on the obligation.

In a separate transaction, one year later, in 1995, Bennett Management transferred a $5.6 million loan receivable from Patrick Bennett to Bennett Funding without evidence of consideration other than an intercompany accounting entry. According to Coopers, "no known documents exist to support the assignment of Patrick's receivable."

Many investor obligations were improperly recorded as well. For example, on May 2, 1995, investor Baeza purchased a lease, according to Tom Lumsden, a partner at Coopers, "and remitted a check payable to [Bennett Funding] in the amount of $103,766.24." Lumsden noted that the statement-of-purchase contract, assignment of contract, confirmation, and all correspondence were in the name of Bennett Funding.

Bennett Funding, however, deposited the Baeza check into a Bennett Management account. Bennett Management booked "the cash as an asset and the obligation to [Baeza] as a liability."

Bennett Management, through its d/b/a "Bennett Processing Company," remitted monthly payments to Baeza. Abruptly, in August 1995, Bennett Funding assumed responsibility for making the remaining payments to Baeza, yet, the obligation remained on Bennett Management's books. No known documents exist that memorialize the transfers and assignments.

As further evidence of the intertwining of the debtors' affairs, the operating activities of Bennett Funding, Bennett Receivables, Bennett Receivables–II, Resort Service, American Marine, the Processing Center, and Aloha Capital were included in the 1994 consolidated audited financial statement. Bennett Funding and the same debtors also filed a consolidated federal tax return.

Patrick was partly able to perpetrate his crimes through the use of the "Honeypot."[5] The Honeypot was a gigantic operating account at Chemical Bank in which virtually all cash received by the Bennett companies was commingled.

The Honeypot (account number 550-004890) was opened on March 21, 1990, in the name of Bennett Funding. The Honeypot account contained various subaccounts. As reported by Shaun O'Neill, the former assistant controller of Bennett Funding, the subaccounts were (1) a controlled disbursement account from which disbursements were made; (2) short term/overnight investment accounts; and (3) a lockbox in which certain payments were received. Each subaccount "had its own account number but was linked to the Honeypot."

Bennett Funding also opened a remote disbursement account at First Bank, N.A., in Minneapolis (account number 160233807660). Proceeds from certain designated collateralized bank loans were deposited into this account. The collateral consisted of leases and membership agreements. As long as there was sufficient funds, Patrick made payments to "investors who had purchased municipal leases" from this account.

The Honeypot was not limited merely to Bennett Funding. Virtually all the related entities dipped their beaks into the trough as well. Billions of dollars flowed daily into and out of the Honeypot over the years from numerous sources.

These sources included: payments from lessees; payments from dealers for inventory promissory notes; misdirected funds, such as payments rightfully belonging to other leasing companies; loan proceeds from banks; proceeds from the assignment of leases and notes to investors; funds raised by Bennett Receivables and Bennett Receivable–II private placements of approximately $155 million; excess funds on deposit in the

Fig. 7. Flow of money into the Honeypot account among the various Bennett companies

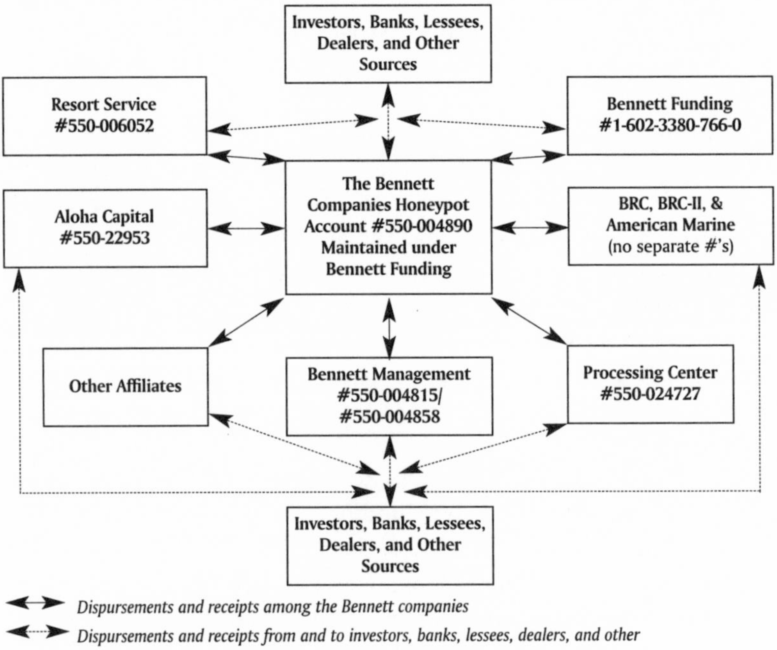

Dispursements and receipts among the Bennett companies

Dispursements and receipts from and to investors, banks, lessees, dealers, and other

Source: Based on Exhibit A from the O'Neill Affadavit in the Substantive Consolidation Motion. The Honeypot diagram can also be viewed at the Bennett web site: <http://www.bennett-funding.com>.

First Bank account; and proceeds from investment accounts held by the Bennett companies, such as CDs and overnight investment accounts.

From 1990 through 1995, the Bennett companies paid out an incredible $3.513 billion from the Honeypot to investors ($1.53 billion), banks ($331 million), equipment vendors and manufacturers ($787 million), trade suppliers, employees, and brokers ($146 million), to Bennett family members, individuals, and entities without specific reference for the use of the funds ($254 million), and nonleasing assets ($465 million).[6]

Because of the sheer volume of transactions in the Honeypot, it was very hard, but not impossible, to trace specific funds. This was a painful but important job so that the trustee's counsel could sue to collect outstanding loans or set aside fraudulent conveyances for significant assets.

That is what the forensic accountants and investigators spent so much time and, despite the substantive consolidation, money on.

According to O'Neill and the other Finance Department employees involved with cash, "Patrick controlled the Honeypot and all other aspects of cash management."[7] The transfers of billions of dollars were accomplished through a computer link to on-line banking services. Yet, the "ability to reconcile the inter-company balances was made difficult, and in some instances impossible, by Patrick's refusal to provide information about the transfers."

Patrick spurned any attempt to gather information concerning the purposes of many cash disbursements. He said to "book the transfers as inter-company receivables." This made "the flow of specific cash untraceable from its source to its ultimate use or investment. . . ."

In cash management, Patrick received a Daily Cash Packet from a Finance Department employee. The packet comprised (1) a Cash Management Transfer Sheet, (2) Account Information Summary Page, (3) Prior Day's Balance Report, (4) Credit Report, (5) Debit Report for the Honeypot and other accounts, (6) a Current Day Disbursement Report, and (7) an Investment Summary Sheet.

Table 5. Significant ($800,000+) Nonleasing Assets

Asset	Amount	Asset	Amount
Aegis Stock	25,809,694	Genovese Partnerships—	
Americorp Loan Receivable	2,224,916	Hemlock & Highwood	
American Gaming Stock,		Loan Receivables	49,942,984
Loan Receivables, Gaming		Hotel Syracuse	26,588,043
Boats and Casinos	79,855,444	Kasarjian House	1,200,000
Ameridata Warrants	7,500,000	KDV Enterprises Loan	4,910,000
Anthony Pavoni Loan Receivable	800,000	Mountaineer Park Mortgage	10,200,000
Aroostook Mall & Theatre	35,849,375	Neil Wager Loan Receivables	10,976,373
Atrium	4,514,217	Patrick's residence at Toad Harbor	2,246,206
Campground Acquisition &		Quality Inn & Days Inn Purchase	
Operation	30,034,152	and Loan Receivables	12,404,280
Carleton Island	956,663	Scriptex Leases & Loan Receivables	88,435,234
Comfort Suites Construction	8,004,600	Sioux City Sue gaming boat	
DBS Loan Receivable	2,714,809	and barge	8,500,000
Drew Schaefer Loan Receivable	3,500,000	Speculator Gaming Boat	22,212,866
Erie Islands Mortgage &		Target Vision	4,776,644
Time-share Financing	4,025,226	Vernon Downs Racetrack	4,741,726
Ferris Industries Stock & Loans	7,225,781		

As witnessed by O'Neill, "Every morning staff would obtain information regarding the previous day's activities in the Honeypot [and] the First Bank Account . . . [through a] PC modem [link]." The information would "be compared to what Patrick . . . had directed on the previous . . . day to verify . . . all transactions had been completed correctly."

From this review, an Account Information Summary Page was prepared. The summary page showed the opening balance for each debtor's account and was forwarded to Patrick for further review.

By midmorning, the current day's disbursement figures would become available showing "the total dollar amount of checks paid out from the Honeypot. . . ." This amount would then be entered on the summary page and deducted from that day's opening balance.

The resultant amount would give Patrick a snapshot of the cash position in the Honeypot, and guide him through his fiscal manipulations.

With this information, in the event any particular Bennett company was cash poor to fund its daily operations, Patrick raided the Honeypot to cover any shortfalls. The Cash Management Transfer Sheet recorded all such intercompany cash transfers.

According to Coopers, "Disbursements were made from the Honeypot to the various [Bennett companies] . . . based on their respective cash needs and irrespective of the source of such funds or . . . such companies' receivables."

Before the close of business, Patrick received an Investment Summary Sheet showing the closing balance remaining in the Honeypot.

Despite the detailed information contained in the Daily Cash Packet furnished to Patrick, "no inter-company ledgers were maintained among the various [Bennett companies] regarding the sources and disbursements of funds." Money transfers into and out of the Honeypot were recorded as Bennett Funding intercompany transfers, "even if Bennett Funding's receipts or disbursements were not involved."[8]

The migration of funds, as Coopers' Lumsden noted, "created a 'pinball' effect where funds bounced around from debtor to debtor making it virtually impossible to trace the source of funds to its ultimate use or investment."

But the Honeypot was more than just a gigantic bank account. Because all funds were commingled and flowed into and out of the Honeypot, each Bennett company shared financial risk and reward of the whole group—akin to a shared-risk pool for young male drivers.

"The use of the Honeypot account created a much wider consolidated financial implication than merely the inability to trace the source of funds," stated Lumsden.

Because institutional lenders relied on the credit of the Honeypot as a whole, all of the Bennett companies were able to share the risk, "such that there was never any financial risk which would be borne exclusively by any individual debtor."

The Honeypot's pooling effect enabled "each debtor to economically share in the gains and losses of the group," as long as the money kept rolling in.

Seven months after their review of the books and records of the debtors, interviews of current and former employees and interested parties, and upon the advice of experts, Coopers found that "there can be no doubt that the debtors operated as if they were one complex business enterprise," a conclusion inevitably drawn from the Bennetts' Janus-faced need to hide and their need to reveal.

As Coopers admonished, "Without substantive consolidation, creditors would be limited to the asset position of a particular debtor to seek repayment of their claims," even though at any time that debtor might have valuable assets "or might be devoid of any assets at all."

In the face of such overwhelming analysis, Judge Gerling ordered the substantive consolidation of the eight Bennett estates in August 1997. The ninth company, Cordoba Corporation, was thrown into bankruptcy solely to rescue the proceeds from the sale of the *Lady Kathleen* from Bud.

Patrick, like Pooh Bear, from time to time, reached his own paws into the Honeypot and drew heavily. The cash stuck to his fingers. Between 1992 and 1995 Patrick personally siphoned off about $13 million from the Honeypot through Bennett Management. This bit of embezzlement, while not as elaborate as the FIN/INV method, was nonetheless highly effective and profitable for Patrick.

To accomplish the embezzlement, Patrick created a series of entities known as Bennett Finance Group I, Bennett Finance Group II, etc. What exactly Bennett Finance Group I, et al., are and who, if anyone besides Patrick, are members is anyone's guess. All we know is the entities exist on the accounting and computer records of the company. There seems to be no independent evidence of their existence.

Once these entities were established, at least on an accounting basis,

Miles of files. Some of the Bennett companies' thousands of banker's boxes containing millions of documents. Exhibit from the litigation files with the non-settling banks.

Patrick had Bennett Management cut about 160 checks to the Bennett Finance entities periodically from 1991 through 1996. The checks varied in amounts and were designated as loan proceeds. Although the checks were payable to the named entities, they were endorsed by Patrick and then deposited into his personal account at a brokerage clearinghouse.[9]

In the summer of 1995, after the SEC inquired about these unlawful diversions, Patrick, aided and abetted by Joseph Canino, CPA, fabricated records to provide the pseudoappearance these diversions were contemporaneously recorded on Bennett Funding's books and records and Patrick had repaid the purported loans.[10]

The dipping into the Honeypot to the tune of $13 million through the

Bennett Finance Group entities was not accompanied by any contemporaneous loan documentation, such as interest and principal amortization schedules, repayment schedules, promissory notes, or collateral security—at least none that have surfaced. None of the largesse has ever been repaid in reality.

After being rejected by numerous lenders, a local real estate developer persuaded Patrick to finance the construction of a mall and theater complex in Presque Isle, Maine. Presque Isle is in Aroostook County in the northeastern quadrant near the border with New Brunswick, Canada. By the way, some of Stephen King's stories are set in Aroostook County.

Construction loans involve two stages of lending. As a rule, the first lender provides construction financing and working capital to the developer. However, such lenders rarely want to be involved on a long-term basis. A prudent construction lender, as a condition precedent to making the loan, will obtain a commitment letter from a permanent lender so as not to be stuck with a long-term loan.

The permanent lender bases its credit decision upon the name recognition of the anchor tenants, such as Sears and Macy's, and the forecasted and projected vitality of the rental base and aggregate gross sales of the smaller stores.

When told about the project, Bennett Funding board member Coach Mac, a native of Maine, said the sparse population did not justify the transaction. After hearing the sales pitch by the developer that droves of Canadians and soldiers from a "not-too-far" military base would de-

Table 6. Nine of the approximately 160 payments to the Bennett Finance Group entities controlled by Patrick Bennett

Payee	Check #	Date	Amount
BFG II	10278	Apr. 10, 1991	$120,000.00
BFG IV	30417	Mar. 12, 1992	$205,921.80
BFG III	31456	Oct. 13, 1992	$261,231.91
BFG IV	249264	Mar. 1, 1994	$300,000.00
BFG II	423182	Feb. 9, 1995	$6,259.70
BFG II	423187	Feb. 9, 1995	$200,000.00
BFG VII	357820	Feb. 9, 1995	$221,246.00
BFG III	527879	Feb. 14, 1996*	$99,954.14
BFG III	527881	Feb. 14, 1996*	$6,668.81

*Bennett Funding filed bankruptcy on Mar. 19, 1996.

scend upon the mall like seven-year locusts, Patrick overruled Coach Mac.

Ultimately, Patrick, through Bennett Management, loaned $37,075,267 to construct the mall and theater despite the absence of a commitment letter from a permanent lender.

Unfortunately, Coach Mac was right. Because of the steep devaluation of the Canadian dollar, the crush of Canadians did not materialize. The military base was closed as part of a round of base closings. Because the traffic was so light, the businesses that paid rent as well as a percentage of gross receipts to the developer were having difficulty making ends meet. The real value of the mall plummeted.

The developer could not get a commitment, and Bennett Management became the de facto permanent lender. In transactions in which the value of the collateral is lower than the amount owed, if the lender forecloses it will not realize enough from the sale of the undersecured property to pay off the loan. The relationship therefore shifts from creditor/debtor to partnership.

Such was the case with the mall. Patrick had no real choice but to continually acquiesce to the developer's requests to extend the maturity date of the loan.

The loan was extended right through the bankruptcy. Eventually, the trustee was able to settle with the developer for $26 million, including $24.5 million in cash and a short-term note for the balance.

However, not long before Bennett filed bankruptcy, Patrick borrowed about $8 million from the First Bank in Minnesota, the same bank that had the mini-Honeypot account. Patrick pledged the Aroostook Mall mortgage as collateral to secure the loan. As First Bank did not perfect the assignment of the mortgage by properly filing it with the Aroostook County clerk, the trustee predicted its claim would be converted to unsecured status. As unsecured creditor, First Bank will receive about $2.4 million for its claim.

The aggregate settlement amount lost on the mall deal will equal about $14.6 million sans interest. This figure assumes neither the developer nor the guarantor of the mall loan files bankruptcy.

Despite the announcement of the settlement, as of this writing, the estate received $18,670,830 on top of previous payments of $921,452, for a total of $19,592,282, a real loss of $20 million.[11]

A lifelong friend of Patrick received "broker's fees" from Bennett Management, the lender, for the mall transaction in excess of $225,000.

Bennett Management's books and records also show the same broker received through an associated business, KDV Enterprises, an undocumented cash infusion of $4.5 million. No paperwork has surfaced for either the brokerage deal or the cash infusion.

Another friend of Patrick's, Joseph Canino helped manipulate Bennett Management's accounting records. He was a longtime Bennett employee who had been fired in 1993 for bad attitude.

It was interesting to see his reappearance in 1995 in the inner sanctum of the Finance Department. As Patrick explained, Canino was hired to bring Bennett Management's tax filings up to date. This was a credible explanation given the fiasco with the West Virginia Lottery Commission.

It took several months of "work" to prepare the respective year's returns, have them reviewed, and then move on to the next year. I say "work" because according to the forensic accountants our friend Canino's major task was to rerecord journal entries on the computer system.[12] Journal entries are the daily recordation of what payments represent. The entries are supported by appropriate documentation.

When the empire fell, Canino's handiwork of changing journal entries was easy to trace, as he left the backup in two banker's boxes at the office. All one had to do, and what was done, was to review journal entries on the system with those in Canino's box and voila! note the difference. For example, an original journal entry listed a certain payment as a commission. Canino reclassified the entry to record the payment as rental expense.

Canino was at the time of the reversing of most of the journal entries a certified public accountant. What went through his mind? Why would he risk his CPA license and face civil lawsuit and imprisonment to change journal entries for Patrick Bennett? True, Canino was an old friend of Patrick's, but would he so simply just do what he was told, turn a blind eye, aid and abet?

To this day, the word on the street is that Canino thinks he has done nothing wrong. He blames the employees who smoked him by finding his boxes of reality left "inadvertently" at his work station. Maybe the boxes were left to assuage a guilty conscience? Maybe they were left because he thought he would be coming back into work the next day? Or maybe he was just stupid?

Patrick's Legal Troubles

IN CONJUNCTION with the SEC civil complaint, a companion criminal complaint was filed by an FBI special agent, John J. Hess, and approved by an assistant U.S. attorney, Michael Sommer, against Patrick on March 28, 1996.[1] The criminal complaint charged Patrick with one count of securities fraud and one count of perjury.

Patrick, accompanied by his lawyer, Charles Stilman, pleaded not guilty at the arraignment in Manhattan. He was released on his own recognizance, based, in part, on his renowned fear of flying and the $500,000 lien on Gwen's house.

Price Waterhouse was Bennett Funding's outside auditors in the 1980s. As part of its audit, PW suggested that, to avoid a catastrophe that may ensue if the board and control group traveled together, half should travel with Patrick by car and the remainder by plane. Patrick joked that with his "luck the airplane would crash into the car."

Throughout the years, Patrick cultivated the notion that he was deathly afraid to fly. He was chauffeured from Syracuse to meetings with his cronies in New Jersey and with the SEC in Manhattan.

Despite the travel card, witnesses reported seeing Patrick in the American Airlines terminal in Chicago and then aboard a plane to Syracuse in February 1997.[2] He was accompanied by an attractive young blonde not his wife.

The witnesses had met Patrick on several prior occasions in the Syracuse area through mutual friends. They were shown pictures of Patrick and identified him. The witnesses said a friend of theirs was on an earlier flight with Patrick from Miami that terminated in Chicago. Most of the passengers on the Miami flight originated from one of the Caribbean islands.

Although this information was upstreamed to the authorities, Patrick's preconviction release on his own recognizance was never revoked.

Not long after the plane trip, Patrick's activities were brought before a federal grand jury convened to probe the improprieties at Bennett Funding. The grand jury issued an indictment for violating federal laws on June 26, 1997. The indictment superseded the criminal complaint.

After the indictment was handed down, Charles Stilman issued a statement on Patrick's behalf:

> In the [last] 15 months . . . Patrick Bennett . . . has assisted the [bankrupt-cy] Trustee in recovering millions of dollars of assets. Although the pendency of the indictment continues to make it impossible for him to comment on the specific charges, [Bennett] expects that the full truth will show that the Bennett Companies were not a "Ponzi scheme" and that the Companies were not run for his personal enrichment. He deeply regrets that any investor has suffered any financial injury, and as a former officer and director of the Bennett Companies accepts full responsibility for his actions.[3]

At the time of the indictment, Special Agent Timothy Dorch of the FBI said of Patrick and the other coindictees, "They were not outwardly dangerous or outwardly menacing individuals, in the sense of the term dangerous . . . [but] they were extremely dangerous . . . in the economic sense."[4]

Patrick was rearraigned on the indictment in federal court in Manhattan. Again, he pleaded not guilty to all charges. Boldly, Patrick requested a court-appointed attorney, because he did not have the means to continue to pay Stilman.

Table 7. The federal counts against Patrick Bennett

Description of Count
Fraud in connection with sale of leases
Mail fraud
Bank fraud
Securities fraud in connection with sale of BRC notes
Money laundering
Money transactions in property derived from specified unlawful activity
Conspiracy to obstruct justice in connection with SEC investigation of 7 percent notes and perjury
Conspiracy to obstruct justice in connection with SEC investigation of financial statement and perjury
Obstruction of justice
Perjury
Conspiracy to commit bankruptcy fraud and conceal assets
Concealment of assets

Stilman, who typically represents the rich and the famous, stated he would lend whatever assistance the new counsel needed because he "would not abandon Patrick."

The request was granted and public defender David Levitt, assisted by Mark Gombiner, took over representation. The trial date was pushed back several times to accommodate Patrick's new counsel and a change of trial judges.

As a tactic, criminal defendants, particularly those not incarcerated, prefer to stretch the proceedings. In this fashion, the natural order of things works to their advantage. Prosecution witnesses die, disappear, or develop faulty recall. Evidence becomes lost. As in Patrick's case, the prosecution team itself may change. The transfers are not always smooth and vital information falls into the cracks.

In a last-ditch effort to prolong the criminal prosecution, the public defender filed a motion in October 1998 before Judge Griesa seeking, among other things, to change venue of the trial from Manhattan to the northern district of New York.

Levitt argued that as Patrick's wife, Gwen, is the primary breadwinner, Patrick is responsible for rearing his two sons. A trial in New York City would visit an unfair hardship upon the family.

To sweeten the pot, Levitt added that if the motion was granted, a former district attorney cum defense attorney from an adjacent upstate county is waiting in the wings to take over the defense at a reduced cost, saving taxpayers the cost of the public attorney.

In papers filed in opposition to the motion, assistant U.S. attorneys Patrick Smith and Richard Owens replied, "[The] request is an affront to the approximately 12,000 victims of the crimes alleged in the indictment."[5] The motion was denied and jury selection commenced on December 7, 1998.

Anticipating a conviction, even Breeden jumped into the act and stated publicly, "Society has a message to send here that if you go into business and fail, it isn't okay to cook the books and cheat people."[6]

Patrick, as did his brother Michael, filed chapter 7 bankruptcy.[7] Chapter 7 is known as a liquidation. In cases in which the chapter 7 debtor has nonexempt assets, the creditors may realize some return on their debts. In cases in which the debtor has no assets or only exempt assets, the creditors receive nothing.

Chapter 7 trustees for individual cases are selected at random from a pool of standing trustees previously approved and selected by the U.S.

Trustee's Office, an arm of the Justice Department. Chapter 11 trustees such as Breeden are selected from a pool of applicants on a case-by-case basis.

During the mandatory section 341 meetings of creditors, Richard Croak, Patrick's bankruptcy attorney, allowed him to testify concerning only his assets not those interrelated with Bennett Funding, its bankruptcy, or those that would readily bury him.

At the meetings, Patrick invoked the Fifth Amendment privilege against self-incrimination about five hundred times.[8] For example:

Q: Mr. Bennett, what is your wife's job at the Comfort Suites Hotel?

A: In response to that question, under the advice of counsel I invoke my right under the Fifth Amendment of the United States Constitution against self-incrimination.

Q: Mr. Bennett, when did you buy the fax machine?

A: In response to that question, under the advice of counsel I invoke my right under the Fifth Amendment of the United States Constitution against self-incrimination.

Q: Mr. Bennett, when did you purchase the couch in your home?

A: In response to that question, under the advice of counsel I invoke my right under the Fifth Amendment of the United States Constitution against self-incrimination.

Even to fundamentally more important questions as to the whereabouts of more than twenty-seven racehorses, Patrick took the Fifth.

Croak, in a surprising move surely to endear him to no one, requested Judge Gerling to permit Patrick to inspect Breeden's personal investment portfolio because of alleged double-dealing in transactions between Bennett Funding and Equivest, which owns the shares of Resort Funding. As you will recall, Equivest is the public time-share company that is the focal point of the bankruptcy reorganization.

In November 1997, Judge Gerling allowed Equivest to give Bennett Funding additional shares in exchange for cancellation of its debt. A few days before the hearing on the proposal, Breeden bought three thousand shares in Equivest but failed to disclose the purchase until January 1998. Breeden was criticized publicly for buying the shares of Equivest without first disclosing the purchase to and obtaining approval from the Bankruptcy Court.

When the story broke, a lawyer for the trustee said, "What [Breeden] was doing was identifying his interests with the investors. It was a symbolic gesture." The three thousand shares represented less than one-tenth of 1 percent of the total issued shares of Equivest. To make the problem go away and avoid any further appearance of impropriety, Breeden donated the Equivest shares to Syracuse University.[9]

Croak's twist on the deal was: "Breeden sought to eliminate the debt Equivest owed to Bennett Funding . . . thereby increas[ing] the value of [Breeden's] interest in Equivest." Croak argued that Breeden's debt cancellation affected Patrick, because he personally guaranteed some of that debt.

Breeden's chief litigation lawyer, George Newcombe, from Simpson Thacher, rebuffed Croak and said that "it was pretty absurd for Patrick Bennett, who has taken the Fifth Amendment at every turn to block our ability to find out where hundreds of millions of dollars in investor money has gone, to think that he can now start asking questions."[10]

Fearing such questioning by Patrick "would be opening the proverbial Pandora's box,"[11] Judge Gerling denied Croak's motion.

Interestingly, before he went freemartin, Croak was the assistant U.S. trustee assigned to the chapter 11 proceeding of the Hotel Syracuse, Inc., in 1993. He opposed adamantly the Bennetts' purchase of the Hotel Syracuse during his tenure. Is Syracuse really that small or are mysterious and inexplicable forces at work?

Eventually, the trustee in Patrick's chapter 7 bankruptcy proceeding, Lee Woodard, petitioned Judge Gerling to seize Gwen's house and sell it for the benefit of Patrick's personal creditors. Woodard theorized that as Gwen did not have gainful employment from 1990 to 1996, she could not have paid Patrick for the house or have the reasonable expectation to repay loans or mortgages.[12]

In his bankruptcy schedules, Patrick stated he owned only a couch and a chair in the entire house. In an attempt to investigate the veracity of Patrick's claim, Woodard requested a visit to determine its contents but was denied access by Gwen.

A few weeks after filing the petition to seize Gwen's house, Woodard, under the same theory, laid siege to a more modest house, in Sherrill, New York, Gwen had purchased for her grandmother in 1991 for $76,000. Title to the house was transferred to a trust created in 1997 for their two sons. Bud and Kathleen also took up residence there, especially during Patrick's trial.

Woodard sought the return of twenty-seven horses listed on Patrick's

1995 income tax return because they were given away or sold below market and stated values.

In the danse macabre that is the Bennett bankruptcy, Patrick filed a proof of claim against Bennett Funding and Bennett Management for more than $800 million. The claim was equitably subordinated to the interests of the Bennett creditors.

White Sands

R ESORT SERVICE Company, fka (formerly known as) Resort Funding, financed membership campgrounds throughout the country. Essentially, Resort purchased membership agreements from campground developers. Akin to financing equipment leases, Resort raised capital by pledging the membership agreements as collateral to support bank loans. Resort also raised money by selling the agreements to investors.

The interest rates charged Resort by the various banks were at the top end of the scale. The high rates were passed through to the campground members as part of the cost of their membership. To ensure those costs did not escalate beyond reasonableness, part of the interest rate inherent in the financed agreements would be absorbed by the developer through discounts offered for the purchase price of the membership agreements to Resort.

For example, if a ten-year membership sold to the public for $5,000, Resort would buy it for $4,000, but bill the consumer/member the full $5,000 plus interest. The agreement purchases were on full recourse so that the developer was responsible to pay Resort the balance due on defaulted membership agreements.

Despite the high rates, forced discounts, and recourse obligations, Resort stayed competitive because of the quick turnaround time for approval, closing, and disbursement of funds. Moreover, many of the developers were subprime borrowers who were accustomed to paying higher rates to borrow funds.

Even after deals closed, money changed hands, and membership agreements assigned, developers continually hunted for cheaper rates. This would allow them to reduce the cost of offered memberships and reduce potential amounts owed by the developer to Resort because of the recourse obligation for defaulted membership agreements.

One such hunter/developer notified Resort he wanted to buy out the campground's portfolio. Armed with the membership agreements and the transference documents, Vice President Al Cerimeli and I traveled to El Paso, Texas, to consummate the deal and receive the payoff amount of about $300,000.

Our travel agent probably never visited El Paso. She placed us in a hotel directly across the road from an active oil refinery. The air was none-too-clean smelling. The city had an unctuous feel. Not long after our return to Syracuse, it was reported a bunch of babies were born with their brains outside of their bodies because of petropollutants in the drinking water.

"Hey, Al, let's take a swim before dinner," I suggested.

We went downstairs and entered the indoor pool area. Slicks of oil floated on the surface of the pool water. We looked at each other in amazement and declined to go in.

As long as we were minimally clad, we opted to take a sauna. We opened the door and were hit by a strong odor of shellac or varnish. We could not tell whether the hotel intentionally coated the sauna with the noxious chemicals that leach in the dry heat of the sauna or whether residue from the refinery adhered to the pinewood. In either event we dared not enter.

"I hope the food's better off," Al said.

The next morning we met the developer at his office, transacted business, and checked out of the hotel.

Al and I were instructed to visit another campground that did business with Resort Funding. Little Creek Resort was just outside Ruidoso, New Mexico, about 130 miles north of El Paso.

Little Creek had sold about three hundred membership agreements to Resort Funding for about $1.5 million. Soon after the sale of the agreements, many of the members stopped paying. The default rate was growing dangerously high. Management was not responding to our inquiries nor was it paying on the charged-back membership agreements and honor its recourse obligation.

About halfway between El Paso and Ruidoso lies White Sands National Monument in the heart of the Tularosa Basin, a mountain-ringed valley at the northern end of the Chihuahuan Desert.[1]

White Sands is 275 square miles of great dunes of white gypsum sand.

The dunes are driven by gale force winds, which relentlessly roar across the desert for days on end.

Only a few species of animals and plants are hardy enough to survive burial by the migrating dunes and the harsh desert environment. Some affect a white tint to blend with the sand.

As we were in no particular hurry to get to Little Creek, we entered the federal preserve. Al and I drove around looking at the sea of endless dunes. After the motor tour we got out and walked around for closer inspection.

I noticed a large insect walking up a dune leaving herringbone tracks in the sand. As I bent down to get a closer look, a sand beetle surfaced, grabbed its prey, and dragged it down under. "Shit."

Within a few minutes of our stroll, the sky darkened and rain fell without warning. "How could it be, a desert visit and it rains?" I wondered. We scurried to the car and drove off to Ruidoso to grab a bite to eat. Al had a hankering for local cuisine. We found a small storefront advertising "Best Bar-B-Q." Although I was a little skittish after El Paso, we entered.

The "restaurant" was maybe 40´ × 30´ The five or six tables were old barrels with square pieces of particle board nailed on top. The grill was a jury-rigged oil drum with hinged door.

"How you boys doin'?" the owner said holding a barbecue utensil. His apron was splattered with oil and drippings. "S'down, s'down," he said with a Western twang.

We obeyed.

"Now, whatta you boys wan' ta eat?"

"What's good on the menu today?' Al asked.

"Whats good?—well, hell, everythin's good. Tell ya what. I be fixin' you a sample of everthin' on the grill," the owner said. He looked like he was a former test pilot out of the *Right Stuff*. Indeed, around the frieze of the restaurant were black-and-white photos of men in uniform.

Mr. Right Stuff lifted the cover to the oil drum, poked the utensil inside, and said, "Boys, you in for a real treat today."

Al and I looked at each other and gulped.

Mr. Right Stuff took out an unidentifiable selection of meats. They did smell good, however.

"Let's see. We got some brisket, some ribs, ah, hell, I'll just give you a piece of everthin'."

After he cleaved a chicken, he held each piece in his hands like Osiris,

Egyptian deity of the underworld, weighing virtue in the hearts of the dead.

He slapped the chicken onto two plates. He repeated the procedure for the beef and the pork, and walked over and plopped the plates down before us.

"Dig in, boys, don't be bashful," he said, leaving us to enjoy the meal.

I gave the pork to Al, making sure Mr. Right Stuff didn't notice, as I was afraid he might get violent because I was rejecting his food. We savored the meal. It was the damned best barbecue I ever had before or since.

We paid and left for Little Creek, about a twenty-minute drive.

Membership campgrounds cater to the recreational vehicle (RV) crowd, who may stay a week at one campground then a week at another as they travel throughout the country under reciprocal-use arrangements with other campgrounds.

The campgrounds are usually near and advertise, make use of, and take the name of, a prominent geologic feature, such as a lake, a river, a cavern, or a mountain.

They offer a myriad of activities, including pool tournaments, sleigh rides, pancake breakfasts, Super Bowl parties, Las Vegas nights, kiddy bingo, Easter egg coloring, arts and crafts, dance nights, dart tournaments, canoe rides, hiking, swimming, horseback riding, and Fourth of July celebrations.

Many campgrounds have swimming pools, horseshoe pits, clubhouses, basketball courts, miniature golf, driving range and putting areas, tetherball, and similar amenities.

Most offer full RV hookups to sewer, water, and power, and are required to build sewer and septic systems and use well water.

The members are a mixture of senior citizens, RV road warriors, and urbanites who like to go out into the country to relax on weekends. Although many have their own RVs, some members stay overnight in stationary mobile homes or in small on-site cabins.

The Company's protocol was to perform extensive due diligence before entering into transactions with the developers. This included on-site inspection by an architect and careful analysis of financial information.

Based on our experience of campgrounds, Al and I expected to see an active resort centered on the water at Little Creek. We expected to see boys and girls having splash fights, teenagers sunning on rafts and floating platforms like seals, people diving and swimming, and lots of water.

Alas, Little Creek was closed, deserted even. No staff, no campers, nobody. We walked around in stunned silence unable to comprehend the ghost town. After a while I talked into a voice-activated recorder: "Little Creek has hookups installed for only about fifteen to twenty of the sixty-plus RV trailers it claimed it could accommodate. No permanent sites are visible. The grounds are unkempt and the vegetation grows wild and untrimmed. There is no creek or any other body of water except for a dry construction culvert about ten feet wide and ten feet deep, which has a large exposed pipe running down the middle and heavy construction equipment nearby. Boy, someone fucked up on this one."

But Al and I should not have been so surprised to see this Potemkin village; after all, the signs preceded us: oil slicks on water and rain at the desert.

More Books to Cook

To ATTRACT investors like moths to a flame, a financial statement has to be appealing, enticing, something to cause an investor to salivate, to die for. Or at least in Bennett Funding's case, post profit.

To help keep it that way, Patrick and his cadre, including Kasarjian and Genovese, entered into sham transactions. The ersatz deals boosted Company income and shielded its actual losses by, for example, failing to establish reserves required by generally accepted accounting principles for nonperforming loans.

The bogus deals created the appearance of income or profitability on the financial statements that were distributed to the banks, brokers, and investors.[1]

Sometime before 1993, to illustrate, Bennett Funding loaned about $10.8 million to American Gaming, fka Gamma International, the New Jersey gaming conduit. The majority stock of American Gaming, a public corporation, was in turn owned by Shamrock Holdings Group, Inc., fka Bennett Holding, Inc., a company owned entirely by Michael Bennett.

From the indictment against Patrick and Michael Bennett and others filed in the U.S. District Court, Southern District of New York, we learn that in the spring of 1993, American Gaming announced that for fiscal year 1992, it "had a net loss of $4,071,919 on sales of $12,651,549." The statement indicated that "there was substantial doubt about [American Gaming's] ability to continue as a going concern."[2]

Based on these public statements, Bennett Funding's auditors at the time, Mahoney Cohen, advised Patrick that the Company "might need to take a reserve against the loan" because American Gaming was in dire financial straits with losses of more than $4 million.

If Patrick acquiesced to the auditor's request and took such a reserve, Bennett Funding's income would have been reduced by a staggering $10.8 million resulting in "a substantial amount of negative income for 1992."

To remedy the situation and "avoid taking a reserve on the loans," Patrick orchestrated a series of sham transactions in which the Company advanced $15.45 million through intermediaries to American Gaming and ultimately winding up in Bennett Funding's coffers to create the impression the outstanding loan was repaid.

Specifically, on April 7, 1993, Bennett Funding transferred $15.1 million to Bennett Management, Patrick's slush-puppy company. Bennett Management then wired on the same day $14.45 million to Kenton Management, a Kasarjian-owned company.

Kasarjian then wired $14.45 million from his company to Mutual Investors Funding Corporation, Inc., MIFCO, a company owned by coindictee Gary Peiffer, a partner in Jeffer, Hopkinson, Vogel, Coomber and Peiffer, a New Jersey law firm. The firm rendered securities opinions and did other work on behalf of the Company and its affiliates.

When Bennett Funding changed accountants in 1992 to Mahoney Cohen, Peiffer's firm wrote a thirteen-page opinion addressing certain issues relating to securities raised by counsel to Arthur Andersen, the former accountant.[3] The opinion was instrumental in securing the engagement of Mahoney Cohen.

On April 8, 1993, Patrick wired, through Bennett Management, another $1 million to Kasarjian's company, which, in turn, wired it to MIFCO.

On April 9, 1993, Peiffer, through MIFCO, purchased 100 percent of a $15 million private placement offering of American Gaming common and preferred stock.

The same day, American Gaming repaid its indebtedness of $10.8 million to Bennett Funding with the money Patrick had secretly laundered through Bennett Management, Kasarjian, and Peiffer. Undoubtedly, some of the wired funds ended up in the pockets of these men as a laundry fee.

In April 1993, Patrick advised Mahoney Cohen that American Gaming had sold $15 million of common and preferred stock to MIFCO. Patrick said American Gaming used those funds, in part, to repay American Gaming's outstanding indebtedness to Bennett Funding.

As a result of the phony loan repayment, Mahoney Cohen "did not require a reserve on account of the non-performing loan. . . ." This enabled Bennett Funding to report a false profit on the 1992 financial statement.

Also from the indictment we learn Patrick did the same type of circle jerk with a promissory note for $10.5 million. In December 1991, Bennett Funding loaned about $9.6 million to Erie Islands Resort and Marina, a time-share and membership recreation project near Lake Erie in Ohio. In consideration, Erie Islands executed a promissory note calling for eighty-six payments to be paid to Bennett Funding.

In August 1993, after making some payments and reducing the principal balance to about $8 million, Erie Islands, claiming poverty, stopped making scheduled payments.

In December of that year, to avoid taking another reserve against the outstanding Erie Islands loan, which would have resulted in a loss on the 1993 financial statement, Patrick sold the Erie Islands note to Hemlock Investor Associates for an amount greater than the balance due on the note.

In 1990, Charles Genovese formed Hemlock Investor Associates, a New Jersey partnership with offices in Franklin Lakes. Genovese, a certified public accountant, was a partner in the accounting firm, Genovese, Levin, Bartlett Co., also in Franklin Lakes.

Hemlock is the name of the street in New Jersey on which Genovese lives. It is also the name of the poison Socrates drank as punishment for his imagined crimes against Athens. Can they pick names or what?

On December 28, 1993, Patrick surreptitiously wired $10.5 million from a Bennett Management account into Hemlock's account. Before the wire transfer, Hemlock had only $14,500 in the account. The next day, Genovese caused Hemlock to issue a check to Bennett Funding for the same amount in consideration for the purchase of the Erie Islands note. Accordingly, Patrick was able to book a profit on the transaction of $2.7 million.

Patrick misled Mahoney Cohen by failing to disclose the funds used by Hemlock to purchase the Erie note originated from Bennett Management, thereby improperly booking the multimillion-dollar profit on the 1993 financial statement.

The boilerplate charge for obstruction of justice is "defendant unlawfully, willfully and knowingly and corruptly influence, obstruct and impede and did endeavor to influence, obstruct and impede a governmental investigation."

The boilerplate charge for perjury is "defendant having taken an oath in a deposition, said that he would testify truly, and that any written testimony would be true, did knowingly and contrary to such oath, stated and subscribed material matter which he did not believe to be true."[4]

Patrick appeared before the SEC Regional Office in Manhattan in June 1993, December 1994, April 1995, and January 1996. He gave hours upon hours of sworn-to testimony.

Based on the testimony, the feds indicted Patrick for, among other things, obstruction, perjury, and conspiracy to commit perjury and obstruction related to the American Gaming repayment and the sale of the Erie note to Hemlock. The italicized portions are the materially false statements.[5]

Q: Can you describe for the terms of that transaction?

A: Hemlock—the general terms?

Q: Yes.

A: *Hemlock purchased an asset. It was about the same period of time, in the area of $10 million plus, you know, approximately $10 million.*

Q: And how did Hemlock Investor Associates come to purchase the Erie Island note?

A: Hemlock had been a—had loaned some money on an unsecured basis to Bennett Management *and some time during the course of the year I remember a conversation with Mr. Genovese that he said he was—*

Q: Is this 1993 when you said, "the course of the year?"

A: *Yes. When he said he was looking—he was going to have some additional funds available in Hemlock, and because of that he was looking to have a—rather than an unsecured loan, he was looking for a secured transaction, so he'd be looking to, you know, purchase an asset and still have one of our companies service it for him but, you know, have a tangible asset as collateral rather than just a, you know, unsecured loan.*

Q: And were there any problems with regard to collecting on the underlying membership contracts which comprised the Erie Island note?

A: *I don't know.*

Q: Do you know if there were any such problems before the note was sold to Hemlock?

A: *I'm not aware of any, I mean as far as I know, they were current in their payments.*

Here, Patrick clearly misled the investigators. In engaging in the campground business, Bennett/Resort Funding would typically purchase the underlying membership agreements, then bill and collect from the members directly.

Unlike most campground deals, however, Erie Islands borrowed money from Bennett Funding and pledged the membership agreements as collateral. Erie received the money from the members directly and paid Bennett monthly to reduce the principal of the loan, which is known as a *hypothecation* in the industry.

Erie Islands was not paying under its various obligations to the Company long before the note was flipped between the conspirators, Patrick and Charles Genovese. Although it had the right to collect from the members directly if Erie Islands was rendered in default, this right was effectively waived by Bennett Funding.

From the same indictment, Genovese, who faced similar charges, went before the SEC on October 19, 1995.[6]

Q: Apart from your counsel, Mr. Genovese, did you speak with anybody about your testimony here today?

A: *No.*

Q: Have you discussed with Mr. [Patrick] Bennett the substance of the testimony that you might be giving today?

A: *No.*

Q: When did Hemlock buy this Erie Island note?

A: *I don't know if it was back in October or November.*

Q: Of what year?

A: *1993.*

Q: What is your attorney finalizing now?

A: *When I went into the agreement back in '93, I had the option at that time to take an equity position any time I wanted it.*

Q: An equity position in what?

A: *In the park.*

Q: In the Erie Island Resort and Marina?

A: *Yes.*

Q: Was there an interest rate that was part of that promissory note that you were buying in '93?

A: *There was an interest rate.*

Q: What was it?

A: *Seven or eight percent.*

Q: Did Hemlock understand that there were certain set monthly payments that it would be receiving on that note?

A: *Yes, but they were received through their administration.*

Q: Let's break that down. What was Hemlock's understanding as to the amount of monthly payments Hemlock would be getting as a result of this note?

A: You mean the amount of the monthly payment?

Q: Yes, yes.

A: *I think it was $60 or $65,000.*

Q: That's what Hemlock understood the note was paying?

A: *Yes.*

Q: To make sure your testimony is clear, Hemlock understood that the Erie Island Resort and Marina would be paying the Bennetts $60 to $65,000 a month? Is that right?

A: Correct.

Q: And that the Bennetts, one of them, would be paying Hemlock that same amount? Is that right?

A: *Yes.*

Q: Now, can you describe for us how it came about that you, you meaning Hemlock, purchased this note? What the negotiations were?

A: Well, Pat really wanted to terminate Hemlock.

Q: What do you mean by that?

A: *I was looking for a specific portfolio not to have this collateral, not that specific collateral do a lot of parks, and when Pat came across this park, I was interested.*

Q: When was that they wanted to terminate the line of credit?

A: Sometime in '93, but I kept—*I asked him for a specific portfolio to purchase.*

Q: So you approached Bennett first?

A: *Yes.*

Q: What did Pat say?

A: *He came back to me with this park.*

Q: About when was that?

A: *Sometime in October of '93.*

Q: Mr. Genovese, how did Hemlock raise the money to pay Bennett Funding Group $10.5 million for the Erie Island note?

A: *Through investors.*

Q: It raised it through investors?

A: *Yes.*

Q: Did Hemlock have cash on hand at year end 1993 or the beginning of 1994 to comprise a $10 million payment to Bennett Funding Group?

A: Did it have the total amount cash on hand? No, it did not.

Q: Where did that cash come from to be able to cut the check to Bennett Funding Group?

A: *I requested my loan account back from Pat on Hemlock and I took a note out with Bennett Management.*

Q: Where did the rest come from?

A: *We borrowed money from Bennett Management.*

Q: How much did you borrow from Bennett Management?

A: *Four million or five million.*

Q: I return to my question. You've accounted for approximately $7.3 million of the $10.5 million that Hemlock paid for the Erie Island note. Where did the rest come from?

A: *I think there's another note, but I don't know which—maybe it's recorded in '94.*

Q: Another note from who to whom?

A: *I don't recall.*

Q: Is it any company that was owned or operated by any of the members of the Bennett family?

A: Michael Bennett.

Q: Michael Bennett? What was the name of that entity? Do you know?

A: *Michael Associates or something.*

Q: Okay. So, let's return to the original question so I understand where the money came from so Hemlock could buy the Erie Island note. Hemlock already had loaned Bennett Management and Development over $3 million and called in $3 million of that loan. That's right?

A: *Yes.*

Q: Separate and apart from that, Hemlock borrowed $4 million from Bennett Management and Development, right?

A: *All right, yes.*

Another sham sale resulted in a pseudoprofit of $3.5 million in 1992. In December of that year, Patrick sold leases that Bennett Funding had purchased previously from Scriptex in June 1992 to Kasarjian's company, Kenton Group, for $21.6 million.

To accomplish this fakery, Patrick gave Kasarjian a document that reflected Kenton's purchase of the Scriptex leases. In fact, Kenton did not purchase the leases nor pay for them either. At Patrick's behest, Kasarjian had directed his secretary to sign the accompanying fictitious bill of sale.

Kenton then resold the leases back to Scriptex before the ball at Time Square fell ushering in 1993. Again from Patrick's indictment:

Q: So [Mr. Bennett,] getting back to the request of Scriptex to repurchase its leases, what happened after that initial conversation with Michael Bennett?

A: As I said, at some point I remember having a conversation with the president of Scriptex and—

Q: Who is that?

A: The president of Scriptex.

Q: What is the person's name?

A: Anthony Pavoni. *And just, you know, discussing his intent and, you know, he notified me that he wanted to use Kenton as an intermediary in effect so that he could obtain a fee on the transaction.*

Q: So that who could obtain a fee?

A: *Kenton. And that's all I remember as a specific conversation.*

Q: The question is, as best as you can recall, at what point in time did you speak with Mr. Pavoni?

A: *I really don't remember. I mean it would have been obviously some time in probably the mid-part of 1992, but I just can't remember.*

Q: And what communications did you have with Mr. Kasarjian regarding the sale of these leases from Bennett to Kenton?

A: *Well nothing more than what I already testified to. I had a conversation with him and, you know, relayed the fact that Mr. Pavoni had wanted to make him an intermediary in the transaction, and I think when I had that conversation he already was aware of that from a conversation he had of his own with Mr. Pavoni. So there wasn't anything more of substance to it than that.*

Q: Do you know why the funds flowed directly from Scriptex to Bennett? . . . Do you know?

A: *Well, they were the funds ultimately, you know, that were used for*

Scriptex to, you know, buy back the transactions from—technically from Kenton.

Q: Do you know where Scriptex got the money?

A: *I'm sure they generated in their course of business.*

Q: Did you have any conversations with anyone regarding the source of the money that Scriptex used to pay for these leases?

A: *No.*

Ultimately Scriptex's debt to Bennett Funding eclipsed $80 million. Scriptex simply did not have the wherewithal to make such purchases unless it used Monopoly money. Charles Genovese was Scriptex's outside auditor at the time.

On or about September 14, 1995, coindictee Thomas Pomposelli, the former controller of Scriptex, appeared before the SEC and gave testimony[7] concerning the Scriptex-Bennett-Kenton lease transactions, and the methodology of payment commonly referred to as the "in and out" of Scriptex/Bennett checks. Again, the italicized portions are the materially false statements.

Q: Did you talk [with Anthony Pavoni] about some of the things that might be asked of you here today when you talked to him?

A: *I don't recall what we discussed, to be honest with you.*

Q: Have you ever talked to Mr. Pavoni at all about any of the questions you thought you might be asked here today?

A: *Again, I don't recall.*

Q: You might have?

A: I may have, yes.

Q: Did he ever make comments to you about some of the things he thought you might be asked about here today?

A: *I don't recall.*

Q: Aside from the one copier, and that one piece of machinery that was sold to them, have there been any other business dealings, to your knowledge, between Kenton and any of the Scriptex entities?

A: Yes.

Q: What was that?

A: *I believe in 1992 there was a—Kenton acted as a broker on some of these transactions, sale lease-back transactions.*

Q: What do you mean they acted as a broker?

A: *Kenton Portfolio acted in bringing the two parties together and acted as the broker for the deal itself.*

Q: Is that to say that Kenton actually provided the introduction of the parties involved?

A: No.

Q: When you say they brought the parties together, what do you mean by that?

A: *They acted—Kenton Portfolio acted—again, as structuring the deal and bringing the two parties together on this particular transaction.*

Q: Who were the parties involved in this transaction, Mr. Pomposelli, this one that started in June and culminated in December 1992?

A: *I believe it was Scriptex Enterprises, Aloha Leasing and Kenton Portfolio.*

Q: What do these checks represent, Mr. Pomposelli?

A: Individually, I couldn't speak, just looking at the checks.

Q: Do you know, Mr. Pomposelli, what it is that these checks are payment for? If you wish, we could go one by one instead of just treating them all as a whole.

A: No. I'll answer to the best of my ability. Could you repeat the question?

Q: Sure. Do you know at all what these checks represent payment for?

A: Yes.

Q: What is it?

A: *To the best of my knowledge, these are payments, a repurchase of a rental portfolio.*

Q: What do you mean by a repurchase of a rental portfolio?

A: *It was a repurchase of a rental portfolio that we did a sale lease-back on in 1992.*

Q: Mr. Pomposelli, if you could provide for me just a brief narrative as to the involvement of this particular transaction from beginning to— and I believe you testified that it started in June. If you could just walk me through the transaction from beginning to end, as best you understand it.

A: *As best as I understand it, in or around June of 1992, we entered into a sale lease-back transaction where we sold a certain rental portfolio, leased it back, and then subsequently, in October through December, we repurchased those leases, or bought out those leases.*

Q: Mr. Pomposelli, do you at all remember discussing the merits of this transaction from the Scriptex standpoint, especially in light of the fact that it would result in a 3.5 million dollar loss to Scriptex?

A: Yes.

Q: Who do you remember discussing that with?

A: Anthony Pavoni.

Q: When was that discussion?

A: *On or around October, I guess.*

Q: Of 1992?

A: *Of 1992.*

Q: How is it that the funds were transferred in connection with the June portion of the 1992 transaction, as well as the December repurchase of the portfolio?

A: In June we sold the portfolio for approximately $18 million. We put approximately $13 million back on deposit with the Bennett Funding Group. We used the remainder for certain debt repayment and lease payments. *Then subsequently in October we received the money that we had on deposit with the Bennett Funding Group. And then borrowed some additional funds and then repurchased the portfolio back starting in October.*

On September 15 and October 31, 1995, Anthony R. Pavoni appeared before the SEC and gave testimony[8] concerning the Scriptex year-end sale of leases.

Q: Mr. Pavoni, in 1992 do you remember having sold do you remember Scriptex having sold to one of the Bennett entities a group of leases for 16.67 million, and subsequently repurchasing it for in the neighborhood of 21 million?

A: *Yes.*

Q: Mr. Pavoni, aside from the scheduling of testimony, have you spoken to anyone regarding your appearance here today, again other than discussions you've already described with Mr. McGillicutty [*sic*]?

A: *At this point no one else knows about my visitation today.*

Q: Did you discuss with anyone what you anticipated to testify to here today?

A: My attorneys.

Q: Other than your attorneys?

A: *Not in detail whatsoever other than to say I'm going to the SEC to talk about the Bennetts and Scriptex.*

Q: Mr. Pavoni, in connection with this transaction we were just discussing [the 1992 Kenton transaction] you mentioned that Mr. Kasarjian and/or Kenton provided services in order to assist in the closing of the transaction. Could you be more specific as to the services that were provided by Mr. Kasarjian in that endeavor?

A: *Mr. Kasarjian acted as a consultant assisting me and Mr. Bennett and consummated this financial transaction.*

Q: Acting as a consultant what did Mr. Kasarjian do?

A: *He helped sell the financial concept of this particular transaction.*

The conspirators fell in lockstep with Patrick's suggestion that Kasarjian and Kenton were acting as honest brokers that structured deals and put parties together. This does not smack true.

These people and their respective companies had been doing business together since the 1980s. Tens of millions of dollars flowed between them annually. They did not need to be further rewarded for structuring deals. All they had to do was call one another on the phone.

Q: Whose idea was it originally, Mr. Pavoni, to unwind the transaction? Do you recall?

A: *It was mine.*

Q: Do you recall generally what his (Patrick Bennett's) words were? Did you propose to him in effect unwinding the transaction?

A: *I had discussions with my ex-partner at the same time. I said we are going to do something to stabilize the company.*

Q: That would be Mr. Kasarjian?

A: That's correct.

Q: Was Mr. Kasarjian at all involved in contacting Mr. Pat Bennett about unwinding the transaction?

A: *He assisted me in regards to unwinding it.*

Q: What role did he play, do you recall?

A: *It was similar in the sense that as a former CFO of the company he worked with me and Pat unwinding the deal.*

Q: Mr. Pavoni, this bill of sale as you mentioned is in effect a bill of sale between Kenton selling contracts as the term is used in this document to Scriptex. Was this document in any way negotiated between Kenton and Scriptex to your knowledge?

A: *It was negotiated between three parties.*

Q: Who were those three parties?

A: *Kenton, Bennett, Scriptex and I talked about Bennett, primarily Aloha.*

Q: Mr. Pavoni, what to your knowledge did Mr. Kasarjian do in order to sell the unwinding of the transaction?

A: Selling is an art of trying to sell the benefits to—

Q: [Question by Pavoni's attorney] What did he do?

A: *He helped me unwind it. He persuaded a certain individual that it would be good for our business to unwind the deal.*

Q: And this certain individual you mean is Pat Bennett?

A: I'm sure it was Pat Bennett.

Q: Were you at all present during the times that Mr. Kasarjian was trying to sell this unwinding of the transaction to Mr. Pat Bennett?

A: *This was done via the phone.*

Q: [Question by Pavoni's attorney] The issue is whether you were present?

A: No.

Q: Were you at all privy to some of the exchanges that took place between Mr. Kasarjian and Mr. Bennett?

A: No.

Q: During the time that you did take part in these discussions, did you play a role at all in setting the terms for the unwinding?

A: *Yes.*

Q: What role is that?

A: I was the President of the company. *I had to make a determination to persuade Mr. Bennett to unwind the deal and help me work through my cash flow problems and unwinding this deal was one of the attempts at keeping the company moving forward. So obviously I had to sell somebody on that and that particular person was Pat Bennett.*

Q: Mr. Pavoni, the document that we have in front of us, the bill of sale of contracts, lists Kenton as the seller. Why was payment made to Bennett rather than Kenton?

A: *They were the actual holders of the paper, the original paper. In reality they were the individuals that we originally had sold it to.*

Q: Mr. Pavoni, is that to say that you signed this bill of sale of contracts with Kenton not knowing whether Kenton actually owned the contracts?

A: *The representation made to me was that they owned the contract. Do I know if they had them physically in their hands, I do not know.*

Q: Who made that representation to you?

A: *The individual right here. Ken Kasarjian.*

Q: If the transaction was unwound in December 1992, why would some of these checks have been written in October 1992?

A: I previously stated that the whole portfolio was unwound in the last 90 days of the year, *so we began to unwind it. I do not understand the accounting terms behind it.*

Here one is reminded of the standard admonition by lawyers to deposition witnesses: do not volunteer information. No one asked Pavoni about accounting terms, yet he mentions them gratuitously. His rehearsal with Patrick no doubt covered this base.

Q: Mr. Pavoni, why did it take 90 days to unwind the transaction?

A: *We made the decision to unwind the agreement in the fall and we made a determination to unwind it in the last 90 days of the year and complete it by year end.*

Q: And why was the transaction unwound over the last 90 days?

A: *That was the way we determined to do it.*

Q: And what was that based upon?

A: *Our goal was to get out of the contract by year end. There was no specific—that was our decision.*

After Pavoni's appearances before the SEC, Bud had a glimmer in his eyes. His walk seemed faster, purposeful.

"Yeah, Tony kicked their ass. He handled them real good," Bud exclaimed.

Tony was Bud's macho poster boy. Tony's bravura was infectious. Tony could handle the SEC with both arms tied behind his back. Tony was in a league by himself, a force to be reckoned with. Bud seemed to rest the fate of the Company upon Tony's performance before the SEC.

But Atlas shrugged. Both Tony Pavoni and Thomas Pomposelli pleaded guilty to the charges of perjury and obstruction. The Company tumbled into the abyss. Pavoni was the first of the criminals to get sentenced. Because of Pavoni's severe health problems and Vietnam War service, the judge sentenced him to two years' probation, six months' home confinement, subject to doctor's visits and legitimate job searches, and a $4,800 fine. One wonders whether the judge took any of the victims' veteran status into consideration as well when meting out punishment.

After Pomposelli's testimony at Patrick's trial in January 1999 in which he detailed the "in and out" of the respective companies check issuances, Patrick stated, "[I]t took me a long time to figure it out, but a number of people . . . that I did business with and trusted for years had both lied to me and apparently cheated the Bennett Companies in their business dealings over the years."[9]

Patrick also entered into fake unilateral consulting arrangements with business associates and affiliated companies. For example, Patrick booked $2.3 million as fee income for bogus consultation on behalf of Aegis, another Bennett Funding affiliate.

Patrick was indicted for perjury on this transaction, because he testified the money was fee income. The president of Aegis testified the money was a simple loan repayment and Patrick's proof, consisting of invoices, was nothing but backdated forgeries.

Q: Mr. Bennett did you ever have any communications about an invoice in the amount of $511,730.25 to Aegis?

A: I don't remember a specific conversation on this invoice. *We did a lot of work for them in 1993.* There's also, I know, another invoice that— also to them, you know, for a much larger amount, and I don't remember any specific conversation on the invoice. I do remember, you know, the nature of all the work that was done.

Q: And what was the nature of that work?

A: *Well, it was a lot of assisting them—Aegis—in structuring, and they went through what I would call a—or we assisted in the buy-out of one of their original principals which is, what I would call unfriendly situation. We really advised them in the structure and the transaction and—*

Q: Who was that principal?

A: A gentleman—I can't think of his first name. Wallace was the last name. *And in exchange for that, we had done—during that process we had done some business with them and ended up as part of that transaction, obtaining some equity in the company in Bennett Management, and all the real work that was done in the structure and over the period of the year was really done by Bennett Funding Group employees, so the fee that was paid, you know, was paid to Bennett Funding Group. I just don't remember the specifics of either one of them.*

Q: If I can show you what's been marked as Exhibit 142, and ask you if you've ever seen this before?

A: I certainly could have. This is the other—I mean we haven't—*I haven't seen a copy of it recently,* but I know that's the amount, you know, of the other invoice we're looking for.

Q: And—

A: *But, and as I said, the income off this transaction was associated with the whole structure of the—which referred to here as the "Wallace buy-out."*

Q: Do you know whether Exhibit 142 was actually ever paid?

A: *No. I don't know, I would think it was, but we can certainly check.*

Q: Do you know how the amount of the invoice on Exhibit 142 was determined?

A: *It was over a period of time looking for—I'm sorry, not looking for, but looking at the services that Bennett provided especially at the time for the company that they were provided. By assisting in the buy-out we, you know, helped this company, you know, avoid a—what could have, been, you know, a serious problem for them, you know, from a conflict standpoint. So it would have been a negotiated situation, but there wasn't any specific tying one to, you know, one amount to another—a part of it type of thing.*

Q: Do you know who negotiated this amount?

A: *I probably would have done, you know, most of the work, I did a lot of the work on the buy-out as it came down to, you know, the fees we were entitled to: I worked on most of it.*

Q: You worked on the buy-out or you worked on the negotiations determining the price, I'm sorry?

A: I'm sorry. *Both.*

Q: And with whom did you negotiate at Aegis?

A: *A number of people—the management people primarily probably the chairman, Angelo Appierto.*

Q: Are there any documents which indicate in more detail the scope of the work that was performed in connection with these invoices or the hours spent?

A: *When we—I think there is, yes, I mean, I can remember—I can remember myself—this is one of the things I know we're looking for, and I think when we find the invoice I think there'll be more there other than just the invoice because I spent the better part of 1993, you know, working on that transaction.*

In these four transactions alone—American Gaming loan repayment, Erie Islands note purchase, Scriptex lease purchase, and Aegis invoice—more than $45 million was deliberately and incorrectly booked and accounted for to create the illusion of profit. After all, people would rather invest in a company with millions in net profits than millions in losses.

Although large year-end transactions may set off red flags, Patrick lied to the auditors and fabricated and backdated documents related to those purported transactions:

Q: You've mentioned the sale of property to Hemlock in 1993. Based on your recollection was Bennett Funding forthcoming with Mahoney Cohen about the substantive aspects of that transaction?

A: *As far as I know.*

Q: Were there aspects of that transaction that were not explained to the auditors to your knowledge? Were there aspects of the Hemlock transaction that were not told to the auditors?

A: *I don't know.*

Q: Was Mahoney Cohen ever misled as to the substantive nature of any transactions that it looked at during the years 1992, 1993?

A: That I'm aware of? *Not from what I'm aware of.*

Q: Okay. Putting aside you personally, do you know of instances where Mahoney Cohen was misled about the substance of a transaction but not because of something you did, but because of something someone else at your company did when telling them about the transaction?

A: *No. My answer "not that I'm aware of" means, you know, same answer, not that I'm aware of.*

Q: You mentioned transactions involving Kenton and Scriptex. Were there aspects of those transactions that were not explained to the auditors at the time?

A: *I—as I said, I don't know.* I wouldn't have direct conversations with them.

Q: Mr. Bennett, to your knowledge, has there been any reason for not having fully disclosed the circumstances surrounding any transactions to the auditors within the last five years?

A: *No. Well, I'm not sure whether it's been done or not been done.* I mean, it's a two—there's two parts to the question. *I'm not sure whether it's a fact, and if it was, no reasons that I know of.*

Q: How were these transactions with Kenton related-party transactions based on your understanding?

A: What I already said, because at the time Kasarjian was an officer of Bennett Funding Group he owned Kenton.

Q: Why were they previously not disclosed as such?

A: *I don't think any reason, I think it was just oversight from everybody's standpoint.*

Q: Why isn't Mr. Kasarjian's name on these two pages?

A: *I don't know.*

Q: Was Mr. Kasarjian's name intentionally left off this list so that the reader of the memorandum wouldn't know that he was a member of Bennett's management?

A: *No.*

In testifying before the SEC, Charles Genovese, Tony Pavoni, and Thomas Pomposelli stated they did not discuss their testimony with one another. In truth, all of them carefully orchestrated and scripted their testimonies with Patrick before taking the oath. This was later admitted by Michael Bennett, Kasarjian, Pavoni, Pomposelli, Cerimeli, Menchella, and even Patrick in open court.

Another accounting scam was known as the "wrap" lease. The wrap lease was a method by which the Company could convert past-due portions of large-ticket equipment leases that appeared on the books but were either fictitious themselves or grossly nonperforming into new "performing leases" with the same lessee.

Bennett-style wrap involved placing, or "wrapping," past-due payments on nonperforming Scriptex leases, to name one lessee, into new Scriptex leases using the delinquent payment amount as the principal amount of the new, or wrap, lease.

Patrick would then cause accounting entries to be made showing Bennett Funding paying Scriptex the purchase amount of the wrap lease and Scriptex paying the past-due amount on the original lease to the Company. Thus, instead of having one lease with $200,000 unbilled stream and $50,000 overdue amount components, two leases would exist in the amounts of $200,000 and $50,000 respectively with no past-due pieces.

Although no money changed hands, the entries created the illusion that fake leases or nonperforming leases were current. Moreover, the wrap leases could be, and indeed were, sold to investors.

In reviewing Patrick's activities outlined above, which includes the ingenious FIN/INV systems lease double-pledging, the sham transactions, the cooking of the books, the creation of wrap leases, the diversion of millions in cash personally, the conspiracy and obstruction, and helping run legitimate enterprises, all the while outside auditors were auditing, outside lawyers were lawyering, and the SEC investigating, one can rightfully wonder when the man slept.

Pick a Bank, Any Bank

THE FOLLOWING is the honor roll of banks and financial institutions that were victimized by Patrick. Spot yours?

Abrams Centre, Amcore Bank, American Banks, American National Bank of Union Spring, American State & Trust Co., American Trust Federal Savings Bank, American Bank, Amerifirst Bank, NA, Amsterdam Savings Bank, Androscoggin Savings Bank, Ballston Spa National Bank, Bank of Bellevue, Bank of Herrin, Bank of Mt. Carmel, Bank of Newberry, Bank of Ohio County, Bank of St. Petersburg, Bank of Sunset, Bank of the Mountains, Bank of Tioga, Bank Of Utica, Bankfirst, Banterra Bank, Bay Area Bank, Bay State Savings Bank, BayBank, Bayside Federal Savings & Loan, Berkshire County Savings Bank, Caldwell National Bank, Canton Federal S&L, Carterville State Savings Bank, CenBank f/k/a State Bank–Buffalo Lake and Tri-County Bank, Central Bank & Trust, Central National Bank, Canajorharie, Central State Bank (Muscatine), Chemical Bank, CIB Bank, Citizens Bank of Princeton, Citizens Bank, Corydon, Citizens Bank, Leon, Citizens National Bank of Albion, Citizens National Bank of Malone, Citizens State Bank (Arlington), Citizens State Bank of Hickman, Citizens State Bank of Milford, Citizens State Bank of Shipman, Citizens State Bank of St. James, Citrus Bank City First Bank, City National Bank & Trust Company (Gloversville), City National Bank & Trust Company (Hastings), City State Bank, Community Bank, FSB (Michigan City), Community Bank, NA (Waynseburg), County Bank, Crawford & Assoc, Cumberland Security Bank, DeAnza National Bank, Deposit Bank, Dime Savings Bank, DDJ Mead Hobbs and Howe, Inc., Douglas County Bank, Douglas Federal Bank, A FSB, East Side Bank & Trust Company, Eaton National Bank, English State Bank, Equality State Bank, Equitable Bank (Compass Bank), Equity Bank, ESB Bank, Etowah Bank, Exchange Bank of Alabama, F&M–Milford, F&M Bank, Fairfield National Bank, Farmers & Merchants–Summerville, Farmers & Merchants Bank–Miamisbur, Farmers State Bank, Fidelity Federal Savings Bank, First Bank Mankato, First Citizens National Bank of Dyersb, First Community Bank, First Federal S&L Association of Coryd, First Federal Savings Bank Of Galion, First Federal Savings Bank Of LaGrange, First Keystone Federal Savings Bank, First National B&T Company of Willis,

First National Bank & Trust, First National Bank & Trust Co. (Ponca City, Okla.), First National Bank & Trust Company (Carbondale), First National Bank (Carmi), First National Bank (Ottawa), First National Bank in Pinckneyville, First National Bank of Alachua, First National Bank of Bridgeport, First National Bank of Central Florida, First National Bank of Cold Spring, First National Bank of Crockett, First National Bank of Dieterich, First National Bank of Elmore n/k/a Pioneer Bank, First National Bank of Herminie, First National Bank of Mapleton n/k/a Pioneer Bank, First National Bank of McCook, First National Bank of NW Ohio, First National Bank of Ottawa, First National Bank of Portland, First Northern B&T, First Security Federal Savings Bank, First Star Savings Bank, First State Bank, First State Bank of Barboursville, First State Bank of Harvard, First State Bank of Livingston, Firstar Bank, Flat Top National Bank (First Community Bank of Mercer), FNB in New Bremen, FNB of Central City, FNB of Longmont, FNB of Waconia, Framingham Co-operative Bank, FSB–Red Wing, FSB–Sauk Centre, FSB of Wyoming, Gloucester Bank & Trust Co., Goodland State Bank, Grand Marais State Bank, Great Falls Bank, Greater Delaware, Green County Savings Bank, Grinnell Federal Savings Bank, Harrisburg National Bank, Hawkeye Federal Savings Bank n/k/a Commercial Federal Bank, Heller, Hibernia Savings Bank, Hicksville Bank, Hillcrest Bank, Home Federal S&L Association of Nebraska, Hudson United Bank f/k/a Urbana National Bank, Illini State Bank, Indiana Lawrence Bank, Interchange State Bank, Iowa State Bank, Iron & Glass Bank, Jacobs Bank, Jefferson State Bank, John Warner Bank, LaCrescent State Bank, LaFayette County State, Lafayette Savings Bank, Leavenworth National Bank & Trust Co.–Liberty, Lockport Savings Bank, Longview National Bank, M&T Bank, Medway Savings Bank, Melrose State Bank, Mercantile Bank of Mt. Vernon (Mercantile Bank of Southern Ill.), Merchants National Bank, Merchants State Bank of Lewisville, Metlife Capitol Corp., Metrobank, Middletown Savings Bank, Minnesota Bankfirst, Minnesota Valley Bank, Monroe County Bank, Mutual Federal Savings Bank, National Bank of Coxsackie, National Bank of the Redwoods, New Carlisle Federal Savings Bank, North Adams Hoosac Savings Bank, Northwestern Savings Bank, Norwest Bank Red Wing, Norwood Co-operative Bank, Ocala Bank, Oswego City Savings Bank, Overland National Bank (First Commerce Bancshares, Inc.), Oxford Bank & Trust, Palos Bank & Trust Company, Park West Bank & Trust Company, Peoples Bank & Trust, Peoples Bank & Trust Company, Peoples Bank (Lebanon), Peoples

Bank (Sandy Hook), Peoples Trust Company, Perpetual Federal Savings Bank, Plattsmouth State Bank, PNC Bank (Midlantic Bank), Potters Savings & Loan, Potters Savings & Loan Company, Republic Bank, Rhinebeck Savings Bank, Rocky Mountain Bank (Security State Bank), Rome Savings, Roundbank, Roxborough, Safety Fund National, Sand Ridge Bank, Savings Bank of the Finger Lakes, Scandia American Bank, Seaboard Savings Bank, Security Bank, Security Federal Savings & Loan Association of Chicago (Pinnacle Bank), Security Federal Savings Bank (Logans), Seguin State Bank & Trust, Seneca Federal Savings & Loan, Skylands Community, Smith County Bank/A Branch of Citizens, Sofco-Mead, Inc., South Trust, Southeastern Bank, Southtrust Bank of Georgia, NA f/k/a Bankers First Savings Bank, FSB, Sprague National Bank, Spring Hill Savings Bank, St. Henry Bank, State Bank & Trust of Kenmare, State Bank of LaCrosse, State Bank of Oliver County, Sterns Financial, Stoneham Savings Bank, Story County Bank & Trust, The Commercial Bank, Texas City Bank (Merchants Bank), The Howard Bank, Third Federal, Third Savings, Tolland Bank, Tracy State Bank, Tucker Federal Savings Bank, Tupper Lake National Bank, Twentieth Street Bank, Union State Bank, United Security Bank, Valley Bank (Citizens–Western Indiana), Washington Savings Bank n/k/a Roosevelt Bank, Watseka First National Bank, Weakley County Bank, West End, Western National Bank of Wolf Points, William Penn S&L Association, Willow Grove, and Yoakum National Bank.

Estate Planning and Other Machinations

FOR AS LONG as I have known him, Bud endeavored to find the elixir that would minimize estate taxes that may be due upon the transfer of Bennett Funding equity to his heirs. He read articles and talked with knowledgeable people. He had a will drawn and redrawn. He had a trust created. Every so often a new tax guru would strut the offices like a colossus only to be discredited soon thereafter.

One day Bud called me into his office to advise of yet another estate planner from among the ranks of Bennett Funding's outside auditor at the time, Mahoney Cohen. Unlike his predecessors, this planner definitely had a comprehensive plan that seemed to be sound and well thought out.[1] At least it was a plan, a written blueprint to transfer wealth from Bud and Kathleen to their sons with minimal taxation.

After an eternity of review and upon advice of yet more consultants,[2] Bud decided to go with the plan a few years later. To lessen the tax due upon the transfer of Bennett Funding common shares to his sons, Bud needed to lower the taxable basis of Bennett Funding over time. To achieve this goal, he sought to create new "asset companies" owned by Patrick and Michael from the get-go.

These companies would, essentially, continue Bennett Funding's business under new names, Aloha Capital Corporation and the Processing Center, Inc., and be free from the valuation of Bennett Funding.

Two problems arose. First, instead of Michael owning the stock of Aloha Capital from inception, the stock was somehow owned by and reported on the interim financial statements of Bennett Funding. Accordingly, the stock of Aloha Capital needed to be sold to Michael *tout de suite*. To that end, an extensive opinion from an outside tax attorney was needed to ensure that the proper valuation of the stock and therefore its purchase price would pass muster from a tax perspective.[3]

The lengthy opinion suggested the proper purchase price should be $1 million. Relying on advice from Aloha Capital's outside director, Merv Goldman, Michael ignored the opinion and tendered only $10,000 in full consideration of the purchase of the stock of Aloha Capital from Bennett Funding.

The second problem was more in appearance. Notwithstanding the creation of the "asset companies" as separate and distinct entities, all of their officers and directors were former Bennett Funding directors and officers who were transferred by Bud without previous notification in September 1995 to assume their new positions.

Coupled with the woefully low purchase price of the stock, the concomitant "transfer" of the officers simply would not pass the smell test. Michael argued vociferously that Aloha Capital did have three "outside" directors and therefore a pleasing aroma.

These individuals, however, were certainly well connected with Bennett Funding. As recently as December 15, 1995, outside director Merv Goldman had a consulting agreement[4] with Bennett Funding to provide diversified corporate and financial services and had brought investor money into Bennett Funding. Outside director Richard Kelley was a longtime associate of Bud and Patrick and had his own and his family's money invested in Bennett Funding financial products.[5]

Mark Scoular, the third outside director, was the former chief executive officer of Erskine Holdings Funding Corporation. Erskine Holdings was a player in the equipment-leasing industry and had long-term contracts and financial arrangements with Bennett Funding. Mark was also a close friend of Michael and helped hold down the fort during the tumultuous days of the Bennett bankruptcy in March 1996.

Despite these improprieties the sale of the shares from Bennett Funding occurred anyway. To complete the transactions, Bennett Funding, the holder of the rights to the name Aloha, the logos, and other goodies that went along with it, needed to transfer such general intangibles to Aloha Capital to consummate and legitimize the transaction.

Accordingly, I was asked to draft the appropriate agreement. By the time the Bennetts finished their talking, almost one year had passed. The Bennetts exerted pressure to backdate the agreement to January 1995, eleven months before its actual execution in December 1995. The Bennetts wanted it to read: "Agreement made the 2nd day of January, 1995."

I declined to honor their request as such opting for the following language: "Agreement made the 2nd day of December, 1995, with an effective date of January 2, 1995, memorializing oral and written agreements and understandings reached prior to the execution date."

Such compromises are common in legal transactions. Nothing hidden. I rendered unto my client what it sought while exercising independent professionalism inside the law.

There is a passage in the Torah that commands: "You shall love your God with all of your mind, with all of your strength, with all your being. You shall bind these words as a sign upon your hand, let them be a symbol before your eyes and inscribe them on the doorposts of your house and on your gates."

The first sentence is inscribed on a miniature parchment scroll, which is placed into a small holder called a mezuzah. I'm sure many have seen small oblong objects affixed to doorways in temples and in Jewish homes. The direction of the posting of the mezuzah on the doorpost, however, is not specified in the Torah. Should it be hung horizontally or vertically?

To the superstitious, a tilted mezuzah is said to allow the dybbuk, the evil one, to slide off and bar entry. Talmudic scholars likened the mezuzah to a man. The scholars said a man at rest generally lies horizontally and a working man is generally upright. A leaning man, however, could be considered both resting (for example, against a post) or working (for example, using his leaning body weight to keep the post upright). Thus, an angled mezuzah can be said to be both horizontal and vertical simultaneously, satisfying both schools of thought.

I cannot say that such heady talmudic thoughts went into drafting the compromise language. Suffice to say what was written was open and truthful. The Bennetts signed my version.

No matter one's religious predilection, all would seem to agree the words "to love God with all you have" should not be lightly taken or easily forgotten.

But should they be literally inscribed on the entrance ways where one lives, on the hand one uses, and held before one's eyes? One can argue the ritual reinforces the importance of the words. That the words be worn and inscribed to underscore their significance. That the ritual is an earthly manifestation of heavenly activities.

But for certain practitioners, the rite seems to have taken on a life of its own, overshadowing the meaning of the words, making them perhaps less important than the ritual itself—exalting form over substance.

By extension, much of our daily lives is bound up in rites, in media worship, and in choosing the appropriate format. This is especially true in the workplace, where every day seems to pay homage to performance by blind rote because "it has always been done that way."

Perhaps the Bennett Funding employees' systemic orthodoxy, their willingness to accept rewards for adherence to and punishments for deviations from accepted rites of conducting day-to-day affairs at the Company allowed the climate of criminality to exist. The employees were far more concerned with getting the format correct than understanding the elements of which it was composed.

This phenomenon helps explain why employees did not question the information contained in collateral listings, financial statements, and business reports, as long as those documents were in proper format. Even if inquiry were made, a plausible response or quip to placate the superstitious surely followed.

Pension Plan De-vesting

U NTIL 1992, Bennett Funding sponsored pension and profit sharing plans (the "plans") for its employees that were completely funded by the Company. Since salaries were below industry standards, the plans were not necessarily generous but essential.

Pursuant to an audit by the IRS, Bennett Funding, as the plans' sponsor, was tagged with a penalty because it allowed improper investments to be made by the plans in leases owned by the Company itself. In the world of employee retirement plans, that is a big no-no.

In 1992, the Company set up a 401(k) that superseded the former pension and profit sharing plans. The money in the former plans was simply to be reinvested without further deposits. Unlike the former plans, the 401(k) was funded by the employees up to 15 percent of their gross salaries. Once a year, Bennett Funding was to match the employee contributions up to 6 percent of gross salaries contributed.

After the Bennetts fled the coop, an exhaustive review and analysis of the plans and the 401(k) revealed that virtually all of the money in Bennett Funding's plans, some $2.5 million, was either looted, raided, or invested in financial products of dubious integrity.[1]

For example, Patrick, through Bennett Management, loaned $250,000 to North American Communications Group, Inc. North American, a company in Missouri, was on the verge of going public at the time. The company claimed it was cornering the market on pay phones installed in prisons. The loan receivable was assigned from Bennett Management to the plans for $250,000.

After repaying only $30,072.92, the company defaulted. When the plans were later scrutinized, the North American–receivable joined a large list of matters to be pursued. Later on, I commenced action against the company and obtained judgment in full.

Within about two months of the judgment, North American agreed to pay principal and interest, about $355,000, over five years to the plans. As of this writing, the plans' new trustee, M and T Bank, reported no funds have been received.

From March 1995 through February 1996, Patrick also arranged for numerous transfers of funds from the plans to Highwood and Hemlock partnerships, both controlled by Genovese. The payments were made to

Table 8. Money Transfers to Highwood Associates

Date	Amount	Action
Sept. 13, 1995	290,000	Wire transfer from plans to Bennett Funding
Sept. 25, 1995	60,000	Wire transfer from plans to Bennett Funding
Sept. 25, 1995	670,000	Wire transfer from plans to Bennett Funding
Feb. 26, 1996	50,000	Check from plans to Bennett Funding
Feb. 26, 1996	150,000	Check from plans to Bennett Funding
Mar. 27, 1996	184,786	Journal entry reflecting a Dec. 31, 1995, transaction that debited Bennett Funding's debt to the plans by $184,786 and credited Highwood the same amount
Total	$1,404,786	

allow the partnerships to repay some $2.4 million in loans from Bennett Management in 1993.

For example, in September 1995, Patrick caused Bennett Management to assign a large loan receivable of Highwood to Bennett Funding. Bennett Funding, in turn, assigned the Highwood obligation to the plans. Patrick then diverted $1,404,786 from the plans to pay Bennett Funding for the assigned Highwood loan. Bennett Funding paid the money to Bennett Management to close the books on the transaction.

In late September 1995, instead of paying the original debt that was assigned to the plans, Genovese gave about $1.4 million of the diverted plans' funds to his family through checks marked "returned principal" and drawn on a Hemlock account.[2] Patrick had signatory authority on the account as well. Additionally, in February 1996, only one month before the bankruptcy, Patrick diverted another $250,000 from the plans directly to Hemlock.

When the lawsuits by the various investors, the SEC, and the trustee started in earnest in April 1996, Genovese was checked into a local hospital and placed on a suicide watch.[3] Somehow I do not believe that the Genovese clan will be paying the funds back voluntarily.

The balance of the funds was "borrowed" by Bennett Funding to help ease the crushing debt burden, at negative $15 million per month. The dent the funds made staved the wolves for only four days. But the improper borrowing broke the pocketbooks and hearts of hundreds of employees who counted on that money for retirement, for their children's education, and other permissible early withdrawals.

Moreover, since about 1994, annual mandatory matching payments by the Company to the 401(k) never materialized or were diverted. Only money the employees contributed to the 401(k) remains intact, because the funds were held in trust by a nonrelated third-party financial agent. Unfortunately, neither the plans nor the 401(k) mandatory contribution piece were insured against any of these losses.

To compound matters, in mid-1997, the U.S. Department of Labor (DOL) sued the Company for improper administration of the plans as well as failing to make mandatory contributions to the plans.[4] The DOL also went after Bud and Patrick as fiduciaries of the plans. Although Patrick's criminal proceeding and bankruptcy placed a practical hold on the action against him, Bud is still defending.

Black's Law Dictionary defines *fiduciary,* a term derived from Roman law, as "a person holding the character of a trustee in respect to the trust and confidence involved in it and the scrupulous good faith and candor which it requires."[5] Bud and Patrick were entrusted with other people's retirement money. That's like letting a pyromaniac stand guard at a match factory.

When the 401(k) records were reviewed it became painfully obvious that Patrick had forged Bud's signature on withdrawal orders. Can you imagine the dilemma visited upon father and son?

DOL Lawyer: Tell me, Mr. Bennett, is that your signature on this withdrawal statement?

If Bud lies and says yes, he is guilty of breaching his fiduciary duty and maybe committing perjury. If he tells the truth and says no, Patrick is guilty of breaching his duty and forgery.

DOL Lawyer: I repeat, Mr. Bennett, is that your signature?

Not long after the review of the plans revealed the improper diversions and investments, Bud and Kathleen publicly questioned why the employees bellyached, because about half of the money missing was credited to the Bennetts' accounts anyway.

Upon hearing this, Breeden moved to block the Bennetts from receiving their share of the 401(k) distribution and to subordinate any claim they may have to the remainder in the other plans. The Bennetts fought the trustee, claiming he had no right to monkey with their retirement money.[6] Only Michael was willing to forego his share of the plans for the benefit of his former employees.

One year later, perhaps coming to their senses, the other family members discussed the pension situation and decided to subordinate their claims after all, "for the good of the employees." Despite this fling with altruism, Bud is still up to his neck in litigation concerning his share of the money.

Michael A. Bennett

MICHAEL BENNETT, 40, is Patrick's younger brother. Unlike Patrick, Michael graduated from LeMoyne College, a Jesuit institution in Syracuse. He is thinner, therefore taller appearing, and generally better looking than Patrick. Naturally, he went into sales. He started working for Bennett Funding immediately upon graduation. He did not have a previous job as an adult.

Before it was all said and done, Michael had obtained ownership of the Hotel Syracuse and Shamrock Holdings, the American Gaming holding company, as well as other assets worth a reported $80 million—paper value, anyway. He gave it all up. He sold the Hotel Syracuse just before the filing of the bankruptcy petition and transferred whatever major stock holdings he had to Breeden, postpetition. Indeed, of all of the Bennetts, Michael was certainly far and away the most cooperative and remorseful.

In observing him over the years, I would say Michael certainly inherited some of Bud's ugly qualities, such as short temper, engaging in loud blowouts, belittling people, a "do what you want" attitude despite advice and guidance from experts, and a profound contempt for lawyers. The only thing we had in common were boyhood beagles named Trixie.

Like his father, but unlike his mother and brother, Michael was quick to forget and forgive the object of his overinflated ire. Soon after the petitions were filed, Michael fled for Florida to be with his parents, to obtain employment his father procured selling boats, and to posture for bankruptcy.

Through the fat years at Bennett Funding, Michael grew accustomed to money and power and comfort and a leveraged unmarried lifestyle. All of his living expenses for housing, food, transportation, and insurance were paid by the Company. He drove a Jaguar and a Special Edition

Michael Bennett standing above the renovated lobby of his Hotel Syracuse. Photo by Dick Blume. Copyright © The Syracuse Newspapers.

Jeep. He even had a box seat at the Carrier Dome to root for his beloved Orangemen. His salary was large and he had no dependents. He was kind to less-fortunate family members and friends, through gifts, loans, and sweet business deals.

Michael was responsible for pushing the various leasing programs with manufacturers, dealers, and master lease accounts with Fortune 500 companies. Through Michael and talented people he hired, Aloha Leasing initiated or fine-tuned some of the most creative programs in the industry, including dealer interim financing for office equipment and cost-per-copy lease agreements.

Although he knew the top investors and the inner circle of coindictees, Michael dealt primarily with the sales force. From my entry into the Company in 1984 until just before we tanked in 1996, Michael went through six sales managers. The fault was never his.

In the hurly-burly of postpetition, Michael granted interviews. When asked about the criminal charges facing Patrick, Michael distanced himself from the financial side of the operations. "I was sales," Michael would say countless times to anyone who would lend an ear, especially the press. One time he broke down on camera and had to cut the interview. It resumed later with a taciturn Michael professing innocence.[1]

But as one investor intuitively asked during a open hearing early in the bankruptcy, "What did the Bennetts talk about when they sat around their dinner table?"

Although the Bennetts engaged in bloodcurdling screaming fights in the office, they basically did not communicate with one another. They preferred middlemen and proxies. One is reminded of the sheriff in *Cool Hand Luke* advising "what we have here is a failure to communicate."

The boat job in Florida his father arranged did not work out. Although Michael liked piloting small vessels and having fun on board, he probably did not know enough to sell them. After all, a good salesman knows his product.

Not long after, believe it or not, a Florida captive leasing company hired Michael in a sales position. One would think the name Bennett anathema in the leasing industry. A captive leasing company is one owned by a bank or other financial institution that supplies all of the funds for equipment purchases and operations. Generally, captives are very competitive because of the low cost of funds, unlike Bennett Funding, which had to borrow every penny at high rates.

Michael was asked to resign when the indictments came down in June 1997. He filed for bankruptcy in Florida in September 1997. Breeden successfully motioned to change venue to the northern district of New York. Lee Woodard, Patrick's chapter 7 trustee, was installed in Michael's case as well.

After the bankruptcy filing, Michael moved to Virginia to design Web pages and work for a friend who creates fashionable dog collars and was a former salesperson at Bennett Funding. But with all the protestations to the contrary, it turns out Michael helped Patrick with the cover-up against the SEC and more.

On November 23, 1998, in the federal courthouse in Manhattan, Michael tearfully admitted before Judge Griesa he conspired with his brother Patrick to obstruct the SEC's investigation and he lied to the SEC concerning a backdated document.

"I did understand what he wanted me to say when the topic came up," he told the judge. No family members accompanied him at the confession. His counsel stated Michael pleaded guilty "to accept responsibility for his acts." Afterward, Michael headed back to Virginia.

His story goes back two and a half years earlier. On March 15, 1996, like Patrick, Michael appeared before the SEC at its Regional Office in Manhattan. The feds indicted Michael for obstructing the SEC's investigation of Bennett Funding's financial statements and the sale of the Erie Islands note to Hemlock.

Michael was also indicted for perjury regarding deposition testimony before the SEC. Contrary to his promise to tell the truth under oath, he lied to and misled the SEC regarding the following italicized matters:[2]

Q: [Michael], have you ever heard of an entity called M. A. Bennett Associates?

A: Yes.

Q: What is it?

A: That's a company I formed to acquire the Hotel Syracuse.

Q: When did you form it?

A: Let's see, this is '96—I think around in '92, '93 range.

Q: And apart from acquiring the Hotel Syracuse, did it have any other purpose?

A: No.

Q: Apart from acquiring the Hotel Syracuse, has it acquired anything else?

A: Has it acquired anything else? Yeah, it acquired a building right next to the Hotel Syracuse. . . .

Q: Okay. Apart from acquiring those two buildings, has it invested in anything else?

A: *Yes, it did make an investment once.*

Q: And what was that investment?

A: It was an investment that was brought to me by Charles Genovese [regarding Erie Islands].

Q: And what particularly was it?

A: *I don't know all the details around it. He was up one time in Syracuse—he primarily comes up to visit Pat, but he knows the whole family. And he explained that he thought he had a good opportunity for me to make some money through the—well, for me. So, I talked to my brother about it, and it sounded like a good opportunity. And I eventually did the investment through M. A. Bennett Associates.*

Q: Was it a loan?

A: *Geez, I'm trying to remember if it was a loan. All I know is it earned interest—I mean, all I can remember is it earned interest. I don't know the exact structure of it.*

Q: How much money did it involve?

A: God, I think it's—is it a couple million—I can't remember the exact number.

Q: Whose couple of million, your personal couple of million?

A: *No, not my personal—I actually—when I talked to my brother, his recommendation, what I was able to do is M. A. Bennett basically made an arrangement with—I think it was BMDC, actually, let me think. They may have BMDC where I basically borrowed from them through a preferred stock type of—I'd have to get the stuff to really remember exactly, but some form of preferred stock where I—actually, I borrowed the money from them, then they had preferred stock in my company. Then I invested it with Charles' company.*

Q: And when did you sign this document [money transfer authorization]?

A: *December 20th* [1993].

Q: You're sure of that?

A: *Yes. . . .*

Charles Genovese also appeared before the SEC in October 1995.[3] He was questioned about the raising of the capital to purchase the Erie Islands note from Bennett.

Q: Finally, Hemlock had on hand $3.5 million from a loan it received from M. A. Bennett, is that right?

A: *Correct.*

Q: [Referring to Exhibit 277] was this note signed on January 3rd, 1994?

A: *I would assume so.*

Q: What do you base that assumption on?

A: Signed this third day of January, 1994.

Q: Apart from what it says, do you have a recollection of it being signed that day?

A: *I don't recall.*

Q: Do you recall signing it back then?

A: *Yes.*

Q: Does this note—I'm sorry—does this Exhibit 278 concern that $3.5 million investment or loan that M. A. Bennett ultimately provided to Hemlock by year-end 1993?

A: *Yes.*

Q: When was the first time that you saw this letter that is Exhibit 278?

A: The date?

Q: Approximately when did you first see it?

A: *I don't recall, but—'93.*

Q: Mr. Genovese, I put before you what has been marked as Exhibit 279. Can you identify that exhibit?

A: A letter from M. A. Bennett Associates to Hemlock, attention to myself, Charles.

Q: When was this document received by Hemlock?

A: The date we received it? Yes. I couldn't tell you from this.

Q: Sometime on or shortly after December 1993?

A: *I would assume so.*

Q: When did you first review this letter?

A: I couldn't give you a particular day.

Q: Generally can you give—

A: *December.*

Q: '93?

A: *Yes.*

Now for the truth. I incorporated M. A. Bennett Associates, Ltd., in New York on December 1, 1992. Its purpose was to acquire the shares of stock of Hotel Syracuse, Inc., the corporation that owns the Hotel Syracuse. M. A. Bennett also acquired the Addis Building adjacent to the Hotel Syracuse. It was to do nothing else.

Several full-time Bennett Funding employees helped minister to the varied needs of the Hotel Syracuse. Kevin Kuppel, Bennett Funding's treasurer, Coach Mac, Patricia Payette, Michael's executive secretary, and I did our part. It was like having two jobs. I did virtually all of the legal work for the hotel, including debt collection, office lease review, franchise agreement review, union grievances, construction contract review, and general legal duties that popped up from time to time.

Our promised reward for all of this extra work never materialized in any practical way. What we got was a minority interest in M. A. Bennett Associates. That's it. Michael owned 76 percent of the stock, the four of us combined had 24 percent. Inasmuch as M. A. Bennett never declared a dividend and owed far more than it was worth, the value of our shares was zero.

Despite Michael's testimony, M. A. Bennett never issued preferred shares in 1993 to any entity except perhaps to Patrick, Michael, and Charles in their minds.

Moreover, not one of Michael's coshareholders, directors, and officers in M. A. Bennett, Kuppel, Coach Mac, Payette, and I were aware of, let alone consented to, a loan to Genovese's company regarding the Erie Islands note or for anything else for that matter. The Genovese loan was in the millions and M. A. Bennett's financial position would have prohibited such matters.

The letter referred to in Michael's testimony that he signed on behalf of M. A. Bennett in December 1993, witnessing the loan and approving of the transfer of the proceeds to Genovese, was not brought to anyone's attention nor accounted for contemporaneously in M. A. Bennett's books and records, in the corporate minute book, or in the legal documents file. Neither was the promissory note Charles signed on behalf of Hemlock in December 1993.

Coopers & Lybrand did find, however, that Bennett Management made payments to or disbursements on behalf of M. A. Bennett Associates in an amount greater than $24 million from January 1, 1993, through June 30, 1995.

During December 1995, the $24 million receivable was transferred from Bennett Management to Bennett Funding through the use of an accounting journal entry.

There was no evidence of any consideration being received or paid for any of the transfers. No bona fide and contemporaneous documents exist to support the transfers, either.

I guess at this point that the transfer of $24 million does not seem like such a big deal in the face of the hundreds of millions already mentioned. But $24 million is a princely sum. It is unbelievable no documents exist to support the various transfers.

In fact, a review of M. A. Bennett Associate's bank statements shows conclusively Patrick laundered money through his brother's company.[4]

All in all, Michael had no choice but to plead guilty to the various charges of perjury and obstruction surrounding Hemlock's purchase of

Table 9. Balances in M. A. Bennett Associates bank statements

Statement Date	Starting Balance	Closing Balance
Aug. 31, 1995	$3,930,764.61	$31,514.30
Sept. 29, 1995	31,514.30	31,589.50
Oct. 31, 1995	31,589.50	31,667.40
Nov. 30, 1995	31,667.40	31,742.97
Dec. 29, 1995	31,742.97	31,821.25*
Jan. 31, 1996	31,821.25	20.21
Feb. 29, 1996	20.21	20.25

*On the Dec. 29, 1995, statement, Michael had written "Closed out with interest to BMDC 1/9/96."

the Erie Islands note. He also lied concerning the issuance of M. A. Bennett preferred shares in 1993, the loan to Genovese, and the execution and date of the agreements in connection therewith.

Without legitimate supporting and corroborating evidence, it was not reasonable for government prosecutors to assume these things happened as Michael and Charles said they did before the SEC in March 1996.

As Ms. White, the U.S. attorney for the southern district of New York, said:

> The pervasive pattern of perjury and obstruction of justice reflects complete and utter disregard and contempt for the SEC and its duty to protect the investing public. These massive acts of brazen obstruction include: the preparation and submission of reams of fraudulent documentation, the suborning of perjury from at least eight people, and carefully scripted testimony. The charged crimes represent a systematic assault on the SEC.[5]

It is interesting the government and society take such a dim and hard view against people who did not participate in the original crime but aided in its cover-up.

Had these people come clean early on, the SEC might have shut down the evil empire much sooner instead of "significantly adding to the amount of investor losses."

But why should anyone express such shock and dismay at the cover-up? Does one really expect criminals to simply leave their trails wide open, to go gently into the night?

In this light, it is easy to understand Patrick's, Ken Kasarjian's, and

Charles Genovese's motivations to lie to the investigators and encourage others to do so as well. Not only was the spigot of easy money threatened to be capped and booty forfeited but also the real fear of incarceration loomed large. What's one more felony in the face of those prospects?

Michael's motivation to lie and obstruct justice was perhaps a bit less selfish but nonetheless suspect. Clearly, from Michael's testimony before the SEC, he was not comfortable with either lying under oath or with the subject of his testimony. His story was rehearsed with insufficient time to fully grasp the nature of the various terms bandied about and the substance of the underlying stock and loan transactions.

By lying and cheating, Michael was proclaiming in fact and in deed he was his brother's keeper, that blood is thicker than water and money. Or maybe he was just trying to protect vested interest—to ensure he would continue to enjoy the good life of globe-trotting, swank hotels, and fast cars.

But what possessed the lesser players to aid and abet the criminals? Were they bribed by Patrick in the form of hidden salaries, bonuses, or some other perks? Were their illegal activities manifestations of misguided loyalty to Patrick and to their fellow employees? Did they even believe their tangled web of intrigue mixed with proper stick-togetherness could vanquish the SEC? After all, with innocent demeanor and friendly gray/blue eyes, Patrick did not look like a mugger of widows. His feigned protestations of innocence proved persuasive to the coconspirators.

During the Spanish Inquisition, the auto da fé was the judgment passed on heretics generally followed by burning at the stake.[6] Tomás de Torquemada, the Inquisitor-General, considered the auto da fé the supreme "test of faith."

In a strange adaptation of the auto da fé, it seems the aiders and the abettors helped Patrick as some sort of test of faith. Although words were exchanged among the coconspirators, they were not really necessary. One simply knew what one had to do. These men were men and could be counted on. Shoulder to shoulder, and all of that stuff.

At Patrick's trial, Tomas Pomposelli, the former controller of Scriptex, testified that he, Patrick, and Anthony Pavoni met half a dozen times in 1995 to backdate documents and plot ways to mislead the SEC. Pomposelli said that although Patrick never directly asked him to lie, he did so "out of some misguided loyalty . . . to my company, my boss and Pat Bennett."[7]

Eight of the heretics pleaded guilty to various charges of conspiracy, perjury, and obstruction of justice. Under the federal criminal system, sentences are imposed based upon a point system. Points are assessed according to the seriousness of the crime, the amount of money involved, and the number of victims. The more points the greater mandatory jail time. Cooperation with authorities, contrition, and restitution all reduce points.

It is not certain how many points will be shaved on account of cooperation, remorse, and recovery of assets in the bankruptcy in the face of a crime in which 12,000 people, 10,000 trade creditors, and 245 banks were swindled out of $1 billion. I'm sure the victims don't want any point shaving and are free to make statements at the sentencing.

Gout is caused by an excess of uric acid in the blood, which forms crystals.[8] The crystals can lodge in and cause painful inflammation of the feet and hands, especially the big toe. It has been said gout is the rich man's disease, because it can be tied to a diet rich in fats, which can trigger the overabundant uric acid. We have all seen old movies in which the mogul sits with a bandage wrapped around his propped-up foot.

After attempting to be the general manager of the Hotel Syracuse for about one year after its acquisition, Michael finally did the right thing and hired a professional hotelier.

Joe Kelly, Michael's selection, was a good and competent manager and administrator, at least to the extent Michael let him alone. He stands about 5'8" with dark hair and handsome looks. During our association, Joe always spoke softly with an authoritative quality, because he knew what he was talking about.

Joe brought the hotel up to speed, introducing the staff to the Star report and other administrative and financial planning tools.

During a meeting at the hotel in early 1995, I noticed Joe was limping. "What's wrong?" I asked him.

He looked at me sadly and answered, "Gout."

Almost feeling those minuscule uric acid crystals invading my own foot, I winced with pain. I expressed my concern for which he thanked me.

After the meeting, I walked over to where Michael and Joe were talking in time to hear Michael make fun of Joe's limp and his ailment. There are many things to poke fun of in this universe, but a disability is not among them.

As stated above, because of perfidy in the campground industry, the Bennetts were forced to gain control of fourteen membership campgrounds in various states. The takeovers were necessitated to avoid wholesale loss of cash coming in from consumers whose membership agreements with the various campgrounds were assigned to Bennett or Resort Funding.

Because of the inherent and widespread consumer fraud that seems to go hand in hand with the industry, the various states attorneys general keep close and watchful eyes on the goings-on at the campgrounds. The members themselves are a litigious bunch. But you can't really blame them, because many of the promises made by management as to existing and contemplated facilities and amenities go routinely unfulfilled.

The paradigm of such campgrounds is Hideaway Harbor, a/k/a Hidden Cove, in Alabama. There came a time when a Bennett Funding affiliate corporation took over the campground from the former owners because they could not repay the recourse obligations from defaulted members whose agreements were assigned to the affiliate. Recourse entails the payment by the campground owner of the balance due on defaulted membership agreements and is known in the industry as a "chargeback."

At Hideaway Harbor, the rate of chargeback of defaulted membership agreements exceeded the rate of return on new and existing agreements and the owners simply could not pay the postman. After lawsuits and countersuits bashed the parties, the owners settled and Hideaway Harbor became another Bennett company.

After failing to keep one promise or other made by either the former owners or Michael Bennett, or both, a member sued for fraud and breach of contract. At that time, Alabama was notorious for awarding deserved compensatory damages but outlandish punitive damages.[9]

As the story goes, the large punitive awards were upheld, at least in substantial part, by the Alabama Supreme Court, which was packed with plaintiff trial lawyers who depended heavily upon healthy contributions from their minions, that is, those who received one-third contingency fees on the enormous judgments.

For example, take the case of a BMW owner who noticed an undisclosed presale touchup on his new car. He sued, and won a $4,000 judgment to compensate for the price differential. The jury also awarded $4 million in punitives to punish the naughty BMW. Although the Alabama Supreme Court reduced the award to $2 million, it took the U.S.

Supreme Court to throw out the punitive award as violative of due process.

Although the case against Hideaway Harbor was weak from the plaintiff's standpoint, nevertheless, the firm did not back down and demanded $150,000 to settle. Michael rejected the offer as outrageous, because the contract was only worth a few thousand dollars. So on the litigation rolled.

Eventually, opposing counsel conducted a deposition of Michael in Syracuse. Our Alabama counsel, I, and another in-house counsel represented Michael. During the deposition it became apparent Michael was an uncontrollable witness. He knew more, much more, than the attorneys representing him. Opposing counsel was eating the tension like a gas-guzzling luxury car.

Toward the end of the morning session, Michael was directed by his Alabama counsel not to answer a certain question. Instead of heeding counsel's advice, Michael leaned over and slapped him right then and there before all of the counsel and the stenographer, and answered the question anyway. A lunch break was called immediately. Michael went his way, and Alabama counsel, associate counsel, and I went to a restaurant to eat and unwind.

We sat down and ordered lunch. The lawyer/victim was a gentleman and shrugged off the incident like so much dandruff on his lapel. Halfway through the meal, we noticed the place grew quiet. It seemed people were turning their attention to the TV near the bar area. It was Oklahoma City just after the bombing.

Bonfire

ON OR ABOUT the same day Bennett Funding filed its bankruptcy petition, Patrick and some of his boys secreted off-site numerous boxes of documents. The posse gathered at the Atrium lot at night and loaded a rented U-Haul. The illegal convoy headed north on route 81 and exited for Patrick's former residence at Toad Harbor on Oneida Lake, just outside Syracuse.

On the beach at Toad Harbor, the group piled wood and other combustibles and kindled a fire. When the flames were high and the heat intense, they heaved the boxes into the roaring blaze. The incriminating evidence turned to smoke and ash. The conspirators breathed in the evidence. It lodged in their lungs and smarted their eyes and sooted their clothes. It seeped into their pores. They became one with the records they so desperately tried to destroy. To complete the job would they need to destroy themselves?

Did they dance about the swirling smoke like primitive men propitiating the gods? Did they chant? Did they drink whiskey and howl? Did they strip naked as if partaking in a secret ritual? Did they wear face paint and carry war clubs? Did they bond in their criminality? Did the hot flames warm their faces during the cold of an upstate New York early spring day? Did mist blow from their muzzles? Did their souls mirror the evilness they did on earth? Did they think themselves immune from the eyes of the world? Oh, but someone saw them prancing on the beach. A reliable witness. An unimpeachable witness.[1] And so did a security video camera at the Atrium lot.

Audits Were Holy Things

PATRICK LAID down the law: nothing was more important than the preparation and publication of Bennett Funding's financial statement. As previously explained, financial statements were used to entice the investors and to urge the brokers to steer their clients' money into Bennett Funding.

The Bennett Funding financial statements helped raise more than $3.2 billion in six years. Funny, Bud told the employees during a Company-wide meeting he had a dream: by 2000, he wanted Bennett Funding to become a $1 billion company. Well, he achieved his dream years early. Too bad the $1 billion was on the wrong side of the ledger.

The audit itself was championed by the Company's chief accounting officer, William Crowley. Because of his cool demeanor and logical presentation, Bill reminds me of Mr. Spock with normal ears and haircut. His late father, a longtime friend of Bud and former controller of the Company, fought in the Battle of the Bulge. I remember one day after complaining to him about the politics of the place. "Don't get angry. It's just silly," he said. Every so often I think of that phrase and the day becomes manageable.

Anyway, the CAO's main focus was to work with the outside auditors to complete the financial statement. No one in Bennett Funding was allowed to deal, communicate, or basically meet with the auditors but through the CAO. In all the years of audits and through all of the auditors including Price Waterhouse, Arthur Andersen, and Mahoney Cohen, I can count the number of meetings between the auditors and members of the Legal Department on the fingers of a farmer's hand.

In the audit process, Legal's basic job was to furnish Crowley with a report on the collectibility of certain leases the auditors selected. The other task was to furnish the auditors with an opinion as to the nature and scope of material litigation in which Bennett Funding was involved that was otherwise unreported by outside counsel. As most material litigation was in the hands of outside counsel, needless to say, the report was skimpy.

When the financial statement was finally ready, Patrick or Bud would announce its publication to the brokers and bankers like the Greek runner dispatched from the battle at Marathon uttering victory before dropping dead from the exertion.

Accounting firms will issue an unqualified independent auditor's report only after an audit of the subject company.[1] The audit comprises a comprehensive and thorough review of the company's books and records and relevant documents in accordance with generally accepted accounting principles and generally accepted auditing principles (GAAP). Deviation from the GAAPs can lead to independent liability to the accountants.[2]

Compliance with auditing standards mandates the completion of a detailed action plan by the accountants as to the parameters of the review and the areas of the company they intend to examine. The guiding principle in performing the audit is to obtain reasonable assurance about whether the company's financial statements are free from material misstatements.

Arthur Andersen (AA) was retained to audit Bennett Funding and prepare financial statements commencing with the tax year 1989. All went smoothly until the preparation of the 1991 financial statement in 1992. Financial statements, like tax returns, are prepared in a subsequent year for the previous year.

It seems AA had growing concerns centered in the nature of the financial products the Company was selling to investors as well as certain basic accounting issues.

At the point AA started raising its concerns, the 1991 financial statement was long overdue. Bankers were demanding to see it, brokers were clamoring for it, and heavy hitter investors needed to see it for assurance like some paper security blanket.

May 1992 rolled around without the Company receiving the unqualified auditor's report. Pressure was building. For without the financial statement, Bennett Funding was in jeopardy of losing its capital sources.

Then the good news. Bill Crowley had discussed and apparently worked through with Arthur Andersen the final changes to the financial statement. On May 5 AA advised it would be sending the signed opinion by express mail delivery.

On that same day, Patrick was in New Jersey meeting with brokers who provided the Company with much of its financing. Crowley relayed the good news to Patrick, who, in turn, advised the brokers that the financial statement could be in their hands by the seventh.

On May 6, when the promised executed statement did not arrive, Crowley called AA. He was told a tracer would be instituted on the missing package. A few hours later, Crowley made another call to AA and was told the package was not sent out but it would be sent by courier that very afternoon.

While the back-and-forth was going on, AA faxed a copy of the financial statement and unqualified report. AA's fax cover page stated "Final footed 5/6—all OK."[3]

On May 7, Patrick and Crowley called AA to complain that the original was not yet in their hands. They were told the issues previously raised were not solidly addressed and AA was willing to execute only a qualified opinion. Bennett Funding had received and disseminated unqualified opinions from AA in the past. A qualified opinion would hint something is wrong and was useless.

The package did not arrive the next day either nor was it ever to arrive. AA advised it had found some more legal issues that needed addressing by an attorney even before a qualified opinion would issue. This statement came after Patrick told the brokers the final statement was ready.[4]

AA's demands sent Company honchos into a tailspin. Pandemonium broke out. Bud asked me to prepare an opinion of counsel to Arthur Andersen. The opinion was to state whether Bennett's direct sale of leases to investors was a security and whether such sales are on recourse to Bennett should the lessee default.

Based on the information given and certain assumptions, I opined that the leases were not securities and their sales were not on recourse.[5]

In that I was in-house counsel to Bennett, AA declined to accept my opinion and requested the Company obtain opinions from outside counsel with extensive experience with the SEC.

Instead of complying with AA's request, Bud got an opinion from a local sole-practitioner with limited securities experience. Another opinion was also offered by a New Jersey attorney presumably at the behest of Ken Kasarjian. Both opinions, which essentially regurgitated my opinion, were rejected because the attorneys were not recognized securities experts.[6]

To backstop my findings, I obtained an opinion from securities counsel from a large Kansas City firm the Company had been using for various matters since the late 1980s. I also obtained an opinion from a local commercial law firm on the recourse issue. Both firms concurred with my opinion that the direct sale of leases did not constitute the sale of securities and that such sales were not on recourse to Bennett Funding.[7]

Unbeknownst to the Company at the time, Arthur Andersen retained Skadden Arps, one of the largest law firms in the world, to address the issues in a ten-page memorandum. The Skadden Arps memorandum,[8] never shown to the Company, reached opposite conclusions, because they were opining as to whether the sale of undivided interests in a pool of leases constituted the sale of securities. I opined as to the sale of specific leases to specific investors, a vast difference.

Within a few days AA advised no report would be issued and further demanded Bennett Funding pull all financial statements issued previously by AA.

In practical terms, AA dumped Bennett. Realistically, AA could not have believed Patrick would tell the aforementioned banks, brokers, and investors it was questioning Bennett Funding's business practices and that financial statements previously furnished were to be returned and not relied upon. That is like the condemned setting up his own execution.

Moreover, AA demanded payment of an additional $90,000 before it was willing to release its file to new auditors.

Bennett Funding had no recourse but to formally terminate the engagement. To that end, the parties had to work a mutually agreeable exit strategy. Bennett Funding needed to get relevant portions of AA's file to the new auditors. AA had to ensure Bennett would send out communications to the investors and banks advising that no reliance could be placed on the financial statements previously furnished.

To aid in the parting, Bud and Patrick retained Lynn Smith of Devorsetz Stinziano, a local firm.[9] Smith, a partner at the firm, had continually represented Bud and the Company since the early 1980s. Smith sent a draft letter to AA with suggested watered-down "pull" language. Before the expiration of AA's deadline to respond to Smith's wording, Patrick sent the letter "as is" to the investors. AA's objection to the language came after the fact.

As this was going on, Bud instructed me to ready trial notebooks. Bennett Funding was going to rumble with AA. I can hear Michael Buffer now: "Let's get ready to rumblllllllllllllllllllllle."

Regardless of the outcome of the AA imbroglio, the Company still needed a financial statement. I believe Kasarjian saved the day by suggesting the regional firm of Mahoney Cohen (MC), in Manhattan. After some quick meetings, MC was retained to audit Bennett Funding and prepare a certified financial statement.

In the transition, Mahoney Cohen asked AA questions concerning the following:

• Integrity of the client
• Nature of disagreement, if any, with the client as to accounting matters or performance of procedures
• General level of the client's cooperation
• Reason for the change in accountants
• Need to perform other accounting services
• Nature of weaknesses, if any, in the client's accounting or bookkeeping system
• Areas that have caused or may cause difficulties[10]

I am not sure MC was shown or privy to all of AA's working papers, but it accepted the job. Apparently, an opinion of counsel from Gary Peiffer's law firm allayed MC's concerns, which were raised by AA's departure.[11] From 1992 through 1995, Mahoney Cohen was the Company's auditor.

Not long after Bennett Funding filed bankruptcy, both Arthur Andersen and Mahoney Cohen were sued by the individual investors, who claimed the accountants failed to detect the Ponzi scheme or any of its constituent parts. The investors also claimed the firms ignored the rubrics incorporated into the GAAPs. The suits were then consolidated into the gigantic class action now pending in the United States District Court in Manhattan.[12]

In particular, the lawsuits allege Bennett Funding's financial statements for 1991 through 1994 were not in accordance with generally accepted auditing principles. The improprieties include:

1. A breach of the standard requiring an auditor exercise due professional care in the performance of its examination and preparation of its report;

2. A breach of the standard requiring an auditor to gain sufficient understanding of its client's internal control structure as a basis for reliance thereon and to determine the extent of the tests to be performed;

3. A breach of the principle that an auditor must obtain sufficient, competent evidence to form a basis for its opinion;

4. A breach of the principle and standard that an auditor must view related party transactions with a heightened level of scrutiny and that financial statements shall disclose related party transactions; and,

5. A breach of the principle and standard that the financial statements should show the company's cash flows sufficiently to provide investors, creditors, and others with reasonable and accurate means to determine the company's ability to meet future cash needs, assess the reasons for cash receipts and disbursements, and assess the effect of noncash investing and financial transactions during the period.

In other words, if they did my taxes I would be very concerned.

AA was also sued because it failed to warn investors that improprieties were discovered and that it had requested Bennett Funding to pull all of the previous financial statements.

Now for generally accepted standards of reality.

1. The 1994 financial statement prepared by Mahoney Cohen did disclose in a footnote Bennett Funding was undergoing an SEC investigation. The footnote reads as follows:

> The Company is the subject of an on-going Securities and Exchange Commission investigation that originated from a review of certain transactions entered into with individual investors. The outcome of the investigation and its effects on the Company is not determinable at this time. It is management's opinion that the investigation will have no impact on the Company's business.[13]

Only God and those involved know what haggling went into the preparation of that footnote. In any event, the brokers, lenders, and investors were put on notice of the SEC investigation. Perhaps they should have made proper inquiry beyond the four corners of the financial statement.

2. I guess when AA chose its course of conduct, it had to balance the potential liability of disgruntled investors versus the immediate threat of Bennett Funding. After all, Bennett Funding discovered AA had obtained an opinion of counsel that it did not share with Bennett Funding concerning alleged securities violations, had faxed a draft of the financial statement to Bennett Funding CAO Bill Crowley, advised the statement was "in the mail" knowing Patrick was in front of investors, and made a ludicrous claim for additional fees in the amount of $90,000. AA had more than a little interest in the success of the Bennett Funding Ponzi scheme.

3. As it turns out, one of the members of Mahoney Cohen, Gene McGillycuddy, happened to be a neighbor of Anthony Pavoni. The same Pavoni who was the owner of Scriptex, friend and partner of Kasarjian in Kenton.

McGillycuddy left Mahoney Cohen to become partners with Pavoni in Castle Office Systems, Inc.[14] Castle was engaged in the business of gobbling up office-equipment dealerships, like Cronus eating his children. The equipment leases generated by the Castle dealers would then be purchased through Bennett Funding. May the circle be unbroken.

It seems somehow the repayment of the $80 million debt of Scriptex to Bennett Funding and the start-up of Castle were bound up together. Curiously, no in-house counsel was ever asked by the Bennetts to help with any part of the transaction that affected some fourscore million dollars of debt.

Indeed, very few people in the Company even knew about the transaction. The corporate culture of secrecy and stealth enveloped like thick fog. I wonder if Patrick was a ninja in a past life. In fairness to Michael, he did ask in the fall of 1995 to "get copies of the documents" long after the deal closed. Pavoni never responded to my request.

A healthy-looking Bennett company meant more business and enhanced financial position for Castle through the purchase of Castle-generated leases and, consequently, more money for the Bennetts, Pavoni, and Kasarjian.

In January 1994, Patrick had Bennett Management set up a $15 million line of credit for the benefit of Scriptex. Scriptex accessed the line specifically to acquire the shares of stock or the assets of office equipment dealers.

Later that year, in April, after the agreement was in place, Scriptex purchased two hundred shares of Castle preferred stock purportedly worth $50,000 per share. The $10 million was advanced over the next several months through the credit facility from Bennett Management.

In September 1994, Castle, presumably with the $10 million from Scriptex, purchased Engle Business Systems for $3.3 million, and in February 1995, D. W. Duplicating for about $2 million.

In November 1994, Scriptex itself purchased the assets of Big Apple, a New York–based dealer, for about $1.5 million.

In the synergy of evil, Castle incorporated Scriptex Acquisition Corp. (SAC). Shortly after the formation, Scriptex transferred all of its operating assets into SAC. The consideration for the transfer of the assets was seven hundred shares of Castle's common stock, allowing Scriptex to gain 87.5 percent ownership.

The operative documents used in connection with these various transactions and issuances were executed by McGillycuddy representing SAC and Pavoni on behalf of Scriptex.

About one year after these transactions, Pavoni entered into a "consulting," or severance, agreement with Castle, receiving $20,000 per month.

Through these gyrations Scriptex became the corporate parent of Castle, which, in turn, became the parent of SAC, Engle, and D. W. Duplicating. By the way, not to confuse things, but in 1997, SAC changed its name to its present style, Northern Business Systems, Inc.

Item 1: In the same month Bennett Funding filed its bankruptcy petition, Castle executed a series of nineteen promissory notes to the Company, totaling $1,457,500. None of the funds have been repaid.

Item 2: In the same month Bennett Funding filed its bankruptcy petition, Castle entered into a series of nineteen equipment leases with it for an aggregate stream of $1,484,000.64. No lease payments were made.

Returning to the faux pas of the auditors:

4. It has also been suggested that the trained eyes of the auditors should have detected that Bennett Funding's sales of leases to investors and pledges to banks generated more income than supported by the leases themselves.

5. As far as can be determined no auditor ever questioned Patrick's use of the Honeypot for all of the cash into and out of the Company. No auditor ever asked to see the Prime Conversion Account deposit slips or even verified a separate account existed for the account at any bank.

Accounting firms maintain errors and omissions policies similar to malpractice insurance carried by lawyers. Unless a settlement is reached with the errors and omissions insurance carriers, the accountants' liability will ultimately be determined by the United States Supreme Court.

The Classless Action

JUST AFTER the Bennett companies tanked, a preemptive class action was filed in the U.S. District Court for the Southern District of New York—federal court in Manhattan. I say preemptive because in the potentially lucrative world of securities class actions, the firm that files first usually controls the action and becomes plaintiff's counsel of record.

In the Bennett case, several other firms also filed suits on behalf of the investors, which were consolidated with the southern district action.[1] The class action complaint has targeted everyone and anyone connected with the Bennett companies in a broad shotgun approach. People have been sued whether they are guilty as sin or as innocent as new-driven snow.

The Bennetts, all of Bennett Funding's directors, officers (including me), outside law firms, outside accountants, outside credit insurance companies, outside brokers, and a few others were named as defendants. Although many of those named deserve what they get, many others do not.

Particularly, most of the former officers of the Company wielded no power. They were not "control persons" under the Securities Act of 1933 as alleged in the complaint.[2] As everyone seems to know, except the class action attorneys, real power and control was reserved in the name of the Bennetts.

Just as, presumably, the class action counsel, those officers and employees who remained with the Company in the bankruptcy proceeding worked hard to recoup as much money as possible for the investors and eke out an existence for themselves. But the class action suit had a chilling effect upon those efforts. It was like the Sword of Damocles hovering above their heads.

It does not seem just that these individuals, who are not under any criminal, administrative, or other official inquiry or investigation concerning their activities at Bennett Funding, must defend themselves in the class action.

To be sure, the officer/employees are victims too. Their pension/profit sharing plans were looted, many lost significant dollars on lease investments, most eventually lost their jobs, and their earned commissions and out-of-pocket expenses were not paid. Early on, they had to endure the ignominies of disgruntled investors and banks, as well as fend off the press.

When I offered these reasons in an attempt to have the officers/employees removed from the class action, one attorney likened us to the Germans who professed innocence at knowing what the Nazis were up to. Another attorney knew the employees don't have assets worth chasing, yet wants to keep them in the suit to "squeeze" out information.

Although the class action counsels' approach to sue all officers at first is the correct procedure, after several years of document review and depositions, the lawyers should have acquired a sense as to who was really responsible for the scam and dismissed the innocent. Unfortunately, the suit rampages like a dislodged mountain boulder crushing everything in its path as it races downhill.

In early 1999, a global settlement was reached among the trustee, the class action attorneys, and Generali insurance. The settlement will be discussed in detail later.

In papers submitted to the District Court for approval of the settlement, class action counsel agreed to release both Coach Mac and Tim White, the former CEO of Aloha Capital, because there was no evidence they participated in either selling the securities to the investors or in the Ponzi scheme itself.

Although the remaining officers were indeed happy for Tim and Coach Mac, nevertheless, their release created the implication the rest of us participated in selling the offerings or in the Ponzi scheme itself. Should such a Hobson's choice been foisted upon those who neither participated in the sales or in the fraud?

To be sure, if there was evidence of participation, dollars to donuts, the trustee, the SEC and the Justice Department would have commenced proceedings a long time ago.

Discovery is the name given to requests by one party for information and documentation from another party during litigation.[3] The most common discovery devices are requests to produce documents and reports of experts, present items for inspection, depositions, interrogatories (questions), and requests for admissions.

The most important and perhaps most abused discovery device is the deposition. Depositions are administered under oath. Generally, no judge is present, just the attorneys for the parties, the deponent (the one being questioned), a representative from the opposing party, and a stenographer.

Depositions give opposing counsel a chance to sum up the performance potential of trial witnesses, test their credibility, assess adversaries, juxtapose documents with testimony. Depositions may also lead to the discovery of new evidence. Other than objections for form, generally, all other objections, such as hearsay, are reserved for trial.

Depositions are grueling. They can and do go on for hours, sometimes days. They can be simultaneously intense and boring, achieving an instantiation of Nietzsche's Apollinian-Dionysian Duality.[4]

Sophisticated lawyers can have the deposition transcripts instantly produced on disc and downloaded into specialized litigation software, which can be reviewed that same night in preparation for the continuance of the deposition the next day or used at trial, particularly for impeachment.

Although many of the participants do not realize it at the time, cases are oftentimes won or lost during depositions.

Since the filings of the Bennett bankruptcy and the class action, countless depositions of parties, nonparty witnesses, and experts have been conducted across the country. Some depositions have been videotaped. The costs for depositions are astronomical because of attorney's fees, and costs for travel, lodging, food, and the transcripts themselves.

As the class action rolls like the rock of Sisyphus, there came a time when discovery deadlines, previously extended twice, were extended once again into the new millennium.

The modified discovery order was drafted by class action counsel, circulated for comment, and forwarded to presiding U.S. District Judge Sprizzo for review and execution.[5]

The preamble, or "whereas" clauses, of the final order suggests the parties "have been litigating . . . in good faith and . . . have concluded that based upon the ongoing discovery process and resulting scheduling difficulties for depositions . . . it is in the best interests of all parties to extend discovery . . . until Nov. 30, 2000."

The class action commenced in April 1996. Four years later discovery will be finally concluded, unless, as the order noted, further "extension[s] . . . shall be made by motion or stipulation prior to the extension of the date deadline. . . ."

This means the class action trial will not be started perhaps until 2001 or beyond. How are witnesses and defendants to remember events or identify documents, in some cases going back to the 1980s, that will be played before the jury as if they happened only yesterday?

How will people explain the appearance of impropriety of a few documents that bear their signature? Can they remember the intent behind the creation of those documents? Will the ten thousand other nonincriminating or exculpatory documents they produced be shown to the jury as well?

Is it fair that people will be judged for events that occurred almost two decades before?

Surely, in such cases, justice delayed is justice denied for both the victim and the accused. Such is the world of big-time litigation in America.

Richard C. Breeden, the Trustee

IRONICALLY, ALL of the Bennetts' immediate prepetition and early postpetition jockeying was taken to avoid the appointment of Richard C. Breeden as receiver or as bankruptcy trustee. Despite these efforts, Breeden was appointed trustee of Bennett Funding on April 18, 1996.

From his testimony in Bankruptcy Court, one learns Breeden graduated from Harvard Law School, taught constitutional law just after graduation, joined a prestigious law firm, became a legal adviser to vice president, then president, Bush, helped orchestrate the bailout of the saving and loan crisis, chaired the Securities and Exchange Commission, and most recently partnered at Coopers & Lybrand.

A few months into the proceeding, Breeden left Coopers to devote his time and attention to the Bennett Funding bankruptcy and the stabilization of Resort Funding in the time-share industry. He also turned his talents to start a consulting business to put his new-found trustee skills to

Table 10. Revenue received by the various debtors for nonleasing assets as of December 1, 1998

Nonleasing Assets	Amount Collected	Nonleasing Assets	Amount Collected
Aroostook Mall	18,670,830	Mountaineer Park Race Track	11,191,105
Bennett Atrium	161,000	Patrick Bennett Restitution	1,001,025
Bob Evans Restaurant Lease	110,000	PIRC Corp.	50,000
Branin Investment	10,000	Sage Recovery	10,556
Bullek Proceeds from sale of Mammoth Caverns	195,283	Schleicher-Soper	110,400
		Service Employees Union Lease	37,926
Cowen & Company	29,028	Sioux City Sue	339,500
Danarb Associates	200,170	Speculator Deposit	40,000
Deposit Certified Checks	25,491	TargetVision	605,371
Ferris Industries	2,944,622	Tax Refund	650,111
Life Insurance Cashouts	52,018	U.S. Die Casting	201,000
KDV Enterprises	654,125	Widewaters Group	921,452
Ken Kasarjian	1,029,642		
Legal Retainer Refunds	250,516	Total	$39,791,171
Lisa Chapman (Kasarjian's former wife)	300,000		

use for other unfortunate companies and to advise businesses on domestic and international capital markets.

Congress has allowed chapter 11 bankruptcy trustees, such as Breeden, to be paid up to 3 percent of all money paid out from the estate to unsecured creditors through reorganization dividends. The money to pay the creditors, himself, and the administrative and legal fees is obtained from the trustee's efforts at collecting assets of the estate.

Breeden is entitled to what Congress has provided subject to Judge Gerling's opinion as to his effectiveness.[1] When all is said and done, after administrative and legal fees are paid, Breeden will probably collect assets and pay out to unsecured creditors about $400–500 million; his fee will be upward of $15 million.

As former head of the SEC, Breeden knows the insidious ways of securities crooks. He despises them so. Early in the Bennett proceeding he wrote to the investors,

> [I]f assets belonging to the bankrupt estate have been diverted or misappropriated, I intend to pursue their recovery in the most vigorous manner possible. During my tenure as Chairman of the U.S. Securities and Exchange

Commission from 1989–1993, I worked on literally hundreds of cases in which we sought to recover assets on behalf of victims of illegality. I will bring the benefit of that experience to the task of recovering the greatest possible value for the estate. We intend to find questionable transactions and any misappropriated assets, wherever they may have been hidden.[2]

Breeden has particular disdain for the Bennett family. Make no mistake, through the Bennetts' misdeeds, a bankruptcy trustee was needed to assume control of the Company.

Maybe the guilty pleas and confessions of Kasarjian, Genovese, Peiffer, Menchella, Cerimeli, Pomposelli, Pavoni, and Michael Bennett and the conviction of Patrick Bennett will once and for all end the weirdest theory you'd ever want to hear, namely, the SEC drummed up the allegations to take over the Bennetts' thriving business and install Breeden, their former commander, as trustee.

Whether the proponents of this bizarre idea truly believe it, are on drugs, are delusional, are trying to blame others for investing their money in such a company ("I told you not to put all the money in one basket, Harry"), are trying to unseat Breeden and put their own boy in charge, are trying to blame others for the misadvice given to invest in Bennett Funding ("Harry, have I got a deal for you"), or are just plain stupid, one can only guess.

In support of the weird theory, in a 1997 letter to the U.S. Trustee's office, one investor suggested,

> The Bennett Company operated perfectly for the ten years I invested with it, prior to the S.E.C. action. Gentlemen, if the operation of the Bennett Company was Fraudulent—SO BE IT—GIVE IT TO ME! This alleged fraudulent operation sent a check every month until the government stepped in to protect me and the other investors? Allegations of Ponzi, double selling of leases, dilapidated Casinos in Reno, off shore bank accounts—I DON'T BUY IT.
>
> Was there something wrong inside the BENNETT COMPANY? PROBABLY!
> Are there things wrong inside GENERAL MOTORS CO.? PROBABLY!
> IS THAT A REASON TO SMASH 12,000 INVESTORS FROM HERE TO HELL?????
>
> The S.E.C. took the first steps in wrecking a company that had been a reliable source of income for many years. It appears that Mr. Richard C. Breeden was involved with the S.E.C. and initiated the action against the Bennett Company. —Certainly others cooperated with him to achieve the trusteeship of the company.[3]

Incredibly, and without knowing any of the facts, another investor, purportedly a representative of the HALO GROUP, wrote, "We have listened to many Bennett Horror stories offered by Trustee Breeden, such as, The Bennetts stole the employees IRA and 401-K Plans money. Absolutely false. The account exists and is ready for distribution. IT IS IN THE HANDS OF THE PROPER AUTHORITIES, UNTOUCHED!"[4]

Even Bud could not resist getting into the act. First, in June 1997, he sent a letter "to our friends" in which he solicited support to make a triumphant return: "There is a growing group of unheard 'investors' who want the help of the Bennett Family to jump-start our former business to return funds to the investors."[5]

In July 1998, the Bennetts filed papers with the Bankruptcy Court alleging Breeden was out to ruin their companies long before he was appointed trustee while he was connected with the SEC.

George Newcombe, Breeden's lead litigation attorney from Simpson Thacher, responded, "[Bud is] patently delusional [and] paranoid."[6]

Then the coup de gràce. In October 1998, just before the commencement of his trial, Patrick sent a fax to the *Syracuse Post-Standard*. According to the paper, Patrick wrote that the Bennett companies were forced to declare bankruptcy because federal officials had accused them of securities fraud, then leaked the information to the press. He stated that until that time the companies were in good financial shape. In March 1996, assets outweighed liabilities "making it impossible to call this a [pyramid] scheme by anyone's definition."[7]

Again George Newcombe's response: "There's overwhelming proof of a [pyramid] scheme . . . [t]he amount and scope of [which] ha[ve] been laid in great detail."

Even the editors of the *Syracuse Post-Standard* wrote, "Yet another outrage emerged last week from the morass that is the Bennett Funding Group." The paper continued,

> We get sick and tired of wrongdoers who claim that their problems were created by the media. If Bennett didn't want to be facing a 34-count indictment, he should have been a lot more careful with his investors' money. This is just the latest load of manure that Bennett has tried to unload on this community. They are too busy blaming everyone but themselves for their problems.[8]

Despite the rhetoric of the Bennetts and their supporters, the SEC did not engender the bankruptcy to install Breeden. Simply, the Bennetts brought it upon themselves.

Breeden is perhaps the quickest study I have known. He possesses the ability to review a report containing various facts and figures, digest it, then talk about the subject at will. The Bennetts, by contrast, had a transparent ability to take over a new concept, brand it their own, wrap themselves in its banner, embrace it, identify with it, and act as if the concept had been ingrained in the Company's ethos from time immemorial. They would look at you with "crazy eyes" if you didn't carry the banner or similar platitude.

His family living in Connecticut, Breeden rents an apartment close to downtown Syracuse. Keeping in tune with the working style in New York City, he usually arrived at work between 9:30 and 10:00 A.M. and stayed into the night. This is in sharp contrast to the upstate ethic of Bennett Funding employees who arrived early.

Breeden is an ardent sailor. He takes great pleasure aboard his racing yacht. Thankfully, I never heard him use sailing metaphors at the workplace.

During the bankruptcy, Breeden became a consultant to the accounting firm of Deloitte & Touche. After he revealed the relationship, it was incumbent upon Deloitte to disclose its client list to the Bankruptcy Court to insure no conflict of interest existed.

Deloitte refused to disclose its clients. Accordingly, Breeden was ordered by Judge Gerling to end the relationship with Deloitte. The court also impliedly ordered Breeden to disgorge $150,000 he had already received in consulting fees from Deloitte. This fee was in addition to draws he received as trustee at the rate of $50,000 per month plus expenses up to $3,500 per month.

When Breeden did not disgorge the money fast enough, Guy Van Baalen, the assistant U.S. trustee responsible for the Bennett case from an administrative point of view, sought Breeden's removal for improper after-the-fact disclosure of material conflicts of interest, such as the Deloitte consulting job and the shareholder interest in Equivest Finance.[9] According to those loyal to the trustee, Van Baalen, for some undisclosed reason, developed a zeal against Breeden bordering on hatred. Or, perhaps, he was simply doing his job "damn the politics."[10]

Although Judge Gerling agreed the return of the money was required under his order, no date was set forth when to do so. In what may have

Trustee Richard C. Breeden in the reception area of the Bennett companies in the Atrium.
Photo by Frank Ordoñez. Copyright © The Syracuse Newspapers.

been a rebuke to Van Baalen, the court left the date to return the Deloitte consulting fee up to Breeden.

Although no one publicly questioned the wisdom of exercising the U.S. trustee's policing powers, nevertheless, did anyone seriously believe Judge Gerling would remove Breeden after two and a half years of service, the recovery of hundreds of millions of dollars, and the chaotic and devastating affect a change in administration would wreck upon the proceeding?

Setting aside the transaction costs inherent in such futile motions, the appointment of a new trustee would undoubtedly usher in new counsel and accountants, who in turn would need to be brought up to speed, costing the bankruptcy estate untold and unnecessary millions of dollars.

Throughout the bankruptcy, Breeden kept the creditors informed through meetings, official reports, and periodic letters. In one such letter, Breeden explained the general workings of a chapter 11, as well as the mechanics of a plan of reorganization. He wrote, "In any Chapter 11 bankruptcy, there must ultimately be a Plan of Reorganization or 'POR.' The POR is a plan for paying off and restructuring debts and allowing the debtor to emerge from bankruptcy. The POR is distributed to creditors along with a Disclosure Statement, which is designed to provide important information to help creditors evaluate the POR."[11]

Once the POR and Disclosure Statement are filed with the Bankruptcy Court, a hearing is convened to consider the approval of the disclosure statement. If approved, the POR and disclosure statement along with ballots are sent to unsecured creditors, that is, those affected most in a chapter 11 bankruptcy, who vote on whether to adopt the POR. A two-thirds majority must vote in favor of the POR for it to be confirmed.

In distinguishing between the Bennett bankruptcy and other chapter 11 proceedings, Breeden wrote, "In a small or purely commercial bankruptcy, the POR typically happens within a few months. This has not been remotely possible in this case . . . due to the massive fraud that took place and the lack of reliable information. Furthermore, it was difficult to identify a specific plan until we became more certain of what the level and type of liabilities were for both investors and the banks."

Early in the proceeding, even Bankruptcy Judge Gerling observed: "Maybe nobody can humanly envision a plan which will once and for all bring finality to the rights of all parties in this case. Maybe none of us sitting in this courtroom have the ability to craft such a plan."[12]

Breeden went on to explain the pivotal role that Resort Funding, Inc., and Equivest Finance, Inc., were to play in the overall reorganization of the Bennett Companies. "Once those entities had a strong capital base and high levels of profitability, we planned to resume leasing activity at [Bennett Funding] with . . . leasing targeted . . . at renewals of our previous office machine business and . . . leasing capital goods to the leisure/vacation industry to complement [Resort Funding's] strengths."

In closing, Breeden predicted the "use [of] The Processing Center as the 'back office' for the leasing and timeshare activities of the future."

After two and a half years, Breeden finally filed the plan of reorganization on December 31, 1998 (the Bennett POR).[13] Along with the Bennett POR, a proposed disclosure statement and report on the fraud investigation were also filed.[14]

The Bennett POR was a series of proposed alternative courses of action the trustee could pursue depending upon the fulfillment of certain conditions and caveats and upon his business acumen.

Couched in general terms and applicable to all chapter 11s, the objectives of the Bennett POR included maximization of the value of the remaining assets and portfolio of leases, streamlining the administration of the bankruptcy and reduction of costs, preservation of favorable income tax attributes to enhance dividends to creditors, and providing speedy cash distributions to creditors.

To accomplish these stated goals, the Bennett POR called for the transfer of the leasing business into a limited liability company. Unlike Kasarjian's LLCs, the leasing LLC, as named in the Bennett POR, would own and service the portfolio of leases until a suitable purchaser was found.

After the leasing LLC was created, certain settlement proceeds received, marketable assets sold, and cash distributed, the balance of the bankruptcy estate would be flipped into a liquidating trust. At such point when the taxable nature of the liquidating trust was optimal, its assets would be liquidated and the proceeds distributed to the holders of allowed claims.

Despite lip service paid to the continuation of the leasing and servicing businesses, the Bennett POR was nothing but a liquidation of the business through attrition or quick sale. Simply, the leasing business died on the vine and the Processing Center never reached critical mass to service third-party accounts.

Indeed, in November 1998, only one month before the Bennett POR was filed and distributed, the local paper quoted Breeden as saying "the Bennett companies cannot be saved."[15]

This prompted Breeden to write a memorandum to the Bennett employees on that same day as the article appeared: "This morning's newspaper contains a story concerning possible liquidation of all of the Bennett Companies. The headline in the article is not accurate as to what has been said by me or by counsel for the Estate . . . please do not pay too much attention to the articles, which are based on conjecture rather than fact."[16]

As relatively few employees are needed to service the diminishing portfolio and perform bankruptcy-related tasks, layoffs started in the second week of January 1999.

To ameliorate the harshness of job loss Breeden offered a plan whereby employees would be given one week's salary for each year of employment capped at eight weeks plus an additional month of Company-paid insurance benefits. Judge Gerling approved Breeden's severance package.[17]

Honestly, though, what kind of idiot would do equipment leasing with Aloha Leasing or servicing with the Processing Center in the face of so much fraud, inaccuracies in books and records, and death blows dealt to numerous dealers and trade creditors?

Aloha Leasing's reputation was so soiled that soon after the bankruptcy was filed, the Equipment Leasing Association of America (ELA), the preeminent national equipment-leasing association, voted to expel the Company for gross violations of its Code of Conduct. In response I offered:

> While violations of the ELA Code may have existed prior to the bankruptcy, they most certainly do not under the present Trustee. Bennett Funding is not the same Company as it was and should not be punished for past sins as it endeavors to free itself from the yolk of impropriety and suspicion. Accordingly, in the spirit or rebirth embodied in Chapter 11 of the Bankruptcy Code, it is respectfully requested the ELA Fair Business Practices Committee take no disciplinary action against Bennett Funding which would thwart its attempt to reorganize.

Whether the ELA would have acquiesced is moot, because the Company did not pay its membership dues.

In a letter sent to the investors one week after the Bennett POR was filed, Breeden announced new estimates for distributions and made comparisons with other bankruptcies in terms of recoveries and expenses.[18]

He predicted ultimately unsecured creditors will receive between $0.36 to $0.43 on the dollar of final claims, after expenses. As detailed in the disclosure statement accompanying the Bennett POR, much of the anticipated distributions is based upon projections of income derived from the sale of Equivest shares on the market, the allocation of default insurance proceeds among the unsecured creditors, and the results of pending litigation.

These significant outcome determining factors are referenced in footnotes and text insets in complicated charts reminiscent of guarded projection language in stock prospectuses.

A serious misnomer that permeated the literature is "final claims" of investors. Final claim, as used in the Bennett bankruptcy, is not the amount set forth in the investors' proof of claims filed with the court. Final claim means "adjusted final claim."

One year before the submission of the Bennett POR, the trustee submitted a proposal to the Bankruptcy Court. The proposal envisioned that the twelve thousand current and former investors and 245 banks who received any interest or profit from the Bennett companies at any time during the six years preceding the filing of the petitions on March 29, 1996, will have that earned interest component deducted from any recovery they might otherwise be entitled.[19]

The plan was an attempt by the trustee to mitigate the losses suffered by more recent investors, whose money, in theory, went to pay principal and interest to earlier investors. It was buttressed by legal precedent in similar Ponzi scheme cases. And under the guise of improper or fraudulent conveyance by the debtor, such allocations are permitted in Bankruptcy Courts applying New York law.

Breeden's plan did have a twist, however. If an investor was paid during that same period (1990–96), and the amount received exceeded the gross amount invested, the investor will be sued and forced to disgorge the surplus. Moreover, any investor or bank that received payments during the three-month preferential period (December 30–March 29) will be required to disgorge those payments as well.

As expected, this part of the plan met with fierce opposition from the investors and the banks who clamored for Breeden's head. Judge Gerling denied the decapitation and adopted the plan in mid-March 1998, exempting from the onslaught investors whose net gain was below $1,000.

By the end of March 1998, about fourteen thousand individual lawsuits, called adversary proceedings in Bankruptcy Court, were instituted against investors and trade creditors, costing the estate more than $1.5 million in filing fees alone.[20] Saperston & Day, a firm with offices throughout upstate New York, was retained just to manage the project at reduced hourly rates.

In fiscal year 1998, which ended on September 30, a record 1.44 million bankruptcy petitions were filed nationwide, representing a 5 percent increase over the year before.[21] The impact of fourteen thousand adversary proceedings on the Northern District Bankruptcy Court clerk's office has got to be an administrative nightmare.

In one typical suit, investor Stephen Thomas had purchased a couple of short-term promissory notes for $10,000 each from Bennett Receivables and Bennett Receivables–II, the special purpose subsidiaries of Bennett Funding. When the notes matured, Thomas opted to roll over the investment by accepting new short-term notes. When these matured, the rollover process was repeated.

On January 1, 1996, Thomas cashed out the notes and ended his relationship with the Company. The trustee sued Thomas for the return of Ponzi interest of $2,783.21, and for $50,000 principal because he viewed each rollover as a repayment in full followed by an immediate reinvestment of the entire amount.

In noting "that it would be grossly inequitable to expose [Thomas] to over $50,000 in potential liability when the amount of capital he risked and the amount of purported profit paid to him barely exceeded $20,000 combined," Judge Gerling found that the rollovers were not independent transactions but allowed the suit to continue concerning the amount actually received by Thomas.[22]

Fallout from the barrage affected employees as well. Employees who purchased leases were treated as any other investor and sued for interest made in excess of investment. One such employee, who still works for the Company and testified for the government at Patrick Bennett's trial, had invested all of her and her immediate family's savings into Bennett Funding financial products.

She was informed her lease account zeroed out, and her parents' lease account netted $2.67. Because her parents were fortunate to have liquidated their prime conversion account, PCA, sometime before the bankruptcy filing, the estate was going to ask for the $70,000 to be returned. She broke down.[23]

All was not bleak, however, as Breeden managed to secure permission from Judge Gerling to make an unprecedented early partial distribution to the investors upward of 6 percent of their adjusted final claims.[24]

In allowing the early distribution, Judge Gerling took an equitable, and perhaps courageous, step, because the Bennett bankruptcy "is a unique case, and it calls for unique measures. . . ."[25]

In exclaiming that "this is the best day of the case so far," Breeden sent out the first payments, totaling $40 million, in August 1998. He said, "It gives you a great feeling to sit in front of a stack of 9,000 checks . . . which represents a meaningful development for a family out there."[26]

Eventually, in October 1998, the trustee, his counsel, counsel for the Unsecured Creditors Committee, and counsel for the Early Investors

Committee filed a joint motion in the Bankruptcy Court.[27] Early investors are those still owed money on the Company's books and records but who received payments from Bennett Funding over a number of years.

Because the "early investors" generally received more payments characterized as interest than later investors, they are more likely to have a larger reduction in their original claim owing to the claims adjustment process.

After hearing arguments on the joint motion, Judge Gerling approved yet another plan, whereby investors who were sued under the adversary proceedings will be able to elect whether to settle their suits by reducing their claim by an additional 30 percent of the already-reduced adjusted claim amount.

Of course, any investor opting out of the settlement was free to roll the dice and continue defending against the adversary proceeding. As this was not an appetizing prospect, because counsel would need to be retained and the prognosis for victory not at all assured, only a few investors declined to settle.

Those investors who went for the plan can hope to have a final claim for 70 percent of their adjusted claims, that is, 70 percent of payments received minus investment made and minus any payment received in the interim distribution. This calculation, then, under the plan of reorganization, is the final claims of investors referenced by Breeden.

To illustrate, an investor purchased one-year leases for $100,000 at 9 percent interest. He expected a return of $109,000. During the year, he received $70,000 before the Company went bankrupt. The investor's adjusted claim, calculated by subtracting $70,000 from $100,000, not $109,000, becomes $30,000. The final claim is 70 percent of $30,000, or $21,000.

Under the Bennett POR, the investor will receive between 36 and 43 percent of that amount, or roughly $8,400. The total received by the investor from the Bennetts and through bankruptcy dividends will be $78,400, a loss of $30,600, including initial investment interest, or 28.07 percent real recovery. The real recovery does not include interest for the loss of use of the funds during the intervening years or lost opportunity costs occasioned by failing to take advantage of other investments. In a footnote to one of his opinions, Judge Gerling rightfully noted:

"Consider the case of a hypothetical innocent investor who deposits $1,000 into a Ponzi scheme and is repaid, one year later, with $1,010.

Though under the Trustee's analysis this hypothetical investor will have received $10 of profit, it is hard to conclude that he is a net winner under this transaction. By spending $1,000 on the Ponzi scheme, the investor gave up the chance to place his money in other investments, many of which presumably would have offered him a better return than the 1 percent actually received. In borderline cases, the legal (and equitable) question of whether an investor benefited from or was victimized by a Ponzi fraud will often depend on whether the fact-finder chooses to take into account such factors as lost opportunity costs and transaction costs, thus making the entire analysis more complicated than the simple comparison of figures on a balance sheet."[28]

According to an excerpt from the 1999 1st quarter operating report, the consolidated bankruptcy estates had total receipts of $417,987,581. $315,121,606 derived from lease and lease related payments, $14,817,033 from interest on money on deposit, and $10,178,646 from the inventory finance program. The balance was from proceeds received from the sale of assets and related transactions.[29] In other words, 81.37 percent of all revenues, $340,117,285, derived from normal business operations.

Clearly, the lion's share of money received flowed from lessees who simply honored their commitments and had little to do with Breeden's efforts, save stabilization of the Company.

Still, Breeden deserves congratulations because the actual rate of return the investors will enjoy is very respectable in a stock fraud case. Indeed, if the trustee's projections in the disclosure statement are accurate, total revenues could reach $720 million by the end of the case. If so realized, Breeden stands to earn $20 million. This amount would be in addition to payment he will receive as executive officer of Equivest at $410,000 per year, bonuses up to $307,500, and stock options which are all contingent upon a successful public offering of the Bennett companies shares of Equivest stock.

Some Figures for Perspective

FROM JANUARY 1990 through December 1995, Bennett Funding and its affiliates raised $1.945 billion from the assignment of leases, promissory notes, and other financial products to investors.[1] In addition, during the same period, the Bennett companies received loan proceeds from 245 banks, totaling $481 million.[2]

In 1995, the company executed an agreement in which MetLife Capital Corporation, a financial subsidiary of the insurance giant, loaned $50 million to the Company, secured by leases.[3] Not long after the MetLife deal was concluded, Resort Funding finalized an eight-month negotiation with ING Bank, a major Dutch-based institution, for a $50 million line of credit secured by time-share receivables.[4]

This is the same ING Bank that purchased Barren's Bank of England for £1 and assumption of $1 billion in liabilities. This is the same English bank laid low by a scamming broker residing in Singapore.

Bennett Funding also obtained a $15 million line of credit with Heller Financial secured by, you guessed it, equipment leases.

With the securing of $115 million from ING Bank, MetLife, and Heller, and an additional $74 million from other sources, Bennett Funding was, ostensibly, able to free itself from the burden of raising capital from private placements to investors, especially in the light of Patrick's agreement with the SEC to stop using PPMs in spring 1995. At least that was the story as pitched by Patrick.

In reality, the sale of securities through PPMs was simply shifted to Kasarjian's limited liability companies, such as Beckett, with proceeds funneled to the Company. Moreover, Patrick's double-dipping went into warp drive as he continued to sell municipal leases directly and through Kasarjian's off-site operations.

In the course of its legitimate leasing business, the Company collected $674 million from lessees under the various lease agreements in place during this six-year period.

This little company from Syracuse was able to get its hooks on $3.289 billion from investors, banks, financial institutions, and lessees. This massive amount was raised by a company that employed twenty people in cramped rented space only twelve years before its fall in 1996.

World-class companies and their agents performed extensive due diligence on Bennett Funding before getting involved. *Due diligence* is a "measure of prudence, activity, or assiduity, as is properly to be expected from, and ordinarily exercised by, a reasonable and prudent person under the particular circumstances."[5]

This means that before the large lenders loaned money, they conducted on-site audits of Bennett Funding's books and records, interviewed personnel, reviewed financial information, the computer system, and reams of accounting information, reports, and trial balances. They reviewed Bennett Funding's financial statements authored by outside auditors. They reviewed the quality of the financial inventory. They asked the right questions, looked at the right documents, spoke to the right people. They were thorough. They were professional. They fucked up.

During the bankruptcy, as is required, the trustee convened periodic meetings of creditors at various locations throughout the country. One meeting was conducted in Florida on February 25, 1997. During that meeting Breeden presented a computerized slide show illustrating the "tragic mathematics" of the Bennett bankruptcy. Some of the more significant figures as of the petition date, March 29, 1996, follow:

• Total lease receivables = $322,401,100.

• Total lease claims by investors and banks = $900,878,178. "For every $1.00 in lease receivables," Breeden noted, "there are $2.79 in claims against leases."

• Total liabilities = $1,003,491,648 broken down into secured—$228,924,682—and unsecured—$774,566,966.

• "Toxic leases," a term coined by the trustee, in which no money has been received postpetition, total $44,000,000. These include Scriptex, Americorp, Hotel Syracuse, and Castle leases.[6]

May 15, 1997, was the official cutoff date for acceptance of proof of claims from investors, banks, and other creditors in the Bennett bankruptcy. The trustee retained an outside professional claims agent, Poorman-Douglas Corp., to administer the mountain of claims and attendant paperwork and data input.

Although budgeted for $68,825, Poorman-Douglas's first fee application sought payment of $242,285 plus $67,618 in expenses. The discrepancy resulted because the Bennett system "was comprised of vendor numbers assigned to each purchase; whereas the creditors often lumped their investments into a single claim or amount." As a result, Poorman-Douglas created a "more substantial database than originally envisioned."[7]

Approximately twenty-one thousand claims were filed, with an aggregate demand for over $5 billion. Through the coordinated efforts of the trustee, in-house staff, and the claims agent, and based upon agreements with creditors and decisions by Judge Gerling, thousands of duplicative, overstated, and erroneous claims were eliminated. When all of the acceptable claims were tallied, the $5 billion shrunk to approximately $1 billion.

Breeden's final report on the fraud, filed in December 1998, stated the investors and banks purchased approximately $2.4 billion worth of commercial and municipal-equipment leases between 1990 to 1996. The Company, however, had only $980 million worth of such leases to hawk.

The bankruptcy process itself has also spawned impressive figures. As of March 31, 1999, the aggregate claims for professional fees for the trustee's lawyers, the trustee's accountants, the counsel to the unsecured creditor's committee, the accountants for the unsecured creditor's committee, the independent fee auditor, and the trustee was $45,232,382, with $34,292,229 paid, $3,229,533 disallowed, and another $7,710,619 authorized and on tap to be paid. A total of $9,983,000 in fees had accrued by the end of the first quarter of 1999, but had not been submitted for approval by Judge Gerling.[8]

In bankruptcy matters, payment for fees earned and expenses incurred by attorneys, accountants, and other professionals, such as appraisers, must be approved by the judge on motion to creditors and other interested parties.

In December 1996, Judge Gerling retained the services of Stuart, Maue, Mitchell and James, Ltd., to ride herd on the feeding frenzy that surely will accompany the fee applications.[9] Stuart Maue, a Missouri-based company, provides accounting, consulting, and professional fee-auditing services.

In accordance with Judge Gerling's standing order, law firms and other professionals must at first submit their fee applications to Stuart Maue. The detail supporting the applications, which consists of time records and receipted expenses, must be tendered to Stuart Maue on disc in universally accepted computer language and by hard copy.

The time sheet entries are separated into scores of different categories to facilitate Stuart Maue's review. The findings are then submitted to the court and served upon the applicant and interested parties. The applicant may choose to respond to the auditor's report. Interested parties and creditors may file objections as well with Judge Gerling serving as the ultimate arbiter if any discrepancies remain.

To illustrate the process, Simpson Thacher filed its fifth application seeking payment of professional fees in the amount $3,046,312.50, and

Table 11. Fee applications of and payments to professionals as of March 31, 1999

Professionals	Fee Applications	Court-Ordered Fee Adjustments	Payments Made to Professionals	Pending Fee Applications
Baker & Botts	520,094.16	–33,213.56	137,608.14	349,272.46
Richard C. Breeden	2,171,150.62	0.00	2,171,150.62	0.00
Coll Davidson Carter Smith Saite	158,796.11	–5,000.00	128,643.33	25,152.78
Coopers & Lybrand	9,410,673.75	–1,463,650.24	7,944,598.28	2,425.23
Cornerstone Research, Inc.	118,073.68	0.00	42,380.00	75,693.68
Curtis Thaxter Stevens Broder	89,205.08	–3,197.00	37,374.20	48,633.88
George Davis	124,000.88	–13,332.96	110,667.92	0.00
Firley Moran Freer & Eassa	103,002.07	0.00	103,002.07	0.00
Harvey and Harvey	54,371.36	0.00	54,371.36	0.00
Kaye Scholer	389,147.12	0.00	320,000.00	69,147.12
Matt Harrison	16,031.04	0.00	16,031.04	0.00
Milligan-Whyte & Smith	57,097.10	0.00	56,184.25	912.85
Poorman-Douglas	309,903.75	–8,666.95	128,156.80	173,080.00
Preston Gates & Ellis	8,035.66	0.00	8,035.66	0.00
Saperston & Day	2,121,448.56	–7,078.27	1,593,524.96	520,845.33
Shanley & Fisher	116,074.20	0.00	82,819.20	33,255.00
William L. Silber	43,640.00	0.00	34,950.00	8,690.00
Stuart, Maue, Mitchell & James	729,168.91	0.00	528,201.71	200,967.20
Shaw, Licitra, Esernio & Schwartz	176,774.27	–108,621.27	68,153.00	0.00
Simpson, Thacher & Bartlett	25,472,934.40	1,561,486.25	18,101,719.35	5,809,728.80
Thomas A. Lihan	100,977.65	0.00	98,443.75	2,533.90
Unsecured Creditor's Comm	49,746.00	0.00	49,746.00	0.00
Wassermann, Jurista & Stolz	1,631,473.62	–15,592.60	1,533,188.12	82,692.90
Whiteman Osterman & Hanna	205,180.86	0.00	167,682.86	37,498.00
Zolfo Cooper	1,055,381.89	–9,694.67	775,596.70	270,090.52
Totals	$45,232,382.74	($3,229,533.77)	$34,292,229.32	$7,710,619.65

Source: Adapted from Bennett Funding records

reimbursement of expenses in the amount of $430,599.76 incurred from July 1, 1997, through October 31, 1997.

The fee auditor's report was filed with the court in March 1998. Simpson Thacher provided replies to Stuart Maue's report and reduced its fee application by $1,831.50 because of duplicate billing errors. It also reduced its expense claim by $133.51.

Both the U.S. Trustee's Office and the Official Committee of Unsecured Creditors filed objections to the fifth application. After a series of adjournments the fifth application came on to be heard by Judge Gerling in May 1998. At that time, the court awarded Simpson Thacher a provisional fee of $1 million and $200,000 in expenses.

In his decision several months later, Judge Gerling noted Stuart Maue's report identified entries in Simpson Thacher's "time records . . . as falling into twenty general categories which appear to violate Court Guidelines." Additionally, the judge said that "the Auditor's Report isolates approximately one hundred fourteen . . . specific . . . categories . . . for review and analysis."[10]

The various categories questioned by Stuart Maue included vaguely described tasks (disallowed $674.50); multiple attendance at events (disallowed $4,855.50); intra office conferences (disallowed $7,599); administrative and clerical tasks (disallowed $80,101); fee application (disallowed $41,701.27); retention of local counsel in certain litigation matters (disallowed $16,449); *Lady Kathleen* (disallowed $4,228); Michael Bennett's change of venue motion (disallowed $6,249.15); database matters for investigation and analysis (disallowed $4,909.50); section 341 hearings preparation (disallowed $1,802); miscellaneous services, such as recruitment efforts for part-time local counsel (disallowed $1,341.50); and expenses (disallowed $54,323.28) for a total allowed payment of $3,201,321.67 and a court-approved savings of $273,626.08.

In this fashion, Stuart Maue has saved the Bennett estate almost $3.2 million in improper billing and expenses as of the end of the first quarter of 1999. The firm earned about $728,000. Although law firms are entitled to bill for the time involved in submitting and defending fee applications, such billing is relatively modest and pales in comparison to the net savings. Yes, Virginia, someone is watching the pot.

But even with the savings and disallowances, professional fees are paid from bankruptcy assets otherwise available for distribution to investors and banks. In this fashion, it is anticipated the bankruptcy estates will pay upward of $75 million to everyone but the aggrieved.

Citing a General Accounting Office report, Breeden wrote that in "chapter 11 cases, combined payments to professionals and trustee represented about 34% of total collections."[11]

In the Bennett case, he continued, "total fees paid to date have been approximately 6% of total collections, or less than *one-fifth* the percentage level of expenses the GAO found as the national average."

In defense of escalating payments to professionals that seem incongruous with the scope of the victimization, Breeden's remarks were reminiscent of the Starkist commercial in which Charlie the tuna is asked if he wants good taste or to taste good:

> Even a child could tell you that a big case will have big expenses. . . . Ask yourself a simple question. What do you most want out of the bankruptcy proceedings? Do you want the maximum possible recovery in the quickest period of time? Or, instead of cash paid to you, would you rather know that the Estate had very low expenses? Of course we could have had extremely low expenses by simply letting the crooks and the banks take all the money, in which event unsecured creditors would have gotten very little. I don't think that more than a handful of people would have wanted that result.[12]

In any event, a comparison between final amounts in other cases versus ongoing expenses in the Bennett matter was perhaps having fun with statistics. Although a footnote in the disclosure statement stated that the "GAO figures are not directly comparable to the Bennett case, but are provided for purposes of perspective," the use of the proverbial statistical apples-to-oranges approach was clumsy.

The disclosure statement stated the national average chapter 11 payout to unsecured creditors is 17.5 percent of total collections. The average chapter 11 rate of return relative to total collections is a non sequitur, because the average percentage of recovery relative to losses or amounts claimed as losses is ignored.

Thus, in chapter 11 cases, unsecured creditors could receive a significant portion of their claims even though receiving only a small percentage of money collected by the bankruptcy estate after the payment of administrative expenses.

For example, a chapter 11 estate receives $825,000 in collections. The trustee pays $400,000 to a secured creditor and $300,000 to attorneys, accountants, and himself. The balance of $125,000 is split among six unsecured creditors who filed claims for $25,000 each. Even though expenses reached 36.36 percent of collections, each unsecured creditor would receive $20,833, or 83.32 percent of their individual claims, but only 2.5 percent of total collections.

The trustee's manipulation of statistical information, "statisticulation,"[13] perhaps a by-product of years of government service, was regrettable. Nevertheless, most cases do not lie in the parallel universe in which the Bennett bankruptcy seems to exist.

The Cover-up Commences—
The 7 Percent Solution

How DID the SEC find out about the goings-on at Bennett in the first instance? After all, Bennett Funding was a privately held company with only a smattering of private placement filings and not subject to the strict rules that govern public corporations.

In 1991, Bennett Funding entered into a program specifically designed for Horizon Securities, Inc., a regional broker that had been selling Bennett Funding financial products. The program offered Horizon investors a 7 percent return on Bennett Funding promissory notes in exchange for a one-year loan. The loan was to be collateralized with specific membership agreements assigned from Resort Service Company, then known as Resort Funding, with an aggregate principal balance of at least 147 percent of the face amounts of the Horizon notes. The amount of the overcollateralization was a product of the face value of the notes, the interest rate paid out to the investors, and the interest rates inherent in the assigned collateral.

To sweeten the investment, the membership agreements were to be insured against default proportionately to the 147 percent overcollateralization to provide complete coverage for the assigned collateral. The insurance was provided by Assicurazioni Generali, S.P.A., an Italian insurance company ranked at the time number 62 in the world. More on Generali later.

Between February 1991 and April 1993, Bennett Funding raised approximately $4 million through the sale of the Horizon notes.

At this point, two stories have emerged concerning the commencement of the SEC's involvement. In 1993, Horizon underwent a routine audit and examination by NASD. NASD made inquiry concerning the nature of Bennett Funding and the Horizon notes. The inquiry somehow kicked upstairs to the SEC.

The other theory holds one of the Horizon investors showed the prospectus to her friend Riva Starr, an SEC enforcement attorney.

The theories converge in May 1993 when the SEC sent Bennett Funding a letter of inquiry and requested production of all documents related to the Horizon notes.

In particular, the SEC staff raised concerns about whether adequate collateral—membership contracts—was assigned to support the 147 percent overcollateralization. The staff also questioned whether the default insurance with Generali was in place as described to the purchasers of the Horizon notes. Lastly, the SEC wanted to know whether the Horizon notes were securities that should have been registered in the first instance.

After two years, the inquiry turned into an investigation. By this time, the Company assembled an armada of securities attorneys to protect its interests before the SEC. These included John Oberdorf from Robinson St. John & Wayne, Bennetts' longtime counsel; Rick Marshall from Kirkpatrick & Lockhart; and Irving Pollack, a securities legend, from Storch & Brenner of Washington, D.C.

Bennett Funding's securities counsel attempted to assuage the SEC's concerns through the joint submission of an extensive explanatory letter with accompanying exhibits, dated June 22, 1995.[1]

Although not rising to the level of a "Wells submission," which is a formal request to the SEC not to file charges, the lawyers' letter suggested that "Bennett Funding is a bona fide company, producing substantial, legitimate revenues." The lawyers sought "to impress upon [the staff] that [Bennett Funding's] errors [in collateralizing the investments] were the result of inadvertence or mistake, not disrespect for the law, and, as a result of the intrinsic value of the company, not a single investor dollar will be lost."

The lawyers advised that before the commencement of the Horizon offering, a method of assigning adequate collateral to each Horizon note was devised and implemented by an experienced and able officer of Bennett Funding.

The lawyers said a worksheet was created from which lower-level employees could determine which membership agreements should be assigned to satisfy the 147 percent requirement.

The firm told the SEC that Al Cerimeli,[2] vice president–finance, created the collateralization models and that Anthony Menchella[3] assumed responsibility for the ministerial task of applying the worksheet and assigning the collateral to the Horizon notes.

Tony was a longtime friend of Patrick. He operated P.T.'s Shortstop, a deli in the northern boundary of Syracuse. P.T.'s leased approximately $600,000 worth of equipment from Bennett Funding—one big fucking deli.

P.T.'s went belly up. Patrick came to Tony's rescue and put him to work for a partnership owned by Patrick and his wife, Gwen, Bennett Financial Associates, doing odd jobs at Vernon Downs Racetrack and at Bennett Funding.

Despite the rhetoric, it turns out the SEC was correct. The Horizon notes were undercollateralized. Mea culpa. Bennett Funding told the SEC that Tony made mistakes in the assignment of collateral, assigning too little collateral to many Horizon notes and far too much collateral to others. That, as Tony's erratic behavior indicates, "his mistakes were not part of a conscious plan to deceive."

Tony testified that horrific personal problems he suffered during the period he assigned collateral, including his bankruptcy, a heart attack, grave family illness, and a death in the family—for which he obtained psychological counseling—so distracted him from the proper acquittal of his duties in many instances that he did not assign proper amounts of collateral to the notes.

In any event, Bennett Funding did not benefit from Tony's mistakes. Indeed, while his mistakes resulted in the assignment of approximately $1.2 million less in collateral than should have been assigned to the Horizon notes, in 1992 and 1993—the period during which he was assigning collateral—Bennett Funding had more than $26 million in excess collateral that could have been, but was not, assigned to any financial products.

Bennett Funding undoubtedly could have and should have done better in supervising Tony. But the task was not rocket science. Tony had the right stuff to perform the assignment, earning a B.S. degree in business administration from the University of Miami.

Added to the calculus was Bennett Funding's purchase of an insurance policy from Generali. As described in the literature given to the Horizon note purchasers, "Generali insured the lesser of 75% of the membership agreements securing payment of the Notes (i.e., 75% of 147% of the face amount of the Notes) or 100% of the principal and interest outstanding on the Notes."

Bennett Funding's securities counsel also advised the SEC that registration of the Horizon note offering was not required for three reasons. First, the notes were not securities under the applicable securities laws. Second, even if the notes were considered securities, they were commercial paper and exempt from registration under the securities laws. Commercial paper is a high-quality short-term obligation of a large issuer such as GM. Third, even if the notes were deemed securities and not commercial paper, nevertheless, the notes were sold in a private placement, and not subject to the rigid requirements of public offerings.

The lawyers added gratuitously, "Even if the [SEC] staff disagrees with this conclusion and now believes that the Notes should have been registered, several factors argue against the institution of enforcement action in that . . . *there is not a trace of fraud*. . . ." If ever an example of "putting one's foot in one's mouth" existed, surely this was it.

While the firm was making its pitch to the SEC following Bennett Funding's receipt of the SEC inquiry letter, Patrick met secretly with Al Cerimeli. In the course of that meeting, according to the indictment, Patrick advised Al that he had not assigned membership agreements to collateralize the Horizon notes at the time they were sold to investors. Patrick told Al the membership agreements needed to be assigned to the Horizon notes after they were sold to the investors "in order to make it appear the collateral had been assigned at the time the Notes were sold" a year or two before.

Based on Patrick's directive "to create . . . documents designed to make it appear membership agreements had been assigned to each of the Notes at the time" those Notes were sold, Al "fabricated the fictitious documents and labeled them 'Attachment To Promissory Note.'"

In June 1993, Patrick produced the fake documents to the SEC, including copies of the promissory notes and the attachments. The attachments were stapled to copies of the documents, which were "actually sent to the purchasers of the . . . Notes" by Finance Department or Horizon employees at the time of sale. This created the appearance the Company had also provided the attachments to the investors at the time of purchase.

Concerning the notes, Patrick testified before the SEC in June 1993:[4]

Q: You mentioned a few moments ago that the note was secured both by an insurance policy through Generali and through specific contracts. Can you give me a bit of description as to how each note is secured by specific contracts, how that works?

A: Yes. The mechanism under which it takes place?

Q: Um-hum.

A: *As part of the insurance process of the insurance being assigned, spe-*

cific contracts are assigned, you know, to each note as collateral for that note, and the insurance policy guarantees the performance of that collateral—those collateral contracts.

Q: And the note which is on page 0009 is accompanied by an attachment similar to 0010 in the case of each note holder?

A: *Yes.*

Q: Let me clarify "accompanied." I just want to clarify that the Attachment to the Promissory Note, which is 0010, is transmitted to each note holder, correct?

A: *Yes.*

After Patrick produced the attachments to the SEC, he directed Al to fabricate the collateral models. The fake models were presented to the SEC to give "the appearance . . . the [company] originally posted the [membership agreements] on the models and used the models to create the . . . attachments"[5] at the time of sale.

Patrick thought it would seem more realistic and believable if Al told "the SEC . . . Tony [Menchella] made a mathematical error in calculating the amount of collateral needed for each . . . Note" under the models he prepared.

Patrick then met with Tony and provided him with the newly created models and the fabricated attachments. Patrick instructed Tony to fill in the collateral and attachment information in his own handwriting. Patrick produced the documents prepared by Cerimeli and by Menchella to the SEC.

Patrick gave more testimony to the SEC in December 1994. The italicized portions are the materially false statements.

Q: Why don't you describe the procedure for the 7 percent Notes?

A: *In the case of the 7 percent note, once the order was processed and the receipt was issued, that information was given to Mr. Cerimeli to process and create a model to ultimately give to a staff person to assign the collateral. And he would have prepared a model of, given a work sheet to a staff person whose job is to assign collateral. That staff person would have access to all the unassigned collateral—all the insured unassigned collateral available at that time. And it was their job to assign a proper amount of collateral. And it's clear from reviewing this note, and I am sure the others we are going to look at—that mistakes have been made.*

Q: Do you know how the mistakes were made, to use your phrase?

A: *No. As I said, I'm, you know, very disturbed with it. The first I became aware of it was Monday and Tuesday as we just reconstructed and looked at some of these documents and these specific Notes. And I am certainly going to find out how they were made and who made them, but at this point, other than somebody doing their job incorrectly, I don't have an explanation.*

After Al and Tony were subpoenaed to testify before the SEC, Patrick met with both men "in advance of their respective testimony." He discussed "the false explanations [the two] were to provide to the SEC concerning . . . the fictitious attachments . . . and models."

Early after the criminal charges were filed, Al sought the advice of Emil Rossi, perhaps the preeminent criminal defense attorney in Syracuse. Al was advised to plead guilty to the charges of perjury, obstruction of justice, and conspiracy. He did and continues to wait more than two years for sentencing.

Not long after, Tony Menchella followed suit and pleaded guilty to the same charges. Unfortunately, all of Tony's personal problems—bankruptcy, a heart attack, grave family illness, and a death in the family—which were stated to the SEC to mask the miscollateralization were true. Added are jail time, the stigma of being a convicted felon in America, and financial ruination.

In the same SEC submission by Bennett Funding's lawyers concerning the 7 percent notes, it was reported the Company used "finance industry standards" and its own historical default rates on leases to establish "a range of reserves which [Bennett Funding] carried [on its books] to account for revenues which [are not], potentially, collecti[ble] due to lease payment defaults."[6]

The submission suggested Bennett Funding's practice was to set aside a reserve each time it purchased a new lease. Although Bennett Funding could have set aside any amount within the self-established range (a blend of industry standards with historical rates), "[Bennett Funding] consistently reserve[d] the very high end of the range required by GAAP."

For example, the lawyers stated that "in 1992, rather than reserving the low-end amount of $5,564,312.00, [Bennett Funding] voluntarily reported reserves of $9,826,818.00. . . ." Again, in 1993, "[Bennett Funding] reported a reserve of $12,750,176.00 . . . when the low-end reserve consistent with GAAP would have been only $7,271,557.00."

Very noble figures, except so many of the leases were multipledged and multisold to investors and banks, that the real reserve needed to be ratcheted fivefold. Further, the income to be held in the reported reserve derived not necessarily from lease payments but from fresh cash generated by the Ponzi scheme. The reserves were illusory.

You remember the story about the accountant asked to add two and two on a job interview. He bolted from his chair, locked the door, pulled the blinds, took the phone off the hook, leaned over the desk of the interviewer, and whispered in her ear, "How much do you want it to be?"

The law firms that issued the submission were sued by the trustee. Ironically, all of the notes were repaid fully in 1994.

WHY?

"There are more things in heaven and earth, Horatio, than are dreamt of in your philosophy."

—*Hamlet*

Hotel Fever

THE BENNETTS loved hotels. The love affair started in 1985 with the purchase of two local hotels that eventually became Days Inn and Quality Inn franchises. The hotels never turned a profit and needed periodic cash infusions from Bennett Funding to stay afloat.

The Bennetts' Days Inn was sold in 1995 for $4 million to an investor/friend of Patrick as a tax shelter. The Company paid $200,000 up front, taking back a note and mortgage for the balance of $3.8 million.[1]

Not long after the Days Inn sale, the $3.8 million note was pledged to a third-party lender, IRR Assets, as collateral for yet another loan to Bennett Funding in the amount of $2 million. After making one payment, the loan was rendered in default because of the Bennett bankruptcy.

The original $3.8 million note was not tendered to IRR Assets at the closing of the loan. Under standard commercial law, IRR did not perfect its security interest in the note, allowing the trustee to leverage a favorable settlement.

The purchaser of the Days Inn made a few payments on his note after the bankruptcy then refused to pay further. The owner resisted the trustee's efforts at foreclosure on the mortgage because of the allegations of fraud and misrepresentation. At the time of this writing, the Bennetts' Quality Inn was still owned by the estate, as no credible buyer emerged.

In 1993, coinciding with a push toward becoming the first family of Syracuse, the Bennetts purchased the Hotel Syracuse and gave it to Michael. The Hotel Syracuse is on the National Registry of Historic Hotels. The purchase was against the recommendation of every person in Bennett Funding who had an opinion on the subject. The numbers were simply not there.

At the time of purchase, the hotel was in bankruptcy itself, a victim of a prolonged union strike by the rank and file. But profit did not matter. Neither did the scarcity of trained hoteliers, the use of already overworked Company personnel to fill hotel spots, nor the lack of a comprehensive marketing plan. None of these mattered. It seemed the motivation behind the wasteful venture was to give Michael the hotel as the lynchpin of a strategy to revitalize downtown Syracuse, with Michael and his family to be hailed as saviors.

The purchase price was a combination of up-front and deferred cash payments, payoff of certain debts and assumption of others, payment of the seller's attorneys' fees of $1 million, and hiring the son of the seller as a consultant. The total package, without applying the cost of renovations, was about $8.5 million, for what one *Wall Street Journal* reporter called the "decrepit Hotel Syracuse."[2]

It is axiomatic if you can walk away from a deal, then walk away. If you cannot walk away, negotiation must ensue. Michael could have walked away. He did not need the Hotel Syracuse. When we were told by the seller's counsel their $1 million fee, which was to be paid by the Company, was nonnegotiable, we should have walked away then and there. But Michael capitulated without blinking an eye. Hell, it wasn't his money, after all.

During a meeting with Bud, he once told me he had about $9 million he needed to give to his boys. The money wasn't in Bud's savings account. It was pent-up cash value in some of his companies.

"You know," he said, "I bought Michael a pool for his house, so I had to buy Patrick a pool too." At the time his "boys" were 39 and 35.

Bud appeared to be almost agonizing over what to do with his money. He settled the matter by giving each brother $4.5 million. With his money, Patrick bought Vernon Downs. Michael pumped his money into the Hotel Syracuse.

But Bud need have not have worried because his sons knew how to and did take care of themselves. Patrick created an irrevocable trust for his two preteenage sons with Michael serving as trustee. His signature was required for all withdrawals from the trust. According to bank statements, all of the trust's $1 million was withdrawn within half a year before the filing of the bankruptcy petition. This was over and above the $13 million Patrick "borrowed" from Bennett Management.

Over a three-year period, Bennett Funding pumped about $20 million into the purchase, renovation, and upkeep of the monolith known as the Hotel Syracuse.[3] Michael "relaunched [the hotel] with a blitz of promotion, including a glossy magazine in which the hotel . . . told its own story: I was conceived in a world of contradictions . . . the roaring 20's, the Jazz Age, the Age of Discontent. . . ."

Table 12. Breakdown of the Intercompany Debt for the Hotel Syracuse

Obligation	Outstanding Debt
Purchase Price and Accrued Interest	$9,300,000.00
Acquisition Funds	$2,660,000.00
Renovation Loans	$3,121,187.00
Preferred Stock	$1,635,025.00
16 Leases	$4,087,653.82
Total	$20,803,865.82

Even with Michael's ceaseless promotional efforts, the hotel barely broke even and that only because no debt service was made to Bennett Funding to repay the $20 million. About the only thing that made money was "Coach Mac's" sports bar.

For a while, and besides his other duties, Michael was the general manager of the hotel. He had absolutely no experience as a hotelier, did not know the lingo, and did not have the contacts. But he looked the part, much the same way James Brolin did in the TV series *Hotel*. Michael even sold his home and moved into his hotel, ostensibly to be where the action was. He must owe a nice capital gain.

The Hotel Syracuse was sold in February 1996 as part of a self-imposed drive to liquidate assets to pay off bank loans. Patrick, however, diverted the sale proceeds to fuel the Ponzi and defer mass resignation of certain key employees who had recently uncovered the double-pledging of leases.

The purchaser, Allegro Property, was a subsidiary of a public corporation traded on the Vancouver Stock Exchange, coincidentally(?!) named Equivest International Financial Corp. The purchase price for the hotel was $18,010,000. Allegro paid net $1.4 million cash ($0.4 million in adjustments). The Company took back a $16.2 million mortgage to consolidate the approximately $20 million debt owed from M. A. Bennett, the holding company of the hotel, and paid $10,000 cash to Michael.

The $10,000 was used to purchase about four thousand shares of Equivest International Financial Corp. Immediately after the filing of the Bennett bankruptcy petition, the stock of the public corporation plummeted and the shares were worthless.

Coopers & Lybrand discovered that Allegro had an undisclosed standing relationship with Patrick before the sale. The trustee sued to gain
control of the Hotel Syracuse based on a fraudulent conveyance theory.

According to papers filed by Simpson Thacher, Bennett Management
owned 2.1 million of the 7.4 million outstanding shares of Equivest International Financial Corp., as of October 25, 1995. The lawyers stated the
president of Allegro advised them that Bennett Management "sold its 2.1
million shares in Equivest . . . in January 1996 so that the . . . [sale] would
not be a related-party transaction."

The attorneys further went on to say that the "sale of the stock was
never consummated, but . . . placed in escrow pending the satisfaction
of certain promissory notes given to [Bennett Management] by the
purchasers."

As Allegro disputed the trustee's allegations, Judge Gerling found
a genuine factual issue and did not grant summary judgment on this
issue but found it "immaterial to the ultimate question of actual intent
[to defraud]."

In granting summary judgment to the trustee, the Bankruptcy Court
noted the transfer was made "with actual intent to hinder, delay and defraud the Company's creditors."[4]

As a result of Judge Gerling's decision, the trustee was given a mortgage on the hotel, albeit much lower than the outstanding balance owed
the Company. When Allegro balked at making payment, the trustee filed
for foreclosure. Eventually, Allegro came up with the juice and averted
the inevitable. At least half of the value of the inflated investment was
lost.

In September 1994, Patrick incorporated Bennett Associates, Inc., a
New York corporation. He held every position and was the sole shareholder. Bennett Associates entered into a long-term ground lease with
Mid-State Raceway, the corporate owner of Vernon Downs, for the purpose of constructing a Comfort Suites hotel alongside the racetrack.

The hotel was patterned after the Sky Dome Hotel at the Blue Jays'
ballpark in Toronto. Patrons could watch races and make wagers in the
comfort of their rooms.

The hotel was also a short drive from the Turning Stone Casino,
owned and operated by the Oneida Nation. The hotel did fairly well until the Oneida's built their on-site hotel.

In December 1995, the name of the corporation was changed to Comfort Associates, Inc. About that time, Comfort Associates entered into a

$8 million line of credit agreement with High Mountain Associates, a partnership directed by Charles Genovese.

Although the records are not clear as to the exact amount, Patrick, through Comfort Associates, accessed the line and borrowed at least several million dollars. To secure the line of credit, the corporation mortgaged the hotel to High Mountain, subject to the rights of the lessor, Mid-State, in the ground lease. Bennett Funding also pledged to High Mountain its payee rights to an outstanding promissory note from another Bennett corporate borrower.

As all of the corporate name changing, loans, promissory pledging, and mortgaging were transpiring, Patrick quietly transferred the shares of Comfort Associates to Gwen. Gwen did not give contemporaneous consideration for the shares spawning suits to control the shares.

After the Bennett bankruptcy petitions were filed, the Genovese faction claimed funds were advanced under the line of credit agreement but remained unpaid. Under the terms and conditions of the mortgage and note, Comfort Associates was in default. Accordingly, title to the hotel should be transferred to High Mountain.

"Not so fast," cried the trustee. Inasmuch as construction financing and other costs for the Comfort Suites emanated from Bennett Management to the tune of $8.5 million, the trustee laid siege to the hotel as well.

The homestretch at Vernon Downs with the Comfort Suites in the background. Photo by Jim Commentucci. Copyright © The Syracuse Newspapers.

As Charles pleaded guilty to the various charges of perjury and con-spiracy, the High Mountain mortgage will be equitably subordinated to the interests of the Bennett creditors.

Just before the bankruptcy, the Bennetts had their sights on a sprawl-ing hotel complex at Alexandria Bay, New York, and several Doral Hotels in New York City. I shudder to think of the skullduggery those acquisi-tions would have spawned had the bankruptcy not nixed the Bennetts' plans.

A Tale of Two Companies

IN SEPTEMBER 1988, the Thing Corporation purchased a building on route 31 in the town of Cicero.[1] Cicero lies somewhat north of Syra-cuse. Route 31 is the main road in the area and sees fairly heavy traffic.

Thing paid $125,000 for the building. Two months after the purchase, Thing raised $175,000 by mortgaging the property to a local bank.

In 1995, Thing leased the property to a partnership named First-N-Goal to operate a pizzeria and deli. First-N-Goal had pool tables, video games, provided fast food and drink, and from all accounts was a fun place to hang out.

Steven Bodnar and his brother-in-law were listed as partners in First-N-Goal.[2] Patrick Bennett was the president of the Thing Corporation. Tony Menchella was the vice president. Bodnar was involved with Menchella in another deli venture, the defunct P.T.'s Shortstop. Bodnar was also seen by the witness heaving boxes into the bonfire at Patrick's Toad Harbor residence. At the time, Bodnar's brother-in-law gave his ad-dress as Shaw Road, the same street as Toad Harbor.

Cellular Enterprises, Ltd., was incorporated in 1981. From a review of the records, it appears the corporation was started by Bud but was never energized and remained dormant—a shelf corporation. Four years later, to avoid the expense of incorporation, Cellular was dusted off, its certifi-cate of incorporation amended, and its name changed to Standardbred Enterprises, Ltd.

At the time of the name change, the shares of Standardbred were owned by Patrick and a cache of his horse-racing buddies. Standard-bred's professed business was brokering leases for horse-training equipment and trailers through Aloha Leasing. For its efforts, Standardbred received commissions in excess of $80,000. Standardbred was paid an additional $7,000 in commissions as late as March 27, 1996, only one day before the SEC lawsuit.[3]

Patrick also used Standardbred to purchase income-producing properties. In May 1989, the Thing Corporation purchased another parcel of land on route 31 for $220,000. Six days later, Thing mortgaged the property back to the seller for $340,000. Four months later, in September 1989, Thing borrowed another $100,000 from a local bank, which placed a second mortgage on the property.

In September 1991, Thing's mortgage to the original seller of the property was assigned to Standardbred. On that same date, Thing's second mortgage to the local bank was also assigned to Standardbred.

In January 1993, Thing deeded the second parcel to Standardbred for $1.00 plus the payoff of the assigned mortgages of $440,000. The source of the funds Standardbred used to make the real estate transactions was also traced to Bennett Management.

Standardbred was also the vehicle Patrick used to gain control of Vernon Downs through the purchase of a majority position in Mid-State Raceway, Inc., the public company that owns and operates the racetrack. Over six years, Patrick used more than $4 million from Bennett Management filtered through Standardbred to make his purchase of the Mid-State shares.[4]

"The racetrack, built deep in the countryside between Syracuse and Utica in 1953 when harness racing was a booming sport, is a pale gray oval three-quarters of a mile around, flanked on one side by gentle green hills and on the other by a sprawl of low white buildings that include an enclosed grandstand, a clubhouse and offices. Below these buildings is a series of stables that can hold almost 1,000 horses."[5]

Through buy-sell agreements among the shareholders, Gwen Bennett eventually obtained a controlling interest in Standardbred. Court documents indicate that in December 1995, Patrick transferred the remaining 126,657 shares of Mid-State to Standardbred, now Gwen's corporation. The consideration for the transfer of the shares was a $1.95 million note. The note provided for annual interest payments $195,000, commencing the following year and was to mature in December 1999.

Since the sale of the shares, which severed his ownership ties with the track, Patrick has been seen watching the horses and working at concession and food stands at various events and concerts.

One of Gwen's major decisions was to appoint her former employer at the Squat and Gobble to the board of directors of Mid-State. Squat, a favorite watering hole of horse people, is the tavern where Gwen once waitressed and met Patrick.

On March 1, 1996, twenty-eight days before the bankruptcy, Patrick sold and assigned his right and interest in the Standardbred note to N. W. Investors, equal to the face amount of $1.95 million. N. W. Investors is a limited liability company managed by longtime Bennett associate Neal Wager.

In June 1996, N. W. Investors notified Standardbred the loan was being accelerated because of a default triggered by Standardbred's purported insolvency. To induce N. W. Investors to forbear exercising its rights as the holder of the $1.95 million note, Standardbred executed a security and escrow agreement. The forbearance arrangement mandated that the Mid-State shares would be held by escrow agents for the benefit of N. W. Investors.

In April 1997, N. W. Investors notified Standardbred of the occurrence of an event of default under the escrow agreement because of its failure to make an interest payment the preceding month.

When Standardbred and the escrow agent refused to tender the shares, N. W. Investors filed suit in Supreme Court of Nassau County (Long Island). Breeden intervened in the action and was successful in removing it before Judge Gerling.

Sometime after the removal, N. W. Investors filed a motion for summary judgment suggesting it had an unfettered right to the stock certificates representing the Mid-State shares because of the default. The trustee's counsel successfully fended off the attack because the initial sale of the shares from Patrick to Standardbred "reeked" with fraud and other improprieties.[6] Wager's alleged payment of $1.95 million for the Standardbred note was also suspect.

Stemming out of Charles Genovese's testimony during Patrick's trial in January 1999, and shortly before Judge Gerling's decision was rendered concerning the Standardbred shares, Wager, 53, of Garden City, was accused by the Justice Department of conjuring documents relative to the Erie Islands note as well as conspiring with and helping to orchestrate Patrick and Michael Bennetts' and Charles Genovese's systematic assault against the SEC.

A criminal complaint was filed against Wager on January 22, 1999, in the southern district of New York.[7] As of this writing, Wager is defending against the charges.

Over the years, through Standardbred and Comfort Associates, Patrick diverted more than $12 million from Bennett Management to prop up his position in Mid-State.

It has been said Patrick paid an inflated price for the Mid-State shares. It has been said Patrick floated Mid-State through cash infusions from Bennett companies' sponsored races. It has been said horse racing corrupted him.

Did the smell of freshly groomed track dirt mixed with manure, horse sweat, and the perspiration of jockeys intoxicate Patrick and compel him to take the quantum leap from patronage to ownership?

Did the sheen of silks and the names emblazoned on winner's circle blankets, the look of well-worked racing forms and spent betting tickets, the sounds of screaming gamblers urging their picks, the easy booze, and the feel of living large compel him to excess?

Can a need to feed a horse habit explain his actions—a habit perhaps so strong that the allure of horseflesh can prove more tempting than a woman?

The Insurance Fronts

CIGNA INSURANCE COMPANY offered the same credit default insurance program to Bennett Funding as did its successor, Generali. The coverage was in effect from 1984 until cancellation in 1986. CIGNA, however, was obligated to pay Bennett Funding on any insured lease that defaulted as long as the premium was paid before cancellation. Inasmuch as many of the leases ran five years, coverage was effective through 1991 for the portfolio in existence at the time of the cancellation in 1986.

In 1990, CIGNA stopped paying Bennett Funding on claims it had been paying, in some cases, for years. Failing to achieve an acceptable resolution of the abrupt nonpayment, the Company sued CIGNA, alleging breach of contract and bad faith.[1]

CIGNA counterclaimed alleging three broad violations of its contract of insurance with Bennett Funding. First, CIGNA claimed it mistakenly paid on municipal leases because the Company did not get proper notices of nonappropriation from the municipalities in question. Nonappropriation is a method by which municipalities can cancel leases for the ensuing year if payments are not allocated for the lease in the annual budget.

Second, CIGNA suggested the Company filed claims on defaulted leases with related parties or Bennett-controlled companies without disclosing to CIGNA the relationship between lessor and lessee.

Third, CIGNA alleged the Company did not tender collected amounts or the value of repossessed equipment on defaulted leases on which CIGNA paid insurance proceeds in the normal course.

The Company denied CIGNA's allegations, because audits conducted by agents of CIGNA did not reveal the alleged improprieties at the time. In fact, the allegations did not surface until CIGNA enticed Bennett to meet with a view toward settlement of all claims in one lump sum just before it stopped paying in 1990.

The Company claimed it acted properly regarding its handling of municipal defaults and had sufficient documentation to support the filed claims.

The Company further argued the insurance contract did not require related-party dealings to be disclosed. Although it was perhaps not wise to file claims on leases in which the lessor controlled the purse strings, the Company was not legally prohibited from so doing.

The third allegation that the Company was hoarding reimbursement for payments received on collections was plain wrong. During the relationship, the Company tendered hundreds of thousands of dollars in collected funds to CIGNA. Moreover, although it was contractually permitted to recoup costs incurred in collection efforts and keep a contingency fee of one-third of all sums collected, all such amounts were never withheld but tendered to CIGNA.

In the course of the litigation, the Company did acknowledge it had repossessed equipment from a lessee from Texas, kept it, but failed to properly credit the value of the equipment to CIGNA's account. Other than this, there is no evidence the Company withheld the value of repossessed items from CIGNA.

The Texas lease story is interesting. In early 1985, Bennett Funding entered into several large-ticket equipment leases with the Craig Germain Company. The parties also entered into a credit agreement in which the Company agreed to lend Germain up to $1.3 million. The leases and loan agreement were guaranteed by Craig Germain individually and ten other subsidiary and affiliate corporations. The leases and the credit agreement contractually placed jurisdiction and venue in Syracuse, New York.

After the deal was consummated, the equipment delivered and installed, and $800,000 paid under the loan, Germain failed to make monthly lease payments and loan repayments. The Bennetts were angry and demanded action be taken immediately.

I commenced action on September 9, 1985, in New York. About one week later Germain commenced an independent action in Texas, claiming Bennett Funding breached the loan agreement by failing to pay the remaining money due under the credit agreement.

Germain retained the venerable New York City firm Cadwalader, Wickersham & Taft, which retained Bond, Schoeneck & King, to serve as local counsel to defend the New York federal action. Shortly after their involvement, the megafirms filed a motion to change venue of the proceeding to Texas.

Such a move would have been disastrous to the Company. We simply could not risk a Texas court applying Texas law in an action involving a "homey." We could not afford having all of the Company's key officers testifying ad nauseum so far from home. Nor could we afford the cost of retaining local trial counsel, and the attendant expenses for travel, food, and lodging for the witnesses.

Talk about David and Goliath—the minions of Cadwalader Wickersham Taft Bond Schoeneck King versus twenty-nine-year-old Stewie Weisman. Enlisting the help of Kenneth Bobrycki of Melvin and Melvin, we prevailed.

Federal Judge Munson denied the venue change. He opined that where, as here, the contract between two sophisticated corporate entities has a venue provision, such a provision will be upheld absent special circumstances that were not present in this case.[2]

Through the efforts of local Texas counsel Kelly Akins, formerly of Gardere & Wynn, we were able to repossess most of the leased equipment. Although Germain's business practices were the subject of litigation, his taste in office art was superb.

The Bennetts became the Medicis of Syracuse with paintings, antique furniture, oriental carpets, and other appointments. Eventually, Germain filed bankruptcy and we never heard from him again.

Because of the intensity of the CIGNA litigation, heightened competition in the leasing and campground arenas, and the SEC investigation, it was decided to sweep the offices for bugs. The players we dealt with had the money and clout to plant bugs. AMRIC Associates,[3] a private investigative firm owned by the former regional director of the FBI, was hired and swept the executive offices and phones. No bugs were found.

After battling with CIGNA for a while, Bennett Funding offered to reconcile the lease portfolio, adjust some figures, and pay CIGNA, assuming the reconciliation was in its favor, even if the payment was in the millions.

To foster settlement, Bud decided to enlist F. Lee Bailey, whom he met while their yachts were docked alongside at the Bahamas. As F. Lee was just getting involved with the O. J. Simpson matter, he recommended the services of his lesser-known but equally well-connected brother, at least in insurance circles, Bill Bailey. When CIGNA found out we were represented by the Bailey brothers, it flipped out.

"They must be hiding something," thundered the response to settlement overtures.[4] CIGNA was going to teach the Bennetts a lesson. CIGNA wanted all of its claim money returned, which was paid out for five years and then some. The suit continued.

The CIGNA litigation was pending as of the filing of the bankruptcy petition and stopped dead in its tracks. It is doubtful whether any of the issues raised in the litigation will be resolved.

CIGNA did not make one dime on the suit from the Bennetts but paid large attorneys' fees to its local counsel, Hancock & Estabrook. In the Bennett bankruptcy proceeding, many banks have taken the same position as CIGNA's: they would rather fight than settle. Hancock also represents many of the fighting banks in the Bennett bankruptcy. It seems that the firm had the Bennetts' fraudulent tendencies pegged years before the public revelation.

My view on settlement is simple. If someone owes money and is willing to pay a substantial piece, take the money and run. Too many things can and do go wrong during litigation. You can lose. You can get awarded a lesser sum than the settlement offered. Your adversary can file bankruptcy. Another judgment can sneak in ahead. Star witnesses die, change their testimony, or become otherwise unavailable.

Sometimes in actions in which people's rights are violated, such as in discrimination suits, attorneys are placed into positions in which their instincts tell them a proposed settlement is fair but the client wants her rights vindicated before a jury in a court of law.

An attorney has a duty to exercise professional independent judgment and strongly recommend settlement if it is in the client's best interest. Yet, despite the risks and the feel of money in hand, a client has a right to go all the way. At that time, an attorney must weigh heavily whether to continue the representation or recommend new counsel be retained. It is a tough decision and should be made on a case-by-case basis. The Bennett lease litigation never rose to that level, however.

After CIGNA departed, the Company went many years without credit insurance for its lease products. It seems the insurance coverage was a large carrot that ensnared many an investor.

"You know, I bought those damn leases because the broker said they were insured. So where's the insurance money?"

No doubt during this lean period the Company had trouble unloading its product. This, along with the campground debacle, probably served, in part, as the genesis for the creative accounting, the double-pledging, and some of the other nefarious activities that kept the Company afloat.

Finally, in 1990, after four years without the ability to offer insurance for new Bennett financial products, Patrick was able to secure default insurance through Assicurazioni Generali S.p.A., Generali U.S. Branch. This was accomplished with the help of Pat Bowling, a longtime Bennett associate and insurance broker from the Pacific Northwest.

In all, from 1990 to 1994, eleven policies were entered into between Generali and Bennett Funding for equipment leases, and Resort Funding for membership agreements.[5]

The Generali/Bennett insurance program was different in kind and scope from most such default insurance programs. In typical deals, the investor or a third-party trustee is named as the loss payee on the insurance declaration. The declaration is the controlling document and evidences an insured's interest in the policy.

In the Generali program, however, the loss payees were other Bennett companies, such as the Processing Center, not the individual investors. To give the investors the impression they were covered by one of the Generali policies, Patrick sent investors copies of insurance certificates bearing the investors' names.

In fact, the insurance policies were devoid of any mechanism for any individual investor to make a claim for payment. According to the trustee's counsel, "The structure made such a claim impossible to administer."

Under the Generali policies, the leases and membership agreements themselves that were purchased by the investors were not insured against default or nonperformance. Instead, the leases and agreements were placed into collateral pools. A separate declaration of insurance for each pool was issued by Generali. The declaration would reference an attached list of the leases and agreements that made up each pool, and was referred to as equipment loan registers. The declaration would then bear the name of one of the Bennett companies or a Bennett broker as loss payee.

In the initial policies, Generali's obligation to pay was triggered by a shortfall in payments received from leases and membership agreements listed in the various insured pools and the amounts due to investors who purchased those leases and agreements or whose investment was collateralized by them.

Thus, contrary to what the investors must have thought they purchased, the nonpayment of any lease or agreement did not trigger a claim against Generali. Such a claim was colorable only when the aggregate nonpayment of the entire pool created a deficiency between the amounts due from lessees and members and the amounts due to investors.

In essence, the policies forced investors to share the risk with other investors in the same pool. These investors had no more in common than their respective leases and agreements, which were listed in an attachment to the declaration for that pool.

Even if such a shortfall occurred, the payment would be made to the Bennett company named as the loss payee, not to the individual investor.

After some policies were in effect, Generali changed the program. Besides the shortfall requirement in the pools, the new policies provided coverage when Bennett Funding itself also failed to make the payments due to the investors.

Arguably, the trustee claimed, the double trigger evidenced Generali's direct or imputed knowledge that Patrick was engaged in a Ponzi scheme. It was reasoned if a lease is double-pledged, only one payment can be made by the lessee. In a pool concept, necessarily, a continuing shortfall would occur between the amounts due to investors and the amounts received from lessees because payment would flow into one pool at the expense of another pool.

The "second trigger" to initiate the claims procedure—when Bennett Funding itself failed to make the payments due to the investors—according to the trustee, "shielded Generali from such claims as long as the Ponzi scheme continued."

In other words, so long as Patrick paid the investors from whatever source derived, no claims could be filed because the double trigger was not tripped.

As a condition to entering into the default insurance policies, Generali made Bennett Funding execute an indemnification agreement. The indemnification agreement provided in the event Generali did pay claims, the Company agreed to reimburse Generali for any such expenditures.

To secure the indemnification agreement, the Company put up a $1 million certificate of deposit (CD) in the name of Generali at Chemical Bank. Actuaries aside, with the double trigger mechanism, the indemnification agreement, and the $1 million CD in place, Generali's was to be insurance without risk.

Claiming it was getting out of the credit default insurance business, Generali terminated the policies in 1994. By that time, Generali insured approximately $79 million value of leases.

When claims were finally filed after Bennett Funding's collapse in March 1996, Generali reneged on paying Bennett Funding or the investors. Accordingly, the trustee and the class action counsel brought separate suits.

Just as the appetizing but fraudulently produced financial statements were crucial to the continuation of Patrick's scheme, so too was the default insurance offered by Generali.

As stated in Bankruptcy Court documents filed by the trustee, "The fact that the various investments were purportedly insured by one of the world's largest and most reputable insurance companies induced thousands of investors and others to invest their money in the various financial instruments sold or pledged by the Debtors."[6]

Generali did not roll over. It claimed, among other things, the eleven policies were unenforceable because Generali itself was defrauded by the Bennetts.

In a separate development about one year after the suits were commenced, the superintendent of insurance of New York secured $1 million in penalties against Generali for its failure to be licensed to engage in credit/default insurance in the first instance.

Then, in August 1998, about two years after the actions were commenced, it was announced the trustee, class action counsel, and Generali reached a settlement whereby the insurance giant will pay $125 million to be administered through the Bennett bankruptcy.

This amount does not include interest that has been accruing, according to the terms of the settlement, at about $17,000 per day from October 1998 through the actual payment after all approvals have been received.

The stipulation of settlement was formally documented and signed on December 21, 1998.[7] The trustee filed a motion to approve the settlement before Judge Gerling. Class action counsel filed a companion motion in the U.S. District Court for the Southern District of New York, which has jurisdiction over the class action cases.

If the fee portion of the settlement is approved, class action counsel will receive 23 percent of the first $75 million, 21 percent of the next $40 million, and 18 percent of the rest, a fee equal to $27,450,000. Breeden will receive 3 percent of the remainder. It is not clear from the documents whether the per diem interest is figured into the fee structure, although I suspect it is. Simpson Thacher will receive fees upward of $2 million commensurate with hours devoted to the matter, subject to application and approval by Judge Gerling.

Because the trustee and the class action counsel entered into a joint prosecution agreement against another insurer, Sphere Drake, and accountants, Mahoney Cohen, attorneys' fees for recoveries in those actions will be limited to a flat 18 percent.

In a letter sent to the investors in early January, Breeden urged the investors to approve the terms of the Generali settlement, including and especially the attorney's fees:

> In looking at the issue of the class counsel's fee requests, one has to start with the accepted system in place for many years throughout the United States. While, many of us might question whether 33% is an appropriate award for a contingency fee, that question is no easier than saying whether it is justifiable for someone to make $15–35 million per year playing basketball, or $100 million for a baseball contract. The market sets such standards, not political processes. Thus, the bottom line for me was that I could not disregard the risk that the Estate alone might win a much lower recovery, and also that if we worked with them but had no agreement, class counsel might be awarded a 33% fee, or perhaps even more.[8]

In a strong condemnation of the fees to be paid to professionals under the Generali settlement, the Official Committee of Unsecured Creditors noted, "[I]f all of the fees, expenses and commissions were allowed by the courts, more than *$34,000,000.00* could be deducted from the Generali proceeds!"[9] The committee urged the investors to write to Judge Sprizzo—who presides over the class action—and protest the proposed fees. The judge received about 1,500 letters.

After several hearings on the matter, Judge Gerling approved the terms of the settlement but stated that "any substantive ruling on the class counsels' entitlement to fees would be an unwarranted interference in the work of the district court." He denied that part of the motion dealing with approval of attorneys' fees inherent in the settlement agreement.[10]

In mid-1997, in an unrelated matter, it was discovered Generali carried many life insurance policies on victims of the Holocaust.[11] After intense negotiations championed, in part, by former senator Al D'Amato, Generali agreed to pay upward of $65 million to settle claims by Holocaust survivors. I guess the living victims are worth more than the dead ones.

After Generali canceled the policies with Bennett Funding, the Company took swift steps to make sure it would not be left in the lurch and be able to offer credit insurance to its investor base. To that end, Bennett Funding started its own insurance company in Bermuda, called Bennett Insurance Company. Later, the name was changed to Capital Insurance.

Capital Insurance is known as a "captive" insurance company, as it did not possess sufficient assets to pay on claims. Captives rely on a fully capitalized reinsurance company that would ultimately pay on filed claims. This was accomplished in October 1994 with Sphere Drake Insurance, PLC, one of the world's leading reinsurance companies. Ultimately, Sphere Drake reinsured about $130 million of leases. Its insurance program was materially like Generali's.[12]

But don't let its pedigree fool you. As with Generali, Sphere Drake made Bennett Funding execute a hold harmless and indemnification agreement and has reneged on paying on claims. Even Sphere Drake's counsel noted, "the existence of a Hold Harmless Agreement between Generali and Bennett . . . or . . . between Sphere Drake and [Bennett] brings into question the very nature of the insurance arrangement and whether it would withstand scrutiny as a bona fide insurance arrangement."

The counsel went on to state, "each of the policy forms . . . requires . . . payments to loss payees, even if the default is brought about by fraudulent act of [Bennett]. There is the potential of a problem under state law, to the extent that some states would find it against public policy to permit insurance for fraudulent acts."

In an attempt to divert attention that the certificate of insurance "be in any way interpreted as a direct contract," on the part of Sphere Drake, its counsel recommended the word "confirmation" be substituted for "certificate,"[13] like the Monty Python skit in which a dog license was altered to read "halibut" license.

In 1998, Sphere Drake changed its name to Odyssey Re London Limited. As depositions, interrogatories, motions, and subpoenas fly, negotiations are under way to resolve the parties' differences. As of this writing, no concord has been reached.

In the early 1980s, Harvey Zelin, an enterprising businessman from Missouri, placed an advertisement in the *Wall Street Journal.* Harvey was looking for leasing contacts to help finance his company, Comp-Tech Manufacturing Company, Inc.

Comp-Tech, headquartered in St. Louis, manufactured pulse meters. The pulse meters were coin-operated devices that measured a person's pulse, which were just becoming fashionable at the time.

Bud read the ad and contacted Harvey. As part of the "due diligence" review, Bud flew to St. Louis, met Harvey, and toured his factory. After the visit, the Company entered into a long-term relationship with Comp-Tech. Bud and Harvey became business associates and friends.

Over the years the Company entered into sale-leaseback transactions with Comp-Tech for various types of vending machines, worth about $10 million. Sale-leasebacks are financing transactions in which a manufacturer sells equipment to a leasing company, which, in turn, leases the equipment back to the manufacturer.

In sale-leaseback transactions, the manufacturer merely pays a security deposit and the first month's rent but keeps the full purchase price paid by the leasing company. Over time, it makes incremental monthly payments under the lease. It is a favored method of raising capital employed by manufacturers and vendors.

After the sale-leaseback agreement is in place, the manufacturer is then free to sublease the equipment to third-party lessees. The subleases, the equipment, and the stream of payments from those subleases are generally assigned to the leasing company as security to insure the payments on the master lease with the manufacturer. Sometimes the manufacturer services the subleases, sometimes the leasing company.

Not long after Bud and Harvey shook hands, a group of about sixty investors, in the Chicago area, purchased Comp-Tech pulse meter leases through their tax advisers, Brennan and Morris. These were not part of a sale-leaseback arrangement but independent transactions.

Unlike the standard deals the Company put together, the relationship between Bennett Funding and the Chicago investors was different. In the Chicago case, Bennett helped the pulse-lease transactions along by supplying lease forms to Comp-Tech and procuring credit insurance on the pulse leases through Rockford Insurance of Illinois, a short-term precursor to CIGNA.

The pulse leases, mostly, were between Comp-Tech and the individual Chicago investor. Most did not even mention Bennett Funding. The records indicate Comp-Tech was responsible for remitting payments directly to the investors, not through Bennett Funding. For each lease transaction, Bennett Funding received a commission. In essence, Bennett Funding acted as a facilitator, not as a lessor.

The pulse-machine investments and the Bennett/Comp-Tech sale-leasebacks paid like clockwork for years. Then, one day, without warning, Comp-Tech stopped paying the investors on the pulse-machine leases and stopped paying Bennett Funding on the sale-leasebacks. Despite Zelin's professed friendship with Bud, he never advised why he stopped paying.

Soon after the money dried up, Comp-Tech was thrown into involuntary bankruptcy by a group of Missouri creditors who weren't receiving payments either. We retained local counsel to shepherd us through.

The Comp-Tech sale-leaseback transactions were default insured by CIGNA. The insurer wound up paying the policy cap for any single claim of $2 million to the Company. Because of the large payout, CIGNA hired its own firm to police the Comp-Tech bankruptcy and audited Bennett Funding's books and records concerning the Comp-Tech transactions. CIGNA paid despite all of this attention. In CIGNA's suit with Bennett Funding, it claimed the Company cheated them on this deal as well.

During the Comp-Tech bankruptcy, a creditor performed self-help by seizing equipment in the field and exercising dominion over the vending routes. He was charged with bankruptcy fraud, like the charges against Ken Kasarjian and Patrick relating to the destruction of the $5 million line of credit note.

Sometime after the Comp-Tech bankruptcy, the Chicago investors filed suit against Bennett Funding and Brennan and Morris.[14] They alleged Bennett Funding was more than a facilitator, that it was in cahoots with Comp-Tech and had direct recourse liability. I called our retained Missouri firm, seeking a recommendation for counsel in Chicago.

"Michael O'Rourke from Winston & Strawn," was the response. Winston & Strawn[15] is a megafirm headquartered in Chicago. Michael O'Rourke was a senior litigator with the firm. He agreed to defend the Company.

After a series of early Bennett victories that dismissed portions of the complaint and fended off an attempt to impound insurance proceeds from Rockford, the litigation hunkered down.

To avoid the mounting legal fees, we offered to settle the case for $300,000. The reply was, "Nuts." I do not know whether the opposing counsel felt he was General McAuliffe at the Battle of Bostogne, but his response was immature and rude.

A couple of years into the litigation, O'Rourke left Winston & Strawn with a few other lawyers, and they opened their own shop. As I developed personal relationships with counsel, not with firms, I allowed him to take the file. The litigation rolled on. Depositions in Syracuse and Chicago were conducted. Demands for discovery of documents were exchanged. Our final offer of $500,000 was met with a counteroffer of $800,000. Both were rejected.

Eventually, the trial was set for October 1995, just before the double-pledging of leases was uncovered. I flew to Chicago. O'Rourke, a Harvard-Oxford graduate, was in Tiananmen Square sightseeing just before the student protest crackdown. He put me up at his house.

Trying to settle the case one last time before trial, the judge spoke with all parties. I had authority to go to $750,000. The amount was high, but it was anticipated the trial would last for months. The Company needed to avoid the costs and tremendous inconvenience of a prolonged trial. Moreover, we were concerned a New York corporation accused of defrauding local investors may not play well before a Chicago jury, which had been some of the same concerns in the Germain matter.

During the litigation, the sixty-odd plaintiffs selected a committee to speak for the group. The committee, however, seemed to consist of one woman who was a friend, neighbor, or former client of the partner prosecuting the claim.

Inasmuch as this was not a class action, we had complained vociferously about the committee. We argued against placing control of settlement discussions in the hands of one or a few people whose interests may be inimical to the group as a whole. The judge agreed in part and required the committee to dutifully advise all members of proposed settlements.

As we had previously offered $500,000 and the plaintiffs counter-offered at $800,000 to settle, the judge asked if the parties would split the baby and pay $650,000. I agreed.

"The committee will take $700,000," opposing counsel announced. The judge looked at me.

"Your Honor, 650 is the best and final offer," I responded, confident that the amount would be palatable. O'Rourke and his partner Mike Moody just sat back and watched the exchange. The plaintiffs' lawyer left chambers allegedly to consult with the committee.

After returning, the lawyer said, "No dice, Your Honor, let's go to trial." "The greedy bastard," I thought, and dug in at the $650,000 figure.

As we entered the courtroom, plaintiffs' counsel made an announcement. "Your Honor, the plaintiffs have decided to discontinue the action."

Everyone in the courtroom was flabbergasted. O'Rourke sprang to his feet. "Judge, this is outrageous. We have spent weeks preparing for this case and my clients have spent tons of money. As recently as yesterday they gave us no indication they were going to do this. We want some kind of sanction imposed."

"Your Honor," opposing counsel said. "We have a right to discontinue the action, plain and simple." That was it. Whatever plan they had in mind had better been worth it, because the lawyers rejected $650,000.

We went back to O'Rourke's office[16] and celebrated. I called Syracuse and relayed the news. Even Bud was happy. O'Rourke drafted a proposed order containing sanctions. Although the judge did not give us all we wanted he did impose a penalty.

A few weeks later, we were served with a brand-new complaint, which sought new causes of action based on developments and rulings during the former litigation. It probably would have been tossed anyway; the Bennett bankruptcy short-circuited the matter.

Late during the Chicago litigation, while reviewing documents in preparation for trial, O'Rourke came across commission statements payable to JB Vending in Syracuse. It seemed that for every pulse-machine lease, JB Vending received a small commission of $75–$100. He asked me what the statements were about. I had no idea. I asked Patrick who JB was.

"Joe Bodnar," he replied flatly. Joe Bodnar, the brother of box-burning Steven Bodnar, was Patrick's longtime friend. Joe was also one of the cooks at the Company's annual clambake.

"What's JB Vending?" I asked.

"It's his vending company," Pat responded, his voice growing taut. Then I asked the $64,000 question.

"Why is JB getting commissions on the Comp-Tech deals?"

"Because he is consulting on the job," Patrick said, and ended the conversation.

The pulse machines and other coin-operated machines were placed in retail stores in designated routes in Missouri. JB was located in Syracuse. Although the arrangement made no sense at the time, the matter was insignificant relative to the millions invested in Comp-Tech by the Company and the investors. I did not pursue it.

Upon reflection there was no legitimate reason why Bodnar's company would have been involved in the Missouri coin-operated routes, especially because they were serviced by local businesses. The commissions were paid in the early and mid-1980s, well before any need was spawned. It was just greed.

During the Chicago litigation, Harvey Zelin was indicted for federal crimes and served a sentence. Joe Bodnar died.

Endless Troubles

STATISTICALLY, the Grand Canyon National Park is impressive.[1] Earning National Park status on February 26, 1919, the park spreads over 1,218,375 acres, about 1,904 square miles. The canyon proper is 277 miles from Lees Ferry to Grand Wash Cliffs. The Colorado River, which rushes at the bottom, is 1,450 miles long, originating in the Rocky Mountains and flowing into the Gulf of Mexico.

The canyon's greatest depth is six thousand feet and greatest width is eighteen miles. Park officials log about 5 million visitors each year.

Sara and I visited Grand Canyon in the summer of 1993. In preparation for the visit we looked at photographs of the canyon taken by people who explored by foot, by helicopter, by mule, and by raft down the Colorado River.

But nothing prepared us or could prepare anyone for an actual visit. To see, hear, smell, feel, and taste the Grand Canyon is different in kind from reading about it in books or viewing it in cyberspace.

The day we visited, the sky at the South Rim was clear and blue with piercing rays. People off-loading from busses and cars milled about pointing and gawking down into and across the canyon.

Holding hands, Sara and I inched toward the edge and beheld the most magnificent of vistas. As President Theodore Roosevelt noted, "In the Grand Canyon, Arizona has a natural wonder, which, so far as I know, is in kind absolutely unparalleled throughout the rest of the world."

We beheld layer upon layer of colored rocks dancing with the changing light of the shimmering summer sun: black Archean, crimson Algonkian, lavender-brown Tapeats sandstone, lavender Devonian, red sandstone of the Supai formation, red Hermit shale, pale pink sand-colored Coconino sandstone, and cream and gray Kaibab limestone. Truly, Grand Canyon was carved by the hand of God.

Gentle winds tickled our faces and filled our nostrils with an admixture of attars from desert cacti, delphinium, white thistle, poppy, scarlet bugle, prickly pears, blue spruce, and Douglas fir.

Although I was with Sara, my soul mate, the Grand Canyon beckoned me to join with it, to become one. I took the leap of faith.

I became the pink-hued rattlesnake lying camouflaged in the crags of sandstone. I became the molecules of desert sand suspended and quivering in 120°F heated air. I ran free with bighorn sheep, mountain lion, and mule deer. I became the Colorado River tearing through the canyon and carving yet deeper into the bed as it had for the last 6 million years. I walked among the ancient Anasazi, whose structures are but ruins today.

I solemnly promised to fulfill Roosevelt's naturalist prayer to, "keep [the Grand Canyon] for your children, your children's children, and for all who come after you, as the one great site every American . . . should see."

Oh, but my reverie was snapped when I heard a child ask, "Mommy, can we go now?"

About four hours after leaving Grand Canyon, we arrived at the Phoenician Resort in Scottsdale, just outside Phoenix, Arizona. Nestled at the foot of Camelback Mountain, the Phoenician[2] was billed at the time as the "world's finest resort."

The resort is spread over 130 acres. It has 605 "guest quarters," and 60,000 square feet set aside for meetings. Boasting a $25 million art collection, the Phoenician has a 5,300 square-foot multimedia theater and state-of-the-art communication system. The concierges are fluent in many languages.

Sara and I stayed in a casita, part of a web of 131 guest houses linked to complete the circular design of the main hotel. Our ritual was to get up early before the oppression of the sun started in earnest, have coffee, and walk the grounds. Waterfalls and gushing fountains flaunted the desert.

One did not simply dine at the Phoenician. One descends the central marble staircase to the gourmet restaurants. With light refracting from Italian chandeliers and music wafting from a Steinway grand, eating itself becomes performance art.

The Phoenician showstopper is the swimming complex, a triad of pools residing on three interlinked tiers. The main Olympic-size pool is completely tiled with mother-of-pearl inlay, which radiates an oasis of prismatic colors.

The pool's water is cooled through an elaborate aeration system guised as a cascade. Swimming lap after lap became obsessive because of the sensation of cool water splashing over sun-baked skin.

The resort has a par 71, eighteen-hole Homer Flint–designed golf course and minions of Hispanic laborers, who arise at the crack of dawn and service the course and the guests while daring to dream that their children will be fortunate to taste the Phoenician's fruits. Truly, the resort was created by the hand of man.

Even though the rooms were off-season priced, why would I take my lovely wife to Arizona in the middle of the summer where temperatures were over 100° daily and cooled to 93° during the night? Temperatures that make you feel like a pizza in the oven.

'Twas Company business that brought us there. You see, the Company was sued by Greyhound Financial Services,[3] not the bus company, regarding the repayment of an inherited loan. Greyhound was headquartered in Phoenix. Terms of the loan placed jurisdiction and venue in that city.

I represented the Company along with outside trial counsel. The matter grew out of a dispute involving the collectability of membership agreements at a campground in Missouri named Endless Trails Resort.

Endless Trails was the only asset of Endless Trails Resort, Inc., the only asset of Continental Recreation Corporation.

Continental was incorporated in Iowa in the early 1970s. From a review of the ledger, most if not all of Continental's shareholders were also members at Endless Trails. It seems besides the memberships, the campers were offered shares in Continental.

Minutes from one early shareholders' meeting reveal some of the shareholder/members were more interested in "when the trout stream would be stocked" at Endless Trails than in who was to be elected to the board of directors.

Although technically a public corporation, Continental's shares were not sold on any exchange nor, as far as we can determine, traded today.

In the mid-1980s Bud was introduced to Continental's majority shareholder, William Wilen, by Harvey Zelin. After a few months of negotiation, Bud and Bill came to terms. They shook hands on a deal whereby Bud, Patrick, Michael, Fran Goffredo (Bud's brother-in-law and president of Resort Funding), and Resort Funding purchased Wilen's shares. The Company also assumed Wilen's debt position relative to Endless Trails. Zelin was going to receive shares as well but could not come up with matching funds, so was excluded.

No matter the amount of due diligence, a buyer never truly knows the scope of evilness and debts the seller of corporate stock has accumulated. It is preferable from a liability standpoint, therefore, to purchase assets and not the stock of a corporation. Bud, however, wanted the stock because Patrick wanted the exploitation rights inherent in public corporations.

Soon after the deal was consummated, Bud installed family members to manage Endless Trails. After they proved unreliable, he hired a former Syracuse police official to move to Missouri and take over management. Soon after the installation of the policeman, the name was changed to Bent Oaks Resort, known as Get Bent Resort by the employees.

For a while, the place earned five stars from Coast-to-Coast, a company that hosts a network of membership campgrounds that offer reciprocal rights of usage at member parks.

The Bennetts' luck would not hold, however, because of certain irregularities in the sale of memberships at Endless Trails before the Company's takeover that formed the basis of Greyhound's suit.

In the initial stage of membership sales in the 1970s, deeded lots were sold. The lots were basic fee simple estates in which the buyers received full title to the property just like any standard house closing. The property could be sold, transferred, or willed to third parties, subject to certain rules and regulations of Endless Trails and outstanding mortgages or deeds of trust.

In the next phase offered at Endless Trails, members were sold undivided interests, UDIs, in a specified area of the campground. UDI buyers were given deeds to the property as tenants in common with other buyers, typically 1/400 interests.

The UDI owners had no rights in a particular piece of property but shared ownership rights with other members who purchased similar UDI deeds much the same way as a husband and wife have an undivided interest in their marital residence. The UDIs were freely transferable.

The third phase and method of sale at Endless Trails was right-to-use. Right-to-use was basically long-term lease agreements akin to apartment rentals. No ownership rights in the land were given. Moreover, unlike lot and UDI owners, the right-to-users could not easily transfer their leasehold interests to third parties.

All of the lot owners, UDI owners, and right-to-use lessees shared basic rights in the common areas and privileges associated with the campground, such as the swimming pool and the clubhouse.

Most of the UDI purchases were financed through Greyhound much in the same way Resort Funding financed membership agreements at the various campgrounds. To secure the performance of the finance agreements and Endless Trail's recourse obligation for defaulted UDI agreements, Greyhound filed an overmortgage on the entire campground with appropriate release language carved out for UDI purchases.

Well, it seems when the UDI purchasers were shown the campground by former owners in the chain, the stakes delineating the lot owners' properties were allegedly improperly set. The lines of demarcation between lot owners and UDI owners were not clear and in many instances overlapped in title documents filed with the County Clerk's Office. Thrown into the mix was a title insurance policy that guaranteed the property rights of the various parties based, however, on the erroneous property boundaries.

At once, the rights of the UDI owners and the lot owners collided. As a result, the rate of default on UDI agreements spiraled. Greyhound demanded the Company, as new owner, honor the recourse obligation and

make good on the bad agreements. The Company refused and Greyhound eventually commenced legal action.

After a couple years of litigation among Greyhound, Bennett, and the
title insurance company, the trial was finally set in Phoenix. The judge,
perhaps sensing the matter was ripe, conducted eleventh-hour mammoth pretrial settlement negotiations.

The judge had the various parties come into chambers one on one
and all together. No matter the Company's claims of lender liability and
other malfeasance on the part of Greyhound, we could not easily defeat
Greyhound's claim concerning the pre-Bennett improper staking of the
various property interests at Endless Trails and the resulting rash of non-
payments.

After hours of browbeating, wailing, gnashing of teeth, and appeals to
common sense, the parties agreed to a global settlement. Bennett Funding wound up paying about only half of the remaining debt, saving more
than $600,000. The trial was canceled.

Michael was elated when I telephoned the news. Upon my return,
though, it did not take Bud long to express his dissatisfaction with the
terms of the settlement and perhaps undisclosed hostility for "vacation-
ing" at Company expense.

Eventually, Endless Trails was sold to a Canadian corporation for
$225,000. The Company took a note from the buyer and transferred title
by quitclaim deed because of the uncertainty of the property lines. Citing one reason or another, the buyer defaulted and the matter remains in
litigation.

Hobnobbing

T HE FINANCING provided by Bennett Funding and its affiliates included turnkey construction loans and the purchase of time-share
consumer obligations.

In 1992, actress Debbie Reynolds purchased the closed Paddlewheel
Hotel lying east of the Las Vegas strip. Ms. Reynolds spent "millions re-
modeling before opening a year later."[1]

In 1994, Ms. Reynolds and her business associates desired to upgrade some of the rooms at the hotel to provide time-sharing to the public. Feelers went out and a deal was struck whereby Bennett Management loaned money to Ms. Reynolds's company to accommodate the expansion, and Resort Funding agreed to purchase time-share receivables.

During negotiations in Syracuse, I recall Debbie's only concern was that no lien would be filed on her memorabilia accumulated over a lifetime of entertainment. She left the terms and conditions of the financial arrangement to others. Ms. Reynolds's reasonable request was honored.

Inasmuch as they were controlling the purse strings, the Bennetts really played up their "relationship" with the star of *Singin' in the Rain* by "ordering" her to come to Syracuse to attend the closing.

The closing occurred in the Bennetts' boardroom in the Atrium. As word got out Debbie Reynolds was in the boardroom, the employees stacked up outside the door like planes queuing to land at O'Hare Airport. But Ms. Reynolds, more than ready for them, had 5″ × 7″ glossies, which she autographed for the workers and, more probably, for the workers' parents.

The closing was extremely difficult because of the constant interruptions. Eventually, I had to lock the door to the boardroom. While Bud acted like an excited teenager on a first date, Ms. Reynolds was the comportment of class.

The deal consummated and the rain fell. Todd Fisher, the son of her marriage with Eddie Fisher, was the general manager of the hotel and became a friend of Michael's. He remarked the Bennetts "were of great assistance to Debbie and I."[2] Well, of course they were. The Company pumped in upward of $27.5 million to the project secured by a mortgage, time-share receivables, and a seat on the board held by Michael Bennett.

I doubt Ms. Reynolds would have touched the cash had she known about its origins from defrauded widows, pension plans, and moms and pops throughout the country.

After Michael left Bennett Funding in April 1996, he worked briefly with Olympus Property Management. Olympus was owned by Michael, and it managed, under contract, the various Bennett local hotels. As the hotels were not cash cows, Michael was forced to look for more suitable and economically rewarding employment.

After several failed attempts at securing employment, Michael contacted Todd and made an arrangement to work as a consultant at Debbie's hotel in Las Vegas. Michael checked out of his luxury apartment at the Hotel Syracuse and was ready for the move. He even threw a party

The Bennetts meet with Debbie Reynolds in Kathleen's office in the Atrium. Courtesy of Randi Anglin.

for himself on the eve he was to leave. Later that night he found out the arrangement fell through. I was told Michael cried.

A rumor circulated that Breeden called his "boys" at the FBI and pressure was brought to bare on Todd. Breeden said he "wished he could take credit for it." The story probably goes like this:

The Nevada Gaming Commission, on its own accord as watchdog agency, told Todd that Debbie's casino license would be yanked if Michael Bennett, the undesirable, became associated with the project. This coming from a state with legalized gaming and prostitution.[3]

With no job, no place to stay, and funds dwindling for living expenses and attorneys, Michael went to Florida to live with his parents in the double-wide trailer. After that, prison may not seem so bad. As Nietzsche said, "That which does not kill me, strengthens me."[4]

Not long after Michael's journey, the corporation that owned Debbie's hotel filed bankruptcy as well. The hotel was sold to the World Wrestling Federation for $9 million. When the transaction receives final approval from the various bankruptcy courts involved, the Bennett estate stands to receive the balance due under its loan, about $5.7 million.

Early on, Michael was one of the first central New Yorkers with money and clout to back George Pataki's run for governor of New York. According to an article that appeared in the *Wall Street Journal*, Michael, through the Company, gave Pataki $13,500. When the governor campaigned in Syracuse, Michael offered "him the Hotel Syracuse's opulent governor's suite."

Michael helped organize and attend fund-raisings. He "asked" certain Bennett Funding employees and staff to work on the campaign and fund-raising activities. None of these were reported to the appropriate election boards or commissions.

When Pataki took the Albany mansion, Michael was given a position as county tourism development board member. This was besides his other "nonpaid" positions with numerous civic organizations.

Former congressman and speaker of the house Newt Gingrich was invited to speak to local businessmen in 1995. The event was facilitated, in part, by Michael and hosted at his Hotel Syracuse. I do not know if Newt was paid for his performance.

The entire Bennett family was ensconced deeply with local politics and politicians. Bud was a friend and associate of the County Republican Committee chairman. Money and office equipment and space were given to people running for office. The Bennetts were apolitical creatures and tended to spread their largess to those in or likely to get power. Even Kasarjian, a New Jersey resident, gave a contribution to local politicians claiming to "have business interests in Syracuse."

In an attempt to reduce attorneys' fees, the trustee decided to retain the services of Harris Beach, a Rochester-based firm with a local presence. Harris Beach had the three essentials: bankruptcy and litigation expertise, political clout, and lower hourly rates than those charged by Simpson Thacher. As most of the local firms were conflicted out, few possessed the essentials.

State senator John De Francisco is a partner in Harris Beach. He invested in leases and was stung by the scam.[5] His complaints about Bennett were reported in the local newspaper.

In his original affidavit filed with the Bankruptcy Court in support of the firm's application, the senator did not mention his Bennett connection save he was a disgruntled investor. When revelations concerning campaign contributions and other services rendered by the Bennetts surfaced, the senator was forced to revise the affidavit.

Although it is debatable whether De Francisco was obligated to disclose the entire Bennett connection in the first affidavit because it was personal, not firm, business, nevertheless he offered to place any proceeds received on his claim into a charitable trust and return campaign contributions if his firm were hired. Indeed, De Francisco is the only politician in the entire mess who has publicly offered to disgorge political contributions.

Counsel to the Unsecured Creditor's Committee, charged with protecting the investors in the bankruptcy proceeding, wanted the senator's proceeds to be distributed to the unsecured investors.

In a letter to Judge Gerling, Dan Stolz suggested, "The Committee wishes to make it clear that the Committee has urged the Trustee to recover all direct and *indirect* payments made by the Debtor companies to political and charitable causes."[6]

To be sure, many local, state, and federal politicians accepted campaign contributions and in-kind support from the Bennetts, their companies, or cronies over the years. Other than a very early "before all of the facts are known" show of support by a few of the politicians, not one of them has shown any support for any of the Bennetts in the same way the Bennetts had shown support for them throughout the years. Not one elected representative volunteered to return the ill-gotten gain back to Breeden for distribution to the victims.

Although the application of Harris Beach was rejected by the Bankruptcy Court, it became counsel to M and T Bank, the new trustee of the Company's 401(k) plan.

In 1993, I was approached by two local postal workers, Joseph and Dominick. The two had invented an Elvis trivia game and were looking for a lawyer to help them bring it to market. I mentioned the project to Patrick Bennett. He expressed an interest but only if a license could be secured from Graceland. The project was abandoned: Graceland refused to grant a license because it had "just" granted one to another company that produced a similar game, after it received our prototype.

About one year later Joe and Dom approached me again. This time they had developed a country music trivia game. A forty-page formal business plan was submitted to Patrick. He agreed, months later, to lend $551,000 through his partnership, Bennett Financial Associates. The proceeds were to be used to pay all costs associated with the production and marketing of the game. Patrick required Tony Menchella be the chairman of the board and CEO, to keep an eye on the company.

The agreement called for repayment of the loan in full before any internal commissions, fees, dividends, or the like are paid to Joe and Dom. Thereafter, the net profits would be split between the owners and the partnership.

At first, the company decided to sell the game, Trivia—Country Style through direct marketing like Popiel's "Pocket Fisherman." A spokesman for the game was needed who could bridge the gap between old and new country.

I met Charlie Daniels ("Devil Went Down to Georgia") at an agent's office in Tennessee. He would not endorse the game unless he first reviewed the trivia questions to ensure they were suitable and not offensive. Within a day, Charlie said he loved the questions and signed the agreement, apparently in record time.

Charlie agreed to endorse the game for one year for a flat fee plus a piece of sales. In return Charlie made appearances on a TV commercial and in magazines' advertisements.

As part of the loan terms, Patrick required the company to pay $25,000 to Vernon Downs directly to sponsor a "Charlie Daniels" race. Charlie made a guest appearance at Vernon Downs to promote the game. He meticulously adhered to the terms of the agreement and then some. He plugged the game on national TV shows in which he was a guest.

The rest of the loan proceeds were spent on production costs, agent fees, and advertising. As anyone in the business can tell you, this is not a lot of money to produce, market, and nationally advertise a game.

After selling about four thousand games through the direct method and pulling in $120,000, it was decided to hire a manufacturer's representative and go the wholesale route.

With that approach, the first run of twenty-five thousand games was sold out the first year, primarily through Kmart. All profits were put back into the company to produce twenty-five thousand more games. The future looked bright.

Inexplicably, the next season witnessed dismal sales. Because of what I consider a bad business decision by Tony Menchella, the company borrowed excessively for advertising it could not afford. It was decided to sell the balance of the games to a liquidator.

After shipping about five thousand games to the liquidator, a middleman who was involved in the chain of production took custody of the game pieces for the remaining twenty thousand games. He held them hostage demanding more money. The shipment went unfulfilled. The liquidator refused to pay for the five thousand games delivered because of the breach of contract to ship all of the remaining games.[7]

Joe was paid a modest salary for a limited time because he reduced his hours at the post office to devote more time to the game. Dom did not take any money. Despite hundreds of hours of work over the years, I received nothing for my troubles, not even the customary Bennett broker/finder/consultant/structurer's fee.

Through forensic analysis, it appears the $551,000 originated from Bennett Management and not from Bennett Financial Associates. Accordingly, Breeden sued Joe and Dom who had personally guaranteed the loan obligation. Joe and Dom filed bankruptcy.[8]

Although the Devil may have gone to Georgia, he started off in Syracuse.

Carleton Island, New York

CARLETON ISLAND lies near the town of Cape Vincent, New York, in the cusp formed by Lake Ontario and the St. Lawrence River just south of the Canadian border. In the late 1980s Bennett Funding of N.Y. Corp., owned at that time by the four Bennetts, purchased a large undeveloped tract of land on the island from the Patten Corp. Supplied with money from Bennett Management, Bennett Funding of N.Y. Corp. paid more than $956,000 for the property, representing purchase price and interest on the mortgage and note.

The Bennetts wanted to develop the land for commercial recreational use. To access the choice waterfront property and to develop it properly, roads would need to be constructed and utility easements granted.

As part of the Thousand Islands Forest Preserve, Carleton Island is subject to strict environmental guidelines concerning development. After spending money for feasibility studies after the land was purchased, the Bennetts abandoned their dream because of the hurdles put up by the preserve and the attendant costs to accommodate them.

The property was never developed and generated no income.

Business Syndromes

HEAVYWEIGHT syndrome. Without doubt the Bennetts' business failed because evil cannot endure. But their business also failed because the Bennetts displayed and repeated certain syndromes. One of these is called the Heavyweight Syndrome.

The Bennetts believed a person who had the proper credentials could do no wrong and was worthy of a priori universal adoration among the workforce. The Bennetts fostered idolatry, a worship cult not only of themselves but of their anointed. They would serve up these would-be messiahs to the employees and demand immediate supplication.

With few exceptions, the saviors would ride into town, make a bunch of money for, in some cases, doing nothing at all, and either ride out or be kicked out after the inevitable fall from grace. Even then, most of them demanded and received money for leaving.

To illustrate, in the late 1980s and early 1990s, the national vogue compelled corporate America to rethink the structure of companies along the lines of the transformation of monolithic departments into interdepartmental teams.

In 1994, the Bennetts were finally persuaded to jump onto the team bandwagon. They employed the services of Mark Scoular, the former CEO of Erskine Holdings and former board member of Aloha Capital. Mark was well versed in the creation and maintenance of teams.

Under his plan, employees from the sales, credit, and application departments were split up and reconstituted into Team East, Team West, etc., such that each team had its own salespersons, credit approvers, and programmers. Departments such as Finance, Accounting, and Legal remained intact.

The reconfiguration occurred at the same time Bud had approved the transfer of the leasing business from Bennett Funding to Aloha Capital and the back-of-the-house functions to the Processing Center for estate purposes.

Bouncing from departments to teams and from company to company, the employees were constantly on the move as if they were in the seasonal mass migrations on the Serengeti Plain.

Inasmuch as "Team Bennett" was a forward-looking company, the deans of change saw fit to terminate the services of the most of the litigation section of the Legal Department.

"Our credit decisions will be computer driven and the Team concept will ensure greater productivity," they posited.

The Bennetts did not review the proposal with the in-house attorneys. Had they done so we would have advised them the future may indeed look bright but a backlog of between $14 and $20 million of defaulted leases mandated the retention of the litigation section.

Unfortunately, the plan was carried out and, predictably, the income from lease collections fell off drastically. After about one year of this nonsense, I was finally able to persuade management to rethink the future and hire a new litigation team.

In another example, a couple of years before the team fiasco, Bud decided to resurrect his first business love, telecommunications. Unbeknownst to and without consulting with anyone from the Legal Department, the Bennetts hired a lawyer freshly resigned from Northern Telecom. One day, Bud simply called me into his office and let me read Paul Willard's résumé after they had already hired him.

"He's a systems man and is a heavyweight, a player in the telecommunications industry. I got big plans for him. He'll get a piece of the action for all business he brings in," Bud boasted.

While I feigned interest by bobbing my head every so often, all I could think was, What the hell is a systems man?

Well, the new man, Paul, was placed immediately in charge of the entire litigation effort of the Company against defaulted lessees until the telecommunications business started in earnest. At the time, lease litigation was quite a large operation, employing lawyers, paralegals, interns, and support staff. Paul's wife even said at her first Company Christmas party that her husband was really the new general counsel, implying I was out of favor and just about out the door.

Paul's résumé was devoid of litigation experience. He was not even admitted in New York at the time and could not make court appearances nor sign pleadings. As a consequence, within a year and a half, the litigation section lay in shambles. And like so many of the Bennetts' best-laid plans, the telecommunications business never materialized in earnest.

Paul's fall from grace was rapid, inevitable and nonappealable. He was relegated to handling time-share closings. Only two years after his hire, just after his mother passed away, and just after undergoing serious surgery, he was forced to resign in June 1994.

Paul was a thorough lawyer who was just way over his head in litigation. He handled the time-share closings well, so I lobbied for his retention despite his earlier Richard III attempts at usurpation. Bud coldly told me the new man was out and I should "mind my own business."

Paul stumbled about searching for employment. It was said he did odd legal jobs and even became a Cadillac salesman. Then, in a bit of luck, he found employment as general counsel to a brokerage house in New Jersey, First Interregional.

I saw Paul again two years later in May 1996 when I was "volunteered" to be the Company representative at the Bankruptcy section 341 first meeting of creditors.

Because a crush of people was expected, the Bankruptcy Court Clerk and the Trustee's Office, a division of the Justice Department, rented the Civic Center. The Civic Center is home to the Syracuse Symphony, plays, and other artistic and cultural events.

Sitting in tiered rows, more than five hundred people attended, including investors and their attorneys, banks and their attorneys, employees and their attorneys, trade creditors and their attorneys, the media, and, of course, attorneys.

Concerned a disgruntled investor or two would wreak vengeance upon me, I demanded metal detectors be installed and armed police serve guard. In preparation, I practiced elocution like Demosthenes shouting above the roar of ocean waves with a mouthful of sand pebbles.

I sat at a table center stage while Breeden, who was appointed trustee one month earlier, asked about twenty questions. The audience was quiet and listened attentively. I wondered whether the assemblage thought I was one of the rats who had been caught and was being forced to spill my guts.

Table 13. Summary of fees earned by the attorneys and accountants for the Unsecured Creditors Committee as of March 31, 1999

Professionals	Fee Applications	Court-Ordered Fee Adjustments	Payments Made to Professionals	Pending Fee Applications
Wassermann, Jurista & Stolz	1,631,473.62	−15,592.60	1,533,188.12	82,692.90
Zolfo Cooper	1,055,381.89	−9,694.67	775,596.70	270,090.52
Totals	$2,686,855.51	($25,287.27)	$2,308,784.82	$352,783.42

The game plan was to have Breeden finish his questions and then I would exit stage left. But not so fast. Dan Stolz, the Unsecured Creditors Committee attorney, wanted to ask some questions as well. Under the Bankruptcy Code such questioning was his right. So he fired away. His questions were intense, pointed, and almost accusatory.

Maybe he needed to show how he was going to earn every penny that he would bill the estate from the pool of money otherwise dedicated to the investors, his clients, through bankruptcy distribution.

After he finished I was asked in front of the entire assembly whether I would mind taking questions from the audience. What could I say? It was like the situation all parents find themselves in when their child asks for something in front of another kid who is the beneficiary of the request.

The extemporaneous questioning went on for hours without the benefit of counsel.[1]

"Were you aware, at what point were you aware and were brokers selling to your knowledge aware of an SEC investigation suspecting a possible Ponzi scheme?"

"[Were] you aware of any major withdrawals from the PCA accounts within 90 days prior to the filing for bankruptcy?"

"Are you aware of a company called the Dollar Capital Corp.?"

"What sort of arrangements is the debtor making to protect the alleged secured interests of the banks?"

"What is the status of Bennett Insurance right now?"

"There are several entities mentioned. I would like to know if they are all separate corporations and whether or not there is a bankruptcy case pending with respect to them?"

"Can you shed any light on the leases that Bennett sold, do you know anything about them?"

"What was built into these transactions so that Bennett Funding could profit from the transactions in a way other than double selling the leases?" Whoa!

"Could you please tell us who those outside counsel were?"

"Who was involved in the audits?"

"Do you know where the pension or 401(k) profit sharing plan assets were invested?"

"Were the lease interests that the debtors were selling registered securities?"

"Were there any other attorneys in the in-house legal department?"

"Was it your intention when you drafted the lease assignments that the purchasers of leases would get outright purchases of copier leases and equipment leases?"

"Are you familiar with a company called Triangle Management?"

"On the interest-bearing loans on the municipal lease equipment, were they supposed to be tax free or tax exempt on the interest?"

"Do you have any knowledge of how [Bennett Management] used the money it raised?"

"When was the last audited financial statement and who was it signed off by?"

"When did you say the Aloha spin-off took place?"

"Is there any way possible just one person in this corporation, Patrick Bennett, [knew the] extent of what happened there?"

At the end of the impromptu questioning, I left the stage and mingled with some well-wishers. I was told I did well. It was easy, I told the truth. Imagine my surprise when Paul Willard said hello after two years. He was there to listen to the speakers, because his new employer, First Interregional, had sold a few Bennett Funding leases to its clients.

We had small talk for a few minutes and left. Imagine my surprise again, about one year later, when the SEC and the FBI shut down First Interregional, for, can you believe this, selling fake leases and double-selling leases.[2]

Called the "Baby Bennett" case by the SEC, the First Interregional investors will probably get only a few cents on the dollar out of $123.9 million in unpaid principal on their investments. Its president pleaded guilty to eight counts, including conspiracy to commit securities fraud, tax evasion, and money laundering.

It is not known whether, like two scientists who develop the same theory independently and win the Nobel Prize, First Interregional copied

Bennett Funding or hosed its clients on its own—a criminal twist on the anthropological phenomenon of parallel cultural development.

Joseph's coat syndrome. The Bennetts' management style created and fostered what would seem on first blush to be petty jealousies among the employees. Upon deeper reflection, the jealousies were reactions to injustice. I call this the Joseph's Coat Syndrome, that is, an employer, through mismanagement, creates and fosters a climate whereby employees are led to believe the company's system of rewards and punishments is unjust or inequitable. To illustrate, I borrow from the Torah.[3]

The coat did Joseph in. And the coat sent him to Egypt and to glory. A many-colored coat. A coat bestowed upon the young boy by his loving father. For Joseph was the favorite son of Jacob, whose sons became the twelve tribes of Israel.

It has been said Joseph's brothers became wildly jealous on account of favoritism bestowed continually upon Joseph. Eventually, their jealousy leapt from silent rage to conspiracy and action.

"Let's kill him," some clamored.

But cooler heads prevailed and a plot was hatched. Simply, while some coaxed him, Joseph was assaulted and bound like an animal for slaughter by others who lay hidden along a roadside. They removed the prized coat and streaked it with blood from an animal killed for that very purpose. Joseph was sold to a passing caravan. As the brothers reached home and told Jacob that Joseph had been slain by a wild beast, the caravan entered the border of the land of Goshen. Jacob wept as he clutched the bloody coat.

Joseph had the ability to interpret dreams. He could decipher Pharaoh's dream concerning the fat and the lean cattle. He rose through the ranks and became a man of importance during the Egyptian administration of the famine that plagued the Middle East. Urged on by hunger the brothers went to Egypt and eventually reconciled with the estranged Joseph.

Thus viewed, was it not a prevailing sense of injustice and not jealousy that drove the brothers to act, just as the whips of the taskmasters drove the Hebrew slaves years later? The brothers' selling of Joseph into slavery was but a manifestation of righteousness, albeit savage and cruel.

The brothers worked hard and jockeyed for respect and for the love of their father, Jacob. Joseph, the son of Jacob's favorite wife, stole their thunder. Jacob gave Joseph tokens of love and material concessions far above those accorded his brothers. Did they not feel a moral imperative to strip Joseph of his specialness and privilege and tip the scales back into their favor, or at least to a neutral position?

Joseph was the focal point of injustice, but not the cause. Jacob's unfair treatment was the true source of the outrage. Although, in religious terms, it was necessary for these events to have happened, nevertheless, Jacob should have not have shown such outward favoritism among his children to engender feelings of actionable injustice.

Despite sensational headlines of workplace rage, few employees would go to the extreme as did Joseph's brothers. Nevertheless, recognized injustices in the workplace can reduce morale, increase angst, disenfranchisement, and disloyalty, spawning high rates of turnover, tardiness, and absenteeism among employees, not the elements so necessary for happy and healthy workers.

The cheeseburger syndrome. Many fast-food places, such as Burger King, pride themselves on their ability to cater to whims by allowing the customer to order a burger custom built, for example, with or without pickles.

Well imagine going to a Burger King and ordering a cheeseburger without the cheese. Despite the stunned look of the order taker, you repeat the request. Eventually, the cheeseburger sans cheese is prepared and payment must be made—payment for a cheeseburger, that is. What a waste! Why not order a plain burger without cheese if you are not going to eat the cheese in the first place?

Frequently, the Bennetts hired employees with special skills, paid them accordingly, but did not put their special skills to use. This is called the Cheeseburger Syndrome. For example, the Bennetts employed Richard MacPherson, the former head coach of the New England Patriots and Syracuse University football teams.

Coach Mac, or "Mac," as he is affectionately known, is one hell of a guy. Warm, friendly, with a kind word about everyone, Mac is always eager to help a friend in need. His love for the institution of the family is legendary.

"I'll be doing community relations, being the spokesman for the Bennett companies, and we'll possibly commit ourselves financially to the hotels when Michael buys them, putting our money where our mouth is. We might even live there, have an apartment right there," Coach Mac said in March 1993 just as he came on board.[4] "I see a rebirth of downtown and I want to be part of it," he added.

"What better person to carry our message into the business and central New York community than Coach Mac," interjected Michael.

Coach Mac is a trained and experienced strategist, who dealt routinely with millionaires, prima donnas, megacorporations, the press, and football groupies. The Bennetts never used his strategic talents for development, settlements, or negotiation. They relegated his existence to corporate relations. They paid for the cheeseburger without the cheese.

The antithesis applies as well. The Bennetts employed people woefully underqualified for positions, or, more fairly, elevated people to management positions without a shred of management experience or education.

Managers at Bennett Funding were generally hired from the ranks of the available talent pool. Little or no support was accorded in formal training, continuing education, or seminars. The hapless manager was expected to tackle management duties and maintain a healthy workload as well. You cannot manage a department and maintain an independent workload without compromising one or the other.

Nowhere was the negative synergistic effect of management felt more keenly than at the managers' meetings. The meetings were to be attended by all managers and supervisors of the Company. It convened once a month in the boardroom.

The dialogue at the meetings ranged generally from "this is what I have done today, aren't I a good boy" to bitching sessions. After a while, it became chic for upper management to duck the meetings, feigning a lack of time, and send proxies. I stopped going because I couldn't stand them anymore.

At the meetings, managers were encouraged by the Bennetts to speak freely and to engage in open discourse and debate. Somehow, minutes were taken and circulated to Bud and Kathleen for scrutiny. They knew exactly what everyone said. After talking the talk about encouraging the managers to show initiative, to speak out, and to be constructive, Bud and Kathleen would lambaste, threaten, and harangue transgressors, that is, managers who said anything of substance other than words of praise.

Management takes talent, education, experience, and dedication. Many of these nouveau managers were unfairly demoted, humiliated, fired, or somehow punished for not managing effectively or unwilling to delegate the workload or some other Company-line label.

Based on Bud's articulated paranoia that you can only trust family because everyone else will "screw you eventually," the Bennetts hired all the family members they could. Besides the four founding Bennetts, on the payroll were Kathleen's sister and brother-in-law and their daughter, Kathleen's younger brother, and Bud's sister and several of her children. Patrick even formed a partnership with his wife Gwen.

Before the bankruptcy, Kathleen's younger sister, Merrilee, a vice president, had been in charge of coordinating payroll with an outside payroll service provider. Her office was in the Finance Department. Soon after the petitions were filed, we intercepted three checks from as many different Bennett companies that Merrilee had cut manually to Patrick Bennett after his resignation. The checks totaled something like $12,000.

"Why did you issue the checks to Pat?" I asked.

"Well, since he resigned, I thought he was entitled to accrued vacation pay," she responded. The checks were not given to Patrick. Merrilee was transferred from the Finance area. Her employment was terminated shortly thereafter.

Maybe Bud's nepotism was borne of realism. I don't know. What I do know is that the Bennetts screwed their relatives by looting their pension plans too. Within a few months of the bankruptcy filing, all of the Bennett clan members either resigned or were terminated.

Although it is not clear if any of the extended family members were involved with the criminal activity, it is clear most of these people were good and honest workers who happened to be related to assholes. In most instances their paychecks were sorely needed and will be missed.

Never Met a Client I Didn't Like

To MISQUOTE Coleridge, "lawyers, lawyers everywhere. . . ."
If the lawyers in the Bennett matter can agree on nothing else they all agree the Bennett Bankruptcy, the class action, and related criminal proceedings have been very good for business. The filing of the bankruptcy petition constituted the passage of the Lawyer's Full Employment Act of 1996. If ever a slogan matched the facts truly it is lawyers in the Bennett case "never met a client they didn't like."

One of the hallmarks of the Code of Professional Responsibility is the "conflict of interest" provision,[1] which forbids lawyers from accepting

Table 14. The lawyers involved in the various Bennett cases

Abbey, Gardy & Squitieri, LLP

Anderson Kill & Olick, P.C.

Archer & Greiner

Arseneault & Krovatin

Baird, Holm, McEachen

Baker & Botts

Baker & Hostetler

Barnes & Thornburg

Barrack, Rodos & Bacine

Berger & Montague, P.C.

Berman, DeVaterio & Pease

Bernard Eyssalenne

Bernstein Liebhard & Lipshitz

Bernstein Litowitz Berger
& Grossmann, LLP

Bizar Martin & Taub, LLP

Bond, Schoeneck & King

Boose Casey Clklin Lubitz Martens
McBane & O'Connell

Borowitz & Goldsmith PLC

Brach, Eichler, Rosenberg, Silver,
Bernstein, Hammer &
Gladstone

Brager & Wexler, P.C.

Brasher & Ginn

Braun Kendrick Finkbeiner, P.L.C.

Brauner Baron Rosenzweig
& Klein

Bressler, Amery & Ross

Budd Lamer Gross Rosenbaum
Greenberg & Sade, P.C.

Chikovsky & Shapiro, P.A.

Chimicles & Tikellis

Clark Hill P.L.C.

Cohn, Lifland, Pearlman,
Herrmann & Knopf

Coll Davidson Carter Smith Saite

Cooper, Erving, Savage, Nolan
& Heller

Costello, Cooney & Fearon

Costigan Hargraves & McConnell,
P.C.

Curtis Thaxter Stevens & Broder

Curtis, Mallet-Prevost,
Colt & Mostle

D'Amato & Lynch

Davis Polk & Wardwell

Denenberg Ament Bell
& Rubenstein, P.C.

Dorsey & Whitney, LLP

Downs, Rachlin & Martin

Drinker, Biddle & Reath

Felt, Evans, Panzone, Bobrow
& Halak

Finkelstein, Thompson &
Loughran

Fisher & Boylan

Fitzpatrick & Waterman

Fleming, Roth & Fettweis

Freeman & Herz LLP

Friedman & Kaplan

Furman & Halpern, P.C.

Gargill, Sassoon & Rudolph

Garwin Bronzaft Gerstein
& Fisher L.L.P.

Gary J. Rotella & Associates

Goodkind Labaton Rudoff
& Sucharow

Green & Seifter

Green Hershdorfer & Sharpe

Greenbaum, Rowe, Smith,
Ravin & Davis

Guy A. Van Baalen, Asst. U.S.
Trustee

Hamilton Law Offices

Hancock & Estabrook

Hannoch & Weisman

Hanzman Criden Korge Chaykin
Ponce & Heise, P.A.

Harold B. Obstfeld, P.C.

Harter, Secrest & Emery

Harstein & Harstein

Harvey Harvey & Mumford

Herrmann & Knopf

Hodgson Russ Andrews Woods
& Goodyear

Iason & Silberberg, P.C.

IRS—Steven Jensen Special
Procedures

Jaroslawicz & Jaros

Joel Leifer & Associates

Jones, Foster, Johnston &
Stubbs, P.A.

Julian Pertz Law Firm

Kaplan Kilsheimer & Fox

Karp & Sommers

Kaufman Malchman Kirby &
Squire, LLP

Kelly & Walthall

Kaye Scholer Fierman Hays &
Handler, LLP

Kilpatrick Stockton LLP

King & Pennington, L.L.P.

Kohn, Swift & Graf

Kraemer, Burns, Mytelka &
Lovell, P.A.

Kreindler & Kreindler

Lacy Katzen Ryan & Mittleman,
LLP

Law Office of Klari Neuwelt

Law Offices of Barry Pinkowitz

Law Offices of Bernard M.
Gross, P.C.

Law Offices of Kenneth A.
Jacobsen

Law Offices of Timothy C. Karen

Law Offices of William E. Easton

Levin Fishbein Sedran & Berman

Lindquist & Vennum

Lowenstein, Sandier, Kohl, Fisher
& Boylan

Lowey Dannenberg Bemporad
& Selinger

Lux & DeCroce

Mackenzie, Smith, Lewis, Mitchell
& Hughes

Mager Liebenberg & White

Table 14 *(continued)*

Martin Martin & Woodard	Saiber Schlesinger Satz & Goldstein	Stroock Stroock & Lavan
McCarter & English	Saperston & Day	Sullivan & Cromwell
McCormick & Matthews	Sargent Cramer & Meyers LLP	Thomas C. Kingsley, Esq.
McDermott Will & Emery	Savett Frutkin Podell & Ryan, P.C.	Tompkins, McGuire & Wachenfeld
McMahon, Grow & Getty	Schneck Weltman Hashmall & Mischel	SEC—New York Regional Office
McNamee, Lochner, Titus & Williams	Schoengold & Sporn	Wasserman, Jurista & Stolz, P.C.
Meisrov Gelman Jaffe Cramer & Jamieson	Scolaro Shulman Cohen Lawler & Burstein	Wechsler Harwood Halebian & Feffer, L.L.P.
Milbank, Tweed, Hadley & McCloy	Seward & Kissel	Weil Gotshal & Manges, LLP
Milligan-Whyte & Smith	Shanley & Fisher	Weitz & Lexenberg
Morvillo, Abramowitz, Grand, Iason & Silberberg, P.C.	Shapiro & Shapiro	Whitman Austrian & Hanna
Much Shelist Freed Denenberg Paragano & Benvenuto, P.C.	Shaw, Licitra, Esernio & Schwartz	Wilentz, Goldman & Spritzer, P.C.
Perkins, Smith & Cohen LLP	Shearman & Sterling	William A. Despo, P.C.
Platzer, Fineberg & Swergold	Sills Cummis Zuckerman Radin Tischman Epstein & Gross, PC	Wilson Elser Moskowitz Edelman & Dicker
Preston Gates & Ellis	Simon, Schindler & Sandberg	Wolf Haldenstein Adler Freeman & Herz
Ravin, Greenberg & Marks P.C.	Simpson Thacher & Bartlett	Wolf Popper LLP
Ravin, Sarashoh, Cook, Baumgarten, Fisch & Rosen	Sinnreich Wasserman Grubin & Cahill, LLP	Wolff & Samson, P.A.
Reid & Priest	Sirota & Sirota	Wright & Manning
Richard & Richard	Smith Sovik Kendrick & Sugnet	Zwerling, Schachter & Zwerling, L.L.P.
Rivkin Radler & Kremer Rosenfeld & Stein, P.A.	Start & Stark	
Rossi, Murnane, Balzano & Hughes	Steel Hector & Davis LLP	
	Stillman Friedman & Shaw	

engagements in which the interests of two or more clients may be adverse to each other.

One can daresay this broad maxim would be universally accepted even if no such code provision existed. How could a lawyer represent both the husband and the wife in an acrimonious divorce battle? How could double representation be extended to opposite sides in a suit for negligence?

The conflicts rule also extends to past representation. It would be improper for a lawyer who once represented a corporation to then sue that corporation in the future on behalf of another client. To prevent adverse representation, firms have careful conflicts checks, ethics committees, and other suitable feedback mechanisms to prevent actual, or even in some cases the appearance of, impropriety.

On occasion, a court will allow a firm to represent a client although a conflict of interest has arisen. This bit of wizardry is allowed through the concept known as a "Chinese wall," an obnoxious algorithm referencing the Great Wall of China. The phrase envisions the creation of blockers within a firm to isolate those individuals working on matters of a client whose interests are adverse to the new client.

Because the set of potential and actual clients is finite and firm economics is a driving force behind a decision to represent a client, many lawyers do, perhaps by necessity, subscribe to this end run of the conflicts provision of the code—as if the files aren't available, as if the attorneys don't get together for lunch or a ball game, as if they attend not the same parties, as if they have no friends in common, as if their spouses did not know one another, as if the new Pharaoh did not know Joseph. Either there is a conflicts statute or there is not.

Without doubt the shameful and shameless scramble for money in the Bennett bankruptcy and its progeny has dismantled the anticonflicts provision of the Code of Professional Responsibility. The time-honored principle of the avoidance of conflicts of interest went out the door the day after the petition was filed.

Even the trustee's counsel represents the largest unsecured creditor, Chemical/Chase Bank, in other matters. Chemical/Chase Bank filed claims totaling $16,305,757.53 in the Bennett bankruptcy. Apparently, the conflict was waived upon full disclosure to all parties.[2]

Simpson Thacher was accused publicly by assistant U.S. trustee Van Baalen of a serious violation of the conflicts rule, because it represented Resort Funding and Equivest in a Bennett bankruptcy matter. As punishment, he wanted the firm to be thrown off the case and disgorge all of its fees received from the bankruptcy proceeding, over $9 million at the time.

George Newcombe from Simpson Thacher stated, "We represented [Resort Funding] only where its interests were aligned with the estate. . . . There are no improprieties. There are no conflicts of interest." He concluded by saying that the U.S. trustee's allegations were "completely unfounded" and "based on significant factual inaccuracies."[3]

Gerling ordered Simpson Thacher not to represent Resort Funding or

Equivest in the future but did not force the firm to resign or disgorge its fees.

Some local firms that represent creditors in the Bennett bankruptcy at one time or another represented the Bennetts, their entities, or related parties. For example, Bond, Schoeneck & King represents seventeen banks that refused to settle with the trustee. Although the firm never represented any of the Bennetts or the debtors directly, in accordance with the letter of the conflicts provision of the code, nevertheless, it represented Mid-State Raceway, Inc., the corporation that owns Vernon Downs Racetrack[4]—the same corporation whose majority shares of stock were once owned by none other than Patrick Bennett and then by his wife, Gwen.

By the way, it is not true that only lawyers make money in bankruptcies. The accountants make a killing as well.

From Sin to Sinai

CHARLES GENOVESE's accounting firm, Genovese, Levin, Bartlett Co., hosted black-tie Christmas parties at the Sheraton Crossroads Hotel in Mahwah, New Jersey.

Although the accounting firm was the technical sponsor, the parties were unmistakably Charles's. He was omnipresent. One minute he was orchestrating who would be immortalized in preparty photo sessions, another minute he would be entertaining the guests by playing a trumpet solo.

Charles's Christmas parties were by invitation only. If one was bestowed the honor, one was expected to go. Any excuse was considered a sign of disrespect to Don Genovese.

The guest list consisted of top tier clients of the firm and investors who bought Bennett products through Charles. Many of the independent Bennett brokers who structurally reported to Charles were invited. Charles, of course, received overrides from Patrick for business generated by his brokers.

The four Bennetts, the rest of the board of directors, employees from the Finance Department who primarily interacted with Charles, executive secretaries, and all of their spouses were invited.

Sara and I were invited to and attended a couple of parties as well. We were happy to go. Not because the who's who of Bennett society attended, but we would be alone and have a nice break for a few days.

Charles treated his guests royally. Although Patrick and some Bennett people went earlier to discuss business, most invitees were provided hotel rooms and meals from Friday to checkout on Sunday.

For the bulk of the Bennett contingent, Friday was reserved for travel from Syracuse to Mahwah, checking in, unpacking, eating, saying hello, and relaxing. Saturday mornings found many of us driving to Manhattan to shop, to get lunch, and return to the hotel to get ready for the party, which started about 6:00 P.M.

Party goers were directed through a narrow entranceway off the main lobby. There, Charles, his partners, and their spouses received us with due solemnity and cordiality like parents at a wedding reception.

Charles needed to take the Christmas party seriously. Most of the guests had income and wealth to easily qualify as "accredited investors," that is, a net worth of at least $1 million. They kept Charles living in the lap of luxury. They paid for his palatial residence and the standard of living as befits a parvenu. Many of the employees from the Bennett contingent by contrast lived well below the poverty line of wealth.

After the formal greeting, we were steered toward the hors d'oeuvres, a perhaps inappropriate word to describe the riot of food: shrimp resting on tabletop ice sculptures; mounds of pâté, smoked salmon, and caviar, waiting to be spread on small slices of bread, biscuits, or minibagels; bite-size omelets sautéed in vodka; haunches of hot roast beef and lamb expertly carved to order; heaps of smoked baby ribs; baked clams, fried clams, raw clams, and oysters; bean and pasta salads; crêpes with choice of vegetable or seafood stuffing; and drinks.

After an hour or so, the doors to the main ballroom opened and live music rushed forth to greet us. The guests were ushered in and looked for their assigned table. Seating was planned. God forbid so-and-so should sit with so-and-so. As the guests were finding their seats, the band played and professional dancers strutted their stuff.

Dinner stretched over many courses. In between, the male and female dancers looked for partners from among the guests, magicians performed tricks, and artists drew caricatures. Only psychics from the psychic hotline were missing.

Mousse or some other confectionery concoction was served as a pre-dessert. Formal dessert came from a Viennese cart. Tired after the orgy of food and drink and dancing my way into oblivion, I sipped coffee and looked around.

Charles's party was the incarnation of the seven deadly sins: pride, covetousness, lust, anger, gluttony, envy, and sloth. Men stuffed into dark tuxedos with designer bow tie and cummerbund or vest combos mingled with their ilk while their svelte trophy wives in strapless dresses low cut to their asses, revealing shoulders, necks, arms, and backs, vomited in the ladies' room as they suffered bulimic episodes.

But I was too harsh. These people were just out trying to have a good time. Who was I to decide for another how to dress, what to eat, or who to fuck? Hell, I was there myself.

Ultimately they paid for the parties, so let them dance! They were all duped by Charles and the Bennetts. These husbands, wives, fathers, mothers, brothers, sisters, sons, daughters, grandparents, philanthropists, atheists, devout, givers, takers, bereaved, fat, slim, tall, short, beautiful, ugly, profound, profane, lost, found, stupid, and intelligent were among the legions of investors who suffered grievous monetary losses. Tens of thousands of dollars. Hundred of thousands. Millions.

On a broader level, the costs of the parties were also borne by taxpayers, as the Bennetts and Charles, through their companies, no doubt deducted the affairs as entertainment expenses. To afford such junkets and parties, the criminals must have allocated a percentage of their Ponzi profits into an entertainment sinking fund.

Although the Bennetts probably did not read books on the psychology of investment, the Bennetts and their proxies certainly knew how to keep the investors happy. They knew how to cater to their nouveau riche tastes and bourgeois attitudes. They knew how to stroke their egos like tender lovers.

Like the faithful who bestow gifts and money upon their religious leaders, the Bennetts, Charles, and the brokers knew that wealth attracts wealth, or, more properly, the appearance of wealth attracts wealth. They knew the power of the trappings of success.

"Hey, you think my people are going to invest in a company unless the owners drive around in fancy cars and live in big homes?"

The Sheraton Crossroads, which hosted Charles's Christmas parties, is not far from the site of George Grimm's suicide.

The Christmas party was but one of the unholy amalgam of techniques the Bennetts and Charles employed to entice and lure investors. The others included puffed-up financial statements, tours of Company headquarters, testimonials from politicians, brokers, and other investors, and promotional materials, such as brochures, press releases, and a video.

In 1993–94, the Company produced a video titled *Turning Visions into Reality.*

After returning from vacation one year, I could not help noticing people with cameras and other equipment scurrying about the offices. "What's going on?" I asked one of the cameramen.

"Ask him," he responded, pointing to a man dressed in producer chic—jeans and blazer. I repeated the question.

"Oh, we're making a video for the company," he answered, keeping his eyes on the production crew.

A video? I thought. "Hey, my name is Stu Weisman. I've been out on vacation and just got back so I don't know what I'm supposed to do," I told the producer, my voice radiating the excitement of appearing on the Company's video.

The producer looked at me as if he were gauging my screen appearance potential. "I don't know, let me find out," he said. He left the scene and returned a few minutes later.

"Stu [baby?]," the producer said. "I understand you're the company lawyer," he continued, as if putting an imaginary arm around my shoulders.

"Yeah?"

"Well, this is more of a marketing video for the investors. They're afraid if attorneys are on the production, people will think lawsuits, trouble, all kindsa negative things," the producer advised, his voice arching to reach "you understand what I mean" tonality.

"Oh, I see," I responded, and retreated to my office, believing "they're" referred to the Bennetts.

A few weeks later I watched the premiere. The thirteen-minute video opens with a view of an upstate New York country vista—tree-covered hills and open spaces. It then focuses on the Company's headquarters, "on the spot where the Erie Canal once stood," intones the narrator.

The video describes the Company's leasing business and the businesses of several other affiliates in vogue at the time, particularly Aloha Telecom, National Club Credit, and GEM.

Aloha Telecom was one of the vehicles Bud used to get reinvolved in the telecommunications industry. National Club Credit's business was to finance golf courses. GEM's purpose was to expand the Company's municipal leasing program. GEM had hired and paid the former mayor of New Orleans to promote business among city officials nationwide.

Aloha Telecom, National Club Credit, and GEM incurred start-up costs, promotional fees, and other transactional costs and barely got off the ground before they were abandoned.

The video presentation, which reminds one of a slick infomercial, highlights the Company's state-of-the-art computer, communication, collection, and mailing systems. One scene shows the processing of an endless supply of checks. Another features the manager of the Collection Department describing the technical workings of the computer-driven, voice-activated collection system.

A flash notes the Company's "sound fiscal principles," as the backbone to its conservative approach to financial matters.

The board of directors, the Executive Committee, some salespersons, and marketing personnel appear on the video. All together twenty-two employees have speaking roles and a dozen others nonspeaking cameos.

Except for a brief appearance in a group picture of the employees' Service Club, not one person connected with the Legal Department was asked to or appears in the video. At the time, Legal had several long-term employees and a staff of about fifteen people.

A couple of years after the production and distribution of the video to brokers, investors, banks, and others, the government indicted Patrick and Michael Bennett and Al Cerimeli. All three have speaking roles in the video.

When Breeden, his counsel, and the accountants from Coopers sat around the board table in April 1996 and watched, I thanked God I do not appear in the video.

The Code

WITH THE indictments, the guilty pleas, the conviction, the class action suit, the bankruptcy, and the bad press in this matter, one would think not one lease in the entire Bennett Funding portfolio was real.

Although many leases have proven to be fakes, at the time of the filing of the petition in March 1996, according to an early report prepared by the trustee, approximately fifty thousand leases, with monthly payments ranging from $50 to $50,000, were real; they just happened to have been sold, pledged, or assigned many times over.[1]

The estimated amounts raised by double-pledging and selling of fictitious leases to investors are: 1990, $49 million; 1991, $163 million; 1992, $254 million; 1993, $349 million; 1994, $409 million; 1995, $319 million. A total of $1.543 billion fake and multiple-pledged leases! Coopers identified 8,329 municipal leases that were double-pledged![2]

The Process Center still bills and collects on the good accounts. This effort is expected to last until the second quarter of 2002. Suits to collect on bad accounts are likely to extend well beyond that.

On the day of filing, March 29, 1996, the combined stream aging of the leases was about $320 million.[3] Stream aging is the anticipated revenue to be generated by all of the remaining monthly lease payments. This figure includes both leases from the Aloha Leasing division of Bennett Funding and from Aloha Capital Corp.

The combined aging also includes commercial and municipal leases that were current in payment as of that date; nonpaying "toxic" leases from Scriptex, Americorp, Hotel Syracuse, and Castle; leases in various stages of collection, litigation, and bankruptcy; and a few leases already written off.

The combined stream aging does not include other amounts the estate may receive for such items as exercised purchase options for the leased equipment and posttermination rentals from lessees.

Based on the $320 million jackpot, the primary issue in the Bennett bankruptcy is whether the banks or the individual investors have direct rights or secured interests in the leases, the equipment, and the stream of payments thereunder. Whoever wins this battle ultimately takes control of the boodle.

Our system of commercial laws is embodied in the Uniform Commercial Code. The code, as are other uniform codes, is a set of suggested statutes that the state legislatures are free to adopt in whole or in part. They differ from federal legislation, which is mandatorily followed everywhere in the country.

The code is designed as a comprehensive and seamless web of commercial principles and rules. It is divided into ten major sections. Each section deals with a particular topic, including sales, equipment leases, commercial paper, instruments such as checks, bank deposits, funds transfers, letters of credit, bulk transfers, warehouse receipts, investment securities, and secured transactions. The code has been adopted in one form or another in every state.[4]

Article 9 of the code deals with granting and perfecting security interests in accounts, goods, chattel paper, and negotiable instruments. A security interest, such as a mortgage, is created when a borrower pledges collateral for a loan. The lender takes a secured interest in the collateral and can exercise remedies against it in the event of default under the loan.

It is well settled under the New York enactment of the code and in Bankruptcy Courts applying that law that equipment leases constitute chattel paper.[5] As defined in the code, chattel paper is evidence of a monetary obligation coupled with an interest in goods. In the Bennett Funding case, the monetary obligation is the monthly lease payment, the goods are the leased equipment.

Article 9 allows a creditor to perfect its security interest in chattel paper by taking physical possession of the instrument itself, in this case, by gaining custody of the original lease agreements.

Perfection of a security interest grants the lender rights in the secured property paramount to all others who may claim similar rights in those goods.

The code also provides that perfection of a security interest can be accomplished, in the alternative, by filing a UCC-1 financing statement in the appropriate county office and, if necessary, in the Office of the Secretary of State.

UCC-1s are intended to give public notice that the named parties entered into a lender/borrower or creditor/debtor relationship and the items or goods described constitute the collateral or security for the loan.

Courts have found consistently if a creditor has a perfected security interest in a lease, the "rent" generated by that lease constitutes "proceeds" in which the creditor also has a perfected security interest.

Some 245 banks loaned money to Bennett Funding. The loans were purportedly secured by equipment leases. This is called an asset-based loan. The economics driving the transaction are bound up in the revenue generated by the underlying collateral, in this case, the leases.

For the loans in question, in compliance with the code, the banks took physical custody of the original leases. The banks further shored up their positions by filing UCC-1 financing statements with the Onondaga

County Clerk's Office and the New York Secretary of State's Office in Albany.

Although the banks as professed secured parties do have possession of the original leases and did file UCC-1 financing statements in the appropriate jurisdictions, the trustee's counsel made two compelling arguments that the banks are not secured parties, because they failed to properly perfect their security interests in the leases, the equipment, and the proceeds.

First, as duplicate originals have been found at Bennett Funding, the banks may not have the "original" leases required to grant a perfected security interest and to pass muster under the code.

Second, certain improprieties in the actual names set forth on the filed UCC-1s have failed to give proper and adequate notice to the investing world of the banks' interests in and to the leases. The trustee argues few banks filed the UCC-1s under the proper name of The Bennett Funding Group, Inc., only under the leasing division trade name Aloha Leasing. As the Bennetts did no financial business under the name of Aloha Leasing per se, effective notice to the financial community and investors was not given.

Commercial law experts agree chattel paper, equipment leases for example, is unique among other documents that purport to transfer title or ownership. The experts suggest one sells chattel paper by following the same regimen one would follow to secure a pledge of chattel paper, namely, take physical possession of the instrument or file appropriate UCC-1 financing statements.

Arguably, then, because many of the investors claim they own the leases, possession of the original or a receipt for a filed UCC-1 financing statement would need to be produced to give them supremacy over the banks who claim a security interest in the very same leases.

Not one Bennett Funding investor can produce either an original lease or a UCC-1 filing receipt despite being given the opportunity by the trustee, the banks, and the court. Under the code, therefore, the investors, as purchasers of the leases, failed to even demonstrate a rudimentary ownership or security interest in those leases.

The trustee's counsel advised during the section 341 first meeting of creditors that Bennett Funding was not responsible for the filing of the UCC-1s on behalf of the investors. The onus fell upon the investors or their brokers and financial advisers. Under this theory, the investors have wound up as general unsecured creditors.

In this light, rather than engaging in Byzantine levels of analysis, the Bankruptcy Court held, and virtually everyone has agreed, the banks and not the individual investors are secured creditors. Whether the banks properly perfected their security interests as described above, however, is another story.

Rather than risk rumbling with the trustee, 197 banks settled. Although the varying settlement terms and conditions read like a primer on quantum physics, most of the banks were given the opportunity to settle under four basic options from payouts of collected funds ranging from 78.5 percent up to 95 percent.

In negotiating with the banks, Breeden took the position that earlier settlers get better terms. Accordingly, banks in the first round of settlements may have received more advantageous settlements than banks in the second round. Some banks were even given the "opportunity" to mesh their recovery with additional priority loans to Resort Funding, the Equivest subsidiary.

In the settlement agreements, the trustee acknowledged the banks' security interests in the leases and that the proceeds were "duly perfected, unavoidable, and first priority. . . ." However, the agreements then required the banks to assign and transfer to the trustee all of the bank's newly "recognized" right, title, and interest in and to any and all collateral security for the loans, that is, leased equipment and proceeds.[6]

The banks also released any claims to insurance proceeds except for a proportional share of the booty relative to the insured leases which comprised the banks' various portfolios up to the settlement amounts, minus attorneys' fees and collection costs.

Inasmuch as the banks assigned their claims to secured party status, the trustee will realize up to 3 percent of all settlement proceeds paid to the banks, and the balance to investors, about $9 million.[7] The balance of his fee will come from the net distribution of the liquidation of non-lease assets and the proceeds from settlements from Generali and other defendants.

Although not getting quite full payment, the banks are receiving a substantial portion of what is due them. Importantly, their money, through periodic payments, was and continues to be liberated shortly after the settlements were approved by the Bankruptcy Court in mid-1997.

The remaining banks have chosen to duke it out with the trustee. At stake is about $50 million. After an initial order appeared to have re-

Table 15. The mathematics of the bank settlements

Date	No. of Banks	Total Claims	Estimated Yield to Unsecured Investors
Round I—12/96	49	31,500,000	15,000,000
Round II—2/97	148	95,700,000	35,000,000
Total	197	$127,200,000	50,000,000

Adapted from the trustee's section 341 slideshow presentation.

solved the conflict in the trustee's favor, Judge Gerling rendered a subsequent decision, holding that, mostly, the banks' security interests in the leases were properly perfected.[8] This required the estate to fork over the millions of dollars it collected on the pledged leases from the lessees. The seemingly contradictory orders were cross-appealed and remain open-ended.

Chapter 11 bankruptcies have checks and balances so that the rights of the differing creditors are not roughshod. Generally, secured parties can resort to their collateral if unhappy with the debtor's performance or repayment plan. Having no equity in the proceeding, however, unsecured creditors are championed by the unsecured creditors committee.

In the Bennett bankruptcy, two such committees were formed—one to protect the rights of unsecured creditors generally and one to protect the so-called early investors relative to settlement proceedings with the trustee.

As trustee, Breeden has a duty to all creditors regardless of their status. Theoretically, it is no skin off his nose if the banks prevailed over the investors and all lease proceeds were awarded to them. However, chapter 11 trustees are compensated based on payouts to unsecured creditors, such as the investors, and to secured parties for liquidated property subject to liens, such as the settled banks. It does not cover cases in which the trustee turns over or abandons secured property, such as to victorious banks.

Tension exists because for Breeden to earn large compensation he needed to defeat the banks' secured position in the leases and the streams of payments. It was in his best interest, therefore, to reclassify the banks so to subject the settlement payouts to the 3 percent fee dragnet, even though the settlements reward the banks with the return of much of their investment. In battling the forty-nine remaining banks, Breeden draws upon the estate's coffers.

But for Breeden's settlement, it was doubtful the unsecured creditors would receive any piece of the remaining stream of lease payments. The drafters of the Bankruptcy Code, in their infinite wisdom, harnessed the capitalist greed factor to work wonders for the investors. The more Breeden gets, the more the investors get.

Despite this, a novel argument can be made that the investors do have an interest in the leases paramount to the banks even in the face of proper perfection of the banks' security interests.

The argument was suggested inadvertently by the SEC. The SEC assumed jurisdiction over the Bennett Funding matter because of the allegation of securities fraud. The SEC argued the selling of the leases to investors constituted the selling of securities. They posit, under certain circumstances, leases are securities.

If we view the leases as securities and not merely as chattel paper, perhaps Article 8, as in force at the time, and not Article 9 of the code, takes precedent. Article 8 deals with the rights of owners of securities and perfection of security interests in securities. Article 9 deals with security interests in chattel paper and other goods.

At the time of the selling of the leases to the investors, one provision of Article 8[9] stated that a person who has been issued or sold a security that was recorded on the records of the issuer takes priority in that security even over a properly perfected secured party under Article 9. The law assumes the purchaser of the security did not have knowledge of the secured party's interest in that security aforehand.

Inasmuch as most of the leases were sold to the investors before the pledging of those same leases to the banks, the investors do not and could not have had notice of the banks' position vis-à-vis the filed UCC-1s.[10] Even if the sale came after the bank pledge, nevertheless, few banks filed the UCC-1s under the name of Bennett Funding. They opted to file under the Aloha Leasing trade name, resulting in ineffective notice to the financial community and the investors of the banks' security interest.

Unfortunately, we will never know whether this argument is bona fide. Although one investor took the position that strict perfection requirements "would be inequitable and contrary to the spirit of the UCC" because the code is intended to "protect consumers," such claim was overruled by Judge Gerling.[11] Not one attorney argued the Article 8 versus Article 9 distinction nor challenged the banks' or the trustee's claims that the investors are unsecured creditors because of failure to adhere to code requirements.

Of Brokers and Banks

R IGHT UP until the Company tanked, it relied heavily upon a Syracuse-based brokerage firm, Crawford and Associates, for placement of its leases with most of the 245 banks. Bennett Funding's relationship with Crawford originated in the early 1980s.

Crawford located the banks, struck the deals, and acted as middleman, including preparation of some of the paperwork required for the loans. In return, Crawford received on the average a fee equal to two and a half points of the face amount of each loan. In its heyday, Bennett Funding sent Crawford $1–3 million in leases every two weeks.

The relationship between Bennett Funding and Crawford has been viewed suspiciously. The suspicion centers on the size of the fee Crawford charged Bennett Funding for its services coupled with the exclusivity of the relationship.

Compared with fees and commissions charged by organizations performing similar brokerage services, the fee was unduly high and "therefore probative of the existence of an impropriety, such as an awareness of the double-pledging," according to one investigative law firm.[1] The investigators found no evidence of criminal wrongdoing by Crawford in that regard, however.

The owner of the brokerage house was, like Patrick Bennett, a horseman who loved to play at Vernon Downs. Although I do not know if Patrick can even ride a horse, he was a dedicated fancier. He frequented the track constantly. He entertained investors there. Patrick's persona seemed to be bound up with happenings at the track. Maybe the addiction to gambling drove him to steal money to feed his habit. According to Frank White, the former chief executive of Mid-State, Patrick "threw down $3,000 a night betting at the track."[2]

Until the Bennetts turned their attention to gaming, the local paper supported all of their activities. It gave them "free press" for local business ventures, such as the purchase and renovation of the Hotel Syracuse.

"But," as an editorial stated, "when we look at the trajectory of the

Bennett family fortunes, a point emerges at which the steepest downhill decline began. And that was when they started investing in gambling."

Even Alfred Luciani, who ran American Gaming for the Bennetts, was quoted as saying, "I think they thought gaming was easy, like a delicatessen; you open up and in two days you get a cash flow. It's not like that . . . it's highly speculative . . . it's high risk."[3]

One of the Crawford brokers introduced me to the sport of summer biathlon. Unlike the winter version, in summer biathlon, one runs cross-country more than three miles, stopping periodically to shoot a .22 rifle at stationary targets. I took my son Sam and we had a ball.

Sometime during this mess, the banks that engaged in litigation with the trustee over the perfection of the security interest in the leases took my deposition.[4] The banks' counsel, Unsecured Creditors Committee, and the trustee's counsel—at least ten attorneys—sat around a large conference table at the Bond office.

I was questioned more than six hours by the banks' counsel concerning what I knew about this and what I knew about that. I was told by an "objective" observer the whole thing was a colossal waste of time.

During the deposition, I was asked about the banks' reliance on my opinion of counsel given along with the other documents for each bank loan, namely,

1. *Promissory Note*—set forth the amount and the terms of the loan.

2. *Amortization Schedule*—set forth the schedule of loan repayment.

3. *Schedule of Leases*—set forth the lease numbers and lessee names for pledged leases.

4. *Assignment of Leases*—assigned an interest in the leases to secure the loan.

5. *Bill of Sale*—granted a further assignment of the leases to secure the loan.

6. *Guarantee*—the company guaranteed to pay the loan regardless if the pledged leases performed.

7. *Guarantee Collateral Agreement*—the company guaranteed the performance of the pledged leases.

8. *Servicing Agreement*—set forth the terms by which the company serviced the individual lease accounts relative to the lessee.

9. *Private Label Due Diligence Agreement*—prevented the bank from dealing with the various equipment vendors directly.

10. *Payment Account Agreement*—obligated the company to keep up

to two months of loan payments in an account at the lending bank.

11. *Incumbency Certificate*—set forth which officers in the company were responsible for the bank transaction.

12. *Corporate Resolution*—acknowledged that the company's board approved the bank loan.

13. *Chief Financial Officer/Treasurer Certificate*—acknowledged that the company's CFO, Patrick, approved the bank loan.

14. *Letter That Leases Are in Good Standing from CFO*—acknowledged that the leases were in good standing and valid.[5]

Although at least four other lawyers had signed opinions as well, because I was the general counsel, the banks' counsel presumed the signatures were affixed under my direction. Imagine their surprise when they learned, for a large chunk of time, the lawyers in the Legal Department reported not to me but to Bud Bennett. I also advised them I did not think the banks relied upon the opinion.

"Why is that?" they asked.

"Because I and all other counsel stopped giving the opinions in November 1995, but the banks continued to do business without the opinions right up until the Company filed bankruptcy in March 1996, five months later."

"They did? What do you mean? Why did you stop?"

"I am directing the witness not to answer the question under the attorney client privilege," interrupted counsel for the trustee, who acted as "my lawyer" during the deposition.[6] The questioning did not last long after that. Had I been allowed to answer, I would have said the following:

"Let me suggest the allegation concerning the double-pledging of leases is true. Virtually every one of the thousands of municipal leases sold by Bennett Funding to individual investors from December 1990 through September 1995 were also pledged as collateral for loans from one of 245 banks. I know this for a fact, albeit after the fact, because I was chairman of a committee, the Bank Committee, charged to investigate such things in the fall of 1995, the beginning of the end of the Bennetts."

October 26, 1995, started just like any other day. In by about 8:00 A.M., I ordered my usual breakfast of black coffee and two bagels from the building café, owned and operated by Bud's nephew. Once in my office, I ate breakfast and began reading through various files that lay atop the desk.

Shortly after picking remnants of bagel from between my teeth with a business card, I received a call from Michael.

"Stu, can you come to my office as soon as you can?"

"Sure, what's up?"

"I'll tell you when you get here."

Michael's voice was anxious. A few minutes later I went into his office. Sitting around the conference table were Tim White, CEO of Aloha Capital, Paul Usztock, CEO of the Processing Center, and Michael. Aloha Capital and the Processing Center were set up to continue the leasing business formerly generated by Bennett Funding.

All three men sported concerned faces—downcast eyes imbued with a slight fever-edge. They reminded me of the illustration in which a bartender asks a customer who is a horse, "Why the long face?"

I sat at the round table like one of the knights, Sir Weisman. Looking around the table, I asked what was going on. Michael began to speak quickly in a nervous ramble that was impossible to follow. Tim cut him off and explained the situation.

"Look, it seems when we audited leases in this one bank loan that were being assigned from Bennett Funding to Aloha Capital, it was determined they have been double-pledged."

"What? What do you mean double-pledged?" I asked.

"Sold to investors and pledged to banks as collateral," Tim answered curtly.

"How many leases?" I asked.

"About fifty in the portfolio. All of them were double-pledged," Tim responded.

"All of them?" I echoed.

"Yes, all of them," Tim said rather emphatically as he rose and began to pace like a fighter waiting for the bell.

What had been uncovered by the Aloha Capital internal audit was simply a repeat of the earlier situation in 1994 in which commercial leases were both sold to investors and then pledged to banks as collateral. In this case, municipal leases were double-pledged.[7]

"Look, Stu, this is criminal. Patrick did something wrong here," Tim remonstrated. Before I could respond, Michael screamed in,

"Listen, Tim, that's my brother and I don't want to hear criminal."

"What the hell do you call it then, Michael?" Tim shot back.

"Hold on, guys, let's calm down. This is not going to do any good. Let Stu speak," intoned Paul Usztock as he looked my way.

"Well," I started, not knowing exactly what to say, "we don't know all of the facts. Let's investigate before any action is taken. In the meantime, let's not use the word criminal until we get all of the facts, okay?" I said to keep the peace.

"Yeah, sure," Tim said.

"Fine, I agree," said Usztock. Michael just nodded his assent.

At this time, October 1995, Michael was the only one in the room who knew about the commercial lease double-pledging that had been going on until at least 1994. This was the first hint anything was wrong at Bennett Funding known outside the Bennett family. I was the counsel and I counseled caution. Hold until the facts were in.

It did not take long to establish the entire portfolio of municipal leases that were to be pledged to the bank was indeed already sold to investors. Every one. "Holy shit."

I contacted Patrick to find out what happened and how the matter could be corrected. He began to go through the story of the lack of failsafe in the municipal allocation system. Patrick explained the municipal fail-safe software program was but one of a dozen or more programs on a punch list of items that still needed attention subsequent to their installation in the Finance Department. He explained the commercial system did contain the fail-safe mechanism. Patrick failed to mention that it too was rogue until the preceding year.

Luckily, we were able to kill the subject transaction before consummation, that is, before the paperwork could be sent to the bank and the loan proceeds distributed. No harm, no foul.

Because Aloha Capital was beginning to phase in the leasing business and needed to borrow money through loans from Crawford-brokered banks, numerous other portfolios of existing leases in the inventory were assigned from Bennett Funding to Aloha Capital.

In that fashion, the probe deepened. A municipal portfolio already pledged to a bank in which proceeds were disbursed was discovered to have been double-pledged. The plot thickened.

During the next days, Tim was convinced Patrick was a crook. Based on advice from Tim's personal attorney, he gave the Bennetts an ultimatum: "Patrick must be fired, the authorities told of his criminal behavior, and full disclosure made to all involved." He told this to Patrick's mother, father, and brother. They did not do as Tim demanded; imagine that.

Within two weeks Tim quit. As he was under contract with the Company, he got a large six-figure severance package. Aloha Capital's general counsel quit. By this time the entire board of directors, several officers, all of the remaining in-house lawyers, and the couple of accountants who spotted the double-pledging in the first instance—about fifteen people—knew about the problem. Probably dozens of others heard rumors.

The resignations of individuals who were so high up in the Bennett Funding food chain were a serious impetus for the rest of us to leave, get severance, and move on. But most stayed, far outnumbering those who quit. We needed to ascertain the scope of the problem and try to fix it. But this was hard—stay and not run from the enemy's charge. To have courage under fire.

Shortly after Tim's resignation, I sent the following memorandum to Bud and Patrick and required their signatures:

Memorandum   *Office of General Counsel*

To: E. T. "Bud" Bennett & Patrick R. Bennett
From: Stu Weisman
Date: November 8, 1995
Re: Investigation

This memorandum is submitted to you as Chairman and Deputy Chairman of the Board of Directors of The Bennett Funding Group, Inc., ("Bennett") respectively, relative to certain improprieties associated with the sale of municipal leases.

On the morning of October 26, 1995, I was invited into a meeting with Michael, Tim, and Paul to discuss a memorandum written by the former General Counsel of Aloha Capital. He advised certain Municipal Leases may have been sold to individual investors and then pledged as collateral to certain banks.

Later that morning I met with Patrick to discuss the situation. He advised he was going to commence an investigation immediately. If the allegation of double-pledging was correct, then the Company would take such action as to prevent its reoccurrence and offer to repurchase the leases from the individuals investors, payoff the debt to the banks, or substitute collateral.

Patrick also advised the cause of the alleged problem is the municipal lease allocation system does not have a "fail safe" program which would prevent double allocation of municipal leases. Upon discovery of the problem, Patrick advised the double allocation problem was stopped immediately.

I have been advised by Patrick and by the accounting department the commercial lease allocation system does prevent double allocation of leases. To ensure the problem was not as wide spread as feared, the accounting department audited municipal leases on a trial (sample) basis. The sample audit, which went back to 1991, has revealed municipal leases have been sold to investors and then pledged as collateral to banks in numerous portfolios.

In light of the potential scope of the problem and Patrick's and the Finance Department's inability to deal with the situation, the following course of action is required:

1. Immediate cessation of the sale of municipal leases and their subsequent use as collateral. This has been reported to have occurred but must be verified by personnel not in or connected with the Finance Department.

2. An oversight committee needs to be formed immediately. The committee should be chaired by myself with the authority to appoint other members and to delegate various tasks to other employees, as the chairman deems fit.

3. A complete and confidential audit of all municipal leases from December, 1990, shall be undertaken to examine the scope of the municipal lease situation.

4. Creation of a software program to introduce "fail safe" into the municipal lease allocation system.

5. Repayment of the banks through the liquidation of unencumbered assets. To that end, management shall submit a plan to the committee which will detail the repayment procedure.

6. A law firm shall be retained by the committee to investigate the improprieties concerning the double-pledging. The firm cannot have represented Bennett previously and must be recognized as an expert in the area of corporate compliance. The committee shall discuss the situation with the counsel as to what additional steps need to be taken. If the counsel advises disclosure to third-parties must be made, then the committee shall recommend that course of action to the Board of Directors.

7. Unannounced and periodic audits by the committee shall be performed to insure compliance with the foregoing recommendations.

Not having received an immediate response from Bud and Patrick, I sent an intranet memo to Patrick: "We still need to get the investigation proposal signed off by both your father and yourself ASAP."[8]

That night, Patrick asked me to meet him at a convenient location to discuss the terms of the memorandum. We met at the lounge at the Hotel Syracuse about 7:00 P.M. We shook hands, sat down, and ordered drinks. After a few minutes of small talk, Patrick said, "Look, Stu, we have no problem signing off on the memorandum. We have no problem carrying through with the proposals."

"That's good," I said.

"But," he continued, "we are concerned the committee members will be preoccupied with committee business and neglect their day-to-day responsibilities. It's one . . ."

"Pat, I don't think that will be a problem," I jumped in.

"Let me finish," he said. I kept quiet.

"It's one thing to fix a problem and insure it won't reoccur. It is another to continue to do one's job so we have a company to continue."

"I understand your concern, Pat, but this is a serious problem. If the Company does not take immediate steps to correct the problem, I am afraid wholesale resignations will follow. Also, the rumors will spread and that will be that," I told him.

Sensing I could not be dissuaded from the mission at hand, Patrick said, "Okay, okay, I guess you got to do what you got to do. Just keep in mind that regular business still needs to be conducted. The Company needs capital, employees need to be paid, investors need their monthly payments, the bank loans need to be met, and so on. The Company still needs to raise money through the new leasing company, Aloha Capital, to meet all of these and more."

I assured Patrick that although committee work was job number one, nevertheless we would still be able to function in our respective positions—albeit with an altered view of reality—to keep things moving along.

After our colloquy, we got up, shook hands, and left. The next day, Bud and Patrick signed the memorandum and returned it to me for safekeeping. From that point on, my mission was to carry through with the various agreed-upon items, including the liquidation of assets to pay back the banks, as well as continue in my daily function as general counsel.

Going forward was easier said than done. Because of the double-pledging, we needed to insure no more hanky-panky in pledged portfolios could transpire.

We settled on having an internal due diligence of all leases to be pledged as collateral, that is, make sure the leases were not already assigned, sold or pledged to any other bank or investor. The task fell upon the Accounting Department. It was tedious but necessary work. We had to make sure we were not compounding the problem in future bank loans.

Bill Lester from the Accounting Department devised and implemented the procedures related to pledging leases as collateral to banks:

1. A search must be performed by a member of the accounting depart-

ment for each lease to verify the collateral has not been previously pledged to another bank or sold to an investor. This review will encompass tracing each lease back to the FIN Loan system to verify Bank, Note date, and payment amount. The specific lease must then be entered into the INV system to verify the lease has not been previously sold to an investor. The individual performing the review will sign off on a copy of the collateral listing upon completion of the review as indication of compliance and approval. The approved, signed off copy of the collateral listing will be retained in the house copy of the loan file prior to the execution of the document.

2. A person not connected with the Finance Department will perform a daily reconciliation of the unassigned lease pool. The reconciliation will trace the source and disposition of all leases into and out of the unassigned pool. The reconciliation will be forwarded to, reviewed by and maintained in the Accounting Department.[9]

At long last, the collateral listing will not be the exclusive domain of the leasemeister, Patrick Bennett. Other no-nonsense personnel would oversee this part of the business.[10]

At the time all of these glorious standard operating procedures were implemented, Patrick had the last laugh, because Kasarjian was doing his voodoo off-site by photocopying leases and creating off-system codes. But the joke was not long-lived.

In April 1997, Kasarjian pleaded guilty to various counts of securities fraud, conspiracy to obstruct justice, perjury, and conspiracy to commit bankruptcy fraud.

The following quotations are taken from the transcript of the hearing in federal court in New York in which Kasarjian entered his guilty pleas.[11]

> Kasarjian: The investors believed "the majority of my funds that I raised would be to purchase assets from Bennett, which never occurred . . ." and they "w[ere] purchasing a certain group of leases, but in essence, they would have been fictitious or certainly air."
>
> "There would have been no collateral, not even a unit of revenue. . . . There would have been absolutely nothing."
>
> "I knew in late 1994 that the amount of money being raised . . . that there was no way that Bennett could support the collateral behind the money being raised. . . ."

"I also engaged in a check kiting activity . . . wherein I tried to support Bennett by giving the chief financial officer blank checks drawn on . . . the Kenton portfolio management bank account . . . knowing that there was no cash in the account . . . to allow Bennett to credit his accounts . . . so that his checks wouldn't bounce."

U.S. District Judge Batts: Mr. Kasarjian, you have acknowledged several acts that you have committed. When you did these acts, as to each of these counts, did you know that what you were doing was wrong and illegal?

Kasarjian: "Regretfully, yes, your Honor, I did know."

Kasarjian's lawyer said the guilty pleas were entered to avoid the prolonged wait and expense of a trial. His client was truly full of contrition and wanted to make amends to the aggrieved investors whom he helped fleece millions upon millions of dollars.

Kasarjian must have been singing like a canary since he was busted in June 1996. He rolled over on the other big wheels in this matter and was an important witness at Patrick's trial where he dressed to the nines.

When Kasarjian was being prepped by the U.S. attorneys, another witness, who was also undergoing preparation in an adjacent office, said he brought the attorneys coffee and made chitchat to ingratiate himself. They told him he was going away a long time.

Until the recommendations in my memorandum to Bud and Patrick were in place, the bank loans repaid, and a comfort level achieved where no more bullshit would occur, no in-house attorney would sign opinions of counsel for the various Crawford bank closings, even though the opinions had been part of the standard documentation for all Crawford bank transactions since the mid-1980s.

No matter the pressure that was brought to bear by the Bennetts, we stood firm. If the transactions could not go through because the opinions were not furnished, then so be it.

Nevertheless, every bank that lent money to Bennett Funding or Aloha Capital after the investigation commenced in early November 1995 did so without opinions of counsel.

The banks kept lending money for another five months until the bankruptcy in March 1996. I guess they never relied on the opinions to begin with. That is what I would have told the banks' lawyers during my deposition.

During the litigation with the nonsettling banks, the trustee enlisted the help of George Davis. Mr. Davis was a former senior executive at Citibank with thirty years of experience and a recognized expert in prudent lending practices.

In a careful analysis of the Bennett/bank relationships, he concluded most of the banks failed to adequately and properly protect themselves in three major areas.

First, the banks relied almost exclusively upon Crawford for information concerning Bennett, the collateral, and the performance of the loans. Such informational requests, Davis maintained, should have been directed toward Bennett Funding not through the broker.

Second, although many of the banks met with Patrick and toured the facility, a significant number did not even bother to perform this rudimentary obligation of a prudent lender. Furthermore, the banks did not seriously question the delay in furnishing the 1994 audited financial statement nor the switch from the global auditor, Arthur Andersen, to the regional auditor, Mahoney Cohen.

Third, the banks abdicated control of the cash generated by the leases that were pledged as collateral enabling Patrick to commingle lease proceeds.

In contrast to most of the banks' lack of following prudent lending practices, MetLife, which entered into a $50 million line of credit, performed proper review, went to the source for information, and established a lockbox to segregate and control the cash generated by the leases pledged to secure the credit line.

"Well, maybe you didn't know what was happening before, but when you discovered the double-pledging in October 1995, why didn't you tell someone what was going on?"

That question has been asked or at least pondered by almost all who fell victim to the Bennetts. I shall try to answer by discussing the restraints imposed upon attorneys.

Although not accepted in all states as synonyms, the terms *lawyer, advocate, attorney, attorney-at-law,* and *counselor* refer to a person whose profession is to represent clients in a court of law or to advise or act for clients in other legal matters.[12] Moreover, the term *lawyer* implies the right or license to practice law as authorized by the various state and federal bars. The unauthorized practice of law is punishable criminally.[13]

Representing a corporation in-house does not alter these basic definitions. An in-house attorney represents the business client in court and gives guidance on legal matters. Such lawyers are bound by all rules regarding professional responsibility as apply to the general bar.

Few things can try a lawyer's soul as the decisions that must be made in discharging one's duties under the ethical, economical, and legal frameworks imposed by society and individual conscience. This is compounded by the tension caused by working as an attorney in the legal department of a corporation—especially where business decisions seem to take precedence over legal ones.

As mentioned above, lawyers are subject to the Code of Professional Responsibility. One important provision of the code holds an attorney may not reveal secrets of his client learned during the attorney-client relationship.[14] This is as sacred as the confessional. Violations of the code can lead to reprimand, censure, suspension, or even disbarment.[15]

This rule is so valued that a lawyer had even refused to reveal to the parents of a murder victim where the body of their daughter was buried, because such information was told to the lawyer by the perpetrator and the revelation might have harmed the client. The lawyer's decision was upheld by the courts. What is money in the face of that?

The code has been described as the ethical standards lawyers are expected to maintain—a set of published rules within a system. Although ethical systems appear to be morals codified, they most assuredly are not. Rules of ethics sometime coincide with moral behavior, sometimes adverse. Doing the ethical thing is not always doing the right thing.

Within their own context, ethical rules make sense. But they are not necessarily intuitive. Ethical violations seem to carry so much tongue-clucking authority than other violations of law by their asymptotical and sometimes coinciding relationship with morality, that is, approaching, even paralleling, but never equaling.

For example, it was ethical under the code for the lawyer not to have disclosed the whereabouts of the body of the dead child to her mother. Yet, it was an immoral act not to have done so. This is perhaps one reason why the public takes such a dim view of lawyers.

"How can they represent that animal?"

"Why can't they just tell the mother where her daughter is?"

In the case of the buried child, for example, situations that compel compliance with ethical codes invariably clash with society's sense of right and wrong.

In following the rules of an organization to which one belongs, the ethical codes of that group may have to take precedence over the general moral rules as long as one is a member and wants to continue to be a member of that organization.

Even though every in-house lawyer wanted to climb atop the Atrium and scream that the Bennetts are crooks, such conduct would have been the greater wrong. *Damned if I do and damned if I don't.*

Thus, neither I, the other in-house attorneys, nor outside counsel could have told any investor, bank, or government authority about the alleged wrongdoings. What we could not do was knowingly help the Company continue to commit crimes into the future. We believe this was accomplished by the thorough postinvestigation due diligence procedures instituted by the in-house lawyers and accountants.

For the next several months after the procedures were enacted, from November 1995 right until the bankruptcy in March 1996, the Bank Committee, working sometimes with the Bennetts, sometimes against them, scrambled to unload assets to gather sufficient funds to pay off the bank loans. This was our raison d'être.

The Bank Committee was under tremendous pressure to carry forth its mandate while servicing the Company in the normal course. The angst was at times overwhelming.

All major assets were fit for the chopping block, including:

1. Time-share acquisition, development, and construction loans valued at $33.2 million

2. Bennett Quality Inn valued at $3.8 million

3. Bennett Days Inn valued at $3 million

4. Hotel Syracuse valued at $18 million

5. 7.5 million shares of Aegis Corporation valued at $10 million

6. Gaming vessels valued at $26 million

7. Note receivable relative to bridge loan financing for a mall valued at $38 million

These assets represented $132 million, more than enough to pay off the $35 million present value of the balances due under the bank loans collateralized with municipal leases.[16]

At no time during the scramble for cash to set things right, though, did any of the Bennetts express an intention to throw their personal assets into the liquidation pot. At no time did the Bennetts express any sympathy for the Bank Committee or its grim task.

Since the beginning of my tenure at Bennett Funding in 1984, I do not recall either Bud or Kathleen working beyond normal hours, 8:30 A.M.–5:00 P.M., or on the weekend, even as the heat intensified in 1996. Their attitude was and remains a resolute "fuck 'em."

In furtherance of the investigation of the municipal lease double-pledging, the Bank Committee retained the services of perhaps the pre-eminent white collar crime investigative law firm in the country, Arkin Shaeffer & Kaplan.

Name partner Kaplan and an associate made several trips to Syracuse from their New York office in December 1995 and January 1996. They interviewed more than a dozen witnesses and reviewed corporate records, including:

1. Memorandum to Bud and Patrick in November 1995

2. Financial statements for the past several years

3. Survey going back five years of the value of those assets owned by Bennett that were unencumbered by any obligations

4. The percentage of $1 buy-out municipal leases held by Bennett relative to the total number of municipal leases

5. Complete list of all banks affected

6. Complete list of those municipal leases that were both sold and pledged as collateral

7. Various documents detailing Bennetts' efforts to sell assets to pay off those loans secured by double-pledged leases

8. Representative master inventory list

9. Representative municipal inventory list

10. Records retention policy

11. Representative financing statement to a bank

12. Representative opinion letter to a bank

13. Representative chief financial officer's certification

14. Representative promissory note with attached amortization schedule

15. Representative bill of sale to a bank

16. Representative guarantee to a bank

17. Representative guarantee collateral agreement to a bank

18. Representative assignment of contract to a bank

19. Representative servicing agreement

20. Representative private label due diligence agreement

21. Representative payment account agreement with a bank

22. Representative bill of sale to an individual[17]

After completing the investigation, the firm issued a report. Simply, while it found no conclusive direct evidence of criminal wrongdoing based on the interviews and the document review, the firm did find credible evidence to support an allegation of gross negligence and dereliction of duty by Patrick. Salient points of the Arkin report are reprinted here.[18]

There is, of course, no doubt that double-pledging occurred, and there is also considerable circumstantial evidence supporting the view that the double pledging was intentional.

Patrick Bennett's explanation of the manner in which the double pledging arose does not fully account for the problem. Finally, there is the disputed evidence of employee suggestions for making improvements to the computer system that would have prevented double-pledging, which were possibly made long before the September 1995 discovery and which were, for whatever reason, not acted upon.

The finance department generally and Patrick Bennett individually were grossly negligent in allowing this situation to develop. Our inquiry revealed no effort whatsoever to prevent double-pledging—hardly an unforeseeable occurrence given the overall laxness of controls—from taking place. This is particularly true given that, with the recent computerization of various finance department functions, preventive measures could readily have been implemented and may indeed have been suggested.

The corporate culture at Bennett at times seemed distrustful and suspicious. Several employees whom the firm interviewed have very little faith in the business ethics of some of the executives.

Further, several employees felt that some executives maintain too much secrecy regarding decision-making, not sharing procedural or substantive information with others.

Because family members are in key executive positions and often make decisions among themselves, a certain amount of what appears to be secrecy is presumably inevitable. The firm has drawn no conclusions from the nature of the corporate culture at Bennett for the very reason that it is a family-owned business, but does note that this climate of distrust created difficulties for the firm in its attempts to discern the nature of the double-pledging error. This is because, in a distrustful environment, some employees may make allegations with no factual or first-hand substantiation but based solely on the corporate culture, whereas others may be averse to revealing truthful negative information because of fear of retaliation.

Aside from Patrick Bennett, the firm has seen *no evidence that any other employee of Bennett . . . would have known of the double-pledging or was negligent in allowing it to occur.*

When I advised Bud that the Arkin report found no conclusive direct evidence of criminality, he cut me off before I could tell its real thrust, namely, there was ample evidence of extreme and gross negligence by Patrick in allowing the double-pledging to occur.

Bud ran with the "good" news to tell his wife and others.

"No criminality, no criminality," I imagined him yelling like Chicken Little advising the sky was falling.

I doubt any member of the Bennett family read the Arkin report. How could they? For it contained the truth about Patrick and how the Company had been improperly raising capital for more than five years.

Shortly after the report was issued in March 1996, Michael was summoned to appear before the SEC to give additional testimony. Michael never mentioned the report, the double-pledging of leases, nor the creation of the Bank Committee charged to investigate it. But, you know, the SEC probably did not ask.

I am sure the Arkin report would have found evidence of criminality had the Bank Committee known of the other wrongdoing at the Company, such as the sham transactions to puff up the financial statements, the prior commercial double-dipping, the changing of journal entries, the New York City Transit Authority leases, and the sale of Kasarjian's off-site, off-coded leases.

We could only share what we knew about. Of course, the firm was sued for failing to uncover the fraud.

Some More Business Syndromes

*T*HE SOCK *syndrome.* Argyle, basic black, white crew, knee high, pattern, cotton, cotton blend, nylon, wool, ragg. Oh, the variety of socks! Socks reflect taste in wardrobe, budget, and the acceptability of certain textures against skin. They should be changed often. Having a teenage son, I cannot say daily necessarily.

So too can companies change plans as if changing socks. One day the company will pursue one goal, one strategy, one end. The next day, like shedding argyles for basic blacks, the company will change its goal. The company blows in the wind. It lacks drive beyond simple survival or immediate profit. It twists and turns, picking up trends, making fashion statements and assuming a face along the way.

In the end, it cannot be said the company had a purpose in the universe other than to gain short-term profits for a privileged few.

Although Nietzsche said "man would rather have the void for his purpose than to be void of purpose,"[1] surely, after so many years of engaging in the corporate experiment, we have aspired to become more than just money grubbers.

Incorporations are very simple to do. Generally, they are inexpensive and not very time consuming. Just about anyone can create a corporation. A service in Albany can get one up and running within forty-eight hours for under $400.[2] But what gives it life, what drives it, what sustains it through the hard times—well, that's another story.

Corporations, particularly small, privately held, or close corporations like Bennett Funding, tend to wear the persona of the person in charge. The corporation will suffer from the same neuroses and psychological conditions as its top dog. If the CEO is viewed as a weak, easily swayed individual, so too will the piranhas of the business world view the corporation.

If the CEO is insecure, always aiming to please, the corporation will be viewed as ripe for the picking. In this fashion, sometimes, it is better to be viewed as almost Mafialike. This does not mean the corporation should be unethical, engage in immoral acts, or pander evil. To the contrary, one can be tough without being a crook. Courage is in the heart and the CEO is in the unique position to foster nobility.

All told, the Bennetts had incorporated, merged, or acquired more than seventy corporations. Although many of these corporations were borne of necessity or through strategic planning, others were created willy-nilly, usually at the whim of Bud.

After the double-pledging was investigated by the Bank Committee and corrective action taken, Bud finally decided to get into the act. His idea was to incorporate Bennett Funding Special Purpose Corp. After incorporation, BFSPC was to acquire certain unencumbered assets from the other Bennett companies. The assets, or shares of BFSPC, were then to be pledged to the 245 banks to give them a comfort level until payoff of their loans was achieved. Bud's plan assumed the banks either found out or were told about the double-pledging.

Several days after BFSPC was incorporated and paperwork drafted to effectuate the transfer of the assets, Bud simply abandoned the plan. Probably at Patrick's behest, he opted for another plan, which was to liquidate the assets and either pledge or tender the cash to the banks directly, that is, without disclosure. Bud changed his socks.

When times were good, Bud wanted to get into the telecommunications business in the worst way. Accordingly, he had me incorporate Aloha Telecommunications. Aloha Telecommunications was to carve out a niche by furnishing turnkey leasing of telecommunications equipment to businesses.

Not long thereafter, Bud had me incorporate Aloha Telecom Funding, which was also to engage in leasing telecommunications equipment specializing in governmental entities. Within a year Bennett Telecommunications was born. Its stated purpose was to break into the consumer telecommunications leasing market.

All of these corporations were to serve the same purpose: telecommunications equipment leasing. Separate corporations were not necessary. The entities could have been consolidated under one roof, under one corporation.

Of the three, only Aloha Telecommunications appears to have done any business. The other two were shelved, not to see the light of day. None of the corporations appeared to have been created to defraud investors. Bud changed his socks again. Nothing more nor less.

In 1994, I grew concerned about the number of new corporations that seemed to serve no purpose other than to satisfy an urge. The Legal Department was busy enough without the additional burden of shepherding unneeded entities. The transaction costs involved in setting up and maintaining the overabundance could be saved as well.

I advised Bud tactfully that long-term planning, due diligence review, tax ramifications, the names of shareholders, types of stock, number of shares, type of corporation, start-up capital, state of incorporation, and other similar considerations need to be threshed out before incorporation.[3]

To that end, I drafted a preincorporation checklist, which contained the foregoing elements. Copies of the memorandum and checklist were circulated to the individuals charged with running the Company. A few of them even responded with comments.

Within several days after the dissemination of the memo and checklist, Bud asked me to incorporate three new corporations. He did so without following any of the suggestions, going through the checklist, or obtaining the sign-offs from finance, accounting, legal, and tax departments as suggested for the new ventures. This is not illegal or even improper, simply poor business judgment.

I do not know whether the rapid incorporations on the heels of my advice was Bud's way of showing who was in charge as opposed to legitimate business concern. The fact is he did not follow counsel's advice even in this rudimentary area. "Cheeseburger, cheeseburger." But, as owner, that was his prerogative.

When the scams were uncovered, third parties looked at the corporate organizational chart I had prepared showing all of the seventy-plus corporate interlinks. Most rolled their eyes in amazement. When told many of the companies were banal creations of Bud's changing socks, the viewers professed disbelief. Some people are so ready to accept conspiracy theories and see the evilness in men. In this case, although there was plenty of evil to go around, the number of interlinked companies was not a mathematical expression of conscious design.

Many of them were incorporated based on a business inspiration. The ventures oft times did not emerge leaving an empty shell like an eaten lobster. Many of the corporations were nothing but abandoned or failed attempts to do new business.

Salad bar syndrome. How many times have you ordered a meal at a restaurant that seemed too big to finish only to find "the damn thing was all lettuce"?

Now, imagine building a salad at a self-serve salad bar only to complain "the damn thing is all lettuce."

I call this, naturally, the salad bar syndrome, that is, an individual's mimicking of destructive institutionalized behavior.

Because the salad bar syndrome is an individual manifestation, its existence is revealed only in anecdote.

In a business context, for example, a manager complains about the boring presentation at a management meeting, only to conduct his department's meeting such that the staff's eyes glaze over like jurors at the O. J. Simpson trial listening to the intricacies and nuances of DNA evidence.

The syndrome is not merely hypocrisy. It is deeply rooted in corporate cultures in which information is withheld from employees, stereotypic viewpoints are maintained, homogeneity is a virtue, and the technobabblespeak of business cool permeates.

Surprisingly, Bennett Funding did not suffer to any great degree from the salad bar syndrome despite the fertile breeding grounds of its infamous culture.

A notable complicated instance does bear mentioning, though. There came a time when the accumulated losses from the Bennetts' foray into gaming were intolerable and had to be dealt with. The losses included investment with American Gaming, gaming vessels, and casinos, about $150 million. According to filings with the SEC, American Gaming alone owed the Bennett companies about $125.5 million.

In late 1995, the Company decided to spin off the gaming assets to a start-up corporation, Pegasus.[4] Pegasus was to manage and ultimately sell the gaming assets on behalf of the Company and scour the country for other gaming opportunities in its own right.

Kevin Kuppel, a Bennett Funding board member and officer, resigned his positions to assume leadership of Pegasus. Pegasus was to be an exception in that Kevin, a non-Bennett family member, would be truly in charge and make all executive decisions. He was assured by Bud that Pegasus was to be independent and under his control.

At first, the several employees of Pegasus who were transplants from Bennett Funding were ecstatic about their new sense of autonomy, like snakes shedding their skin.

But Patrick, as much a progenitor as a procreator of Bennett Funding's corporate culture, wanted to secretly pull the strings and extend his style of business to Pegasus. The hapless employees were caught in the middle of a power struggle between Patrick and Kevin. They were fearful of backing the wrong horse.

Kevin stood his ground and would not acquiesce to Patrick's machinations. In late 1995, he resigned to help run TargetVision, Inc., a software company in Rochester, New York, with loose ties to the Company. Pegasus never got off the ground. The employees were not invited back to Bennett Funding.

Patrick's last days at the Company were spent in a tiny office at Pegasus coordinating his departure and defense—an individual mimicking destructive institutionalized behavior.

THE ANSWER?

"If I am not for myself, who will be for me? But if I am only for myself, what am I? And if not now, when?"[1]

—Hillel

A Word to the Wise

LOOK, THE rate of return was not too good to be true but I got burned on those damn Bennett leases anyway. Is there anything I can do to protect myself in similar investments?"[1]

After reviewing the source documents and the computer system used in perpetrating the Bennett Funding financial scam, talking to witnesses, relying upon court decisions, trends in the industry, applicable statutes, new legislation in the offing, and the benefit of hindsight, experts agree steps can be taken to avoid the major pitfalls inherent in lease investing. Those pitfalls are: (1) mistakes in documentation, (2) miscalculation of yields, (3) fraud by broker, servicer, or issuer (4) bankruptcy of issuer or servicer, (5) commingling of payments, (6) lessee defaults and collection problems, and (7) loss of tax exempt status (for municipal products).

General observations first.[2] As I tell every new attorney who works with me, just because we are lawyers working in a legal environment does not mean there is a legal solution to every problem. Do not forget common sense! This same admonition applies to investments as well. Don't forget common sense when deciding to spend your hard-earned dollars. Antennas should be tingling in terms of the promised rate of return, the reputation of the issuer and broker, and the availability of documents to review.

Although the rates of return on some of the Bennett financial products were higher than prevailing rates, they were not much higher.[3] Others were commensurate with offerings of similar scope. This is one reason why people trusted the Bennetts and gobbled the products. But as a rule, if it sounds too good to be true, it probably is: "if too high take a bye."

"The vast majority of reported Ponzi scheme cases involve investors who are promised profits far too good to be believed, and in any case far greater than the roughly market rate return received by [many of the Bennett investors] ... no court, however, has ever incorporated a minimum rate of return into its definition of a Ponzi scheme."[4]

Usually, one can rightfully depend upon the credentials of well-established brokers and issuers. But don't be overimpressed because many such "masters of the universe" are nothing but manipulating, self-dealing, inside-trading money grubbers who could care less about the investing public or their clients.

But also don't be suckered in because the brokers, issuers, or their agents speak like you, "derefore dey mus be okay guyz."

As in the law of supply and demand, with any investment the amount and scope of documentation must be balanced with the size of the investment. However, do not be lulled into a false sense of security because a deal is papered to death. Read all of the documents and ask questions. If the questions cannot be answered, or the issuer/broker is afraid to put it in writing, walk away.[5]

If your common sense is still not offended, continue. If something is not kosher, tread lightly.

In a classical lease-security transaction in which the value of the investment justifies the effort, a host of documents should be reviewed and obtained.[6]

First on the list is the original lease properly executed with ink signature. Although duplicate originals can exist, as in the Bennett case, having an original minimizes the risk and, from a commercial viewpoint, increases the chance of proper perfection of security interest or evidence of transfer of title.

Generally, an original signature makes a document an original, not the thickness or quality of the paper it is printed on.

Sometimes leasing companies enter into a master lease with a lessee, typically a major user such as General Motors. The master lease concept allows a leasing company to accommodate the continuing needs of a customer without the preparation and execution of a new lease with each order.

In such transactions, the master lease, TotaLease in Bennettspeak, contains the standard terms and conditions, such as default clauses and warranty provisions. The leased equipment is referenced in schedules. The schedules describe the type and amount of equipment, the monthly rent, and incorporate by reference the master lease for the other terms and conditions. As the lessee needs equipment over time, new equipment schedules are executed. It is not uncommon for a master lease to have several, if not scores, of equipment schedules.

When an investor purchases a master lease schedule, a certified copy of the original master lease coupled with the original ink-signed schedule must be given.

Although the general stability of government agencies, school districts, and the like is taken for granted, catastrophes do happen, and such municipalities default under their obligations. The most recent example is the massive default of Orange County.

Other municipalities do not pay on time, and collection techniques must be employed. Still others elect not to encumber funds to pay on certain obligations and cancel under a nonappropriation theory.

Despite these risks, investors love municipal leases because they generally are stable and tax exempt. To afford a level of comfort, investors should obtain a credit rating of the municipality from Standard and Poor's or Moody's before entering into a municipal lease investment.[7]

To ensure the interest component is indeed tax exempt, the investor must receive a copy of the properly executed and filed IRS Form 8038G. This form is prima facie evidence the municipality is accorded tax-exempt status. The municipality is responsible for executing and filing the form.

Moreover, an opinion from qualified tax counsel should be furnished. The opinion should unequivocally state the transaction is tax exempt. The opinion should either be addressed to the investor or have language that indicates the opinion is intended for use and reliance by the investor. Otherwise, the law firm issuing the opinion may defeat a claim because of lack of privity.

Leases may be sold or assigned either by direct language on the lease instrument itself, through an allonge,[8] a bill of sale, or a separate assignment. An allonge is an attachment, or rider, to the granting instrument acknowledging the transfer or sale and must be attached firmly. In all cases, originals with ink signatures must be tendered.

To further ensure a proper sale or assignment of a lease, both UCC-1 and UCC-3 financing statements should be filed in the appropriate jurisdictions under the correct names. Many times, although not absolutely required, leasing companies will obtain UCC-1 financing statements from leases for protection in case the lessee files bankruptcy. Those UCC-1s are filed in the lessee's hometown, not the lessor's.

Unless the lessor/lessee UCC-1 included an assignment to the investor on its face, or a separate UCC-3 assignment statement is executed, simply having the leasing company execute and file a UCC-1 for the benefit of the investor without the concomitant assignment of the UCC-1 from the lessee may be insufficient to perfect a secured or other interest in the underlying equipment in the name of the investor should that become necessary.

It would also be beneficial to have the lessee acknowledge the assignment of the lease, equipment or stream of payments or both to the investor.

The payments received from the lessee should flow into a segregated account or lockbox in the beneficial name of the investor. Proof of such segregated account or lockbox arrangement should be tendered.

When the leasing company uses an outside servicer to bill and collect from the lessee, a copy of the service contract should be provided.

If the transaction is credit insured, a copy of the policy, the original certificate or declaration of insurance with the investor named as loss payee on both, financials of the insurer, a copy of the reinsurance contract if applicable, and proof of paid premium are all required.

Keep in mind that it is not customary for an insurer to guarantee the performance of the leasing company, only the payments from the lessee. Be wary of any deal to the contrary.

Obtain a guarantee of the leasing company should the lessee default if the economics of the transaction indicate recourse liability.

Miscellaneous documents should be provided to ensure the leasing company is, in corporate terms, in good standing and authorized to enter into the transaction.

If the lease has a purchase option, a copy of the residual/wholesale agreement with third-party liquidators should be reviewed should the lessee decide not to purchase the equipment at lease end.

At this juncture it may be instructive to view the actual risk language in a Bennett Receivables Corporation–II offering. As you may recall, Bennett Receivables Corporation–II is a wholly owned special-purpose subsidiary of Bennett Funding.

Its "special purpose" was to make loans to Bennett Funding that were to be collateralized by an assignment of a security interest in leases, consumer receivables, and inventory finance promissory notes generated by Bennett Funding.

Bennett Funding, in turn, would use the loan proceeds to make purchases of new income-producing items. Patrick Bennett failed to collateralize the loans with the leases, receivables, and notes.

The "Bennett Receivables Corporation–II, $80,000,000 Short &

Medium Term Notes, dated October 1, 1994, Private Placement Memorandum" contained a generous helping of risk factors:[9]

Preamble

The Notes are speculative and prospective purchasers should consider the
following factors, among others, in evaluating Bennett, its business, [Bennett
Receivables], and the Notes being offered hereunder.

No Trustee or Indenture for the Notes

The Notes will not be issued pursuant to . . . a Trust. . . . Consequently, holders of the Notes will be required to rely on their own resources, rather than
upon the resources of a trustee, to enforce the terms and provisions of the
Notes against [Bennett Receivables]. Additionally, the lack of . . . trustee increases the risk of improper acts or omissions by [Bennett Receivables].

Availability of Recourse

Bennett has guaranteed payment of the Notes and has granted Note holders
full recourse to it. In the event of default, however, there can be no assurance
to investors that Bennett will be able to meet its guaranty obligations.

Availability of Credit/Capital Requirements

Although Bennett believes it has adequate sources of funding and although it
is constantly attempting to expand its financing sources, there can be no assurance of Bennett's continuing ability to maintain adequate funding.

Ability of Bennett to Service Receivables

[T]here can be no assurance . . . that Bennett will not file for protection from
its creditors under . . . Bankruptcy laws or be in a position to service and
manage the receivables which are collateral for the loans which the Company
makes to Bennett.

*Bennett and [Bennett Receivables] are under control of the same persons and
Bennett will retain control of the collateral*

Bennett Receivables and Bennett are under the control of the same persons
and [Bennett Receivables] has no assets other than the notes from Bennett.
Although [Bennett Receivables] will enter into a security agreement whereby
Bennett will pledge certain leases and contracts to [Bennett Receivables] to
secure this debt, [Bennett Receivables] security interest in the Collateral and
the lease and contract payments Bennett will use to repay its loan from [Ben-
nett Receivables] are not perfected as they will remain in the possession of
Bennett. Therefore, no independent third party is in a position to enforce
Bennett's promises with regard to the handling of the security for the debt.

The stated risk factors should have planted the seeds that the lack of a trustee increased the risk that improper acts or omissions by Bennett would not be discovered or remedied. The lack of assurances Bennett would be able to meet its guaranty obligations and continue to maintain adequate funding was an important disclosure. Likewise, the absence of assurance Bennett would not file for protection from its creditors under bankruptcy laws and that no independent third party would be in a position to enforce Bennett's promises with regard to the handling of the collateral were compelling.

Indeed, the preamble to the PPM stated:

> Bennett Receivables will make available, prior to the consummation of the transactions contemplated herein, to each prospective investor and his representatives and advisors the opportunity to ask questions of, and receive answers from, [Bennett Receivables] or from any person acting on its behalf concerning the terms and conditions of this offering and to obtain any additional information, to the extent that [Bennett Receivables] possesses such information or can obtain it without unreasonable effort or expense, necessary to verify the accuracy of the information contained in this memorandum.

How many investors who purchased Bennett Receivables' notes took advantage of this invitation to make inquiries beyond the four corners of the PPM? Indeed, how many investors read the PPM and assessed the various risk factors?

To avoid some of the risks associated with investing, even when such risks are disclosed and published, a savvy investor may turn to lease securitization packages[10] for incorporating most of the safeguards mentioned before.

In lease securitizations, the leasing company sells the leases to a special-purpose corporation that is considered a bankruptcy remote entity (the SPC). Although the shares of the SPC are typically owned by the parent leasing company, the two do not have interlocking boards or common officers, do not share the same office, or even have the same phone number.

Thus, in theory, the SPC will survive the bankruptcy of the leasing company so that the securitization leases are not hotchpot and considered part of the bankruptcy estate.

The SPC then sells the leases to a trust or another special-purpose corporation established by an institutional lender.

Fig. 8. Typical lease securitization program

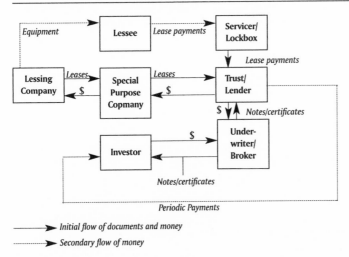

——————▶ Initial flow of documents and money
·············▶ Secondary flow of money

The trust or institutional SPC retains the original lease agreements and issuances notes or trust participation certificates through underwriters. The notes or certificates are rated and sold to investors in the usual ways.

An independent servicer then bills and collects the monthly lease payments from the lessees. The money flows into a lockbox for the benefit of the trust or institutional SPC. The trust then makes periodic payments to the investors according to the terms and conditions of the notes or certificates.

The securitization can become more complicated. For instance, sometimes the leasing company will borrow money from the SPC and pledge the leases as collateral which upstreams to the trust. This allows the leasing company to have a healthy mix of sales and loans on its books and gives it flexibility to have off-balance sheet treatment of the transaction.

Sometimes the rate of return on the notes or certificates sold to investors floats with market rates. In these cases, the leasing company may be obligated to purchase hedge insurance to maintain the stability of the rate.

Although investors should not ignore the foregoing general observations and should be comfortable with both the concept of and the documentation supporting it, securitizations seem to be safe because they segregate the cash flow generated by the lessees and impose an extra layer of sophisticated third-parties, such as insurers, auditors, and rating agencies, in the process.[11]

Good luck.

Crime . . .

WHY DOES society enact so many laws that tend to govern every facet of our existence? Some would say more and more laws are needed because people are bad and things are getting worse. The increase is a reaction to the lack of personal morality exhibited by so many people. We need a battery of ordinances to mask insipid achievements on the moral scale; we are not as advanced morally as we purport to be, and the vacuum must be filled by legislation.

Others may respond that the laws themselves may be responsible for the degeneration of individual morality and not authored in response to it. The ever-widening spiral of laws, rules, and regulations has resulted in the vestigial effect of personal morality; as long as the law is obeyed, individuals do not have to develop their own sense of right and wrong, in essence, abdicating their sense of right and wrong to society's legal mandates. The more laws a society creates, the less moral its citizens need to be; moral education becomes neither mandatory nor required.

Some would go so far as to suggest the legislation is a product of a self-fulfilling prophecy, a movement to arrest moral development and substitute the rule of law—a movement to make us sheep, to strip away our humanity, to dance through life and never have to sit down and think, What is the right thing to do?

With such conflicting viewpoints, and too few people willing to engage in discourse, what, then, can be said of a society too "wrapped up in legislatin' and not enough in educatin'"?

Acknowledging most people would not like toxic chemicals dumped into their drinking water or released into the air their children breathe, one federal environmental regulation[1] restricts the amount of pollutants that factories release into the environment.

For example, annually, a factory is permitted to pour so many cubic tons of sulfur dioxide into the air. The same regulation allows the factory which pollutes less than its quota to sell the differential to another polluter who is in danger of exceeding its pollution limit.[2] From a holistic viewpoint, an acceptable amount of pollution is released into the air. A steady state is achieved. Brokers even transact this kind of business.

In suggesting compliance can be purchased like so many indulgences, the regulation intimates pollution is just another commodity. If a factory pollutes less, wonderful; but if it is helping another factory pollute more, is that wonderful too?

Is this the endgame of more than two hundred years of American jurisprudence—selling rights to pollute? Is this the ideal to which we aspire? If I go below the speed limit, can I give the extra miles to someone else, who is then allowed to exceed the limit so long as equilibrium is achieved?

What face will justice wear when dealing with the Bennetts and their conspirators? What lessons will be learned by those involved? By society as a whole? Will the collective conscience laugh at our feeble attempt to dispense justice?

The protracted nature of the trial processes—already more than three years—the uncertainty of the decisions because of appeals, the enormous cash payments to the lawyers and the accountants, the costs to the taxpayers for the SEC and Justice Department investigations and criminal trials, the loss of life, the altered destinies, the changes of fortunes, and the roller-coaster ride of the bankruptcy, surely serve to dampen the victims' faith in the system.

The long-term employees who suffered stoically the abuses of the Bennetts' management style, which included screaming, public ridicule, ignominies, and punishment for trivial activities, suffered while the Bennetts operated a huge criminal enterprise.

Imagine being called on the carpet for failure to file some form or other while your boss was bilking the corporation, investors, and banks out of hundreds of millions for racehorses, hotels, casinos, stocks, yachts, cars, and general self-aggrandizement.

The employees toiled away at the daily grind. They felt satisfied at night after a good, honest day's work. They earned bread by the sweat of their brows. The employees bought Bud and Kathleen Christmas gifts every year, even when raises were severely limited or cut. The Bennetts were honored even when they bought a yacht and huge homes while giving the employees Thanksgiving turkeys instead of bonuses.

All said, if the Company were to die, it should have died a natural death years ago before the Bennetts fell into the dark side. It should not have been kept alive by artificial and criminal means and crumble like dry filo dough. The employees could have lived with a normal business failure instead of the taint of criminality that pervades their working days. They would have obtained different jobs, maybe making less money, maybe more. But they would never have been maligned and stigmatized. To be sure, reputations were soiled, faith in people shattered, and futures dimmed.

Does the world view the employees as the little girl in the old Shake-n-Bake commercial who refrained, "and I helped"? Is it a physical law that the employees should feel ashamed to have worked for such people?

Those who should feel shame have been indicted. Guilty pleas have been accepted from eight of the perpetrators. Another has been charged with similar offenses. Patrick was convicted. The inevitability of karma, the great cosmic equalizer; the irresistible force of creation driving relentlessly toward justice—If not in this lifetime, perhaps in the next.

As Ms. White, the U.S. attorney, said at a press conference that heralded the issuance of the indictments against Patrick, Michael, Kasarjian, Pavoni, Genovese and several others:

> This indictment charges a massive carefully executed investment fraud, one of the largest in United States financial history. Patrick Bennett is charged with systematically bilking more than 12,000 investors out of hundreds of millions of dollars by selling them fictitious, fraudulent, and worthless lease contracts and promissory notes. Patrick is also charged with taking elaborate steps to launder the proceeds of these crimes, then squandering investors' hard-earned money on himself and his family and on wildly speculative and ill-conceived investments. Calling this white-collar crime may trivialize the enormous hardship and economic devastation suffered by the thousands of hardworking investors who were victims of these crimes. Such wanton disregard for the welfare of others cannot be tolerated.

Ms. White should have added that pounds of flesh will be extracted.[3]

Country Bumpkin—Patrick's Trial

AFTER THE jury was selected, opening statements in Patrick's trial were made on December 14, 1998, my sister's birthday. As is customary in federal trials, Patrick Smith, representing the government, went first.[1]

He told a story of how Patrick sold and pledged the same equipment leases repeatedly. Through Patrick's manipulations, Smith highlighted, the Bennett companies sold more than $1 billion worth of leases than they had in inventory. Although the date when Patrick orchestrated the first phony deal is uncertain, Smith told the jurors that it could have started as early as 1988 with bogus leases supporting Tony Menchella's deli, P.T.'s Shortstop.

Smith went on to talk about Patrick's conspiracy to obstruct justice by creating fake documents and coordinating phony testimony to the SEC, sham transactions, and the blatant embezzlement of $13 million.

Smith emphasized Patrick committed these wrongful acts for personal gain.

In securities fraud cases, defense counsel typically tries to blur the line separating criminal conduct and poor business judgment. Blame is laid at the door of others. Defense attorney Levitt addressed the jury with a provocative rebuttal of the government's case, which took the customary defense tactic into territory heretofore unexplored.

"Patrick Bennett is a country bumpkin,"[2] Levitt announced to Judge Griesa, the jury, a few spectators, and the Bennett family entourage—Bud and Kathleen, Gwen and her two sons, Patrick and Andrew, and her parents.

So that was the grand stratagem—the geography card. Levitt's plan was built upon the stereotypical views held by New Yorkers who live "upstate" (most counties above Westchester) versus those who reside "downstate" (basically, the five boroughs of New York City and Long Island).

Most upstaters see New York City as dirty and crime infested, a place where the residents would kill you so much as look at you. Downstaters view upstaters as yokels. Patrick, a dyed-in-the-wool upstater, certainly fits the troglodyte profile. Surely, the bumpkin defense would play well before a New York City jury.

Levitt told the jury Patrick was not qualified to run Bennett Funding, which he characterized as an out-of-control company run by amateurs. That no doubt will endear him to the employees.

Incredibly, Levitt suggested Patrick did not know his business associates were peddling phony leases. When the SEC began its investigation, Levitt noted, Patrick simply panicked. Any actions taken by him were not malevolent but a knee-jerk reaction to the pressure of keeping the Bennett companies going.

Also appealing to prejudices some of the jurors may have had toward the heavy-handed tactics of the government, throughout the trial Levitt intermeshed the bumpkin story with tales of federal intrigue. He pedaled the bologna that Breeden spun his web during his tenure at the SEC and parlayed it into multimillionaire status as titular head of the Company.

Although there is some truth to the assertion that he was a rube, Patrick was more country squire than country bumpkin. He owned a racetrack, drove around in a Jaguar and a Mercedes Benz, built an eight-thousand-square-foot house and horse farm, drew an enormous salary, owned racehorses and stocks in private and public corporations, and had unfettered control over billions of dollars for a decade.

After seven weeks of testimony from thirty-one witnesses including coindictees, former and current Bennett employees, government investigators, and victims, the government rested on February 4, 1999.

The defense commenced on February 8—Sara and my anniversary. With no witnesses to support his rube's view of the universe, Patrick took the stand himself. In an emotional outpouring that forced Judge Griesa to call a recess, a tearful Patrick admitted he lied to SEC investigators as early as 1993.

Patrick told the jury he discovered Bennett Funding did not assign leases to secure the Horizon 7 percent notes. To protect Horizon, then a client of Ken Kasarjian, and to insure continuity of the business, Patrick admitted he asked both Al Cerimeli and Tony Menchella to backdate documents and lie to the SEC.

From the stand, he apologized to both Cerimeli and Menchella, whose motives were simply to help their friend Patrick. He cast aspersions upon the motivations of the coconspirators and blamed others for failing to keep him informed about proper accounting procedures. Patrick never publicly apologized to the employees, investors, or his other family members for the grief he caused.

Although he admitted there was fraud at the Company, Patrick emphatically denied he was involved with selling bogus leases and double-pledging leases to investors and banks.

Cross-examination started the next day. Under questioning by Richard Owens, predictably, Patrick laid the blame for the double-pledging and selling of fake leases on the shoulders of Kasarjian. Although Kasarjian previously testified he took part in the scheme, he said Patrick was fully aware and took an active role.

During the testimony from other Finance Department employees earlier in the trial, it was learned Patrick even sold double-pledged and fake leases to employees who invested with the Company. Owens, reminding the jury of this unkindest cut, asked Patrick why leases he purchased were genuine.

"I wouldn't know," Patrick responded.

Patrick testified he and Gwen stopped buying leases in April 1993 because they did not have excess cash. Of course, in May 1993, the SEC sent Bennett Funding a letter of inquiry and requested production of all documents related to the Horizon 7 percent notes.

Continuing on the theme that Patrick misled the SEC, Owens had Patrick admit he lied during every one of the ten sessions. He even told the SEC he had a B.A. in business from Syracuse University. At trial he said he did not take business courses, let alone graduate.

During the next day of cross-examination, Owens handed Patrick copies of financial statements that were circulated to the investors and banks. Patrick was asked how Bennett Funding could have transferred more money to Bennett Management than it earned as reported in the 1993 Consolidated Financial Statement.

"I don't think the one number has anything to do with the other," Patrick answered.

During a short jury break, Judge Griesa, appearing confused over the inconsistencies in the reported numbers, echoed Owens's question out loud. The judge, 68, was appointed by President Nixon.

Without calling any other witness, the defense rested its case on February 11, 1999. In rebuttal, the prosecution called FBI Special Agent John Hess to the stand. Hess interviewed Patrick in June 1997. During those interviews, Patrick admitted he engaged in sham financial transactions to hide Scriptex's and American Gaming's default status on loans and leases owed to the Company.

After the presentation of evidence in a criminal trial, it is customary for the defense to make motions to dismiss the matter on various grounds. Levitt requested dismissal of the money-laundering charges, because they occurred in the northern district and not in the southern district.

Judge Griesa, although noting the scarcity of proof of activities in the southern district, denied the motion the same afternoon, leaving the door open for the inevitable appeal.

On February 16, the prosecution delivered its closing argument. Patrick Smith urged the jury to reject the country bumpkin defense.

"How many people . . . own a racetrack?" he asked. He reminded the jurors of the sham accounting transactions and intercompany money transfers.

"There he is, Mr. No Real Training in Accounting, Mr. Country Bumpkin, using technical terms," Smith thundered.

The next day, Gombiner delivered his remarks. He reiterated the theme that, although his client "fessed-up" to making mistakes, "you have to look west across the river to New Jersey" to find the fraud orchestrated by Kasarjian, Pavoni, and Genovese.

In a strange meteorologic metaphor, Gombiner suggested Patrick was in the eye of a "hurricane of paper." He said, in effect, that, although the eye lies in the center, it does not control the storm.

Prosecutor Richard Owens then delivered the closing rebuttal, in which he said the mountain of evidence proved the scheme was intentional.

At the behest of Judge Griesa, the prosecutors agreed to drop 40 of the 104 counts to aid the jurors in considering the volumes of evidence. The judge then instructed the jury on the remaining charges and bid them to deliberate.

During the deliberations, the jury repeatedly sent written questions to the judge. They asked whether all the leases sold by Bennett Funding were securities and, if so, whether the leases should have been registered. Judge Griesa said the issue was irrelevant. Their focus of inquiry should center on whether the leases were double-pledged to investors, he suggested.

The jury asked whether evidence was presented to show Patrick transferred money to his wife and kids or hid assets, such as the millions placed into the Bennett Finance entities. That question was left open.

Surprisingly, the jury even asked whether Breeden, during his chairmanship, had any role in the SEC's initial inquiry into Bennett Funding. They also wanted to know how much money he earns as trustee. Griesa told the jurors their concerns were again irrelevant.

Other questions centered on payments received from the New York City Transit Authority leases and the status of civil suits against Patrick.

They also asked to have testimony read back from Kasarjian's secretary and about the multimillion-dollar loan from the Company.

To observers, the questions asked and trial testimony read back indicated that some of the members of the jury believed Patrick's story that he knew nothing of the double-pledging or that he did not take money from the Company. No doubt the question about Breeden's involvement with the SEC investigation and trusteeship fee sent a surge of "I told you so" down Bud's spine.

A scare arose on the fourth day of deliberations when the jury announced an impasse. Judge Griesa told them, "The case will need to be decided, it will not go away," and sent them back to decide.

In a burst of frustration precipitated by the jury's inability to render a verdict, the judge said there was "sufficient evidence" to make a determination. That prompted Patrick's counsel to request yet another mistrial. Although the judge agreed he may have gone too far in his remarks and instructed the jury accordingly, the motion was denied and the jury was sent back.

On March 2, 1999, the seventh day of deliberations, the jury advised, "Although we have reached an agreement on some of the charges, we have been and continue to be at a stalemate on the majority of them. We have tried to reach an agreement on what most of us consider to be the basic counts, however, our efforts have been unfruitful.

"We have been deliberating since Feb. 18 and our positions have not changed since then. We argue with no resulting change and we feel that no unanimous decision can be reached by this jury."

After receiving the jury's missive, Judge Griesa told the attorneys he could order the jury to continue deliberations, seek a partial verdict on the unanimous counts, or declare a mistrial on the whole. During the selection process, none of the jury panel of seven men and five women professed to having a business background. One juror worked for the Department of Corrections, another for the Parks Department, while another was a nurse. A few were retired. They were sent back again.

Two hours later, the jury found Patrick guilty on seven lesser counts of perjury and obstruction of justice arising out of the SEC investigation. They were hopelessly deadlocked on all of the remaining fifty-three material counts, including securities fraud, money laundering, and bank fraud.

Oh, but what a blow! Eight conspirators, including Patrick's brother, admitted the scheme and the jury failed to convict. Reams of documents and the jury failed to convict. Testimony of eyewitnesses and experts and the jury failed to convict. Millions of dollars spent for investigation, preparation, and appearance at trial and the jury failed to convict. Patrick's tearful, pathetic performance of admissions of ineptitude and the jury failed to convict.

Some observers at the trial were not surprised at the outcome given the complicated nature and presentation of the prosecution's case. Moreover, the heavy reliance upon shady characters, such as Kasarjian, who admitted lying under oath to the SEC, may have been offensive to the jury.

As rumors flew after the prosecution's posttrial debriefing of some jurors, a theory arose that at least one juror bore animosity toward the government, squeaked passed *voir dire* (jury selection), and let loose a fusillade of venom by refusing to acknowledge the omnipresence of the evidence.

Juror-X may have been audited by the IRS, may have lost a spouse to a postal worker, may be a militia person, or may believe the government overreached at Waco and Ruby Ridge. To hide his or her agenda, juror-X threw the prosecution a bone (a much beloved expression of Patrick Bennett) and agreed to the convictions on the admitted charges of conspiracy, perjury, and obstruction.

Another theory suggested that a juror was bribed by the purloined funds Patrick claimed he did not have. In any event, soon after the verdict, an official of the U.S. Attorney's Office stated, "We fully intend to retry Mr. Bennett on all counts for which the jury did not deliver a verdict." Patrick's attorney, David Levitt, said that "next time we'll convince all of them [of Patrick's innocence]." Sentencing was delayed until after "round two."

Within a week of the verdict, the local paper that had covered the Bennett story since inception ran an article that suggested the prosecution's mountain of evidence buried the jurors.[3] "It was boring stuff. Throughout the trial one juror played with her long brilliantly red acrylic fingernails. Several giggled or stared blankly into space daydreaming. Juror number six regularly took cat naps, eyes closed until another juror prodded him awake. The creak of the courtroom door as someone opened it for a peek inside was a welcome distraction."

Based on statistics from Syracuse University's Transactional Records Access Clearinghouse (TRAC), the article suggested that "[f]rom 1993 to

1997, the federal government won convictions in just 58 percent of the securities fraud cases it prosecuted in the Southern District of New York, where the Bennett case was heard."

"Some years," the article continued, "have a better conviction rate than others, from a high of 88 percent in 1994, to just 23 percent in 1997."

These sentiments were echoed in an editorial that appeared in the same paper on the same day and even offered legal advice and strategy to ensure conviction, "[T]here is no need to overwhelm the jury with volumes of confounding details. It is more important to show how some of those details are linked together to form a web of deceit that snared thousands of victims who thought they were dealing with an honest company."[4]

Of course, a conviction based on a theory that reduces the elements of fifty-three counts, including securities fraud and money laundering, to simple Web site–type links would be doomed to reversal on appeal.

Despite the mistrial, the editorial concluded without mercy for the perpetrators, "Bennett and his fellow conspirators deserve to sit in cells for a good long time and contemplate what they have done. The fact that they wore wingtips instead of sneakers does not make them morally superior to a garden-variety mugger."

Three weeks later, the paper printed a reply by U.S. Attorney Mary Jo White, in which she blasted the reporter who, "[d]espite warnings [that the statistics were inaccurate] published the article with the inaccurate statistics included."[5]

Ms. White suggested that "[i]n calendar years 1993 through 1997, the . . . Southern District . . . obtained convictions, by way of guilty pleas or jury convictions, in approximately 99 percent of the securities cases it prosecuted." She concluded by stating, "[I]naccurate statistics such as those published by your newspaper undermine the public's faith in the efforts being made every day by prosecutors and other dedicated law enforcement professionals."

The paper ran a rebuttal article in the same edition suggesting the issue was not the accuracy of the reporting of statistics but the constituents of the database and interpretation thereof. "The Justice Department and TRAC," the article stated, "have a long-standing conflict over data. TRAC is in litigation with two U.S. Attorney's offices . . . over this issue."[6]

While the debate raged over the heady stuff of trial tactics and statistical analysis, Bud Bennett and a die-hard supporter from the HALO

Group of investors circulated letters among HALO's 350 members and sent a lengthy diatribe against Breeden disguised as correspondence to U.S. Attorney Mary Jo White and significant others.

Emboldened by the mistrial on the fraud counts, Bud demanded that "Richard C. Breeden's Fraud, Conspiracy and Illegal Acts are just cause for the court removal and censure of Richard C. Breeden as Trustee of BFG."[7]

Unbelievably, Bud offered again "to help jump-start the Bennett Companies . . . for the benefit of the company and creditors, and not the millions of dollars that Richard C. Breeden has cherry picked and squirreled away to satisfy his obvious greed." He concluded by requesting that the "prosecution focus their attention on Richard C. Breeden's Huge Fraud, Conspiracy, and Trustee's Illegal Acts." He signed the letter "Semper Fi."

Beseeching Ms. White to investigate and remove Breeden for cause, the HALO Group suggested, among other things, that a prosecution witness who is a longtime Bennett Funding employee was bribed in exchange for her testimony at trial.

The employee purchased Bennett Funding leases over the years and fell victim when the Company tanked. The HALO Group maintained that she was given preferential and unique treatment in the calculation of her final allowed claim in the bankruptcy.[8]

The savage and untrue attack on the integrity of both the employee and Breeden necessitated a written response, supported by corroborating documents, affirming that the employee was treated as all unsecured creditors were treated.[9]

The second trial saw changes in personnel. Owing to calendar congestion, Judge Griesa reassigned the case to Judge John S. Martin.[10] Patrick's lead counsel, David Levitt, moved to Virginia and was replaced by Ian Yankwitt. As befitting, Yankwitt had worked for the trustee's law firm, Simpson Thacher & Bartlett, but left in 1997. A spokesman for the firm stated that "Yankwitt never worked on the Bennett bankruptcy case."[11]

A couple of weeks before the trial was to commence, on Saturday, May 1, 1999, at 9:23 A.M., I received a call from the author of the HALO Group letter, eighty-year-old Henry Schaeffer. Henry said he was at a hotel in Vernon on business and just wanted to say hello. The hotel was not too far from Bud Bennett's residence in Sherrill and the racetrack. After exchanging pleasantries for a moment, I cut to the chase and asked what he wanted.

Henry sought to solicit my help in going after that "fraud Breeden." I declined and suggested that he was not only wasting his time but hurting his constituents because the money used to combat the salacious allegations also came from the same pot of money otherwise available for distribution to the investors. He said good-bye and hung up.

Did Henry (and Bud) think I would join their ragtag army? Because he still had money and perhaps nothing better to do, did Henry (and Bud) think I was so weak-willed, so easily manipulated, that I could be recruited with one good talking to? What chutzpah! Especially, because only two weeks before, I told Patrick's attorney, Mark Gombiner, that I was subpoenaed by Justice to testify at the second trial.

Jury selection for round two started on May 17, 1999. In a pared down version of the first trial, the prosecution called fewer witnesses and condensed much of its direct examinations. The government rested its case on Friday, June 4, 1999. Incredibly, the defense rested on the same day without calling Patrick, or any witness, to the stand.

Although no explanation was offered by counsel for the change in tactic, Patrick's conviction for perjury, conspiracy, and obstruction in the first trial would have been admissible to impeach him if he did take the stand in his own defense.

No doubt the D-Day weekend at the Bennett residence was a sad and weepy time. The family probably instinctively felt lightning would not strike twice and that Patrick would be convicted. His young sons would suffer the loss of guidance and companionship during their formative years and bear the bitter fruits of their father's infamy. Gwen would feel the pangs of the emptiness of her marital bed and suffer the economic and psychological scarring occasioned by her husband's incarceration for crimes against so many people.

Closing arguments, limited to two hours each side, were presented on June 7, 1999. Judge Martin then instructed the jury and bade them to deliberate.[12]

Late afternoon on June 9, the jury reported they reached a verdict on forty-two counts of fraud and money laundering, but could not agree on eleven counts of securities and mail fraud. The proceeding was adjourned for the day without revealing the verdict.

The next morning, it was announced that Patrick stood convicted of two counts of securities fraud, five counts of bank fraud, thirty counts of money laundering, and five counts of conducting transactions in property derived from illegal activity.

Based on the conviction on the money laundering charges, Judge Martin instructed the jury to decide whether Patrick was to forfeit $109 million, as urged by the prosecution. The judge requested the jury to try to render a verdict on the eleven charges as well.

Not long after, the jury announced that Patrick owed the government $109 million, but that it was deadlocked on the remaining charges. Judge Martin thanked the jury and declared a mistrial on those counts.

After revoking Patrick's bail because of "risk of flight," Judge Martin stated, "Mr. Bennett is a totally amoral individual who would engage in any criminal conduct that would benefit him in any way." He "lined his own pockets" at the expense of the investors.

Before Patrick was hauled off to jail awaiting sentencing in September, 1999, the judge said that unless the titles to his house, racetrack, and the Comfort Suites were turned over, Patrick would get the maximum punishment.

On the heels of the verdict, Michael Pinnisi, a well-known appellate attorney from Cornell Law School, announced that he was handling Patrick's appeal. Judge Martin granted Pinnisi's request to delay Patrick's sentencing so he could file post-conviction motions. And the beat goes on.

. . . and Punishment

THE SIGHT of him in manacles was something [the investors] very definitely wanted to see," was Breeden's last word on Patrick's conviction.[1] In this swirling mess of frenetic activity, no voice of reason, no call for clarity, no cry in the wilderness has been heard. There is only the clamor—for blood and money. So I hearken upon the words of Hillel, "When everyone about you fails to behave like a human being, you must strive to be human."[2]

Some of the punishments that have been devised for offenses both real and imagined are cruel and inhuman. Although Patrick and Michael are convicted felons with loss of privilege and jail time, Bud and Kathleen will perhaps receive the biggest punishment of all. For many punishments do pale in the face of that which is self-imposed—the clanging bell of guilt, shame, and humiliation.

One day they were the king and queen of Gotham. They lived in the same nice house in Syracuse's Northside for many a year. They had friends and family and contacts all over the place. They were headlined in the paper. They attended lavish parties and fund-raisers. They went shopping at the best stores. They relaxed aboard their motor yacht. They had a legion of dedicated employees, who would go through the wall for them. They had lots of disposable income.

A few days after the bankruptcy petitions were filed, Bud and Kathleen left town secretly and in disgrace. They moved into a double-wide trailer in Florida. About one year later, their sons were indicted on the same day and the indictments were carried on national news. Bud and Kathleen lost all of their corporate holdings and the love and respect of their workforce. They are anathema to the community.

Worst of all was the impact on their family name, Bennett. Like Ponzi, Bennett now stands for a type of criminal activity unsurpassed in the annals of jurisprudence. The Bennetts' family name has transcended what you call people and has become synonymous with crime, with evil, with misery. Indeed, the sobriquet "Baby Bennett" was attached to the First Interregional brokerage scam as early as May 1997.

The Bennetts' name has been stripped from them unceremoniously. My God, they have lost their name! For surely, the crown of a good name exceeds all.[3]

Ultimately, the Bennetts were compelled by a confluence of personality and circumstance to lie, to cheat, and to steal from everyone and anyone who had the misfortune of trusting them. Undoubtedly, they will need to reincarnate, for whatever lesson they were to have learned went unheeded.

As with insults inflicted by age, it is hard to accept so many years have passed since I answered a newspaper ad in 1984. From my twenties into my forties in the blink of an eye. So much of the best years of my life during the most creative and productive hours of the day spent unwittingly perpetuating the criminal enterprise.

During my sojourn both before and after the fall of the Bennetts, I have tried to maintain the virtues of compassion, humility, and humanity. It has not been easy. But surely now my debt service to the Bennetts and those they have hurt has been paid. The ledger is balanced. It is time to move on.

And let us say, "Amen."

APPENDIXES

NOTES

INDEX

Appendix A

Bennett Companies Management

The officers and directors of the Bennett Companies within two years of the filing of the bankruptcy petitions

Name	Age as of Mar. 96	Year Hired	Positions Held
Edmund T. Bennett	68	1977	Chairman of the Board and Chief Executive Officer
Kathleen M. Bennett	65	1977	Director and President
Patrick R. Bennett	43	1977	Director and Chief Financial Officer
Michael A. Bennett	38	1977	Director and Deputy Chief Executive Officer
William P. Crowley	38	1981	Director and Chief Accounting Officer
Kevin J. Kuppel	42	1989	Director and Treasurer
Joanne M. Corasiniti	34	1982	Director and Chief Operating Officer
Richard F. MacPherson	65	1993	Director and Senior Vice President
Stewart L. Weisman	40	1984	Vice President, Secretary, and General Counsel
Paul J. Usztock	45	1994	Executive Vice President
Robert S. Bryant	54	1987	Vice President—Investment
William R. Lester	33	1994	Controller
Kenneth P. Kasarjian	51	1990	Vice President—Investment
Merrilee M. Goffredo	53	1981	Vice President—Human Resources
Robert F. Ruckel	44	1991	Vice President—Credit
Albert C. Cerimeli	36	1983	Vice President—Investor Relations
Timothy J. White	42	1993	Vice President—Sales
John J. Sullivan	62	1993	Vice President—MIS
Lisa Henson	32	1985	Assistant Treasurer
Linda L. Calabria	43	1983	Assistant Vice President
Shaun W. O'Neill	33	1988	Assistant Controller
Tom Barber	*	1995	Vice President—Sales
Robin Kershner	*	1995	Vice President—Sales
Robert H. McCarthy	50	1987	Vice President—Resort Development
John Root	*	1995	Controller—Processing Center

Boldface denotes guilty plea or conviction

*Information unavailable

Name	Age as of Mar. 96	Year Hired	Positions Held
Carmen F. Goffredo	55	1984	President, Resort Service Company
Edward Guardino	*	1994	Secretary, General Counsel—Resort Funding
William Fedorich	*	1994	Secretary, General Counsel—Aloha Capital
Mark Scoular	*	1995	Director—Aloha Capital
Richard Kelley	*	1995	Director—Aloha Capital
Merv Goldman	*	1995	Director—Aloha Capital

Appendix B

Time Flow of Events

Nov. 1977	Aloha Communications Systems incorporated in New York.
Apr. 1984	Name changed to The Bennett Funding Group, Inc.
July 1984	Stewart Weisman starts employment with Bennett Funding.
Dec. 1990	First recorded instance of double-pledging of leases.
Mar. 1992	Arthur Andersen resigns as auditor and pulls financial statements.
June 1992	Mahoney Cohen starts auditing Bennett Funding.
May 1993	SEC inquiry commences against Bennett Funding.
June 1993	Hotel Syracuse purchased by Michael Bennett.
Mar. 1995	Last audited financial statement of Bennett Funding produced for the year ending 1994.
May 1995	SEC orders Patrick to stop selling PPMs.
Oct. 1995	Double-pledging of leases discovered by employees.
Nov. 1995	Bank Committee formed to investigate double-pledging.
Feb. 1996	Hotel Syracuse sold; Bennett Funding acquires Equivest.
Mar. 1996	SEC lawsuit filed against Bennett Funding, three affiliates and Patrick Bennett; criminal charges filed against Patrick Bennett; Bennett Funding and the three affiliates file chapter 11.
Apr. 1996	Four more affiliates file bankruptcy.
May 1996	Richard C. Breeden appointed trustee.
June 1996	Breeden sues the Bennetts for $1.8 billion.
Feb. 1997	A total of 197 banks settle with the trustee.
Apr. 1997	Ken Kasarjian pleads guilty.
Oct. 1998	Investors receive first distribution in the bankruptcy.
Nov. 1998	Michael Bennett pleads guilty.
Dec. 1998	Patrick Bennett's trial starts; Genovese pleads guilty; plan of reorganization filed.
Mar. 1999	Patrick Bennett convicted for perjury, obstruction, and conspiracy; hung jury on remaining counts; government requests second trial.
June 1999	Patrick Bennett convicted on 42 counts, including fraud and money-laundering.

Appendix C

Patrick and Michael Bennett's "Key Man" Life Insurance Policies at New England Life

Insured	Policy No.	Beneficiary	Face Value
Patrick	8832094	Bennett Funding	1,500,000
Patrick	882525	Bennett Funding	1,500,000
Patrick	Z127029	Gwen Bennett/ Bennett Management	3,000,000
Michael	8832093	Bennett Funding	1,500,000
Michael	8833341	Bennett Funding	1,500,000
Michael	Z144044	Bennett Management	3,720,000
Total			$12,720,000

Appendix D

The Nine Bennett Debtors and the Nondebtor Resort Funding, Inc.

Name of Debtor	State and Date Incorporation	Shareholder and Date of Ownership	Percentage
Aloha Capital Corporation f/k/a Bennett Leasing Corporation	Del.—Dec. 30, 1994	BFG—12/94–1/95 Michael Bennett—1/95 to postpetition surrender to trustee	100% 100%
American Marine International, Ltd.	N.Y.—July 19, 1994	BFG—current	100%
Bennett Management & Development Corp.	N.Y.—Apr. 16, 1985	Patrick Bennett —current	100%
Bennett Receivables Corporation	Del.—Feb. 4, 1992	BFG—current	100%
Bennett Receivables Corporation–II	Del.—Aug. 18, 1994	BFG—current	100%
Cordoba Corporation	N.Y.—Nov. 10, 1993	BMDC—current	100%
Resort Service Company, Inc., f/k/a Resort Funding, Inc.	Del.—Dec. 13, 1984	BFG—current	100%
The Bennett Funding Group, Inc. ("BFG")	N.Y.—Nov. 16, 1977	Kathleen and Bud Bennett—current	100%
The Processing Center, Inc.	N.Y.—Jan. 19, 1995	Michael Bennett —1/95 to postpetition surrender to trustee	100%
Resort Funding, Inc., f/k/a Bennett Funding International, Ltd., f/k/a The Processing Center, Inc.	Del.—June 6, 1991	Equivest	100%

Appendix E

Trademarks of the Bennett Companies

Name/Logo	Registration No.	Registration Date
"AL" stylized and design	1605931	July 10, 1990
"TotaLease"	1678772	Mar. 10, 1992
"A" stylized and design	1588121	Mar. 20, 1990
Design (sunrise & waves)	1953214	Mar. 6, 1995
"Resort Funding"	74/496226	Mar. 3, 1994
$ sign	1806392	Nov. 23, 1993
CRUSA logo	1589316	Mar. 27, 1990
GEM logo	1925831	Oct. 10, 1995

Appendix F

The Campgrounds Owned by the Bennett Companies

Name of Campground	State
Beaver Valley	Ohio
Bent Oaks	Missouri
Big South Fork	Tennessee
Deerland Park	Ohio
Eagles Landing	Georgia
Hidden Cove	Alabama
Lazy Creek	Arkansas
Mammoth Caverns	Kentucky
Okatoma	Mississippi
Red Oaks	Iowa
Serendipity	Texas
Southern Leisure	Louisiana
Timberline	Tennessee
Trapper Johns	Ohio

Appendix G

Major Known Assets of Bennett Management

Asset	Value
Note and mortgage on Mountaineer Park Racetrack	$10.2 million
405,000 common shares in Mountaineer	Market
80% ownership of Equivest	Market
250,000 shares of Aegis Funding	$9.5 million
Mall and Theater in Maine	$38 million
Hotel Syracuse mortgage	$16.2 million
Quality Inn	$3.5 million
Days Inn mortgage	$3.8 million
Gold Shore Casino	$34 million
Sioux City Sue Casino	$8.5 million
Total	$123.7 million plus the value of the marketable securities

Appendix H

*The Bank Fraud Counts Contained in the
Indictment Against Patrick Bennett*

Date of Financing	Amount	Bank
June 1993	448,278.87	Middleton
Sept. 1992	246,748.80	Rhinebeck
Sept. 1992	253,248.11	Rhinebeck
Dec. 1992	461,544.70	Rhinebeck
Apr. 1993	264,731.20	Rhinebeck
Apr. 1993	235,257.29	Rhinebeck
May 1994	500,004.79	Rhinebeck
June 1995	1,000,000.00	Rhinebeck
July 1992	864,101.92	Union
Sept. 1992	499,983.98	Union
Oct. 1993	1,199,980.05	Union
July 1994	1,000,000.15	Union
Aug. 1994	999,983.96	Union
Oct. 1994	1,999,990.29	Union

Appendix I

The Categories of Fees in the Bennett Bankruptcy

Code	Description of Project
AA	Asset Analysis and Recovery: Identification and review of potential assets, including cause of action and nonlitigation recoveries.
AC	Accounting/Auditing: Activities related to maintaining and auditing books of account, preparation of financial statements, and account analysis.
AD	Asset Disposition: Sales, leases (sec. 365 matters), abandonment and related transaction work.
AP	Adversary Proceedings: A separate matter should be established for each adversary proceeding.
BA	Business Analysis: Preparation and review of company business plan; development and review of strategies; preparation and review of cash flow forecasts and feasibility studies.
BO	Business Operations: Issues related to debtor-in-possession operating in chapter 11, such as employee, vendor, and tenant issues.
CA	Case Administration: Coordination and compliance activities, including preparation of statement of financial affairs, schedules, list of contracts, United States trustee interim statements and operating reports, contacts with the United States trustee, general creditor inquiries.
CC	Cash Collateral Agreements
CF	Corporate Finance: Review financial aspects of potential mergers, acquisitions, and disposition of company or subsidiaries.
CM	Claims Administration and Objections: Specific claims inquiries; bar date motions, analyses, objections and allowances of claims.
DA	Data Analysis: Management information systems review, installation and analysis, construction, maintenance and reporting of significant case financial data, lease rejection, claims, etc.
DF	DIP Financing Agreements
EB	Employee Benefits/Pensions: Review issues such as severance, retention, 401(k) coverage, and continuation of pension plan.
EC	Executory Contracts: Review, assumption, or rejection of executory contracts.
ET	Examiner and/or Trustee: Motions, hearings, and orders on the appointment of a chapter 11 examiner and/or trustee.
FA	Fee/Employment Applications: Preparation of employment and fee applications for self or others; motions to establish interim procedures.

Code	Description of Project
FO	Fee/Employment Objections: Review of and objections to the employment and fee application of others.
GM	Board of Directors/General Corporate Matters
LC	Litigation Consulting: Providing consulting and expert witness services relating to various bankruptcy matters, such as insolvency, feasibility, avoiding actions, and forensic accounting.
MC	Meetings of Creditors: Preparing for and attending the conference of creditors, the section 341 meeting, and other creditors' committee meetings.
PR	Prepetition Invoices
RC	Reclamation Claims
RE	Real Estate Matters
RS	Relief from Stay Procedures: Matters relating to termination or continuation of automatic stay under section 362.
SI	Securities Issues
ST	Plan and Disclosure Statement: Formulation, presentation, and confirmation; compliance with the plan confirmation order, related orders and rules; disbursement and case closing activities, except those related to the allowance and objection to allowance of claims.
TL	Tort Litigation
TV	Nonworking Travel Time
TX	Tax Issues: Analysis of tax issues and preparation of state and federal tax returns.
UC	Unsecured Creditors' Committee: Formulation and operation of the Unsecured Creditors' Committee.
VL	Valuation: Appraise or review appraisal of assets.
IC	Insurance Claims: Evaluation of potential claims against insurance policies on financing.
BS	Bank Settlements: Negotiation and documentation of settlements with banks releases.
AV	Avoidance Actions
FI	Fraud Investigations: Investigation of potentially fraudulent activities.

Adapted from Stuart Maue's project billing categories

Appendix J

Nonsettling Banks

Amcore Bank

American State & Trust Co.

American Trust

Federal Savings Bank

Americom Bank

Androscoggin Savings Bank

Bank of Utica

Citrus Bank

Deposit Bank

ESB Bank

Farmers State Bank

First Community Bank

First Federal Savings

Bank of Galion

First Federal Savings

Bank of LaGrange

First National Bank & Trust Co.
(Ponca City, Ok.)

First National Bank (Carmi)

First National Bank (Ottawa)

First National Bank of Crockett

First National Bank of Northwest Ohio

First Star Savings Bank

First State Bank

Firstar Bank

Gloucester Bank & Trust Co.

Henry Absher Oil Co. (First National Bank
of Carmi)

Jefferson State Bank

LaCrescent State Bank

M&T Bank

Merchants National Bank

Metlife Capitol Corp.

Metrobank

Minnesota Valley Bank

Northwestern Savings Bank

Norwest Bank Red Wing

Oxford Bank & Trust

Peoples Bank & Trust

Potters Savings & Loan

Security Bank

Seguin State Bank & Trust

South Trust

Sprague National Bank

State Bank & Trust of Kenmare

Stoneham Savings Bank

Story County Bank & Trust

The Commercial Bank

The Howard Bank

Third Savings

Tolland Bank

Tucker Federal Savings Bank

Union State Bank

United Security Bank

Appendix K

"Risk Factors" from the Bennett Receivables PPM

The full text of the "Risk Factors" set forth in the Bennett Receivables PPM is as follows:

The Notes are speculative and prospective purchasers should consider the following factors, among others, in evaluating Bennett, its business, the Company, and Notes being offered hereunder.

No Liquidity of Notes; No Registration Rights

The Notes must be acquired by each purchaser for investment purposes only and not with a view to, or for resale in connection with any distribution. The Notes will be issued in reliance upon an exemption from registration contained in the Act, and when issued, will not be registered under the Act. Purchaser of the Notes must bear the economic risk of the investment for an indefinite period of time. Holders of Notes have no registration rights with respect thereto, and the Company does not intend to register the Notes under the Act in the future.

Arbitrary Determination of Offering Price and Interest Rate

The offering price and interest rate of the Notes offered hereby has been determined arbitrarily by the Company and bears no relationship to any established criteria of value such as the Company's operations, assets, book value or net worth. The offering price should not be considered an indication of the actual value of the Notes.

No Trustee or Indenture for the Notes

The Notes will not be issued pursuant to an Indenture or Trust, nor will the Notes be qualified under the Trust Indenture Act of 1939, as amended. Consequently, holders of the Notes will be required to rely on their own resources, rather than upon the resources of a trustee, to enforce the terms and provisions of the Notes against the Company. Additionally, the lack of an indenture or trustee increases the risk of improper acts or emissions by the Company.

No Sinking Fund

The Company has not created any sinking fund or other similar reserve fund for the payment of principal and interest on the Notes. If the Company does not generate sufficient cash flow from operations or is not successful in refinancing the Notes, the Company may not have sufficient funds to provide for the payment of accrued interest and principal owing on the Notes.

In the event that the Company has insufficient funds to liquidate the Notes at maturity, they will self liquidate over the term of the collateral. The maximum term of collateral used for Notes one year or less will be 12 months.

Availability of Recourse

Bennett has guaranteed payment of the Notes and has granted Note holders full recourse to it. In the event of default, however, there can be no assurance to investors that Bennett will be able to meet its guaranty obligations.

Availability of Credit/Capital Requirements

Bennett's operations are dependent upon its continuing ability to obtain financing by pledging equipment leases, consumer receivables and dealer inventory finance notes as collateral to banks or other lenders and/or to sell leases or contracts on terms which will permit it to earn a profit. Although Bennett believes it has adequate sources of funding and although it is constantly attempting to expand its financing sources, there can be no assurance of Bennett's continuing ability to maintain adequate funding.

Use of Leverage

Although Bennett's leverage has declined in the past five years, it has depended upon borrowed funds in its operations and is highly leveraged i.e., a substantial portion of its assets are funded by borrowings rather than by stockholders' equity. Were Bennett to experience significant losses, leverage would be further increased and there would be a negative impact on its ability to borrow funds from banks or other lenders.

Competition

The equipment leasing market in which Bennett operates is highly competitive. It competes with other leasing companies, equipment brokers and dealers, manufacturers who lease their products, and subsidiaries, affiliates or divisions of financial institutions, many of whom are larger than Bennett and able to obtain funding at more attractive rates. The consumer financing market is not believed by Bennett to be as highly competitive as equipment leasing, but nonetheless there are a number of competitors with greater access to financing sources than Bennett.

Dependence upon Key Personnel

The success of Bennett and the Company is substantially dependent upon the efforts of its officers and directors who hold executive positions. Decisions concerning Bennett's business and its management are, and will continue to be, made or significantly influenced by these individuals. The loss or interruption of their continued services would have a material adverse effect on Bennett's business operation and prospects. Additionally, Bennett's operations would be materially adversely affected if it is unable to obtain and maintain qualified personnel.

Ability of Bennett to Service Receivables

Bennett currently manages and services approximately 60,000 individual transactions (leases, consumer receivables and dealer inventory notes) and for this purpose has developed a sophisticated computer system and effective administrative procedures. Nonetheless, there can be no assurance in the future that Bennett will not file for protection from its creditors under Federal or State Bankruptcy laws or be in a position to service and manage the receivables which are collateral for the loans which the Company makes to Bennett.

No Resale of Notes

These Notes have not been registered under the Securities Act of 1933, as amended, and accordingly may not be offered, sold, resold or delivered in violation of the Act or of any applicable state law. The purchasers of the Notes, by their acceptance thereof, represent that they are acquiring the Notes for investment and not with a view to any resale or distribution thereof. There is no foreseeable public market for the Notes and, they must be considered by purchasers as having no liquidity.

Amortization of Principal

As noted herein, the Company intends to use the proceeds from this issue to make loans to Bennett which loans will be collateralized by the grant of a security interest in certain income-producing Receivables whose performance (sufficient to repay Bennett's loans) is insured. While Bennett and the Company believe that there will be sufficient Receivables for collateral and insurance available for the loans made by the Company to Bennett in the future, there can be no absolute assurance of these assumptions. In the event that there are not sufficient Receivables or that similar insurance or credit enhancements are unavailable, the Notes will become monthly amortizing obligations (both principal and interest will be paid monthly) based upon a term equal to the average remaining term of the insured Receivables collateralizing loans then outstanding to Bennett. In the event that the Notes become monthly amortizing obligations, there is no assurance that holders of the Notes will be able to reinvest principal at the same interest rates as the Notes then bear.

Insurance Coverage

Bennett will have insurance coverage in place to cover defaults. While specific Receivables are covered for their entire term once insured, a significant number of defaults could hamper Bennett's ability to renew the insurance policy for subsequent years.

Bennett and the Company Are under Control of the Same Persons and Bennett Will Retain Control of the Collateral.

The Company and Bennett are under the control of the same persons and the Company has no assets other than the notes from Bennett. Although the Company will enter into a security agreement whereby Bennett will pledge certain leases and contracts to the Company to secure this debt, the Company's security interest in the Collateral and the lease and contract payments Bennett will use to repay its loan from the Company are not perfected as they will remain in the possession of Bennett. Therefore, no independent third party is in a position to enforce Bennett's promises with regard to the handling of the security for the debt.

Notes

WHO?

A Grimm Tale

1. George Grimm was employed at Creative Benefits Consultants, Inc., of New City, N.Y.

2. One of the early newspaper accounts of the Bennett scandal was "Overreaching: Syracuse, N.Y., Sees Proud Local Business Shattered by Scandal—Bennetts, Pillars of the City," *Wall Street Journal,* Apr. 17, 1996.

3. The missing persons report, incident no. 96-11987, was filed by George's wife, Marion B. Grimm. Marion suggested in the missing persons report that her husband "probably learned yesterday morning [Apr. 16] that the clients fund[s] . . . will not be returned . . . and that it would be on the front page of today's [Apr. 17] Wall Street Journal and therefore felt responsible." George also left behind two children.

4. An account of Grimm's death is found in "Bennett Dealer's Death Is One Sad Tale among the Numbers," *Syracuse Post-Standard,* Aug. 3, 1996.

5. Although the Grimm missing persons report and the *Syracuse Post-Standard* article "Bennett Dealer's Death Is One Sad Tale among the Numbers" claim Grimm brought $50 million to Bennett Funding, a search of Grimm's commission records maintained on the Bennett Funding, Processing Center, and Bennett Management computer systems shows only about $5 million was invested. The same records indicate Grimm received $184,079.87 in commissions, which corresponds to a brokerage fee of about 3.68 percent, a typical rate the company paid. Further corroboration is found in the New City investor records maintained on Bennett Funding and Bennett Management computer systems as well as the Bennett Funding's Bankruptcy Schedule F of Unsecured Creditors, Bankr. N.D.N.Y., No. 96-61376, 1996.

6. The quoted material concerning the size of the Bennett Ponzi scheme is from "Trustee Faulted for Buying Stock," *National Law Journal,* Mar. 9, 1998. As noted by Judge Gerling, "[t]he litigation at issue . . . arises out of what the Trustee has elsewhere described as the 'largest Ponzi scheme ever carried out against individual investors and financial institutions in U.S. history.'" *Breeden v. Bennett,* 220 B.R. 743, 747 (Bankr. N.D.N.Y. 1997) reprinted in Order, J. Gerling, Bankr. N.D.N.Y., No. 96-61376, Mar. 18, 1999. Indeed, "large-scale pyramid schemes . . . appear to be on the rise." Investors lost almost $500 million investing in bonds and notes sold by Tower Financial, a failed bill-collection agency run by a former publisher of the *New York Post.* "They're Off and Running, But With Whose Money?" *New York Times,* June 1, 1997.

To accommodate the general readership, strict adherence to the uniform system of legal citation was not followed.

7. Justice Department Press Release concerning the indictments of Patrick R. Bennett, et al., June 26, 1997, p. 6. Some background information concerning the early charges is found in "Bennett Exec Charged with Fraud, Lying," *Syracuse Post-Standard*, Mar. 29, 1996.

8. The amount of the losses suffered by the investors, employees, banks, and trade creditors as tallied in claims filed in the Bennett bankruptcy is more than $5 billion. The trustee pared the amount to $1 billion. See also an article describing Hibernia Bank's losses in the Bennett fraud, *Business Wire*, Apr. 1, 1996.

9. Assets and their approximate valuations are from Bennett Funding's Bankruptcy Schedules of Assets and the Statement of Financial Affairs, Bankr. N.D.N.Y., No. 96-61376, Sept. 1996. Trustee Richard Breeden reported the asset schedules were contained in twenty-eight binders with more than sixty-four hundred pages. Press Release of Richard C. Breeden, Sept. 9, 1996; Letter from Richard C. Breeden to the Investors, Sept. 27, 1996. Most of the Trustee's press releases and letters to investors can also be found at the Company's website: <http://www.bennett-funding.com>.

10. The SEC complaint against Patrick R. Bennett, and others, S.D.N.Y., No. 96-2237, Mar. 27, 1996, and served on the Company's attorneys on Mar. 28, 1996.

11. Bennett Company bankruptcies: Aloha Capital Corporation; American Marine International, Ltd.; Bennett Management & Development Corp.; Bennett Receivables Corporation; Bennett Receivables Corporation–II; Cordoba Corporation; Resort Service Company, Inc.; The Bennett Funding Group, Inc.; The Processing Center, Inc.; and, Shamrock Holdings, Inc., filed in late 1998.

12. Professor LoPucki of Cornell Law School maintains a bankruptcy research database that covers public companies filing chapter 11 from 1980 to the present with assets greater than $200 million. According to the database, there are 309 such companies nationwide with 61 filed in the Southern Dist. of N.Y. No such filings are in any other district of New York. Also, the clerk advised the Bennett bankruptcy is the largest the court ever administered. See also "Patrick Bennett's Big Gamble," *Syracuse Post-Standard*, Nov. 29, 1998.

13. Richard C. Breeden, a Bush appointee, was chairman of the SEC from 1989 to 1993. Breeden noted that the Schedules of Liabilities consists of thirty-three hundred pages. Breeden, Press Release, July 29, 1996. The schedules themselves are found in Bennett Funding's Bankruptcy Schedules of Liabilities and the Statement of Financial Affairs, Bankr. N.D.N.Y., No. 96-61376, July 29, 1996.

14. The SEC published Litigation Release Nos. 15324, Apr. 10, 1997, and 15398, June 26, 1997, concerning Bennett Funding and the indictments.

15. In the reincarnation process, karma is a manifestation of the spiritual lessons that need to be learned on the path of a soul's advancement toward perfection, toward nirvana. For example, sometimes the rebirth allows the soul to feel the pain it inflicted while corporeal by returning, say, as a hostage, a victim, a battered woman. Sometimes, the rebirth teaches the soul humility or to care or allows it to glimpse the oneness of humanity. Sometimes, the soul needs simply to learn not to be afraid. Only when there are no more debts to be repaid, no more lessons to be learned, can nirvana be achieved—the release from the endless cycle of reincarnation by the extinction of the self. General discussion of Hinduism and reincarnation can be found in Y. Kirimura, ed., *Outline of Buddhism* (Tokyo: Nichiren Shoshu International Center, 1981); and Geoffrey Parrinder, ed., *World Religions* (New York: Facts on File Publications, 1983).

16. The Bennett Funding Web site provides an array of information: <http://www.bennett-funding.com>.

Beginnings: My Path to Bennett

1. The name of the Queens law firm was Gitomer, Schwimmer & Gitomer, since disbanded.

2. I attended Syracuse Univ. College of Law from August 1977 to May 1980.

3. The name of the Syracuse law firm was Scott, Sardano & Pomeranz, since disbanded.

4. For a discussion of attorney-billing practices, see Richard Reid, ed., *Win-Win Billing Strategies* (Chicago: ABA Publication, 1992) and *Beyond the Billable Hour* (Chicago: ABA Publication, 1989).

5. Concerning the senior partner with bad karma, see "Holiday Spirit Cheers Scott," *Syracuse Post-Standard,* Dec. 24, 1998.

6. The Federal Rules of Bankruptcy Procedure § 9009 and Official Forms set forth the basic forms used in bankruptcy proceedings.

7. The constitutional language from Article 1 sec. 8 is reprinted here: The Congress shall have power to lay and collect taxes, duties, imposts and excises, to pay the debts and provide for the common defense and general welfare of the United States; but all duties, imposts and excises shall be uniform throughout the United States; To borrow money on the credit of the United States; To regulate commerce with foreign nations, and among the several states, and with the Indian tribes; *To establish a uniform rule of naturalization, and uniform laws on the subject of bankruptcies throughout the United States. . . .* (emphasis added).

8. For a detailed explanation of Tay-Sachs, see the Web site of the National Tay-Sachs & Allied Diseases Association, Inc., at: <http://www.ntsad.org/ntsad/t-sachs.htm>.

9. The Fair Debt Collection Practices Act, 15 U.S.C. § 1692 (1977).

Bennett Land

1. Assets and their approximate valuations are from Bennett Funding's Bankruptcy Schedules of Assets and the Statement of Financial Affairs, Bankr. N.D.N.Y., No. 96-61376, 1996. See also "They're off and Running, But with Whose Money?," *New York Times,* June 1, 1997, describing Vernon Downs racetrack, Ponzi scheme, and treatment of investors.

2. Affidavit of Stewart Weisman in support of Trustee's Motion for Substantive Consolidation, Bankr. N.D.N.Y., No. 96-61376, Oct. 29, 1996. Exhibits K, L, M, and N to the Weisman affidavit are copies of standard operating procedures for the Legal Department regarding bank loans documentation, litigation, handling complaint letters, and bankruptcies.

3. "The Art of Leasing with Aloha," promotional brochure used by Bennett Funding. The Equipment Leasing Association has a Web site at: <http://www.elaonline.com>. See also the *Monitor Daily* Web site at: <http://www.monitordaily.com>.

4. See volume by equipment type chart prepared by the ELA at: <http://www.elaonline.com/annvol.htm>.

5. See trends and forecasts for equipment leasing in the U.S. chart prepared by the ELA at: <http://www.elaonline.com/FASTGROW.HTM>.

6. Letter from the bankruptcy trustee to investors and creditors concerning status of the Bennett bankruptcy, Sept. 27, 1996.

7. The costs to sponsor a hospitality tent at the Ryder Cup Golf Competition included travel, lodging, extras at the tent, additional security, and related costs.

8. At the time, the statute regulating ticket scalping was New York Arts & Culture Law § 25.09 (McKinney).

9. Ultimately, the trustee was able to settle with the borrowers on the mall project, and received about $18 million out of the $38 million loaned.

The Incident

1. The SEC complaint is captioned *SEC v. The Bennett Funding Group, Inc., Patrick R. Bennett, Bennett Management & Development Corporation, Bennett Receivables Corporation, and Bennett Receivables Corporation–II*, S.D.N.Y., No. 96-2237, Mar. 27, 1996.

2. Chapter 11 bankruptcy petitions by The Bennett Funding Group, Inc., Bennett Management & Development Corporation, Bennett Receivables Corporation, and Bennett Receivables Corporation–II, Bankr. N.D.N.Y., Mar. 29, 1996.

3. Information concerning Charles Ponzi is from "There's a New (Ponzi) Sucker Born Every Day," Dec. 23, 1994, reprinted at <http://www.sddt.com/files/library/94headlines/ DN9/STORY94_12_23_05.htm>. See also Mary Darby, "In Ponzi We Trust," *Smithsonian*, Dec. 1998, p. 135. The details of the Ponzi scheme are set forth in *Cunningham v. Brown*, 265 U.S. 1 (1924).

4. The Second Circuit case is *Hirsch v. Arthur Andersen & Co.*, 72 F.3d 1085 (1995).

5. The SEC Web site, at: <http://www.sec.gov/invkhome.htm>, is a good starting place for a discussion of various types of securities frauds. The investor education Web site, at: <http://www.investoreducation.org>, also provides good information.

6. Apparently, lease securities fraud is a booming business. As reported in "Trouble," *Governmental Leasing Digest*, Apr. 1997, an office-equipment leasing company manager was sentenced for telling school district lessees wrongly that their old lease would be paid off to make way for new equipment. The SEC also went after Robert Gersh of Boston Municipal Securities, Inc., for false offerings totaling $14 million, and against First Interregional Advisors Corp., for an alleged Ponzi scheme involving $50 million of leases. Copytech Systems, Inc., a lessor of office copiers, was telling its customers that it would service the machines at no further cost to them, but was not telling its bank assignees about these "secret side agreements," a crime of making a false statement to a federally insured bank.

7. See Exhibit E, a brochure entitled "The Bennett Companies," and Exhibit F, a brochure entitled "The Bennett Funding Group, Inc.," attached to the Affidavit of Thomas Lumsden, partner at Coopers & Lybrand, in support of the Trustee's Motion for Substantive Consolidation, Bankr. N.D.N.Y., No. 96-61376, Oct. 29, 1996.

In filing any documents with the Bankruptcy Court, Coopers used the following disclaimer: "Coopers did not participate in or have a first hand knowledge of the business activities and record keeping practices of the debtors. Consequently, Coopers, in making the statements in this affidavit must rely upon reconstruction and analysis of the debtors' books and records, and upon information obtained directly from current and former employees, interested parties and other individuals and entities who transacted with the debtors."

8. *Merrill v. Abbott* (*In re* Independent Clearing House Co.) 77 B.R. 843, 860 (D. Utah 1987) reprinted in Order, J. Gerling, Bankr. N.D.N.Y., No. 96-61376, *Breeden v. Thomas,* Adv. Pro. No. 98-40892A, Bankr. N.D.N.Y., Apr. 29, 1999.

9. About ten thousand investors were still receiving payments from the company at the time of the filing of the bankruptcy petitions in March 1996. The remaining two thousand had already been paid as of the date of the bankruptcy but were dragged back in when the trustee sought a return of any profit they made in the preceding six years.

10. The names and dates of the investors whom I spoke with are set forth in Weisman record of telephone calls with investors, May 1, 1996 (on file with the author). "At Bennett Trial, Investor Tries to Tell Story," *Syracuse Post-Standard,* Dec. 23, 1998. See also "They're Off and Running, But With Whose Money?" *New York Times,* June 1, 1997; "Investor Follows Bennett to Court," *Syracuse Post-Standard,* Dec. 8, 1998; "Testimony Begins in Second Bennett Trial," *Syracuse Post-Standard,* May 20, 1999.

11. Viktor Frankl, *Man's Search for Meaning* (New York: Pocket Books, 1963).

12. Viktor Frankl, *Man's Search for Ultimate Meaning* (New York: Plenum Press, 1997), p. 123.

13. Although some vendors owed the Company money as well, oftentimes the captured funds were less than the amount of vendor service fees held by the Company. For example, as of Nov. 6, 1997, ABCC, a large vendor, owed the Company $225,000. However, the Company held $648,482.09 it collected from lessees for service fees that rightfully belonged to ABCC, yielding a net loss of $423,482. Eventually, the account was reconciled and the money was liberated. See "20 Largest On-Hold Vendors as of 11/06/97," a Company-generated report.

Daze of Reckoning

1. The SEC Web site contains information about the role and function of the agency, at: <http://www.sec.gov>.

2. The Department of Justice Web site contains information about the role and function of the agency at: <http://www.usdoj.gov>.

3. Richard D. Marshall was the senior associate regional administrator in the New York office of the SEC and, before that, branch chief in the Division of Enforcement of the SEC in Washington, D.C.

4. Kirkpatrick & Lockhart is a law firm of more than four hundred lawyers, with offices in several major cities. See its Web site at: <http://www.kl.com>.

5. Robinson, St. John & Wayne is now known as St. John & Wayne, and has offices in several cities. See its Web site at: <http://www.stjohn-law.com>.

6. Shaw Licitra is now known as Shaw Licitra Bohner Esernio & Schwartz, P.C.

7. At the time of the transaction, the Hotel Syracuse, Inc., owned the Hotel Syracuse. Hotel Syracuse, Inc., was itself in chapter 11, Bank. Ct. N.D.N.Y., No. 90-02921, 1990.

8. A detailed description of the New York City Transit Authority lease scam is set forth in the Affidavit of John Martello, the Assistant Chief Facilities Officer for the NYCTA (Mar. 21, 1996), and the Declaration of Ira B. Spindler, Supervisory Criminal Investigator (Mar. 27, 1996), both submitted in conjunction with the complaint by the SEC against Patrick R. Bennett, and others, S.D.N.Y., No. 96-2237, Mar. 27, 1996.

9. To initiate a chapter 11 bankruptcy proceeding, a corporation needs to file a two-

page petition, a list of the largest twenty unsecured creditors, a list of all creditors, a mailing matrix of the addresses of the creditors, a corporate resolution authorizing the filing of the petition, and an $800 check.

10. Professor LoPucki of Cornell Law School maintains a bankruptcy research database that covers public companies filing chapter 11 from 1980 to the present with assets of more than $200 million. According to the database, there are 309 such companies nationwide, 61 filed in the S.D.N.Y. No such filings are in any other district of New York. Also, the clerk advised the Bennett bankruptcy is the largest the court ever administered. Also, according to Charley Hannagan, who has covered the story for the *Syracuse Post-Standard* since its inception, "I believe we've always called it the largest bankruptcy case in the Northern District of New York." See also "Patrick Bennett's Big Gamble," *Syracuse Post-Standard,* Nov. 29, 1998.

11. See 11 U.S.C. § 1107 (1984) for a definition of and the rights of a debtor-in-possession.

12. See 11 U.S.C. § 1104(a) (1986) concerning the rights of a party in interest to request the appointment of a trustee.

13. An examiner may be appointed under 11 U.S.C. 1104(c) (1986).

14. Matthew C. Harrison Jr. is a partner at Budetti, Harrison & Nerland, a company specializing in interim management and turnaround. See the firm's Web site at: <http://www.budetti.com>.

15. Harrison's book about the WedTech scandal, *Feeding Frenzy: The Inside Story of Wedtech* (New York: Henry Holt and Company, 1980).

16. Bud and Kathleen retained the law firm of Scolaro Shulman Cohen Lawler & Burstein, P.C., of Syracuse to represent them. The chief lawyer was Alan Burstein.

17. The other members of the SEC staff involved with the Bennett matter were Andrew J. Geist, Eric Schmidt, Peter D. Goldstein, Al J. Troncoso, Riva Starr, Barbara Bailin, Ira Spindler, and William Johnson, all under Deputy Regional Director Edwin H. Nordlinger. FBI Special Agent Anthony Zampogna was heavily involved in preparing witnesses for trial.

18. See 11 U.S.C. § 1104 (1980) and § 1109 (1978) concerning the SEC's right to intervene and appoint a trustee.

19. SEC Motion to Appoint a Trustee, Bankr. N.D.N.Y., Nos. 96-61376–79, Apr. 3, 1996.

20. According to documents on file with the clerk of Onondaga County, Bud and Kathleen Bennett lived at 240 Ross Park in Syracuse. The house was purchased in 1959 and the mortgage paid off in 1972. Inasmuch as the house was purchased and paid off five years before the Company came into being, the trustee could not place a prejudgment lien, called a *lis pendens,* on the residence. New York Civil Practice Law & Rules § 6514 and § 6515 (McKinney).

21. An article concerning James Hassett's appointment is "Savior of CIS to Lead Bennett," *Syracuse Post-Standard,* Apr. 17, 1996.

22. Hassett was the chapter 11 trustee of CIS. CIS Corporation is the main operating subsidiary of Continental Information Systems Corporation, a NASDAQ Small Cap Company (Ticker Symbol "CISC"). CIS was founded in 1968 as a finance company that buys, sells, and leases productive capital assets. See its Web site at: <http://www.ciscorporation.com>.

23. Order Appointing Richard C. Breeden as Trustee, J. Gerling, Bankr. N.D.N.Y., Apr.

10, 1996. Judge Gerling's Bankruptcy Court Decisions can be viewed at: <http://www.nynb .uscourts.gov/uticadecision/utidecmenu.html>.

24. At the time of the filing, most of the 275 employees still worked for the Company in the Atrium.

25. Alan Marder of Shaw Licitra was Stuart Gordon's partner.

26. Simpson Thacher & Bartlett was established in 1884 and has 499 lawyers, including 123 partners. It has offices throughout the United States and the world. See its Web site at: <http://www.simpsonthacher.com>.

27. Coopers & Lybrand merged with Price Waterhouse in 1998. Details of the company can be found at the Price Waterhouse Coopers Web site at: <http://www.pw.com>.

28. See the Pinkerton, Inc., Web site at: <http://www.pinkertons.com>.

Kathleen McCarthy and Edmund T. "Bud" Bennett

1. Bennett Funding was on *Inc.* magazine's 500 list three times—205th, 73rd, and 19th—between 1984 and 1995.

2. Lincoln allegedly said the remark in a speech in Clinton, Ill., on Sept. 2, 1858. In 1905, two newspapers, the *Chicago Tribune* and the *Brooklyn Eagle,* gathered testimony to see if Lincoln really said it. The evidence was conflicting and dubious in some particulars. No contemporary accounts of the text of the Clinton speech contain this utterance. However, tradition still attributes the quote to Lincoln, and it has remained a favorite in popular usage. Information concerning Lincoln's quote was supplied by Lincoln aficionado R. J. Norton. See Web site at: <http://members.aol.com/RVSNorton/Lincoln2.html>. Norton advised the source of his information is Roy P. Basler, ed., *The Collected Works of Abraham Lincoln* (New Brunswick: Rutgers Univ. Press, 1953).

3. The Atrium is at Two Clinton Square, Syracuse, N.Y., and is directly across the street from the Federal Building, which houses the Department of Justice. See "Bennett Buys Atrium," *Syracuse Post-Standard,* Apr. 8, 1993.

4. See Internal Revenue Code 26 U.S.C. § 1031 (1990) concerning taxation of like-kind exchanges of real property.

5. A layout of the Company's offices is in the "Grand Opening Dedication" brochure, June 12, 1992.

6. The CIGNA complaint is captioned *Bennett Funding v. CIGNA, et al.,* 91 CV 229, N.D.N.Y. (1991).

7. The information about Bud Bennett comes from discussions I have had with him over the years, from court documents in the Venrock litigation, and from promotional materials and articles.

8. Alan Burstein of Scolaro Shulman Cohen Lawler & Burstein, P.C., represented Bud in the bankruptcy proceeding.

9. Aloha Communication Systems, Inc., a New York corporation, was authorized to issue two hundred shares of stock.

10. F. Lee Bailey is a partner in the law firms of Bailey, Fishman & Leonard in Boston, and Bailey, Fishman, Freeman & Ferrin in West Palm Beach, Fla. See the Web site at: <http://www.cbclegal.com/authors/bailey.htm>.

11. Trustee's Adversary Complaint against the individual Bennetts, and others, Bankr. N.D.N.Y., Nos. 96-61376–79, Adv. Pro. No. 96-70154, June 6, 1996, amended Sept. 3, 1996.

12. When Bud and Kathleen testified they took the Fifth on virtually all questions save their names and addresses. "Elder Bennetts Allege Scheme by Breeden," *Syracuse Post-Standard,* July 3, 1998; "Judge Demands Bennetts Appear," *Syracuse Post-Standard,* Apr. 1998.

13. The captain of the *Lady Kathleen* was Don Carroll. He instituted a suit against the Company, *Carroll v. Bennett Funding,* Sup. Ct. State of N.Y. Cty. Onon., 95-4363 (1995).

14. The payments for all of the items associated with the *Lady Kathleen* were found in the Company's computer records.

15. Homestead and other exemptions in Florida are in Florida Statutes § 222.01 (1869 revised 1998).

16. William Gregory bought the yacht for a reported $600,000. After paying the balance of the ship's mortgage, commissions, and other costs, the sale netted about $78,000. See payoff letter from NationsBank, Nov. 24, 1993, showing amount of $435,429.05. The proceeding instituted by the trustee in Bankruptcy Court is captioned *Cordoba Corporation, Bennett Funding Group, Inc., and Bennett Management Development Corp. v. Edmund and Kathleen Bennett,* Bankr. N.D.N.Y., No. 96-61376, Adv. Pro. No. 96-70132A (1996). See also "The Bennett File," *Syracuse Post-Standard,* Aug. 1, 1996.

17. The initial filed affidavit of Bud Bennett in the Cordoba proceeding was not notarized.

18. Order, J. Gerling, in the matter of *Cordoba Corporation, et al., v. Edmund and Kathleen Bennett,* Bankr. N.D.N.Y., No. 96-61376, Aug. 3, 1998. The Bennetts' reliance on the Fifth Amendment was commented upon by Judge Gerling in the opinion.

19. As to the Rescue Mission scam, see SEC Litigation Release No. 15095, Sept. 30, 1996.

20. The information supplied about Kathleen Bennett comes from discussions I have had with her and others about her over the years, from court documents, and from promotional materials and articles.

21. Elie Wiesel, *Night* (New York: Bantam Books, 1960), p. 9.

22. The Bennett Funding Group, Inc., Certificate of Amendment to the Certificate of Incorporation filed with the Secretary of State of N.Y., Jan. 1994, sets forth the increase in the number of authorized shares to 10 million.

23. David Barrett, of the firm Barrett & Schuler, was the trustee for Bud and Kathleen's shares from Dec. 1995 through Mar. 1996. Barrett served as special counsel, U.S. House of Representatives, Committee on Standards of Official Conduct, 1979–80. He was also the independent counsel for the investigation of Henry Cisneros, Office of Independent Counsel, 1996. His letter of resignation is dated Mar. 28, 1996.

Alms to the Poor

1. The hierarchy of giving is reprinted from *The New Union Prayer Book, Gates of Power* (New York: Central Conference of American Rabbis, 1975), p. 15. The book is used by the Temple Society of Concord of Syracuse. Rabbi Ezring heads the congregation.

2. Rabbi Rapoport of Chabad House of Central N.Y., Syracuse, N.Y., advised that all giving is good.

3. The mission of Make-a-Wish is "to grant the wishes of children with terminal or life-threatening illnesses." Web site at: <http://www.makeawish.org>.

4. Mrs. Bennett's comments were related to me through a conversation with Tom Kingsley.

5. "Bennett Trustee Sues Charities," *Syracuse Post-Standard,* Apr. 18, 1998.

The Evil Empire

1. Most of the entities were found openly in the books and records of the Company. Some of the entities, such as Bennett Finance I-V, Exponential Business Development, Liberty Helicopter Tours, Inc., Meridian Helicopter, Inc., and OnGard Systems, Inc., surfaced either through reviewing the mail addressed to Patrick Bennett as an officer of Bennett Funding or Bennett Management or in boxes left behind by Patrick's henchmen.

2. The term "insider" includes people or entities that have a close blood or financial relationship with the debtor. In essence, an insider is one who has a sufficiently close relationship with the debtor that his conduct is made subject to closer scrutiny than those dealing at arms length with the debtor.

For a corporate debtor, the term "insider" includes all officers, directors, and controlling persons of the debtor, a partnership in which the debtor is a general partner and general partner of the debtor as well. Also included are relatives of a general partner, director, officer, or control person.

An affiliate or insider of an affiliate is also considered an insider if such affiliate has at least 20 percent voting control over the debtor or a corporation 20 percent or more of whose outstanding voting securities are directly or indirectly owned, controlled, or held with power to vote by the debtor. This basic definition of "insider" was used in completing the Bennett Debtors' Statement of Financial Affairs.

Another Boat

1. The relevant part of Immanuel Kant's famous Categorical Imperative: "Act so that you treat humanity, whether in your own person or in that of another, always as an end, never as a means only." Arnulf Zweig, ed., *The Essential Kant* (New York: Mentor Books, 1970), p. 28.

2. Niccolò Machiavelli's famous aphorism "The end justifies the means" is in Daniel Donno, ed., *The Prince* (New York: Bantam Classic, 1984).

The Mastermind, Patrick R. Bennett

1. Trustee's Adversary Complaint against the individual Bennetts, and others, Bankr. N.D.N.Y., Nos. 96-61376–79, Adv. Pro. No. 96-70154, June 6, 1996, amended Sept. 3, 1996, p. 21.

2. Apparently, for the first time in Company history, all of the investor checks for the Jan. 1996 payment bounced.

3. The quoted material is from the Declaration of Ira B. Spindler, Supervisory Criminal Investigator, Mar. 28, 1996, submitted in conjunction with the complaint filed by the SEC against Patrick R. Bennett, and others, S.D.N.Y., No. 96-2237, 1996, p. 20.

4. Ibid.

5. Ibid., p. 19.

6. Ibid.

7. Ibid.

8. Ibid.

9. Ibid.

10. Municipal Tax Opinion Letter from Lasser Hochman Marcus Guryan and Kuskin to Bennett Leasing, Jan. 2, 1992. The firm opined that Internal Revenue Code § 103(a) provides "gross income does not include interest on any state or local bond." Local bond includes an "obligation of a state or political subdivision thereof." Under the scenario presented by Bennett Funding, leases are included in this definition.

11. The trustee disseminated over the Internet "a list of 8,249 specific cases of documented multiple sales involving $96,389,568 in leases." Letter of Richard C. Breeden, Oct. 2, 1997, at: <http://www.bennett-funding.com/index/munipk.html>. See also Breeden's letter to Daniel Stolz, counsel for the Unsecured Creditors Committee, Aug. 12, 1997.

12. The quoted material and analysis is from the Confidential Report to the Board of Directors of The Bennett Funding Group, Inc., Bennett Leasing Corporation, and The Processing Center, Inc., prepared by Arkin, Schaeffer & Kaplan, Mar. 7, 1996, p. 17.

13. Ibid., p. 18.

14. Ibid.

15. John Sullivan was the director of MIS, who told me about the 1994 conversation with Bud and Kathleen in which he advised them of the double-pledging. Based, in part, on this conversation, the trustee's complaint against responsible persons was amended in Sept. 1996.

16. The "look into it" quote was revealed during a conversation with a former employee.

17. The "totally audit" quote was made by Kathleen Bennett to the SEC on Dec. 1, 1994, reprinted in the Trustee's Adversary Complaint, p. 22.

18. The Company had offerings which were noncollateralized straight equity or debt positions, such as the private placement of shares of Resort Funding and debentures totaling about $120 million.

The Mechanics of Lease Fraud

1. As one of its financial products, the Company issued debt and equity instruments through private placement memoranda. The SEC targeted the PPMs because they believed they contained false financial information that was disseminated to investors.

2. The Securities Act of 1933 is found at 15 U.S.C. § 77a (1933 amended 1980). The Securities Exchange Act of 1934 is found at 15 U.S.C. § 78a (1934). For a good discussion of the securities laws generally, see the Web site at: <http://www.law.uc.edu/CCL/intro.html>.

3. Exemptions are found in regulation D, section 4(6), of the Securities Act of 1933. From regulation D, we learn:

Accredited investor shall mean any person who comes within any of the following categories, or who the issuer reasonably believes comes within any of the following categories, at the time of the sale of the securities to that person:

i. Any bank as defined in section 3(a)(2) of the Act, or any savings and loan association or other institution as defined in section 3(a)(5)(A) of the Act whether acting in its in-

Notes to Pages 66–67   335

dividual or fiduciary capacity; any broker or dealer registered pursuant to section 15 of the Securities Exchange Act of 1934; any insurance company as defined in section 2(13) of the Act; any investment company registered under the Investment Company Act of 1940 or a business development company as defined in section 2(a)(48) of that Act; any Small Business Investment Company licensed by the U.S. Small Business Administration under section 301(c) or (d) of the Small Business Investment Act of 1958; any plan established and maintained by a state, its political subdivisions, or any agency or instrumentality of a state or its political subdivisions, for the benefit of its employees, if such plan has total assets in excess of $5,000,000; any employee benefit plan within the meaning of the Employee Retirement Income Security Act of 1974 if the investment decision is made by a plan fiduciary, as defined in section 3(21) of such act, which is either a bank, savings and loan association, insurance company, or registered investment adviser, or if the employee benefit plan has total assets in excess of $5,000,000 or, if a self-directed plan, with investment decisions made solely by persons that are accredited investors;

ii. Any private business development company as defined in section 202(a)22 of the Investment Advisers Act of 1940;

iii. Any organization described in section 501(c)3 of the Internal Revenue Code, corporation, Massachusetts or similar business trust, or partnership, not formed for the specific purpose of acquiring the securities offered, with total assets in excess of $5,000,000;

iv. Any director, executive officer, or general partner of the issuer of the securities being offered or sold, or any director, executive officer, or general partner of a general partner of that issuer;

v. Any natural person whose individual net worth, or joint net worth with that person's spouse, at the time of his purchase exceeds $1,000,000;

vi. Any natural person who had an individual income in excess of $200,000 in each of the two most recent years or joint income with that person's spouse in excess of $300,000 in each of those years and has a reasonable expectation of reaching the same income level in the current year;

vii. Any trust, with total assets in excess of $5,000,000, not formed for the specific purpose of acquiring the securities offered, whose purchase is directed by a sophisticated person as described in Rule 506(b)(2)(ii) and

viii. Any entity in which all of the equity owners are accredited investors.

4. Municipal Federal Securities Opinion Letter from Robinson St. John & Wayne to Bennett Funding, May 1, 1992. Municipal "blue sky" Securities Opinion Letter from Robinson St. John & Wayne to Bennett Funding, June 17, 1992. Municipal Federal Securities Opinion Letter from Rosenman & Collin to Bennett Funding, Mar. 10, 1995.

5. The quoted material is from the Trustee's Amended Adversary Complaint against the individual Bennetts, and others, Bankr. N.D.N.Y., Nos. 96-61376–79, Adv. Pro. No. 96-70154, Sept. 3, 1996, pp. 16–20. Moreover, as Breeden stated in a letter to Daniel Stolz, counsel for the Unsecured Creditors Committee, Aug. 12, 1997,

This process is demonstrated by the case of two Sharp copiers leased to the Oklahoma Medical Center in lease numbers 91090642 and 91090644. Exhibit B contains the documentation covering these machines. Both machines had a monthly payment of $508.29, and they are the only two machines leased by Oklahoma Medical Center that have a $508.29 payment. Both of these leases were pledged to St. Henry Bank. In addition, both leases were sold by Cantelmo & Associates to Joseph and Theresa Lupo of Bloomfield, New Jersey. Though both lease number 91090642 and lease 91090644 had each already been pledged twice, the two leases were also sold in a Kasarjian package to four additional purchasers. Wallace and Marilyn Klarman, Remo & Janet Koivunon, Mrs. Marion Messinger and Helen Tinn all purchased one of those two leases through the Kenton Group as lease "BMDC-51M", with Oklahoma Medical Center as the lessee and payments of $508.29. Because the Kenton "pool" sold to the four purchasers included both Oklahoma Medical Center leases, it is difficult to say which of the four investors bought which of the two leases. However, in the aggregate lease number 91090642 and lease number 91090644 were purchased eight times, or four purchasers of each lease. Since only two "double" sales of these leases are listed in Attachment A, when there were at least four such sales, the Attachment A printout understates the magnitude of double sales of the Oklahoma Medical Center leases by 50%.

6. The information concerning the record number of pledges and double-selling to the same individual was advised by Coopers & Lybrand and is reiterated in a letter from Breeden to Congressman Rothman of New Jersey, Sept. 4, 1997.

The NYC Transit Authority Needs Copiers

1. SEC Complaint against Patrick R. Bennett, and others, S.D.N.Y., No. 96-2237, Mar. 27, 1996. Attached to the complaint are exhibits that were used as a reference for the allegations: (1) Bennett Receivables Corporation–II private placement memorandum (PPM); (2) Bennett Management PPM; (3) testimony of Patrick Bennett; (4) Bennett Receivables Corporation PPM; (5) testimony of Ken Kasarjian; (6) Scriptex consolidation agreement; (7) Bennett Funding, June 22, 1995, submission to SEC; (8) testimony of Anthony Pavoni; (9) Hemlock Investor Associates, 1992 and 1993 tax returns; (10) testimony of Charles Genovese; (11) Bennett Funding, financial statements, Dec. 31, 1994; (12) Bennett Funding letter, June 4, 1992, to Arthur Andersen & Co.; (13) Cohen analysis, "Lease Assignments" (total sales); (14) Bennett Funding municipal lease brochure; (15) tax exemption opinion letter; (16) memorandum to investors from Patrick Bennett, Jan. 30, 1996; (17) statement of purchased leases, Paley Construction Co.; (18) statement of purchased leases, David Able; (19) customer order forms; (20) inventory sheets; (21) confirmation tickets; (22) Cohen analysis, N.Y. City Transit Authority leases sold; (23) affidavit of John Martello, Asst. Chief Facilities Officer of the NYCTA, Mar. 21, 1996; (24) Stoever Glass sample portfolio—lease assignments; (25) Stoever Glass sample portfolio—underlying leases; (26) lease assignment documents pertaining to Allan Eyre clients; (27) State of Alaska Department of Administration agreement (produced by Bennett Funding); (28) Federal Aviation Administration agreement (produced by Bennett Funding); (29) Alan Eyre sample portfolio; (30) City and County of Denver agreements (produced by Bennett Funding); (31) The Bennett Funding International Ltd., PPM; (32) The Bennett Funding Group, Inc., PPM; (33) checks from The Bennett Funding Group, Inc., to Scriptex totaling

$18,677,000; (34) thirteen checks payable to Aloha Leasing; (35) Bennett Funding journal entry recording $3,500,000 of income for Dec. 1992 Scriptex transaction; (36) testimony of William Crowley; (37) documentation for June 1992 purported transfer of six leases; (38) documentation for the 1990–91 leases that Bennett Funding acquired in 1990 and 1991 from Scriptex; (39) checks from Scriptex Enterprises Ltd., to Bennett Funding (Aloha Leasing), June 25, 1992; (40) Mahoney Cohen's work papers illustrating calculations of $3,500,000 gain from Dec. 1992 purported transaction with Scriptex; (41) testimony of Thomas Pomposelli; (42) analysis of Herbert Cohen summarizing payments from BMDC to Scriptex and payments from Scriptex to Bennett Funding; (43) Scriptex financial statements for year ended Dec. 31, 1992; (44) testimony of Thomas Caulfield; (45) Dec. 31, 1992, bill of sale of contracts between Bennett Funding and Kenton Portfolio, Inc.; (46) Gamma International news release, Jan. 18, 1993; (47) memorandum from Patrick Bennett to Gene McGillycuddy, Apr. 9, 1993, and attachments from Mahoney Cohen's work papers; (48) Bennett Funding 550-004890 Chemical Bank account statement for Apr. 1993; (49) BMDC 550-004815 Chemical Bank account statement for Apr. 1993; (50) Apr. 7, 1993, wire transfer instructions for $14,450,000 transfer from BMDC to Kenton and Apr. 8, 1993, $1,000,000 transfer from BMDC to Kenton; (51) wire transfer instruction from Kenton to MIFCO dated Apr. 7, 1993, and Apr. 8, 1993; (52) Oct. 15, 1993, invoice from Bennett Funding to Aegis Holdings, Inc., for "due diligence" and Bennett Funding Dec. 1, 1993, invoice to Aegis Holdings, Inc., for "services rendered"; (53) testimony of Angelo Appierio; (54) Hemlock Investor Associates Dec. 1993 financial statements; (55) Hemlock Investor Associates 1993 tax return; (56) testimony of Kevin Kuppel; (57) Herbert Cohen analysis of Bennett Funding funds transferred to Bennett Management; (58) letter from Kirkpatrick & Lockhart, LLP, Aug. 15, 1995, to Barry Rashkover of the SEC; (59) testimony of Allan Eyre.

2. Copies of the approval, purchase orders, inventory registers, and other NYCTA documents were kept in the Company's microfiche center.

3. As to investor tax liability, see the letter from Hiscock & Barclay to the Company, Apr. 11, 1997.

4. Information concerning the other fraudulent leases was from the Trustee's First Amended Complaint against Scriptex, et al., Bankr. N.D.N.Y., No. 96-61376, Adv. Pro. No. 98-70602A, Dec. 16, 1998.

5. Charles Genovese individually, and through his accounting firm, Genovese, Levin, Bartlett Co., in Franklin Lakes, N.J., raised tens of millions of dollars by steering his accounting clients to invest in lease and other financial products of the Company. He also was instrumental in raising vast sums for noncore assets, such as the Comfort Suites Hotel.

6. Detailed information concerning the various limited liability companies created by Kasarjian is set forth in the Beckett Reserve Fund, LLC, Proof of Claim for $16,423,709.46, Parker-Devon Fund, LLC, Proof of Claim for $1,341,123.61, Stafford Fund, LLC, Proof of Claim for $1,040,229.11, and Sterling Reserve Fund, LLC, Proof of Claim for $7,629,973.45, Bankr. N.D.N.Y., No. 96-61376, Dec. 30, 1996; Objection to the Beckett Reserve Fund, LLC, to the Transfer of its Claim, Bankr. N.D.N.Y., No. 96-61376, June 2, 1998; and Master Purchase and Assignment Agreement and Servicing Agreement between Bennett Funding and Parker-Devon Fund, LLC, Jan. 9, 1996. See also Opinion of Counsel from Okin Hollander to the members of the Parker-Devon, Sterling Reserve, Stafford and Beckett Reserve Funds, LLCs, regarding the Bennett Bankruptcy, Jan. 2, 1997.

7. The dream house was at 44 Midvale Mountain Road, Mahwah, N.J. The house was deeded to Lisa Chapman, Kasarjian's wife, who deeded the property back to herself. The original deed was dated Oct. 24, 1991, and recorded in the Bergen County Clerk's Office on Oct. 25, 1991. Kasarjian executed a $5 million Revolving Credit Note-Security Agreement and Revolving Credit Note on Jan. 1, 1992, in favor of Bennett Management.

What Did You Do in the War, Daddy?

1. The standard definition of *corporation* can be found in *Black's Law Dictionary*, 5th ed. (St. Paul: West Publishing Co., 1979), p. 307.

2. For a good discussion of the tangible and intangible powers of corporations, see Robert Monks and Nell Minow, *Power and Accountability*, at Web site: <http://www.lens-inc.com/power/chapter2.html#section2>.

3. A nonexclusive itemization of the powers of corporations in New York is found at Business Corporation Law § 201 and § 202 (McKinney).

4. The Securities Act of 1933 is found at 15 U.S.C. § 77a (1933 amended 1980). The Securities Exchange Act of 1934 is found at 15 U.S.C. § 78a (1934). General Business Law § 339 (McKinney) regulates the selling of securities in New York.

5. Pursuant to section 13 of the Securities Exchange Act of 1934, a public reporting corporation is required to file an annual report on Form 10-K, quarterly reports on Form 10-Q, and current reports on Form 8-K.

6. Rule 144 exempts from registration the sale of securities by directors and officers pursuant to certain well-defined criteria. General Rules and Regulations 17 CFR § 230.144 (1998).

7. See the Affidavit of Scott Butera in support of the Motion by Trustee to Sell Common Stock in Equivest Finance, Inc., in Registered Public Offering and to Exchange Preferred Stock in Equivest for Common Stock, Bankr. N.D.N.Y., No. 96-61376, July 7, 1998.

8. For example, in New York, automatic lease renewals, known as evergreen provisions, are disallowed unless notice is given to the lessee. General Obligations Law § 5-901 (McKinney).

9. In New York, public contracts for equipment leasing and purchasing are governed, in part, under General Municipal Law 103 and 109-b (McKinney).

10. On municipal cancellation, see Weisman memorandum to Michael Bennett, Apr. 10, 1991.

11. The cancellation of government contracts and leases are governed by Federal Acquisition Regulations, 48 CFR § 49.103 (1997).

12. The name of the investigative firm is AMRIC Associates, Ltd.

13. The Records Retention Plan was drafted on May 21, 1993. The quoted material is from the plan.

14. The process to draft the Business Interruption Plan was started in late 1994 and concluded with a working draft on May 11, 1995. The quoted material is from the plan.

15. The litigation section was headed by Paul Willard, from 1992 to 1994.

16. See the memorandum from E. T. "Bud" Bennett to all employees, Sept. 21, 1994. Edward Guardino became the general counsel of Resort Funding, Inc., the time-share company. William Fedorich became the general counsel of Aloha Capital Corporation.

17. The Company primarily relied upon Robinson St. John & Wayne as its securities counsel.

18. The Code of Professional Responsibility can be found at the N.Y. State Bar Association Web site: <http://www.nysba.org/opinions/codes/anchor1.html>. The quoted material is from the preamble to the code.

19. Zealous representation of one's client is from Canon 7 of the code.

20. Transcript of Weisman testimony, Bankr. N.D.N.Y., No. 96-61376, May 18, 1996.

It's in the Air

1. "SEC Questions Bernardi," *Syracuse Post-Standard,* Apr. 5, 1999.

Pennies from Heaven

1. The incident was reported by Breeden in a letter to the investors, Nov. 24, 1997. The quote is from the Bennetts' lawyer. See also the testimony of Ken Kasarjian as reported in "Witness Maps Bennett Shadow Business," *Syracuse Post-Standard,* Jan. 8, 1999.

The Businesses of the Debtors

1. Much of the specific information relative to the various Bennett companies is from the Bennett Corporations Binder, Defendant's Exhibit B, *Lady Kathleen* Hearing, May 23, 1996; and from the Affidavit of Stewart Weisman in support of Trustee's Motion for Substantive Consolidation, which describes, among other things, the operations of the debtors, Bankr. N.D.N.Y., No. 96-61376, Oct. 29, 1996.

2. Information concerning the origin of the name "Aloha" was furnished by Bud Bennett to me. See also the transcript of Weisman deposition relative to the litigation with the various banks, Bankr. N.D.N.Y., No. 96-61376, July 16, 1997.

3. A good short article about reverse mergers is Stephan J. Mallenbaum, "Alternative to Public Offering—Reverse Mergers Breathe New Life into 'Public Shell.'"

4. Equivest Finance, Inc., is now headquartered in Greenwich, Conn. Its ticker symbol is EQUI (NASDAQ). As Breeden noted in excerpts from a letter to the investors, dated May 29, 1998,

> The plan is to build up Resort Funding, Inc. and its parent, Equivest Finance, Inc. This is why the developments at Equivest Finance, which I have written about in every letter, have been so critical, because it is the engine for the recovery train. I might add that so far it has proven to be a small but very powerful engine. Each $1.00 in revenue earned by the Estate is worth $1.00 to our creditors, and goes in a bank account earning 5%. However, at Equivest's current price/earnings ratio, each $1.00 in after tax net income of Equivest is currently capitalized at approximately $28 in market value (about $25 of which belongs to the Estate). The potential advantages to the creditors of the Estate of strong earnings in Equivest are readily apparent. Under the POR, the shares of Equivest that are owned by the Estate will be sold to the public in an underwritten secondary offering. Each BFG creditor will have the opportunity to take their recovery entirely in cash. However, I hope to be able to give each creditor the right to elect to take a portion of their estimated recovery in stock of Equivest at whatever the IPO price turns out to be.

5. See the Affidavit of Richard C. Breeden in support of the Motion by Trustee to Sell Common Stock in Equivest Finance, Inc., to Underwriters in Registered Public Offering

and to Exchange Preferred Stock in Equivest for Common Stock, Bankr. N.D.N.Y., No. 96-61376, July 8, 1998, p. 1.

6. Ibid., p. 3.

7. Ibid., p. 4.

8. Notice of Evidentiary Hearing on Trustee's Motion Under 11 U.S.C. § 363(b) To Sell Common Stock In Equivest Finance, Inc. To Underwriters in Registered Public Offering and to Exchange Preferred Stock in Equivest for Common Stock, Bankr. N.D.N.Y., No. 96-61376, July 10, 1998.

9. Eastern Resorts had total assets of approximately $29 million, revenues of approximately $9.5 million, and net income of approximately $1.2 million for the five-month period ended May 31, 1998.

10. Motion by Resort Funding, Inc., and supporting affidavits of T. Hamel and G. Klaben to Correct Order which exchanged debt due to the debtors from Resort Funding, Inc., for shares of Equivest, Bankr. N.D.N.Y., No. 96-61376, July 29, 1998.

11. Affidavit of Stewart Weisman in support of Motion by Resort Funding, Inc., to Correct Order, unfiled.

12. See Objection to Correct Order, Harter Secrest & Emery, attorneys for several banks, Bankr. N.D.N.Y., No. 96-61376, Aug. 10, 1998.

13. "Bennett Affiliate Firm Plans to Buy Six Resorts," *Syracuse Post-Standard*, Feb. 18, 1999. See also "Equivest Rises from Bennett's Ashes," *Syracuse Post-Standard*, May 3, 1999.

14. The shipbuilder, Freeport Shipbuilding & Marine Repair, Inc., was sued by the trustee, Bankr. N.D.N.Y., No. 96-61376, Adv. Pro. No. 98-70474A, 1998. Judge Gerling decided that all prepetition contract claims and counterclaims be sent to arbitration. Order, J. Gerling, Bankr. N.D.N.Y., No. 96-61376, Oct. 29, 1998.

15. Information concerning the estate's attempt to get up to $2 million of insurance proceeds for the *Sioux City Sue* is set forth in the Trustee's Motion for An Order Approving Assignment of Rights Agreements and supporting documents, Bankr. N.D.N.Y., No. 96-61376, Jan. 5, 1999.

16. On Mar. 5, 1996, Commercial Union Insurance Company and HIH Casualty & General Insurance Limited, which had jointly provided marine insurance coverage to the vessel and barge, filed suit against Bennett Management, seeking a declaratory relief that the insurers are not responsible to pay on any claims for damage or vandalism to the vessel or barge. Dist. N.J., No. 96-1043, Mar. 6, 1996. See the Amended First Interim Application of Bennett Management's outside counsel, Shanley & Fisher, for a detailed description and analysis of this matter, Bankr. N.D.N.Y., No. 96-61376, May 1, 1998.

17. Memorandum from E. T. "Bud" Bennett to Don Carroll, Nov. 4, 1993, concerning the *Spirit of Ecstasy*; Letter from NationsBank to Bud Bennett concerning the payoff of the ship's mortgage, Nov. 24, 1993.

18. Harold's Club information is set forth in Shamrock's petition and schedules, Bankr. N.D.N.Y., 1998, as well as appraisal information supplied to the trustee. See also "Casino Sale Could Help Bennett Investors," *Syracuse Post-Standard*, June 11, 1998.

19. For a discussion of a settlement reached concerning another gaming vessel, the Gold Shore floating casino, which cost the Company almost $40 million, see the Notice of Debtor's Motion to Approve Compromise of Controversies and supporting documents, Bankr. N.D.N.Y., No. 96-61376, Sept. 18, 1998.

With Apologies to Melville

1. The reference of the heading is to Herman Melville's description of the whiteness of the whale in *Moby Dick*.

2. I attended Brooklyn College from 1973 to 1977.

The Quiet Company That "Made" Hundreds of Millions

1. The terms of the transaction between Chase and Bennett are set forth in a letter agreement dated Apr. 15, 1985. All of the Chase debt was not forgiven, however. As the parties went their separate ways, Chase's company still owed Bennett Funding $306,556 in lease payments and $1,282,656 for various loans and nonperforming receivables assigned to the Company.

2. Memorandum form Stewart Weisman to Patrick Bennett concerning transfer of shares of Bennett Management and the status of the repayment plan, Dec. 26, 1995.

3. Patrick Bennett's horse farm is at 3695 Peterboro Road in Vernon, New York. Information concerning payments from Patrick to his wife, Gwen, were obtained from papers filed by Lee Woodard, the chapter 7 trustee administering Patrick's case, Bankr. N.D.N.Y., No. 97-65399, 1997.

4. West Virginia Code, Chapter 29, "Racetrack Video Lottery Act."

5. Order, J. Gerling, approving sale of Ferris stock, Bankr. N.D.N.Y., No. 96-61376, Oct. 8, 1998. See also "Former Fay's Execs Buy Bennett's Share of Ferris," *Syracuse Post-Standard,* Oct. 9, 1998.

Substantive Consolidation and the Honeypot

1. Paul Szlosek in particular needs mentioning for his efforts in tracing the sources of money bouncing between companies and out the door.

2. Quotes about commingling, analysis, attendant expenses, and risk of the Honeypot are from the Affidavit of Thomas E. Lumsden, a partner from Coopers, in support of Trustee's Motion for Substantive Consolidation, Bankr. N.D.N.Y., No. 96-61376, Oct. 29, 1996.

3. The analysis of the commonality of the debtors is from the Affidavit of Stewart Weisman in support of Trustee's Motion for Substantive Consolidation.

4. The information concerning inter-Bennett company transfers is from the Lumsden Affidavit, p. 3, et seq., and Exhibits B and E.

5. The information concerning the Honeypot is furnished, in part, from the Affidavit of Shaun O'Neill, former Processing Center Controller, in support of Trustee's Motion for Substantive Consolidation.

6. Figures of where the Bennett money went are from the Report of Richard C. Breeden, Trustee, Submitted Pursuant to 11 U.S.C. § 1106, Bankr. N.D.N.Y., No. 96-61376, Dec. 30, 1998, pp. 70–75.

7. Information and quoted material concerning the disbursement accounts, daily cash packet, and payment accounts are from the O'Neill Affidavit and the Affidavit of P. Szlosek, Bennett Funding Director of Accounting, in support of Trustee's Motion for Substantive Consolidation.

8. Szlosek also prepared a twenty-five-page spreadsheet containing a list of select re-

cipients of checks and wires from the various Bennett companies from 1991 through the petition filing date. The report is dated May 14, 1997.

9. The siphoned funds were traced by Paul Szlosek and recorded on a BMDC REMIT-TANCES spreadsheet. See also the Affidavit of P. Szlosek, Bennett Funding Director of Accounting, which describes cash flow positions of the company, Bankr. N.D.N.Y., No. 96-61376, Dec. 12, 1997.

10. Information concerning the diversions aided by Canino is from Trustee's Adversary Complaint against the individual Bennetts, and others, Bankr. N.D.N.Y., Nos. 96-61376–79, Adv. Pro. No. 96-70154, June 6, 1996, amended Sept. 3, 1996, ¶73, p. 26. Joseph J. Canino is a named defendant in the Trustee's Adversary Complaint.

11. The amount of payment to the mall developers is from the Company's records.

12. An example of a journal reclassification is "$50,000 reclassified 1/1/95 Journal Entry on the General Ledger Masterfile Maintenance of Bennett Management for NY Golf Group." See also letter from Paul Szlosek to Simpson Thacher, May 1, 1997, which describes various Canino reclassifications.

Patrick's Legal Troubles

1. Criminal Complaint, *United States v. Patrick R. Bennett*, S.D.N.Y., No. 96-0657, 1996.

2. Details from a memorandum concerning Patrick's trip, dated Dec. 17, 1998:

When Patrick was formally charged in March 1996, he was released on his own recognizance, based in part, on his renowned fear of flying. Rudy and Joya (friends of a Bennett Funding employee) told the employee, at a recent family function, that they remember seeing Patrick in the American Airlines terminal in Chicago and then aboard a plane to Syracuse in *late February 1997*. Rudy remembers hearing an announcement in the terminal for the Syracuse flight for "standby passenger Patrick Bennett." Rudy then saw Patrick sitting on his flight to Syracuse accompanied by an attractive young blonde.

Rudy had met Pat on several occasions in the Syracuse area through mutual friends and knew what he looked like. Both witnesses were shown pictures of Pat last week and identified him. Rudy said that a friend of his, Coach Spartano from Utica College, was on an earlier flight with Pat from Miami that terminated in Chicago. Many of the passengers on the Miami flight, Spartano told Rudy, were from a group tour emanating from one of the Caribbean Islands.

At the time, Bud and Kathleen Bennett lived in Ellenton near Tampa over 200 miles from Miami.

QUESTIONS

i. Did Pat have business in Miami, if so, what?

ii. If Pat was visiting his parents in Ellenton why not fly from Tampa/St. Pete?

iii. Who was the blonde?

iv. Was Pat on the flight from the Caribbean or elsewhere into Miami? If so, from where? What was he doing there?

v. Were the tickets purchased in Pat's name, or the blonde's?

vi. Did Pat hide assets at any point during his trip? If so, when, where and what?

vii. Was Pat's fear of flying a carefully cultivated fiction? Or, did desperation/greed overcome his anxiety?

viii. Who else knew about the flight?

3. Stilman's statement was reprinted from "Bennett Scandal Extends to Cover-up Conspiracy," *Syracuse Post-Standard*, June 27, 1997.

4. Special Agent Dorch's comments were reported in "Patrick Bennett's Big Gamble," *Syracuse Post-Standard*, Nov. 29, 1998.

5. Smith's quoted material is reprinted from "Bennett's Request Called 'Affront,'" *Syracuse Post-Standard*, Oct. 27, 1998.

6. Breeden's comments are reprinted from "Patrick Bennett's Big Gamble," *Syracuse Post-Standard*, Nov. 29, 1998.

7. Chapter 7 petitions of Patrick, Bankr. N.D.N.Y., No. 97-65399, 1997, and Michael, Bankr. N.D.N.Y. (transferred), No. 98-62437, 1998.

8. "Bennett Answers with No Answers," *Syracuse Post-Standard*, Oct. 9, 1997.

9. Concerning the Equivest flap and Breeden's fee, see "Trustee Faulted for Buying Stock," *National Law Journal*, Mar. 9, 1998; "Breeden Donates Equivest Stock to Syracuse University," *Syracuse Post-Standard*, Aug. 3, 1998; "Judge Delays Exam of Bennett Trustee's Investments of Equivest," *Syracuse Post-Standard*, July 31, 1998; "Bennett Trustee Switches Gears, Urges Sale of Equivest," *Syracuse Post-Standard*, July 21, 1998; and "Judge Questions Bennett Trustee's Bill," *Syracuse Post-Standard*, May 26, 1998.

10. The quoted material from Croak's motion and Newcombe's response is reprinted from "Bennett Wants to See Trustee's Finances," *Syracuse Post-Standard*, June 13, 1998.

11. Judge Gerling's quote is reprinted from "Judge Denies Bennett's Inquiry Request," *Syracuse Post-Standard*, Aug. 14, 1998.

12. Besides the Bankruptcy Court documents filed by trustee Woodard, information concerning the attempt to get control of Gwen's real estate holdings is described in "A Fight for Bennett's Farm," *Syracuse Post-Standard*, Jan. 19, 1999; "Trustee Goes After Second Bennett House," *Syracuse Post-Standard*, Jan. 27, 1999.

White Sands

1. Information on White Sands was provided at the National Park service Web site: <http://www.nps.gov/whsa>.

More Books to Cook

1. In his report on the fraud, Bankr. N.D.N.Y., No. 96-61376, Dec. 1998, the trustee stated on page 18,

Even the published [Bennett Funding] financial statements, which were replete with Patrick Bennett's manipulations, did not show it to be a strong company if one looked at all beyond the surface. Indeed, [Bennett Funding's] financial statements, even after being fortified through series of sham transactions, showed anemic results each year ranging from a loss of approximately $560,000 in 1994 to a profit of only approximately $3.1 million in 1993. Over the period from 1990 through 1994, the last year for which audited financial statements were available, Bennett had only $7.24 million in total profits.

Despite this observation, the Company still managed to raise enormous sums and placed great importance upon the financial statements as integral to its continued financial operations.

2. The quoted material is from the Indictment against Patrick R. Bennett, Michael A. Bennett, Charles Genovese and Gary Peiffer, S.D.N.Y., 1997, concerning American Gaming, pp. 18–21, concerning the Erie note, p. 2.

3. Opinion of Jeffer Hopkinson Vogel Coomber & Peiffer, Aug. 22, 1992, and addressed to Eugene McGillycuddy of Mahoney Cohen. McGillycuddy later became Tony Pavoni's partner in Castle.

4. The definitions of obstruction and perjury are from the indictment, pp. 64 and 65.

5. The transcript of Patrick's testimony before the SEC concerning the Erie note is from the indictment, p. 74; concerning the purchase of Scriptex lease, p. 67; concerning the Aegis invoice, p. 69; concerning misleading Mahoney Cohen, pp. 72 and 75.

6. The transcript of Genovese's testimony before the SEC concerning the Erie note is from the indictment, p. 81.

7. The transcript of Pomposelli's testimony before the SEC concerning the Scriptex leases is from the Felony Information against Pavoni and Pomposelli, S.D.N.Y., 1997, p. 15.

8. The transcript of Pavoni's testimony before the SEC concerning the Scriptex leases is from the Felony Information, pp. 11–14.

9. Patrick Bennett's quote concerning others who cheated the Company is in "Bennett Knew about Check Scam, Witness Says," *Syracuse Post-Standard,* Jan. 6, 1999.

Estate Planning and Other Machinations

1. Letter from Mahoney Cohen concerning estate planning, Dec. 10, 1992.

2. Jerome Deener, "Transfer of Significant Wealth: Techniques to Retain Control, While Minimizing Estate and Gift Tax Consequences," Apr. 1995.

3. The Aloha Capital tax opinion was furnished by Devorsetz Stinziano Gilberti Heintz & Smith, PC, Jan. 1995.

4. Goldman's letter agreement for consulting services is addressed to Patrick Bennett, Dec. 15, 1995.

5. Kelley was also Bennett's first choice to serve as responsible person before Harrison's short-lived appointment to that position. Because of his relationship with the Company and his unwillingness to forgo all of his and his family's claims, the SEC batted him down.

Pension Plan De-vesting

1. The information concerning the diversion of funds in the chart is from the Trustee's Adversary Complaint, Bankr. N.D.N.Y., No. 96-61376, Sept. 1996, pp. 45 and 46.

2. For example, checks totaling more than $1.35 million were distributed by Genovese to his relatives in Dec. 1995, noted as "return of principal."

3. Pursuant to a conversation with local law enforcement personnel, Genovese was found in a motel room. According to police investigators on the scene, a journal was recovered at the scene that details his role in helping Patrick with the obstruction of the investigation and the laundering of the funds.

4. The action was filed by the Department of Labor, N.D.N.Y., 97-CV-0148, 1997.

5. The definition of *fiduciary* is from *Black's Law Dictionary,* 5th ed. (St. Paul: West Publishing Co., 1979), p. 563.

6. As to the Bennetts and their benefits, see "Elder Bennetts Stripped of Benefit," *Syracuse Post-Standard,* June 21, 1996.

Michael A. Bennett

1. A description of Michael's appearance is set forth in "Tearful Bennett Admits He Lied," *Syracuse Post-Standard,* Nov. 25, 1998.

2. The transcript of Michael's SEC appearance concerning the Hemlock note is from the indictment, S.D.N.Y., 1997, pp. 77–81.

3. The transcript of Genovese's SEC appearance concerning the Hemlock note is from the indictment, pp. 87–88.

4. The Bennett bank statement is from Chemical Bank, account number 550-024204.

5. Justice Department Press Release concerning the indictments of Patrick R. Bennett, et al., June 26, 1997, p. 8.

6. Cecil Roth, *Spanish Inquisition* (New York: W. W. Norton, 1996 reissue).

7. Pomposelli's testimony is from the transcript of Patrick's trial, Jan. 6, 1999. See also "Witness Denies Bumpkin Defense," *Syracuse Post-Standard,* Jan. 7, 1999.

8. See the gout Web site at: <http://www.rheumatology.org.nz/nz08003.htm>.

9. In *Mutual Life Insurance Co v. Haslip,* the U.S. Supreme Court upheld the award of punitive damages, 499 U.S. 1 (1991). *BMW of North America, Inc., v. Gore,* 517 U.S. 559 (1996). Although eventually the Alabama Supreme Court reduced the punitives to a mere $2 million, the U.S. Supreme Court reversed and remanded the case, as the amount of punitive damages awards did not comport with due process.

Bonfire

1. The witness, a former Bennett employee, asked me not to reveal her name because she is afraid of retribution.

Audits Were Holy Things

1. Typical language included in audited financial statements as set forth in Mahoney Cohen's *Independent Auditor's Report,* Mar. 25, 1995, is as follows:

> We have audited the accompanying consolidated balance sheet of The Bennett Funding Group, Inc. as of December 31, 1994, and the related consolidated statements of operations and retained earnings and cash flows for the year then ended. These consolidated financial statements are the responsibility of the Company's management. Our responsibility is to express an opinion on these consolidated financial statements based on our audit.

> We conducted our audit in accordance with generally accepted auditing standards. Those standards require that we plan and perform the audit to obtain reasonable assurance about whether the financial statements are free of material misstatement. An audit includes examining, on a test basis, evidence supporting, the amounts and disclosures in the financial statements. An audit also includes assessing the accounting

principles used and significant estimates made by management, as well as evaluating the overall financial statement presentation. We believe that our audit provides a reasonable basis for our opinion.

In our opinion, the consolidated financial statements referred to above present fairly, in all material respects, the financial position of The Bennett Funding Group, Inc. as of December 1, 1994, and the results of their operations and their cash flows for the year then ended in conformity with generally accepted accounting principles.

2. The 330,000-member American Institute of Certified Public Accountants Web site has useful information concerning the various standards: <http://www.aicpa.org>.

3. Arthur Andersen's fax cover page and financial statement addressed to Bill Crowley, May 7, 1992, who was indicted for his alleged role in the fraud in July 1999.

4. Information about the chain of events in early May 1992 is in a letter from Patrick Bennett to Stan Konopko at Arthur Andersen, May 29, 1992.

5. Opinion of Stewart Weisman to Arthur Andersen, May 6, 1992. It has been suggested that since all cash payments to investors were made from the commingled Honeypot account and not directly from the purchased leases, the leases were securities because payment flowed from the coffers of the issuer, Bennett Funding, and not from the investment itself.

6. The other opinions furnished to Arthur Andersen were from Carl Guy and David Slaff, both dated May 15, 1992.

7. The securities opinion was rendered by Smith Gill Fisher & Butts, May 13, 1992, and the recourse memorandum by Melvin & Melvin, May 12, 1992.

8. Skadden Arps Slate Meagher & Flom memorandum, June 9, 1992.

9. Bennett retained the firm of Devorsetz Stinziano Gilberti Heintz & Smith, P.C., to negotiate the "pull" letter with Arthur Andersen.

10. Letter from Eugene McGillycuddy of Mahoney Cohen to Arthur Andersen, June 22, 1992.

11. Opinion of Jeffer Hopkinson Vogel Coomber & Peiffer to Mahoney Cohen, Aug. 10, 1992.

12. The nine individual investor suits against the accountants are now consolidated in the matter of Bennett Funding Group, Inc., Securities Litigation, S.D.N.Y. MDL No. 1153, Master Docket No. M-21-72, 1996.

13. The footnote appears in NOTE 9—COMMITMENTS AND CONTINGENCIES, p. 9 of the Financial Statement.

14. Information concerning Castle was from the Trustee's First Amended Complaint against Scriptex, et al., Bankr. N.D.N.Y., No. 96-61376, Adv. Pro. No. 98-70602A, Dec. 16, 1998.

The Classless Action

1. All of the federal civil actions against the Bennetts, brokers, accountants, insurers, attorneys, and others have been consolidated in the S.D.N.Y. The cases are known as "The Consolidated Class Actions," 96 Civ. 2583. The action consolidated principally Kronfeld (96 Civ. 5318), Bernstein (96 Civ. 5322), Barnett (96 Civ. 5323), Aylward (96 Civ. 5321), Stern (96 Civ. 2816), Greenfield (96 Civ. 2903), Spencer (96 Civ. 2989), Glaser (96 Civ. 3567), Wil-

helm (96 Civ. 3614), Wosnack (96 Civ. 4186), Verrillo (96 Civ. 4304), Gralla (96 Civ. 4417), Brum (96 Civ. 4487), and other cases. Several state class actions were also filed, including Thornton (Supreme Court, N.Y. County 96-602297), Moritt (Supreme Court, N.Y. County 96-601927), and Walker (Supreme Court, N.Y. County 96-602779).

2. For a discussion of "control persons" in the context of the Bennett brokers, see the Affidavit of Patricia Gillane in Further Support of Plaintiff's Motion for Class Certification, Bennett Funding Securities Litigation, S.D.N.Y., 96 Civ. 2583, May 22, 1998.

3. Discovery requests are codified in the Federal Rules of Civil Procedure §§ 26–37.

4. Walter Kaufmann, ed., *Basic Writings of Nietzsche* (Modern Library Series, 1992).

5. Pre-Trial Order No. 5, J. Sprizzo, Bennett Funding Securities Litigation, S.D.N.Y., 96 Civ. 2583, May 28, 1999.

Richard C. Breeden, the Trustee

1. Trustees are compensated pursuant to the guidelines established under 11 U.S.C. § 326 of the Bankruptcy Code.

2. The quoted material is from the letter from Richard C. Breeden to Investors, Apr. 30, 1996.

3. Disgruntled investor Theodore Andreozzi's letter addressed to Assistant U.S. Trustee Van Baalen, June 10, 1997.

4. Unhappy investor Henry Schaeffer's letter addressed to members of the HALO investor group, July 25, 1997. He also wrote a letter on Sept. 9, 1997. Mr. Schaeffer said he is not related to Drew Schaefer. Drew Schaefer was mentioned and accused of participating in the scheme by Genovese during his testimony at Patrick's trial in Jan. 1999. "Witness: Scheme Born in Meeting," *Syracuse Post-Standard*, Jan. 30, 1999.

5. One-page handwritten letter from Kathleen and Bud Bennett to "the friends," June 12, 1997.

6. "Elder Bennetts Allege Scheme by Breeden," *Syracuse Post-Standard*, July 3, 1998.

7. "Bennett: Bad Publicity Led to Bankruptcy," *Syracuse Post-Standard*, Oct. 8, 1998.

8. "Blaming All the Wrong People," *Syracuse Herald-Journal*, Oct. 12, 1998.

9. Concerning the Equivest flap and Breeden's fee, see "Trustee Faulted for Buying Stock," *National Law Journal*, Mar. 9, 1998; "Breeden Donates Equivest Stock to Syracuse University," *Syracuse Post-Standard*, Aug. 3, 1998; "Judge Delays Exam of Bennett Trustee's Investments of Equivest," *Syracuse Post-Standard*, July 31, 1998; "Bennett Trustee Switches Gears, Urges Sale of Equivest," *Syracuse Post-Standard*, July 21, 1998; and "Judge Questions Bennett Trustee's Bill," *Syracuse Post-Standard*, May 26, 1998.

10. As to the "vendetta" of Van Baalen against Breeden, see "U.S. Trustee Wants Breeden off Case," *Syracuse Post-Standard*, Nov. 5, 1998, and "Breeden Allowed to Stay as Bennett Trustee," *Syracuse Post-Standard*, Dec. 4, 1998. See also "As Irked Creditors Wait, Officials Squabble in Syracuse Bankruptcy," *Wall Street Journal*, 1998.

11. The quoted material concerning the Plan of Reorganization is from the Trustee's Letter to Creditors, May 8, 1998.

12. Judge Gerling's comments are reprinted in the Trustee's Letter to Creditors, May 8, 1998.

13. Plan of Reorganization, Bankr. N.D.N.Y., No. 96-61376, Dec. 31, 1998.

14. Proposed Disclosure Statement, Bankr. N.D.N.Y., No. 96-61376, Jan. 4, 1999; and

Order and Notice on Trustee's Proposed Disclosure Statement, Bankr. N.D.N.Y., No. 96-61376, Feb 2, 1999. A second hearing on the Proposed Disclosure Statement was held in June 1999, six months after the initial filing. Due to irregularities in certain figures used for comparisons, the hearing was adjourned, once more, to July 1999.

15. Breeden allegedly made his statements to *Syracuse Post-Standard* reporter Charley Hannagan in "Breeden: Bennett Cos. Can't Be Saved," *Syracuse Post-Standard*, Nov. 13, 1998.

16. Memorandum from Breeden to the Bennett Employees, Nov. 13, 1998.

17. Concerning the severance package to employees, see Trustee Motion, Bankr. N.D.N.Y., No. 96-61376, 1999. "Trustee Seeks Severance Pay for Bennett Employees," *Syracuse Post-Standard*, Jan. 29, 1999.

18. Letter from Richard Breeden to the investors, Jan. 8, 1999.

19. First Omnibus Motion to Allow Investor Claims; Objections to Investor Claims; and Motion to Approve Adjustment of Investor Claims, Bankr. N.D.N.Y., No. 96-61376, Dec. 19, 1997.

20. Concerning the suits against investors, see "Lawsuits vs. Bennett Investors Challenged," *Syracuse Post-Standard*, June 12, 1998; Motion to Dismiss Fraudulent Conveyance Count by Counsel to the Early Investors, Bankr. N.D.N.Y., No. 96-61376, May 6, 1998. In addition, approximately eleven hundred actions were commenced against trade creditors to recover preferential payments made within three months of the filing of the bankruptcy petitions. Order, J. Gerling, Bankr. N.D.N.Y., No. 96-61376, Mar. 19, 1999.

21. Bankruptcy filing statistics from "Agency Watch," *National Law Journal*, Dec. 14, 1998. See also "Business Bankruptcies: Room to Grow," *Syracuse Post-Standard*, July 18, 1998.

22. Concerning the Thomas Adversary Complaint, see Order, J. Gerling, Bankr. N.D.N.Y., No. 96-61376, Adv. Pro. No. 98-40892A, Apr. 29, 1999.

23. A local firm even solicited the sued investors. See letter from Harris Law Office to the investors concerning representation in the trustee's suit, May 13, 1998. The Harris Web site at: <http://www.bennettinvestordefense.com>.

24. Notice of Trustee's Motion Regarding Interim Distribution Procedure, Bankr. N.D.N.Y., No. 96-61376, June 10, 1998. See also Affidavit of C. Pulver in Support of Motion for Interim Distribution; Statement of Committee of Unsecured Creditors in Support of Motion to Make Interim Distribution, July 2, 1998; and Response to Trustee's Motion Regarding Interim Distribution Procedure, Bond Schoeneck & King, banks' counsel, July 2, 1998.

25. Quoted material is from Judge Gerling's order authorizing early distribution, Bankr. N.D.N.Y., No. 96-61376, July 9, 1998.

26. Quoted material is from "Breeden Mails Money to Investors," *Syracuse Post-Standard*, Aug. 18, 1998. Concerning the early distribution to investors, see "Bennett Payout Could Begin in August," *Syracuse Post-Standard*, June 9, 1998; "Bennett Creditors to Get Payment," *Syracuse Post-Standard*, July 14, 1998; "Bennett Investors Get Good News," *Syracuse Post-Standard*, Aug. 7, 1998; and "Victims to Get Payback at Last," *Syracuse Post-Standard*, Aug. 9, 1998.

27. Concerning the adjustment plan, see Notice of Motion and Motion of Trustee for Order Authorizing the Consolidated Estate to Enter Into Settlements With Current Investors, Bankr. N.D.N.Y., No. 96-61376, Oct. 2, 1998; and "Court Considers Plan to Settle

Bennett Claims," *Syracuse Post-Standard*, Oct. 22, 1998. See also letter from trustee to the investors, Apr. 23, 1999, and Letter from A. Steinberg, counsel to the early investors committee, to Investors, Apr. 1, 1999.

28. Order, J. Gerling, Bankr. N.D.N.Y., No. 96-61376, Apr. 29, 1999.

29. The Bennett Funding Group, Inc., Statement of Cash Receipts and Disbursements for the period ended Mar. 31, 1999.

Some Figures for Perspective

1. Press Release from Breeden, July 29, 1996: "Since 1990, The Bennett Companies sold more than $2.14 billion in unregistered securities to investors. Using the proceeds of sales to new investors and bank borrowings to make payments on earlier investments, more and more cash was consumed in maintaining a massive pyramid scheme."

2. At the time of the filing, about $215 million was still owed to the banks and about $674 million to individual investors. Trustee's Press Release, July 29, 1996.

3. Becky Morrison from MetLife executed a "due diligence" letter on Nov. 8, 1994, addressed to Chief Accounting Officer William Crowley. The approval letter is dated Dec. 14, 1994.

4. Resort Funding, Inc., f/k/a Bennett Funding International, Ltd., entered into the time-share receivables securitization with ING.

5. The definition of *due diligence* is from *Black's Law Dictionary*, 5th ed. (St. Paul: West Publishing Co., 1979), p. 411.

6. The figures are from the Company's records and from the slide presentation available at the Bennett Web site: <http://www.bennett-funding.com>.

7. Order concerning Poorman-Douglas, J. Gerling, Bankr. N.D.N.Y., No. 96-61376, Mar. 31, 1999.

8. "Bankruptcy Fees Could Hit $70 Million," *Syracuse Post-Standard*, May 18, 1999.

9. Amended Order Appointing Fee Auditor (Stuart Maue), J. Gerling, Bankr. N.D.N.Y., No. 96-61376, Dec. 2, 1996. Stuart Maue's Web site: <http://www.smmj.com>.

10. The quoted material is from Order, J. Gerling, Bankr. N.D.N.Y., No. 96-61376, Nov. 16, 1998. See also the Supplemental Statement of Position of Committee of Unsecured Creditors Regarding Fifth Fee Application of Simpson Thacher, Bankr. N.D.N.Y., No. 96-61376, May 14, 1998. A random review of other fee applications is also interesting. For example, see Fourth Application of Stuart Maue for $89,695, May 13, 1998, and the Sixth Application of Zolfo Cooper, accountants for the Unsecured Creditors' Committee for $92,786.04, June 30, 1998, Bankr. N.D.N.Y., No. 96-61376.

11. "Report of Richard C. Breeden, Trustee, Submitted Pursuant to 11 U.S.C. § 1106," Bankr. N.D.N.Y., No. 96-61376, Dec. 30, 1998. "Report: How Bennetts Failed," *Syracuse Post-Standard*, Jan. 12, 1999.

12. The quoted material is from the trustee's letter to investors, Jan. 8, 1999.

13. The word "statisticulation" was coined by Darrell Huff. Darrell Huff, *How to Lie with Statistics* (New York: W. W. Norton, 1954), p. 100.

The Cover-up Commences—The 7 Percent Solution

1. The letter and quoted material contained therein was drafted by Bennett Funding's outside SEC counsel, June 22, 1995, and submitted to Eric Schmidt, assistant director, Northeast Regional Office, SEC in New York City. The letter is forty pages long and contains the following attachments: (1) analysis of insurance expense; (2) analysis of initial direct costs; (3) affidavit of Patrick Bowling, insurance broker; (4) letter from Schluntz describing payout of insurance, June 1, 1995; (5) affidavit of Glenn Perry from Peat Marwick describing Bennett Funding's accounting practices, June 21, 1995.

An earlier Preliminary Submission to SEC by Bennett Funding's outside securities lawyers was made Aug. 24, 1993, and contained the following exhibits: (1) request for no-action letter to the SEC from Bennett Funding's outside securities counsel, Mar. 16, 1990; (2) memorandum from Patrick R. Bennett concerning no-action; (3) testimony of Harvey Merkin before the SEC, July 15, 1993; (4) Horizon Brokers advertisement for 7 percent notes; (5) Harvey Merkin Affidavit, Aug. 24, 1993; (6) letter from Patrick R. Bennett to Horizon Securities, Apr. 1, 1992; (7) testimony of Patrick R. Bennett before the SEC; (8) Horizon schedule of commissions received from 7 percent note sales; (9) list of 7 percent note purchasers from Feb. 1991 to Apr. 1992; (10) net worth of note purchasers; (11) Horizon internal securities SOP; (12) broker's letter of due diligence review of Bennett Funding; (13) Arthur Andersen & Co. financial statements for 1988 and 1989; (14) Mahoney & Cohen financial statements for 1991 and 1992; (15) Chemical Bank lockbox procedure letter to Bennett Funding, May 21, 1990; (16) Kasarjian letter to Horizon, Apr. 10, 1992; (17) sample 7 percent note and description; (18) letter from investor asking for $5,000 withdrawal from another short-term note program; (19) sample short-term note and insurance certificate; (20) complete Generali Insurance package; (21) completed 7 percent note and attached insurance certificate; (22) Bennett Funding Company Overview; (23) FAQ concerning Resort Funding program; (24) letter concerning insurance to investor; (25) various news articles concerning the economy and interest rates.

2. Both Al Cerimeli and Tony Menchella pleaded guilty to charges of conspiracy, obstruction of justice, and perjury.

3. The information concerning the conspiracy among Patrick, Cerimeli, and Menchella is from the indictment.

4. The transcript of Patrick's testimony before the SEC is from the indictment, pp. 38–41.

5. The quoted material is from the indictment, pp. 37, 38, 39, and 41.

6. The quoted material is from the SEC submission, pp. 8 and 9.

WHY?

Hotel Fever

1. The payments are recorded in the Company's books and records.

2. The decrepit quote and hotel brochure description are from "Overreaching: Syracuse, N.Y., Sees Proud Local Business Shattered by Scandal—Bennetts, Pillars of the City," *Wall Street Journal,* Apr. 17, 1996.

3. The renovation fees are detailed in the Company's books and records.

4. Order, J. Gerling, Bankr. N.D.N.Y., No. 96-61376, Oct. 9, 1997. The figures were set forth in the Order, p. 7. The quoted material from the Order, pp. 23, 24, and 26.

A Tale of Two Companies

1. The transfer and financing documents for Thing's and Standardbred's real estate holdings are as follows: Deed from Estate of Wisinski dated Sept. 28, 1988, and recorded Nov. 16, 1988; Deed from Marra to Thing dated May 11, 1989, and recorded May 17, 1989; Deed from Spera to Thing dated May 11, 1989, and recorded May 17, 1989; Mortgage from Thing to Spera dated May 11, 1989, and recorded May 17, 1989; Assignment of Mortgage from Spera and Marra to Standardbred dated Aug. 22, 1991, and recorded Sept. 24, 1991; Discharge of the Standardbred Assignment of Mortgage dated Sept. 30, 1993, and recorded Oct. 8, 1993; Mortgage from Thing to Skaneateles Bank dated Nov. 16, 1988, and recorded Nov. 16, 1988; Deed from Thing to Standardbred dated Jan 27, 1992, and recorded Jan. 27, 1992; Mortgage from Thing to Norstar Bank dated Sept. 6, 1989, and recorded Oct. 26, 1989; and Satisfaction of Norstar Mortgage dated Sept. 30, 1993, and recorded Oct. 8, 1993. All these instruments were recorded in the Clerk's Office of Onondaga County.

2. Information on the First-N-Goal entity is derived from Dun & Bradstreet Information Services Business Information Report, June 12, 1996.

3. Payment information is from Bennett Management computer printout, June 12, 1996.

4. According to Company records and as determined by Coopers & Lybrand, the cash used by Patrick to make the purchases of Mid-State shares was diverted from Bennett Management. See Trustee's Adversary Complaint against Standardbred Enterprises, Ltd., Bankr. N.D.N.Y., No. 96-61376, Apr. 25, 1997.

5. "They're Off and Running, But with Whose Money?" *New York Times,* June 1, 1997.

6. Information concerning the sale of the Mid-State shares to Standardbred and their subsequent pledging to N.W. Investors is in the Opinion of J. Gerling, Bankr. N.D.N.Y., No. 96-61376, Feb. 1, 1999.

7. Criminal Complaint against Wager, *United States of America v. Neil Wager,* S.D.N.Y. 99 MAG. 0117, Jan. 22, 1999. See also "Man Indicted in Bennett Case," *Syracuse Post-Standard,* Jan. 26, 1999.

The Insurance Fronts

1. The caption of the CIGNA suit is *Bennett Funding v. CIGNA Property & Casualty Companies, et al.,* N.D.N.Y., 91-CV-229, 1991.

2. The Germain matter, *Aloha Leasing v. Germain, et al.,* is set forth in J. Munson's decision at 644 F. Supp. 561 (N.D.N.Y. 1986).

3. AMRIC's Web site at: <http://www.amric.com>.

4. The quoted material is from CIGNA's in-house counsel to me during settlement conversations.

5. Copies of the Generali policies are set forth in Exhibit G to Sphere Drake's Motion to Dismiss the Trustee's Adversary Complaint, Bankr. N.D.N.Y., No. 96-61376, Adv. Pro. No. 97-70049A, Oct. 19, 1998.

6. Affidavit of Richard C. Breeden, Dec. 22, 1998, and the Notice of Motion and Motion of the Trustee to Approve the Generali Settlement, Bankr. N.D.N.Y., No. 96-61376, Dec. 22, 1998.

7. See the Notice of Motion and Motion of the Trustee to Approve the Generali Settlement, which contained copies of the Stipulation and Agreement of Settlement, Memoran-

dum of Understanding between the parties, and Joint-Prosecution Agreement.

8. Letter from Richard Breeden to the investors, Jan. 8, 1999.

9. The letters from the Official Committee of Unsecured Creditors of Bennett Funding Group, Jan. 6, 1999, and Feb. 26, 1999.

10. Orders Approving Settlement, J. Gerling, Bankr. N.D.N.Y., No. 96-61376, Mar. 18, 1999, and Apr. 9, 1999. See also "Legal Fees Outrages Bennett Investors," *Syracuse Post-Standard,* Mar. 18, 1999; "Judge Rejects Bennett Trustee's Legal Fee Pact," *Syracuse Post-Standard,* Mar. 19, 1999.

11. A California court allowed the heir of a Holocaust victim to sue Generali for refusing to honor a life insurance policy. "Holocaust Heir Can Sue," *National Law Journal,* Feb. 8, 1999.

12. Copies of the Sphere Drake documents are set forth in Exhibits A–F, in the Second Amended Adversary Complaint by Trustee against Re-insurer Sphere Drake, Bankr. N.D.N.Y., No. 96-61376, Adv. Pro. No. 97-70049A, 1997, and in Exhibits M and N to Sphere Drake's Motion to Dismiss the Trustee's Adversary Complaint, Oct. 19, 1998. See also the Third Party Complaint, *Lloyd Thompson, et al., v. Sphere Drake, et al.,* S.D.N.Y., 97-Civ-9485, MDL No. 1153, Jan. 1, 1999; Memoranda from Lloyd Thompson to Dick Small, Sept. 9, 1994, and Sept. 23, 1994, concerning the terms of the reinsurance program.

13. Letters from Wilson Elser Moskowitz Edelman & Dicker to Sphere Drake, Sept. 14, 1994, and Sept. 28, 1994, concerning the change of the Certificate of Insurance.

14. The suit is captioned *Ambos, et al., v. Bennett Funding, et al.,* Circuit Court of Cook County, Ill., 95 L 18010.

15. Winston & Strawn's Web site at: <http://www.winston.com>.

16. O'Rourke and several others left and started O'Rourke McCloskey & Moody.

Endless Troubles

1. Information concerning the Grand Canyon can be found at several Web sites: <http://www.thecanyon.com>; <http://www.nps.gov>; and <http://www.gorp.resoure/US_National_Park/az_grand.htm>. The quotes from President Roosevelt are from: <http://www.grandcanyonfoundation.org/faq.htm>.

2. The Phoenician's Web site is at: <http://www.thephoenician.com>.

3. Greyhound changed its name to The Finova Group, Inc., at: <http://www.finova.com>.

Hobnobbing

1. The quoted material concerning the purchase of the hotel is from "Wrestling Federation Buys Debbie Reynolds' Casino," *Syracuse Post-Standard,* Aug. 6, 1998.

2. Todd Fisher's comments are from "Overreaching: Syracuse, N.Y., Sees Proud Local Business Shattered by Scandal—Bennetts, Pillars of the City," *Wall Street Journal,* Apr. 17, 1996.

3. General information about the Reynolds's transaction can be found in "Debbie Reynolds Casino on the Block; Proceeds Will Help Bennett Creditors," *Syracuse Post-Standard,* Aug 4, 1998.

4. Walter Kaufmann, ed., *Basic Writings of Nietzsche* (Modern Library Series, 1992).

5. Sen. John De Francisco, a partner at Harris Beach & Wilcox. Its Web site is at: <http://www.harrisbeach.com>.

6. Daniel Stolz's letter to Judge Gerling, Dec. 19, 1997.

7. *Troiano-Scerbo v. POKO, et al.*, N.D.N.Y., 97-CV-266, 1997.

8. Petitions, Bankr. N.D.N.Y., 98-67940 and 99-60364.

Business Syndromes

1. Transcript of Weisman testimony, Bankr. N.D.N.Y., No. 96-61376, May 18, 1996, pp. 11–24.

2. SEC Litigation Release No. 15276, Mar. 7, 1997, regarding First Interregional Equity Corporation. "N.J. Company Faces $271 Million in Fines," *Syracuse Post-Standard*, May 26, 1999.

3. The story of Joseph is in Genesis 37.

4. "Coach Mac to Call the Plays at Hotel," *Syracuse Post-Standard*, Mar. 13, 1993.

Never Met a Client I Didn't Like

1. Regarding lawyers conflicts of interest, the Code of Professional Responsibility, DR 5-105 [1200.24], "Refusing to Accept or Continue Employment if the Interests of Another Client May Impair the Independent Professional Judgment of the Lawyer.," is reprinted as follows:

A. A lawyer shall decline proffered employment if the exercise of independent professional judgment in behalf of a client will be or is likely to be adversely affected by the acceptance of the proffered employment, or if it would be likely to involve the lawyer in representing differing interests, except to the extent permitted under DR 5-105 [1200.24] (C).

B. A lawyer shall not continue multiple employment if the exercise of independent professional judgment in behalf of a client will be or is likely to be adversely affected by the lawyer's representation of another client, or if it would be likely to involve the lawyer in representing differing interests, except to the extent permitted under DR 5-105 [1200.24] (C).

C. In the situations covered by DR 5-105 [1200.24] (A) and (B), a lawyer may represent multiple clients if it is obvious that the lawyer can adequately represent the interest of each and if each consents to the representation after full disclosure of the possible effect of such representation on the exercise of the lawyer's independent professional judgment on behalf of each.

D. While lawyers are associated in a law firm, none of them shall knowingly accept or continue employment when any one of them practicing alone would be prohibited from doing so under DR 5-101 [1200.20] (A), DR 5-105 [1200.24] (A), (B) or (C), DR 5-108 [1200.27], or DR 9-101 [1200.45] (B) except as otherwise provided therein.

E. A law firm shall keep records of prior engagements, which records shall be made at or near the time of such engagements and shall have a policy implementing a system by which proposed engagements are checked against current and previous engagements, so as to render effective assistance to lawyers within the firm in complying with subdivision D of this disciplinary rule. Failure to keep records or to have a policy which complies with this subdivision, whether or not a violation of subdivision D of this disciplinary rule occurs, shall be a violation by the firm. In cases where a violation of this subdivision by the firm is a substantial factor in causing a violation of subdivision D by a lawyer, the firm, as well as the individual lawyer, shall also be responsible for the violation of subdivision D.

2. The Chemical/Chase bank claim is detailed in a Stipulation between the trustee and the bank, Sept. 24, 1998.

3. The quoted material appeared in "Trustee Wants Simpson Thacher Cut from Bennett Funding Case," *Wall Street Journal*, and in "Briefly," *National Law Journal*. See also "Law Firm in Bennett Case Denies Conflicts," *Syracuse Post-Standard*, May 13, 1998.

4. See Memorandum of Law on Behalf of Mid-State Raceway to Operate a Simulcast Theatre in Syracuse, filed by Bond Schoeneck & King, Mar. 22, 1994. See also Letter from Bond, Schoeneck & King to Patrick Bennett concerning outstanding invoices, June 27, 1994.

The Code

1. Information concerning the number of leases is from Breeden's letter to investors, June 18, 1997.

2. Statistical information was obtained from the Report of Richard C. Breeden, Trustee, Submitted Pursuant to 11 U.S.C. § 1106, Bankr. N.D.N.Y., No. 96-61376, Dec. 30, 1998, pp. 31–32.

3. The combined stream-aging calculation is from the "Bank Portfolio Analysis," Mar. 17, 1997.

4. Although the Uniform Commercial Code has not been adopted in Louisiana, the legislature enacted commercial laws incorporating most of its articles.

5. In the Bennett bankruptcy, the court follows the Uniform Commercial Code as adopted in New York.

6. A letter from Breeden to the settling banks, Feb. 3, 1997, highlights frequently asked questions about the settlement options. A typical settlement agreement is between the Trustee and CenBank, Bankr. N.D.N.Y., No. 96-61376, July 23, 1997. A spreadsheet, June 5, 1997, listed the status of the settling banks and the options they agreed upon. See also "Settlement Offers," which further describes the various settlement terms applicable to all banks, Feb. 5, 1997.

7. The bank settlement figures are from the Trustee's Special Meeting of Creditors slide presentation available on the Web site: <http://www.bennett-funding.com>.

8. Opinion of J. Gerling about whether the banks perfected their security interests in the leases, Bankr. N.D.N.Y., No. 96-61376, Oct. 22, 1996. See also Robert Ihne, "Chattel Paper and the UCC," *Equipment Leasing Today*, Sept. 1996, p. 33.

9. The analysis is applicable to Article 8 before it was revised in 1997. U.C.C. § 8-601(b) states that "this Act does not affect an action or proceeding commenced before this Act takes effect."

10. Under the pre-1997 Article 8, U.C.C. § 8-302 controls the priority of competing interests in securities.

11. Order, J. Gerling, Bankr. N.D.N.Y., No. 96-61376, Apr. 16, 1999.

Of Brokers and Banks

1. The quoted material and analysis is from the Confidential Report to the Boards of Directors of The Bennett Funding Group, Inc., Bennett Leasing Corporation, and The Processing Center, Inc., prepared by Arkin, Schaeffer & Kaplan, Mar. 7, 1996, pp. 11, 12, 18, and 19.

2. The quoted material by Frank White, "They're Off and Running, But with Whose Money?" *New York Times,* June 1, 1997.

3. The editorial and Luciani quote are from "Bennett Bankruptcy Gambling Fueled the Free Fall," *Syracuse Post-Standard.*

4. Transcript of deposition of Stewart Weisman, July 16, 1997, taken relative to the litigation with the various banks.

5. The closing documents referenced were part of each separate bank loan closing.

6. The quoted material is a composite of dialogue from the transcript, pp. 191–205. Since the deposition, the matters under the alleged attorney client privilege have been disseminated to third parties or have become public record.

7. The municipal double-pledging was discovered by John Root, an accountant with Aloha Capital. His findings were reported to Aloha Capital's general counsel, William Fedorich, who circulated a memorandum dated Oct. 25, 1995.

8. The intranet memo was sent to Patrick on Nov. 9, 1995.

9. The due diligence memorandum was drafted by William Lester, Nov. 10, 1995.

10. Other important source documentation concerning the Bank Committee's endeavors are: (1) memorandum and exhibits from W. Lester, CFO of Bennett Funding International to Weisman concerning double-pledged municipal leases, Jan. 10, 1996; (2) memorandum and exhibits from W. Lester, CFO of Bennett Funding International to Michael Bennett concerning securitization of leases, Jan. 9, 1996; (3) memorandum from W. Lester, former CFO of Bennett Funding International to Michael Bennett concerning the double-pledge investigation, Nov. 13, 1995; (4) memorandum from E. Gaudino, former general counsel of Bennett Funding International to Michael Bennett concerning the double-pledge investigation, Nov. 13, 1995; (5) memorandum from Root to Weisman confirming the fire wall, Nov. 28, 1995; (6) memorandum from Patrick Bennett to Weisman concerning repayment of bank loans, Dec. 28, 1995; (7) memorandum from Weisman to Bud Bennett concerning bank repayment plan for double-pledged leases, Jan. 4, 1996; (8) memorandum from Weisman to J. Kaplan concerning the sale of Aegis stock for $35 million and supporting documents, Dec. 21, 1995; (9) second memorandum from Weisman to J. Root, CFO of Aloha Capital concerning the fire wall in the computer system to prevent municipal double-pledging, Nov. 28, 1995; (10) memorandum from Weisman to MIS requesting security clearance to access the FIN System, Nov. 10, 1995; (11) memorandum from Weisman to Kaplan of Arkin, Schaeffer & Kaplan, Mar. 7, 1996, concerning repayment of municipal lease loans.

11. Kasarjian's admission is from the Bennett Funding Web site: <http://www.bennett-funding.com/index/kasarj.html>.

12. The definition of *attorney* is found in *Black's Law Dictionary,* 5th ed. (St. Paul: West Publishing Co., 1979), p. 117.

13. In New York, the unauthorized practice of law is a felony. Education Law § 6512 (McKinney).

14. The Code of Professional Responsibility Disciplinary Rule is DR 4-1-101.

15. The Code of Professional Responsibility discusses the philosophical and ethical considerations underpinning the rule as well as the disciplinary rule itself which a lawyer is bound to follow. From CANON 4, entitled "A Lawyer Should Preserve the Confidences and Secrets of a Client" the ethical consideration we learn, in part: "The proper functioning of the legal system requires the preservation by the lawyer of confidences and secrets of one who has employed or sought to employ the lawyer." The actual disciplinary rule, in part: "Confidences and secrets gained in the professional relationship that the client has requested be held inviolate or the disclosure of which would be embarrassing or would be likely to be detrimental to the client shall not knowingly be revealed by a lawyer."

16. The assets were described in letters from Weisman to the investigative counsel, Jan. 15, 1996, and to Michael O'Rourke, Jan. 11, 1996. The sale of the Aegis shares was referenced in a press release put out by Schwartz & Co., Inc. (undated).

17. The document listing is from the Arkin investigative report, p. 7.

18. The quoted material is from the Arkin investigative report, pp. 28, 29, 30 (footnote 18), and 31 (and footnote 19).

Some More Business Syndromes

1. Nietzsche's famous aphorism in Walter Kaufmann, ed., *Basic Writings of Nietzsche* (Modern Library Series, 1992).

2. Some corporate services are found at: <http://www.empirecorp.com>. Also <http://www.incorporate.com/home.html> and <http://www.win.net/~isl/>.

3. Corporate memorandum to Bud Bennett, Sept. 30, 1994.

4. The full name is Pegasus Entertainment & Funding Group, Inc.

THE ANSWER?

1. The adage is by talmudic sage Hillel, 70 B.C.E.–C.E. 10, reprinted from *The New Union Prayer Book* in *Gates of Power* (New York: Central Conference of American Rabbis, 1975), p. 18. See also Rabbi David Cooper, *God Is a Verb* (New York: Riverhead Books, 1997).

A Word to the Wise

1. The materials available in this chapter are for informational purposes only. The materials are not nor should be construed as providing legal advice to you. You should seek the advice and counsel of an attorney concerning any issue or problem discussed in this chapter. No attorney-client relationship or privilege has been created between Stewart L. Weisman and you relative to this chapter.

2. The SEC's Web site also provides good information: <http://www.sec.gov/consumer/askginv.htm>. See also the Web site of the Alliance for Investor Education: <http://www.investoreducation.org/ktfraud.htm>.

3. "Unlike the garden-variety Ponzi scheme, which typically draws in its victims by promising quick, astronomical profits, the Bennett leasing program was marketed to individuals seeking conservative, low-risk, and long-term investments." Order, J. Gerling, Bankr. N.D.N.Y., No. 96-61376, Mar. 18, 1999.

4. Order, J. Gerling, Bankr. N.D.N.Y., No. 96-61376, Adv. Pro. No. 98-40892A, Apr. 29, 1999.

5. For a discussion of the Bennett fraud and general investment in lease securities, see Alexander Dill, "Bennett Funding Group, Inc.: Are There Lessons for the ABS Market?," *Structured Finance,* May 17, 1996. In Sept. 1996, Moody's Investors Service ran a seminar called "Case Study in Servicer Fraud: Bennett Funding Group, Inc."

6. As to some of the specifics to prevent leasing fraud, see the opinion of J. Gerling about whether the banks perfected their security interests in the leases, Bankr. N.D.N.Y., No. 96-61376, Oct. 22, 1996. See also Robert Ihne, "Chattel Paper and the UCC," *Equipment Leasing Today,* Sept. 1996, p. 33.

7. For a discussion of the SEC's office on Municipal Securities, see "Riding Herd on the Muni Market," *Business Law Today,* Nov./Dec. 1996, p. 29.

8. Allonge is described at U.C.C. § 3-202(2).

9. The complete text of risk factors is set forth in Appendix K.

10. Lease securitization is described in the Dill article and in "Securitization, Critical Evaluation of Funding Alternatives," *Monitor Leasing and Financial Services,* July/Aug. 1997, p. 1.

11. Resort Funding entered into a lease securitization transaction with ING Bank before the filing of the bankruptcy. Perhaps that is why ING did not suffer the fate of most of the other lending institutions.

Crime . . .

1. See, generally, 1990 Clean Air Act, 42 U.S.C. § 7401, et seq.

2. The not-for-profit Adirondack Council was given five thousand pollution credits and will retire one credit for each $50 donation. "A $50 Gift with the Mountains in Mind," *Syracuse Post-Standard,* Dec. 5, 1998.

3. Justice Department Press Release concerning the indictments of Patrick R. Bennett, et al., June 26, 1997. The full statement is as follows:

This Indictment charges a massive, carefully executed investment fraud, one of the largest in United States financial history. PATRICK R. BENNETT is charged with systematically bilking more than 12,000 investors out of hundreds of millions of dollars by selling them fictitious, fraudulent, and worthless lease contracts and promissory notes. PATRICK R. BENNETT is also charged with taking elaborate steps to launder the proceeds of these crimes, then squandering investors' hard-earned money on himself and his family and on wildly speculative and ill-conceived investments. Calling this white-collar crime may trivialize the enormous hardship and economic devastation suffered by the thousands of hardworking investors who were victims of these crimes. Many are elderly and face the loss of their life savings and their hopes for a secure retirement; others now cannot obtain necessary medical treatment or provide for their children's education. Such wanton disregard for the welfare of others cannot be tolerated, and will be prosecuted to the full extent of the law.

Country Bumpkin—Patrick's Trial

1. Just before Patrick's trial commenced, he was placed on notice that if found guilty of defrauding investors, the government will force him to forfeit $150 million under federal forfeiture laws. In that Patrick used court-appointed counsel, claimed he has no assets, and filed bankruptcy, it is doubtful whether the government will be able to secure any portion of the $150 million. "U.S. to Seek $150M from Bennett," *Syracuse Post-Standard,* Dec. 6, 1998.

2. The quoted material in this chapter is from a compendium of newspaper articles covering the trial as follows: As to testimony from Patrick Bennett: "Cover-up Admitted in Ponzi Case," *National Law Journal,* Feb. 22, 1999; "Bennett Says He Can't Follow Cash Flow," *Syracuse Post-Standard,* Feb. 11, 1999; "Bennett Fingers Former VP as Mastermind," *Syracuse Post-Standard,* Feb. 10, 1999; "Witness Admits Coverup in $700 Million Securities Fraud," *Reuters,* Feb. 9, 1999; "Pat Bennett Admits Lies, Not Schemes," *Syracuse Post-Standard,* Feb. 9, 1999; and "Bennett Funding Ex-CFO Says on Stand He Lied to SEC Officials," *Bloomberg News Service,* Feb. 8, 1999. Testimony from some of the government's thirty-one witnesses: "Former VP Says He Asked Bennett for an Out," *Syracuse Post-Standard,* Jan. 13, 1999; "Exec Takes Bennett Jury on Paper Tale," *Syracuse Post-Standard,* Jan. 12, 1999; and "Chasing Paper: Bennett Worker Testifies," *Syracuse Post-Standard,* Dec. 24, 1998. As to the verdict and jury deliberations: "Bennett Is Convicted of Perjury and Obstruction," *Wall Street Journal,* Mar. 3, 1999; "Guilty on 7, Hung on 53," *Syracuse Post-Standard,* Mar. 3, 1999; "Bennett Convicted on Some Counts," *Associated Press,* Mar. 3, 1999; "Patrick Bennett Found Guilty of Perjury, Obstruction," *Bloomberg,* Mar. 2, 1999; "Mistrial Declared on Major Counts Against Bennett," *Reuters,* Mar. 2, 1999; "Bennett Funding Jury Stalemated on Most Counts in Fraud Case," *Reuters,* Mar. 2, 1999; "Bennett Funding Ex-CFO's Trial Jury Says It's at an Impasse," *Bloomberg,* Feb. 23, 1999; "Bennett Funding Jury Told to Continue Deliberating," *Reuters,* Feb. 23, 1999; "Bennett Jury Comes Back with More Questions," *Syracuse Post-Standard,* Feb. 23, 1999; "Bennett Jury Deliberations to Continue," *Syracuse Post-Standard,* Feb. 20, 1999; and "Bennett Funding Ex-CFO's $700 Million Fraud Case Goes to Jury," *Bloomberg,* Feb. 18, 1999. As to Patrick's defense and trial motions: "Careless, Not Criminal," *Syracuse Post-Standard,* Feb. 18, 1999; "Some Charges Dropped in Big U.S. Fraud Case," *Reuters,* Feb. 17, 1999; "Judge Questions Jurisdiction of Trial," *Syracuse Post-Standard,* Feb. 12, 1999; "'There's Got to Be an End,' Judge Says," *Syracuse Post-Standard,* Jan. 14, 1999; and "Bennett's 'Bumpkin' Defense," *Syracuse Post-Standard,* Dec. 15, 1998.

3. "Mountain of Evidence Buried Bennett Jurors," *Syracuse Herald American,* Mar. 7, 1999.

4. "Dumb and Dumber," *Syracuse Herald American,* Mar. 7, 1999.

5. "Conviction Rate in Securities Fraud Cases Very Different Than Bennett Story Showed," *Syracuse Herald American,* Mar. 28, 1999.

6. "Prosecutors Dispute SU Data on Convictions," *Syracuse Herald American,* Mar. 28, 1999.

7. Letter from E. T. "Bud" Bennett to "Friends," Apr. 13, 1999.

8. Letter from HALO Group to members and others, Mar. 29, 1999; letter from HALO Group to Mary Jo White, U.S. Attorney, S.D.N.Y., Apr. 13, 1999.

9. Letter from Simpson Thacher & Bartlett to Daniel Stolz, attorney to the Unsecured Creditor's Committee, Apr. 19, 1999.

10. "Bennett Case Gets New Judge," *Syracuse Post-Standard,* Mar. 26, 1999.

11. "Patrick Bennett Gets New Lawyer for Second Fraud Trial," *Syracuse Post-Standard,* Apr. 16, 1999.

12. A compendium of articles concerning Patrick's second trial is as follows: As to the trial: "Bennett Funding Ex-CFO Stands Retrial in $700 Million Fraud Case," *Bloomberg News Service,* May 18, 1999; "Patrick Bennett," *Dow Jones Newswires,* May 18, 1999, <http://dowjones.wsj.com/archive>; "Bennett Trial Opens on Familiar Foundation," *Syracuse Post-Standard,* May 19, 1999; "Testimony Begins in Second Bennett Trial," *Syracuse Post-Standard,* May 20, 1999; "Last Chapter Being Written in Bennett Saga," *Syracuse Herald American,* June 6, 1999; "Bennett Funding Ex-CFO's $700 Million Fraud Retrial Goes to Jury," *Bloomberg News Service,* June 8, 1999; and "Two Views of Bennett Presented to the Jury," *Syracuse Post-Standard,* June 8, 1999. As to jury deliberations: "Deliberations Under Way in Bennett Case," *Syracuse Post-Standard,* June 9, 1999; "Partial Verdict in Bennett Funding Ex-CFO Retrial," *Bloomberg News Service,* June 9, 1999; "Jury Reaches Partial Verdict in Bennett Case," *Reuters,* June 9, 1999; and "42 Charges Down, 11 to Go," *Syracuse Post-Standard,* June 10, 1999. As to the verdict: "Bennett Is Convicted on 42 Counts of Fraud and Money Laundering," *Wall Street Journal,* June 11, 1999; "Jury Convicts Bennett of Money Laundering, Deadlocks on Key Charges," *Dow Jones Newswires,* June 11, 1999, <http://dowjones.wsj.com/archive>; "Bennett Found Guilty of Money-Laundering," *Reuters,* June 10, 1999; "Patrick Bennett Fraud Jury Delivers Partial Guilty Verdict," *Bloomberg News Service,* June 10, 1999; "Judge Revokes Bail, Cites Risk of Flight," *Syracuse Herald-American,* June 10, 1999; "Man Convicted in Big Pyramid Scheme," *Associated Press,* June 10, 1999; and "Patrick Bennett Jury Returns Partial Guilty Verdict," *Bloomberg News Service,* June 10, 1999.

. . . and Punishment

1. The Breeden quote is from "Bennett Verdict Is Some Satisfaction to Investors," *Syracuse Post-Standard,* June 12, 1999.

2. The adage is by talmudic sage Hillel, reprinted from *The New Union Prayer Book* in *Gates of Power* (New York: Central Conference of American Rabbis, 1975), p. 19.

3. The adage is by Rabbi Shimon. Ibid., p. 24.

Index

Note: Italicized page numbers indicate figures, tables, illustrations, and appendixes.

surance and, 219–22; distributions to, 58,
112, 187–91, 333n. 2; enticements for,
254–56; fraud's impact on, 19–21, 254,
329n. 9; IPOs and, 78; Legal's relation to,
84; liabilities of, by state, *20*, 349n. 2;
longer term vs. more recent, 188–83; opposed to SEC investigation, 181–83,
347nn. 3–4; payments from, 110–11;
PPMs and, 65–66, 74, 91, 96, 289–90,
321–24; protection for, 24, 334n. 1; in
pulse meters, 224–28; reassurance for,
180–82, 187; rights in claims of, 257,
259–63; solicited by lawyers, 348n. 23; tax
liability of, 337n. 3; Web site for education of, 328n. 5; "wrap" leases sold to,
146. *See also* class action suit
Investor-X, 76
INV (inventory) computer system: internal
investigation and, 271–72; leases tracked
in, 54, 59–61, *61*, 63–64, 66–68, 267–69
IPO (initial public offerings) process, 77–79
Ireland, children from, 49
IRR Assets, 207
IRS (Internal Revenue Service), 153, 287
It's a Wonderful Life (film), 3

Jameson-Dewitt & Associates, Inc., 52
Japan, equipment lease vendors from, 80
Jaru, Inc., 97
JB Vending (Syracuse), 227–28
Jeffer, Hopkinson, Vogel, Coomber and
Peiffer, 130
Jewish tradition, 49, 151–52
Johnson, William, *71*, 330n. 17
Joseph's coat syndrome, 245–46
justice, possibility of, 6

Kant, Immanuel, 55, 333n. 1
karma, notion of, 6, 9, 48, 326n. 15
Kasarjian, Kenneth: accusations against,
296–98; audits and, 171, 172; charges
against, 74, 225, 271, 296; counsel for, 84;
double-pledged leases sold by, 68–69,
335–36n. 5; Equivest Finance and, 92;
fake leases sold by, 70–73, 75; guilty plea
and confession of, 271–72, 355n. 11; home
of, 75; limited liability companies and,
96, 192; partner of, 174; perjury of,
163–64, 300; political contributions of,
236; revenue received by, *180;* sham
transactions by, 129, 130–31, 136–37,
139–42, 145
Katz, Jonathan, 24
Kaye Scholer (firm), *195*
KDV Enterprises, 119, *180*
Kelley, Richard, 150–51, 344n. 5

Kelly, Joe, 165
Kenton Group: charges against, 74; check
kiting and, 272; multiple-pledged leases
sold by, 71, 335–36n. 5; sham transactions
by, 130–31, 136–42, 145
Kenton Portfolio, Inc.: as broker in Scrip-
tex-Bennett transaction, 137–41; owner-
ship/control of, 52
King, Stephen, 117
Kingsley, Thomas, 43–44, 50, 81, 333n. 4
Kirkpatrick & Lockhart, 25, 26, 199, 329n. 4
Klarman, Marilyn, 335–36n. 5
Klarman, Wallace, 335–36n. 5
Kmart, game sales of, 239
Koivunon, Janet, 335–36n. 5
Koivunon, Remo, 335–36n. 5
Kosmas Group International, Inc., 95
Kuppel, Kevin, 86, 161, 162, 282

Lady Kathleen (yacht): Cordoba Corporation and, 97, 115; description of, 39; pho-
tograph of, *41;* proceeds from, 40–41,
332n. 16; professional fees and, 196; purchase of, 39, 41, 54; records on, 332n. 14
laws: code for commercial, 257–63; discourse on need for, 292–93;
gaming/gambling (W.V.), 102–3; leasing
(N.Y.), 338n. 9; pollution, 292–93. *See
also* securities laws; *specific acts*
lawyers: absent for Executive Committee
meetings, 109; attitudes toward, 274–75;
in Bennett cases, *249–50;* billing practices of, 9; conflict of interest for, 248,
250–52, 353–54n. 1; definition of, 273;
need to consult, 356n. 1; profits for, 252;
responsibilities of, 85–86, 151–52, 218–19,
248, 250, 274, 339n. 18, 356n. 15; restraints
on corporate, 274–75; unauthorized,
355n. 13. *See also specific firms*
Lazy Creek Resort, Inc., 52
lease litigation: CIGNA and, 216–19; Legal
Department's role in, 81, 218–19, 241–42;
settlement preferred in, 43, 218, 226
leases: application process for, 79–80; as
chattel paper, 258–59; computer tracking
of, 54, 59–61, *61*, 63–64, 66–68, 267–69;
defaulted, 81, 82, 199–200, 203–4, 216–17;
for deli, 199–200; double-pledged,
60–76, 192, 203–4, 244, 257, 265–73,
276–78, 334n. 11; evergreen provisions of,
338n. 8; examples of fraud in, 65–69, 194;
insurance for, 14, 21, 35, 216–28, 288; legal
forms for, 79; as loan collateral, 67,
68–69, 96, 192, 265–73, 335–36n. 5; master
type of, 286–87; original of, 286–87; payments for, 63–64; pension funds used

Need and Greed: The Story of the Largest Ponzi Scheme in American History was composed in 10.5/13 Adobe Minion in QuarkXPress 4.04 on a Macintosh by Kachergis Book Design; printed by sheet-fed offset on 55-pound Sebago and Smyth-sewn and bound over binder boards in Arrestox B-grade cloth with dust jackets printed in black and three PMS colors and laminated by Quinn-Woodbine of Woodbine, New Jersey; designed by Kachergis Book Design of Pittsboro, North Carolina; published by Syracuse University Press, Syracuse, New York 13244-5160.